DATE DUE

#47-0108 Peel Off Pressure Sensitive

Peasants, Rebels, and Outcastes

BY

MIKISO

HANE

Pantheon Books ◆ New York

PEASANTS

REBELS AND

OUTCASTES

The Underside of Modern Japan

PUBLISHED IN THE UNITED STATES BY PANTHEON BOOKS,

A DIVISION OF RANDOM HOUSE, INC., NEW YORK,

AND SIMULTANEOUSLY IN CANADA BY RANDOM HOUSE

OF CANADA LIMITED, TORONTO.

LIBRARY OF CONGRESS CATALOGING IN PUBLICATION DATA

HANE, MIKISO.

PEASANTS, REBELS, AND OUTCASTES.

BIBLIOGRAPHY: P.

INCLUDES INDEX.

1. JAPAN—SOCIAL CONDITIONS.

2. JAPAN—HISTORY— 19TH CENTURY.

3. JAPAN—HISTORY—20TH CENTURY.

I. TITLE.

HN723.H36   952   81–18912

ISBN 0–394–51963–9   AACR2

ISBN 0–394–71040–1 (pbk)

MANUFACTURED IN THE UNITED STATES OF AMERICA

FIRST EDITION

BOOK DESIGN BY ELISSA ICHIYASU

MAPS BY HARRY SCOTT

HN
723
.H36
1982

TO MY MOTHER AND LATE FATHER

Contents

Japanese Weights and Measures

	Japanese	*U.S. or British*
LENGTH:	1 *ri*	2.44 miles
AREA:	1 *chō* = 10 *tan*	2.45 acres
	1 *tan* = 10 *se*	0.245 acres
	1 *se* = 30 *tsubo*	0.0245 acres
	1 *tsubo* = 1/30 *se*	3.95 square yards
VOLUME:	1 *koku* = 10 *to*	4.96 imperial bushels/5.119 U.S. bushels/47.6567 U.S. gallons
	1 *to* = 10 *shō*	0.496 imperial bushels/0.56567 U.S. bushels or 1,216.429 cubic inches
	1 *shō* = 10 *go*	0.05667 U.S. bushels or 121.64 cubic inches/0.47657 U.S. gallon
	1 *go* = 1/10 *shō*	0.04766 U.S. gallon or 12.164 cubic inches
WEIGHT:	1 *kan* = 1,000 *momme*	8.267 pounds
	1 *momme* = 1/1000 *kan*	0.13228 ounce
MONEY:	1 yen = 100 sen	In 1940, equaled 0.2344 U.S. dollar*
	1 sen = 1/100 yen	

Traditionally in Japan, when calculating age, a person is considered to be age one at birth, two on the first New Year's Day and so forth. Thus, ordinarily, there is one year's difference between the Japanese and Western versions of the same person's age. To indicate a person's age in Western terms, the prefix *man* ("full," "fully") is used. People of the older generation still calculate age in the traditional way.

*Currently the official exchange sets the yen at 360 yen per U.S. dollar, but in July 1981 one dollar was worth about 220 yen. The sen is no longer in use today.

Preface

Much attention has been paid to the "miracle" of Japan's process of modernization, which began in the mid-nineteenth century and culminated in the spectacular leap forward of the postwar years. Changes in political institutions and practices, commercial and industrial growth, technological advances, the assumption of a Western facade for the major cities, military expansion, and educational progress all appeared to underscore the "modernity" of Japan when it challenged the Western nations in 1941.

The Meiji leaders set *fukoku kyōhei* ("enrich the nation and strengthen arms") as their overriding goal and channeled all their country's energy and resources toward this end. In this they were remarkably successful, if enriching the nation means the construction of effective instruments of power and the intrenchment of an elite rather than the enhancement of the well-being of the masses. But what, in fact, did this process of modernization mean to the vast majority of the population? How did modernization affect the lives of the people who carried its burden and paid its costs?

The literature on political, economic, social, intellectual, and cultural developments in modern Japan is copious, but relatively little has been written about the actual experiences of "ordinary" people. Even sociological studies about "functions," "structures," "systems," and "attitudes" complete with interesting paradigms, charts, surveys, and statistics do not tell us what life was really like for the peasants or the urban poor. In fact, many of these studies have an antiseptic quality. One does not get a sense of the pain and sorrow, the anguish and anger, the hunger and disease, the stench and filth that continued to be ever-present realities for the vast majority of Japanese.

What remains to be done is to get at "the voices of human experience" at the lower levels of society. A number of Japanese scholars and writers have begun this process of listening to people whose experiences, thoughts, and feelings had formerly been deemed unworthy of consideration by "serious" scholars. They are recording and transcribing the comments and memories of old peasants, retired textile workers, former prostitutes, aging miners, former outcastes, urban slum dwellers, former prison inmates, and so on. Carolyn Lougee of Stanford University speaks of the need to pay attention to "the authentic and compelling expressions of the human enigma in whatever form they assume." I was guided by a similar principle in reviewing the lives and thoughts of the rural populace and of the poor who came out of the villages to enter the mines, the factories, and the brothels.

I have tried as much as possible to rely on personal testimony and eyewitness accounts, utilizing memoirs, diaries, and individual recollections gathered by Japanese social scientists and journalists. Whenever possible I have allowed people who experienced the conditions, events, and developments under discussion to tell their own stories of those years—almost a century—when Japan was undergoing its "modernization."

In general, the chronological limits of this study extend from the beginning of the Meiji era to the outbreak of war in the Pacific. The changes that have taken place in Japan since the end of World War II have been so drastic that the postwar era constitutes an entirely new stage in Japan's history. As a result, I have confined my study primarily to the prewar years, except for a brief impressionistic concluding chapter. Here, I have focused primarily on the peasantry. I shall examine the lives of the urban poor and workers in a subsequent study.

Japanese names have been given in the traditional style; that is, surname first and given name second. For the transliteration of Japanese names and words, I have used the Hepburn system. A diacritical mark over the vowels (ˉ) indicates a long vowel. These marks were not used for widely known place names like Tokyo and Kyoto, which would otherwise be rendered Tōkyō and Kyōto. There is no distinction between singular and plural nouns in Japanese. So *samurai, daimyō,* etc., could be singular or plural.

Many friends, colleagues, and institutions have supported me in completing this book. The grant from the National Endowment for the Humanities enabled me to take a year's leave from teaching to work on this project. The Association for Asian Studies and Knox College also provided research and travel grants. The curators and staff members of the East Asian libraries of Stanford University, the University of Michigan, and the Library of Congress have assisted me on numerous occasions. I am grateful to Professor Ishida Takeshi and the staff of the Social Science Research Institute of Tokyo University for their assistance and for providing me with a research base in Japan. Among fellow students of Japan, I am especially indebted to John W. Dower of Wisconsin for his advice and encouragement. My friends and acquaintances in the village where I spent the formative years of my life helped me refresh my memory and sharpen my perception about prewar Japanese village life, and friends elsewhere facilitated my research and visits to different regions of Japan to enable me to gather data and acquire a sense of time and place about the material discussed here. I am particularly grateful to Mr. Tanabe Sadayoshi and Mrs. Tanaka Michiko for their support and assistance.

I am heavily indebted to many Japanese scholars, journalists, writers, and editors whose publications have been rich sources of information. The memoirs, diaries, and records of interviews with members of the social groups discussed here have been especially valuable. I wish to express my special appreciation to the author, Yamashiro Tomoe, for allowing me to translate and include here a considerable portion of her account of the young farm wife in the chapter "Rural Women" and to the family members of Shimomura Chiaki for permission to translate and include his article on the famine of 1933–1934.

I am deeply obliged to the editorial staff of Pantheon Books for the most extensive and assiduous editorial assistance I have received in my publishing experience. I am particularly indebted to my editor, Tom Engelhardt, not only for his encouragement and counsel but for going over the manuscript with painstaking care and patience. I also wish to express my gratitude to Lorraine Alexander Veach for her meticulous editorial work. Needless to say, whatever defects remain in the book are entirely due to my own deficiencies.

As with all my endeavors in preparing a manuscript, my wife, Rose, has patiently typed and retyped the manuscript from nearly illegible drafts. I am grateful to her and to my daughters, Laurie and Jennifer, for their unwavering support, and for tolerating months of my absence from home as I went off by myself on research jaunts.

Mikiso Hane
Knox College

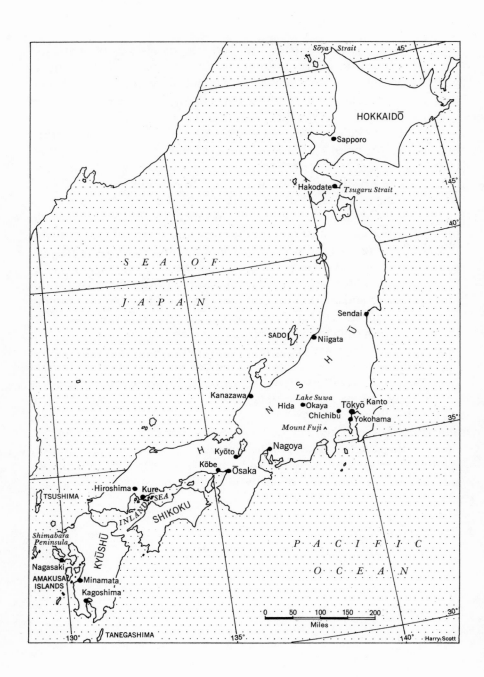

Modern Japan

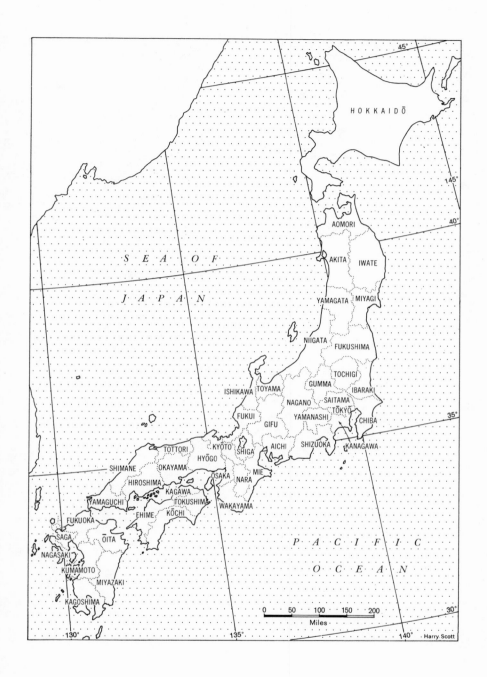

HOKKAIDŌ

SEA OF

JAPAN

AOMORI

AKITA   IWATE

YAMAGATA   MIYAGI

NIIGATA   FUKUSHIMA

TOCHIGI

GUMMA   IBARAKI

ISHIKAWA   TOYAMA

NAGANO   SAITAMA

FUKUI   YAMANASHI   TŌKYŌ

GIFU   CHIBA

KYOTO   SHIGA   KANAGAWA

TOTTORI   AICHI   SHIZUOKA

HYŌGO

SHIMANE   OKAYAMA

OSAKA   NARA   MIE

HIROSHIMA   KAGAWA

YAMAGUCHI   TOKUSHIMA   WAKAYAMA

EHIME   KŌCHI

FUKUOKA

SAGA   ŌITA

NAGASAKI

KUMAMOTO

MIYAZAKI

KAGOSHIMA

PACIFIC

OCEAN

0   50   100   150   200
Miles

Harry Scott

Japanese Prefectures

Peasants, Rebels, and Outcastes

MODERNIZATION

AND THE

PEASANTS

In Dante's *Inferno,* Count Ugolino, gnawing on Archbishop Ruggieri's skull, recounts how he and his sons were starved to death in a prison that was sealed off by the archbishop. Ugolino's sons first asked him to strip off their flesh and eat it to allay his hunger pains; but in the end each cried out, "Father, why don't you help me?" and expired at his feet. What excruciating agony parents must experience in seeing their children starve to death. Yet throughout history this has been the fate endured by countless parents. What could they do to escape such torment?

When famine struck the Japan's peasantry in the Tokugawa period (1600–1868), they starved to death, sold their daughters to the brothels, or practiced infanticide. Satō Nobuhiro, writing late in this period, lamented:

[Infanticide] is particularly widespread in the northeast and in the eastern regions. It is also widespread in the Inland Sea region, Shikoku and Kyushu, but there the children are killed before their birth, thus making it appear that there is no infanticide. The one place where infanticide seems to be extremely rare is Echigo [Niigata prefecture], but in its stead the practice of selling girls over seven or eight years of age to other provinces for prostitution prevails on a large scale. . . . Some consider this practice inhuman, but to think so is a great mistake. It is far more humane than either abortion or infanticide. I was told that long ago in Central Asia there was a large country whose king killed 3,300 children annually to obtain their livers, with which he made a medicine for the kidney to be used for sexual purposes. No one who is told of this practice can help but feel a sense of shock and revulsion . . . but, later, as I reflected on it deeply, it occurred to me that, while the king's act . . . was indeed inhumane, it was not as barbarous as the practice of infanticide prevalent today. In Mutsu and Dewa [northern provinces] alone, the number of children killed annually exceeds sixty or seventy thousand.[1]

Starvation, infanticide, abortion, and selling daughters into prostitution did not cease in Japan even after the Tokugawa era ended and Japan entered her "modern" century. When Yanagida Kunio, a prominent Japanese anthropologist, was working in a governmental legal department, he came across the records of a man who had been convicted of murdering his children in the late 1880s.

About thirty years ago, when there was a severe Depression, a man about fifty years of age was eking out a living as a charcoal maker in the hills of Nishi Mino [Gifu prefecture]. His wife had died some years before, and he was left with a thirteen-year-old son. He had also taken in a young girl about his son's age and was raising them both in a hovel in the hills. The times were so bad the man had trouble selling his charcoal. He would go down to the villages day after day but return each afternoon without even a handful of rice to feed his children. One day he came home empty-handed as usual. He could not bear to look at the starving children's faces, so he stole into the hut and fell asleep.

When he woke up, the evening sun was pouring in through the doorway. It was toward the end of autumn. He found the two children squatting in the sunlight, concentrating on some task. When he approached them he found them busily sharpening the axe he used to chop down the trees. They pleaded with him, "Papa, please take this axe and kill us." The two children then lay on the ground with their heads resting on the woodpile. When the charcoal maker saw this, he felt dizzy and his mind went blank. He took the axe and chopped his childrens' heads off. But he was unable to kill himself, and was arrested and put in prison.[2]

As late as the 1930s, in the famines that struck the northern villages, similar tragedies beset the peasants. All of which leaves one to ask: "How 'modern' was 'modern' Japan?" The year 1868, when the imperial court regained political power from the "feudal" Tokugawa government, is customarily regarded as the beginning of the modern age in Japan. The new rulers then launched Japan on a path of militarization and industrialization, effecting a revolution rather than a simple transference of power or a gradual transition from the "feudal" to the "modern" age. But even a revolution does not result in the total abandonment of the old. After the Meiji restoration, much was held over from the Tokugawa era. Moreover, some historians contend that numerous aspects of modernity can be detected in what we refer to as "feudal" Japan. Undeniably, the linkage between Tokugawa and Meiji Japan is a profound one. "Modern" Japan cannot be understood without an awareness of the Tokugawa background, especially as it relates to rural areas, in which tradition persisted much more tenaciously than in urban centers.

The Tokugawa Background

For more than two centuries before Commodore Matthew C. Perry arrived in Tokyo Bay in 1853, demanding that Japan establish diplomatic relations with the United States, Japan had been virtually sealed off from the outside world, except for a small "opening" at Nagasaki, where the Dutch, Chinese, and Koreans were allowed to come and trade under tight restrictions. During this period, Japan was ruled by the Tokugawa shogunate (Bakufu), which had been established in 1603. Under the Tokugawa rulers, there were about 270 feudal lords *(daimyō)* with domains *(han)* of varying sizes. These lords had autonomous authority over their *han,* but they were in effect vassals of the *shōgun* ("overlord"), and their political conduct was strictly regulated by the Bakufu. The *shōgun* as well as the *daimyō* had their own retainers who, in most instances, were allotted a fixed stipend in return for their services. Unlike the vassals of medieval Europe, the warrior-retainers of Tokugawa Japan were not granted fiefs and did not reside in manorial estates but in "castle towns" where their feudal lords were ensconced. In this sense they were military bureaucrats.

The founders of the Tokugawa shogunate divided the society they ruled into four main classes: the warriors *(samurai),* the peasants, the artisans, and the merchants. At the bottom of society were the outcastes (formerly referred to as *eta* and *hinin,* now as *burakumin*), who may have numbered close to half a million or so by the end of the Tokugawa era. In addition to these strict strata there were the priests, and, at the very top, court aristocrats and, of course, the *daimyō.*

In theory, class divisions were fixed; distinctions between the *samurai* and commoners were strictly observed. Intermarriage was prohibited, although toward the end of the Tokugawa era financially hard-pressed *samurai* sometimes formed marital ties with wealthy merchant houses. Peasants were officially forbidden to leave the land they worked, but those located near towns and cities often did leave their villages in quest of jobs. In general, however, one could say that the official policy of freezing the sociopolitical order was remarkably successful. The peasants, who constituted the vast majority of the population, labored on the land for over two-and-a-half centuries, doing the bidding of the *samurai* class. Only commoners dwelling in towns and cities managed to enjoy some of the benefits of commercial growth.

Since the *daimyō* and their retainers lived in castle towns, merchants, artisans, and workers congregated there to serve the needs of the ruling class. A sufficient number of large urban centers existed to qualify Tokugawa Japan as more than merely a rural-agrarian society. The mid-eighteenth-century population of Edo (Tokyo), the headquarters of the shogunate, is estimated to have been about one million, half of whom were townspeople, the other half the *daimyō* (who had to spend alternate years in the capital) and their retainers. The population of Osaka, the commercial center of western Japan, was about 400,000.[3]

Japan's population went from close to 20 million at the outset of the Tokugawa era to about 30 million at its close. The *samurai* population is estimated to have been about 1.8 million by the end of the Tokugawa period. The number of commoners was officially estimated at about 26 million in 1721,[4] remaining nearly constant for the rest of the Tokugawa era; the peasantry constituted over 80 percent of this figure, so townspeople probably numbered between 3 and 4 million. The bulk of the population, then, consisted of peasants, nominally placed right below the *samurai* in the social order because they were engaged in what the ruling class regarded as essential work. In reality, their plight was much worse than that of the townspeople.

In theory, the land belonged to the *shōgun* or the *daimyō,* and the peasants who tilled the soil were simply given plots of land to produce rice and other crops for the lord. The farmland was not theirs to buy or sell. Actually, however, peasants who were registered by the authorities as *honbyakushō* (full-fledged farmers) held rights over the plots that they tilled, as if they were their own private property. Over the years, some *honbyakushō* managed to acquire a considerable amount of land by either gaining possession of plots belonging to peasants who fell into debt or by reclaiming wasteland. Later, as wealthy townspeople and moneylenders also began to acquire land, absentee landownership began to penetrate villages near urban centers. Those who lost their farmlands became tenant farmers or hired workers laboring for wealthy farmers and absentee landowners in semi-serflike fashion.

The size of peasant holdings varied from region to region. Under the Tokugawa demesne the average was probably about 1 *chō,* the Bakufu prohibiting further fragmentation for fear that the peasants would be unable to pay their taxes and sustain their families on smaller holdings. In areas where land was scarce, such as out-of-the-way hamlets located in mountainous areas, holdings were, however, much smaller, frequently less than a half *chō.*

The peasants were required to turn over to the *daimyō* or Bakufu anywhere from 40 to 50 percent of their harvest as a land tax. As the economic needs of the ruling class became more acute, some *daimyō* collected as much as 70 percent of the yield. In addition to the land tax, a large number of miscellaneous taxes—taxes on doors, windows, female children, cloth, sake, hazel trees, beans, and hemp—were levied on the peasants.[5] The peasants were also called upon to provide corvée to maintain roads, bridges, and other public facilities as well as to repair horse stations along the main roads.

The ruling class regulated the lives of the peasants in minute detail, periodically issuing sumptuary decrees to curb peasant consumption, or proclaiming moral injunctions exhorting them to be frugal, diligent, and self-denying. The ruling class determined what the peasants could plant and grow; what they could eat, drink, and wear; and the kind of houses they could live in.[6] In some instances the *daimyō* even regulated daily work hours. These pronouncements were backed by the sword; little wonder that the ethos and mores of the Japanese peasantry came to be characterized by diligence, frugality, submissiveness, subservience, and self-denial.

However, the peasants could be driven to shatter the psychological barriers of servility and obedience, striking out in blind anger against the authorities, when their situation became desperate enough. In most instances, they sought redress through nonviolent means, submitting petitions to the *shōgun, daimyō,* or other high officials even though they knew they faced certain death because direct appeals to higher authorities were strictly forbidden. When their petitions failed to produce results, which was most often the case, they often turned to mass demonstrations or to violence. Between 1590 and 1867, there were over 2,800 peasant disturbances, most of them erupting in the latter half of that Tokugawa era. The number of peasants participating in these "uprisings" also increased, particularly in the latter stages of Bakufu rule. For example, in 1764, 200,000 peasants in the Kanto region near the capital rioted, protesting the onerous burden of corvée for the post-horse stations.[7]

Such uprisings erupted most frequently in years of major famines, when the peasants were literally driven to starvation. There were at least fifteen serious famines during the Tokugawa era, and, just as in the modern age, villagers in the northern areas suffered most severely. Especially severe famines occurred in the 1730s, the 1780s, and the 1830s. In each instance, hundreds of thousands of people starved to death. It has been said that 2 million people died of starvation in the Tenmei Famine of the 1780s. No doubt this figure is inflated, but it is believed that at least several hundred thousand people did indeed starve to death at that time.

During the Tenmei Famine, Sugae Masumi, an itinerant scholar, traveled through the northern villages and recorded his observations. In the late summer of 1785, when he was walking along the Tsugaru Peninsula, he came across mounds of bleached bones. While he was gazing in horror at the gruesome sight, a peasant came along and spoke to him:

These are the bones of people who starved to death. During the winter and spring of the year before last, these people collapsed in the snow. Some of them were still breathing as they lay on the ground. Their bodies blocked the road for miles and miles, and passersby had to tread around them carefully. At dusk and at night, one had to be careful not to step on corpses and snap bones or step into rotting guts. You probably cannot imagine the terrible stench that filled the air. In order to keep from starving to death we used to catch the horses roaming about, tie ropes around their necks, bind them to posts, cut into their flesh with swords or knives, cook the bloody meat with some grass, and eat it. We also used to catch chickens and dogs running around in the open and eat them. When we ran out of animals, we stabbed and killed our children, our brothers, or other people who were on death's door with some disease, and ate their flesh. We would bite into the flesh from their breasts to stay alive. The eyes of people who have eaten human flesh glisten in an eerie manner, like the eyes of wolves. The harvest this year is likely to be poor again so we will no doubt experience another winter of famine.[8]

Then the peasant burst into tears and walked away.

Our aim here is not a detailed exploration of the plight of the Tokugawa peasants. However, it is important to emphasize that, despite the recent tendency to question the characterization of Tokugawa Japan as feudal and its peasants as serfs, those peasants were, in fact, subjects whose reason for living, as the ruling class saw it, was solely to work the land and provide for the economic needs of the *samurai.* If 6 percent of the population expropriates 50 percent of the land's bounty, and leaves over 80 percent of the population to subsist on what remains, one does not have to be a Marxist to see in this system a classic case of exploitation. This was the conscious policy of the Tokugawa ruling class. An eighteenth-century Bakufu official asserted, "Sesame seeds and peasants are very much alike. The more you squeeze them, the more you can extract from them." Ieyasu, the founder of the Bakufu, said that the *samurai,* in their behavior toward the peasants, should act as arrogantly as they wished. "When the peasants see ordinary *samurai* behaving in such a manner, they will be terrified all the more of high officials and will not dare harbor treacherous thoughts. If the peasants are allowed to be self-indulgent, they are bound to stage peasant uprisings." Another high Bakufu official told his subordinates, "The peasants constitute the foundation of society. To govern them, a certain principle must be followed. First of all, the boundaries of each peasant's plots must be firmly established. Then, they should be allowed to retain what they must actually consume during the year. The rest should be taken up as annual contributions. The peasants must be governed in such a way that they have what is essential but no more."[9] The Tokugawa ruling class also believed in keeping the peasants ignorant. "A good peasant is one who does not know the price of grain" was a saying common among officialdom. "Peasants and townspeople," it was said, "should be forbidden to attend school."[10]

In 1868, the old order was overturned, and Japan entered a new era with the establishment of the Meiji government. The new leaders launched Japan on a path of "modernization," to make Japan rich and powerful. Although the downfall of the Bakufu was largely the result of internal developments, it was the advent of influence from the Western powers, with their insistence that Japan abandon its seclusionist policy and open itself up to international commerce, that contributed most profoundly to the difficulties confronting the Tokugawa government. The Bakufu complied with the Western powers' demands, and this then became its opponents' rallying point as they joined forces against the Tokugawa government in the name of "reverence for the emperor and exclusion of the barbarians." Once in power, however, the Bakufu's opponents dropped their isolationist position and set Japan once and for all on the course of Westernization. Although the methods favored by both the proponents of expelling Westerners and the advocates of opening the nation to external contacts were different, their objectives were the same. Well aware of Western encroachments on China, India, and other Asian nations, the political leaders of both groups strove to preserve Japan's independence.

In 1858, Tokugawa officials decided to conclude a commercial treaty with the United States, despite vehement opposition from powerful domestic forces. They were persuaded, in large part, by the arguments of U.S. envoy Townsend Harris: He contended Japan would be better off dealing with peace-minded Americans than awaiting the arrival of English or French agents who, fresh from their triumph over the Chinese in the so-called Arrow War, would demand greater concessions from the Japanese and be more willing to resort to force to extract them.[11] The transfer of power from the Tokugawa Bakufu to the Meiji government occurred without serious military conflicts largely because key advisers to the *shōgun* feared that a divisive power struggle would present the Western powers with an opportunity to intervene and compromise Japan's independence.[12] This external threat called forth in Japan those elements that Arnold Toynbee has categorized as Herodians. "The Herodian is the man who acts on the principle that the most effective way to guard against the danger of the unknown is to master its secret; and, when he finds himself in the predicament of being confronted by a more highly skilled and better-armed opponent, he responds with the enemy's own tactics and own weapons."[13] The Meiji leaders and their successors, it could be argued, were highly successful in pursuing the Herodian path. Fukuzawa Yukichi, a liberal advocate of Westernization, wrote in 1875, "Our goal is the preservation of our national independence. There is no other way to do so except through the adoption of [Western] civilization. Japan must advance toward civilization for the sake of preserving [that] independence."[14]

The proponents of Westernization, or modernization, in Japan were primarily interested in Western science, technology, and weaponry, not the West's moral or political ideals. This line of thinking, followed by the architects of Meiji Japan, was well expressed by a late Tokugawa Confucian scholar, Sakuma Zōzan (1811–1864), who stated, "In teachings concerning morality, benevolence and righteousness, filial piety and brotherly love, loyalty and faithfulness, we must follow the examples and precepts of the Chinese sages. In astronomy, geography, gunnery, commerce, medicine, machinery, and construction, we must rely mainly on the West."[15]

While its initial motivation for building a rich and powerful nation was defensive in nature, Japan soon joined the Western powers in competing for political and economic gains on the Asian continent. Increasingly, however, such a policy led to conflicts of interest with those Western powers, including a United States that, while professing the highest moral and idealistic motives, pursued a foreign policy of economic imperialism. The significance of the United States's "open-door policy" toward China—adopted in the name of international justice but, in fact, designed to protect U.S. economic interests in that country[16]—was not lost on the Meiji leaders.

Competition for international markets and resources as well as political advantages in Asia exerted a profound influence on Japanese leaders, whose perception of the Western powers as potential threats provided an excuse to demand of the Japanese people their continued personal sacrifice for the good of the nation. Hence, the new order that was established by the Meiji government failed to improve significantly the condition of the people at the lower levels of the social order. In fact, for many it meant greater hardship and suffering. In particular, the peasantry (already expected to provide the resources and manpower to build the wealth and power of the nation) was asked to sacrifice its lives, material resources, labor, and individual interests for the sake of the nation-state and, of course, for the benefit of the small elite at the top of the social pyramid. Still treated like sesame seeds, they were not allowed to share fully the fruits of modernization; little of the new "wealth" trickled down to the masses, and the powerful elite enjoyed as much wealth and influence as had the major Tokugawa *daimyō*. For example, in 1930, 84 percent of the populace —peasants and workers—possessed only 50 percent of the nation's household income, while 24,000 families, or 0.0019 percent of Japan's households, held over 10 percent of the aggregate family income of the nation. At the very top of this pyramid were nineteen families with annual incomes of over a million yen each, while, at the bottom, 2,232,000 families each had incomes of 200 yen or less.[17] As for power, political authority remained in the hands of an oligarchy that emerged to replace the Bakufu and its regional rulers; meanwhile the masses ended by sacrificing their lives on the battlefields or in the burned-out cities of 1945 Japan.

The Meiji Restoration

The Meiji restoration, in 1868, affected all levels of Japanese society in a dramatic fashion. The peasants, who constituted about 80 percent of the population, felt the impact of the transition from Tokugawa rule as powerfully as other segments of the society. Little wonder, since the new order involved the replacement of the Bakufu-Han system with the centralized authority of the new government, the official abolition of feudal class divisions, the termination of the feudal land-tenure system, the adoption of a new land-tax arrangement, recognition of private land ownership, the initiation of major measures to industrialize the nation, the establishment of an army and navy modeled after Western armed forces, and the adoption of a universal educational system.

Even before the actual restoration took place, the authority of the ruling Tokugawa Bakufu had been challenged by rival regional powers, and anti-Bakufu sentiments had begun to spread not just to certain segments of the *samurai* class but also to the peasantry. While, among the *samurai,* this sentiment took the form of *sonnō jōi* ("reverence for the emperor and exclusion of the barbarians"), peasant discontent took the form of *yonaoshi ikki* ("uprisings to remake the society").

As already noted, the number and scale of peasant uprisings began to increase during the second half of the Tokugawa era. The peasants' most numerous complaints concerned their heavy taxation, but the burden of the corvée, abusive officials, the growing concentration of land in the hands of wealthier peasants, difficulties resulting from the penetration of a money economy into the villages, the establishment of *han* monopolies, new administrative measures, food shortages, and the need for aid and relief were all causes of peasant unrest.[18] Between 1865 and 1867 alone, there were seventy-five peasant disturbances, and, while these incidents were not directly responsible for the downfall of the Tokugawa government, they added to the general erosion of the sociopolitical fabric that had sustained Tokugawa rule for over two and a half centuries.

Some *han,* hostile to the Bakufu, introduced a policy of enlisting the common people, including the peasants, into their military units. The most notable example of this policy was seen in Chōshū, the leading anti-Bakufu domain, where Takasugi Shinsaku (1839–1867) organized the *kiheitai* ("shock troops") in 1863. The function of the *kiheitai* was to support the regular troops and stage something like guerrilla warfare against the Tokugawa regime.[19] Before the Tokugawa regime fell, imperial authorities sought to turn peasants under the Bakufu against it by permitting freebooting *rōnin* ("masterless warriors") to spread word among the peasants that a 50 percent reduction in taxes would be effected if the imperial forces came to power. This ploy was persuasive in some areas.

The Bakufu took steps of its own to incorporate peasants into its military forces. In 1863, peasants numbered among its constabulary; and in 1864, when the Bakufu was faced with an insurgent Mito-han (one of its collateral houses), it enlisted as many as 1,500 peasants into its army. In 1865, it mobilized two battalions of peasants in the Kyoto area and armed them with rifles. By the end of its rule—far too late to affect events—the Bakufu was pursuing a general policy of enlisting peasants and other commoners into its infantry.[20]

The peasant disturbances that plagued the Tokugawa government in the closing years of its rule continued into the early Meiji years as the peasants, often led by prominent village landowners, demanded that the new regime fulfill its promise to reduce taxes by 50 percent and improve the peasantry's lot. Because peasant unrest endangered the imperial authorities' plan to effect a rapid transition from Tokugawa to imperial rule, the new rulers resolutely set out to quash peasant troublemakers. They also retracted the promise to reduce taxes by half. It is believed by some historians that the opposing regimes' decision to peacefully transfer control of the capital city of Edo (Tokyo) was made in part because the ruling class feared that infighting might touch off widespread peasant uprisings.[21]

The New Order

The abolition of the feudal order and the establishment of a centralized political system did not affect the political life of the vast majority of the peasants immediately because, at the village level, they still had to deal with the same community leaders who had traditionally served as agents of the feudal lords or the Bakufu. That is, former village leaders, variously known as *shōya, nanushi,* and *toshiyori,* depending on the locality, retained their special status as local leaders. In most instances they were appointed to the newly created post of *kochō* ("chief magistrate"), an office that was established in 1872.[22] When a system of local self-government was instituted in 1888, the old-line village leaders were again chosen, in most instances, as village heads *(sonchō).* A system of village councils was introduced at the same time, but the franchise was given only to those who paid a land tax or a direct national tax of at least 2 yen. These taxpayers were divided into two classes: the major taxpayers, a small group who paid half the tax of the community and had the right to choose half the local council members; and the minor taxpayers, who chose the other half. For example, in one village the major taxpayers, twenty-six landowners, elected the same number of council members as the 449 minor taxpayers. To qualify for the franchise for the prefectural assembly, one had to pay a tax of at least 5 yen, and, to be eligible to serve in the assembly, one had to pay at least 10 yen. For the national Diet, which was convened in 1890, the right to vote and the right to serve in the lower house were limited to those paying at least 15 yen in taxes. This meant that one had to own at least 2 *chō* (4.9 acres) of land. When the first election for the Diet was held, only 1.14 percent of the population was qualified to vote.[23]

The fifteen highest taxpayers in every prefecture had special representation in the upper house of the Diet in that they were entitled to choose one of the men in their circle to serve in that body.[24] Consequently, for the vast majority of the peasants the new political order offered no direct, or even indirect, access to political power. Universal manhood suffrage was not introduced until 1925, and not until 1947 did women gain the right to vote.

The changes that affected the lives of the peasants more directly were the abolition of the feudal class system and the elimination of many social restrictions. During 1869–1871, feudal domains were eliminated as the former feudal lords relinquished their authority to the imperial government. In the process, the class divisions of *samurai*, peasants, artisans, and merchants were abolished and the populace was reclassified as *kazoku* ("peers"), *shizoku* ("gentry"), and *heimin* ("commoners")—not for legal purposes, it was said, but for purposes of identification in the family registers kept in the village and town offices. Legal barriers against interclass marriages were removed and people were granted the freedom to pursue any vocation and live in any district they wished. The common people were now permitted—in fact, required—to adopt family names, a privilege denied them under the old regime. Restrictions formerly imposed on their dress, hairstyles, and mode of travel (travel on horseback had been forbidden) were abandoned, and they were no longer required to grovel in the dirt in the presence of *samurai*. Moreover, they no longer had to fear being arbitrarily cut down by an indignant *samurai* for some slight or imagined offense.

Needless to say, the removal of legal distinctions and restrictions did not mean that the common people were now accorded complete equality with the upper classes, particularly in the social realm. The patricians expected them to continue to be humble and respectful in manner and speech. After World War II, a woman who had been born in 1858 recalled:

We were told [at the time of the Meiji restoration] that the lord of Satsuma was the greatest person in Satsuma [Kagoshima prefecture], and the emperor was the greatest person in Japan. Well, even though the lord of Satsuma was replaced by the emperor, it was something that happened high above and had no relation to us. There were no longer any *samurai* with swords on their hips, but up until the end of the last war the former *samurai* class still distinguished between *shizoku* and commoners and behaved as if we were their servants and were to take care of them as if they were gods. Until the end of the war the *shizoku* addressed us peasants in insulting terms.[25]

The commoners in turn found it difficult to overcome the sense of inferiority that had for centuries been instilled in them at the point of a sword. Fukuzawa Yukichi (1834–1901), a propagator of Western ideas and knowledge as well as an advocate of individualism and freedom, claimed that he was dismayed when he discovered that the new order had not changed the common people's thinking and behavior. Soon after the restoration, he had the following experience with a peasant:

Once when I was taking my children to Kamakura and Enoshima on a holiday, we met a farmer coming on horseback as we were passing along the seashore. As soon as he saw us he jumped off the horse. I caught hold of his bridle and said, "What do you mean by this?" The farmer bowed as if in great fear and began to apologize in his voluble way. "No, no," I said. "Don't be a fool! This is your horse, isn't it?"

"Yes, Your Honor."

"Then why not ride on your own horse? Now, get back on and ride on." The poor fellow was afraid to mount before me. "Now, get back on your horse," I repeated. "If you don't, I'll beat you. According to the laws of the present government, any person, farmer or merchant, can ride freely on horseback, without regard to whom he meets on the road. You are simply afraid of everybody without knowing why. That's what's the matter with you." I forced him to get back on the horse and drove him off. . . .[26]

Fukuzawa also found that the peasants behaved differently toward him depending on the manner [in which he spoke]. In 1872, when he was walking along a road near Osaka, he "stopped a man who looked like a farmer and asked him the way. Probably there was something of the *samurai* manner in my speech and, without realizing it, I may have sounded commanding. The farmer replied very politely and left me with a respectful bow." When he spoke in the haughty tone of a *samurai* to another peasant, "The poor fellow shivered at the roadside." Fukuzawa then spoke to another peasant using the obsequious demeanor of a merchant. The peasant "eyed me haughtily and went on his way without giving me much of an answer." He tried alternating his manner and speech in this way to test the reactions of passersby and found that "people would respond according to the manner in which they were addressed—with awe or with indifference."[27]

While retaining their sense of humility and deference toward the former *samurai,* the peasants expected those who were formerly beneath them in status—the outcastes (then known as *eta* or *hinin*)—to stay in their places. Some of the peasant riots and demonstrations that broke out in the early Meiji years were triggered by peasant objections to dealing with outcastes as equals.

LAND OWNERSHIP

Immediately after the Meiji restoration, rumors began to spread that the government was planning to confiscate all land and redistribute it in equal portions among the farmers. A village elder in a northern hamlet observed in his notebook in 1868 that "there is a rumor that each farm family will be given equal allotments of land worth 6 *koku*. I wonder if such a thing is possible? In our village of Okubo, the total yield is 700 *koku*. There are 300 families, so each family's receiving 6 *koku* would require 1,800 *koku*. In some villages the situation must be the reverse. I can't figure out how they intend to implement this policy."[28] He need not have worried about the practical implementation of equal land distribution; the rumors were false.

In the province of Hiroshima the new government officials felt it necessary in 1871 to issue a proclamation squelching such rumors. "It has been bruited about recently that all debts will be canceled and all the farmlands and woodlands will be expropriated by the government and then redistributed in equal portions to the people. These rumors are wholly without foundation. Such measures will absolutely not be adopted. Everyone should stop worrying and go about his business as usual. If anyone is found to be spreading such rumors, report such activities immediately to the prefectural office."

Similar rumors existed in other areas of the country. A merchant from central Japan, doing business in Yokohama, heard that all the *daimyō, samurai,* and court aristocrats, except those with special talents, were giving their land to the government and becoming ordinary farmers. He also heard that all farmlands would be confiscated and redistributed; thus, he advised his son back home to sell as quickly as possible all the land that they had been holding liens on. "These rumors have been going around for some time but people have been saying such things could not possibly happen. Now we find that other rumors are turning out to be true, so it is not entirely unlikely that the farmlands will be confiscated and redistributed."[29]

This was a time of revolutionary change, and it was not surprising that such rumors spread. One story had it that "Japan will soon be turned over to France. They say that the French flag will soon be hoisted over the imperial palace in Edo [Tokyo]. The emperor will leave by boat for Satsuma on May 23 [1872] and from there will sail for a foreign land. These are absolute facts, I am told."[30]

Although a redistribution of land was never even considered by the authorities, the government did recognize private ownership of land. Deeds on plots of land were turned over to the peasants who had been tilling them on behalf of their lords. These peasants were also granted the right to buy and sell land as they pleased, and to raise whatever crop they chose.

Recognition of private ownership of land was accompanied by a new system of taxation. Instead of exacting the 40 to 60 percent of harvest demanded by the Tokugawa regime and its feudal lords, the Meiji government imposed a tax at the rate of 3 percent of the assessed value of the land. This came to about 33 percent of yield. Since the new tax had to be paid in currency, the amount of rice that had to be set aside to pay the tax depended on the price of rice; so the economic well-being of landowning peasants was now linked to fluctuations in the value of rice.

At the same time, the government deprived villagers of the right to make free use of village woodlands and meadows. These lands had previously been accessible to all the villagers for the gathering of timber, firewood, fodder, and edible plants. Now, the new regime claimed them as government property. In some cases, the village leader (shōya), in whose name they were officially registered, actually laid claim to them as his own personal property. The rich timberlands of the Kiso region in central Japan were turned into the private property of the imperial family, and anyone who poached in these imperial forests was treated as a criminal.[31]

The heavy cost of the Meiji government's determined program of modernization was to be borne primarily by the agrarian sector. During the years from 1875 to 1879, 80.5 percent of the government's revenue came from the land tax; between 1882 and 1892, 85.6 percent. Two decades later, due to the growth of the industrial sectors of the economy, the percentage dropped to 42.9 percent. Meanwhile, the absolute value of the land tax doubled.[32] The land tax, coupled with the fluctuation in the price of rice, caused small and medium-sized farmowners to fall increasingly into debt, with many ultimately losing their land.

Among the numerous measures introduced by the Meiji government, the adoption of compulsory military service in 1873 may have had the most far-reaching implications for the masses. Until the closing years of the old regime, warfare was solely the business of the *samurai*. Now the entire male population was eligible for military service.

Initially the government emphasized that conscription was based on the principle of extending freedom and equality to all. In its proclamation, the government asserted, "First there is military service. After that, the people are free to pursue their chosen occupations. . . . If people want freedom, they must take part in military service."[33] Nonetheless, the peasants' reaction was negative; they were not overly impressed with the fact that they were now being allowed to perform a function formerly reserved for the privileged *samurai* class.

The term *ketsuzei* ("blood tax") was often used to describe the conscription system. Many peasants took this to mean that actual blood would be extracted from them. In Shizuoka prefecture, rumors spread that "they will draft young men, hang them upside down, and draw out their blood so that Westerners can drink it. What the Westerners in Yokohama are drinking—something called wine, it is said—is actually the blood of these young men. The blood is also used to dye the army blankets, uniforms, and caps."[34] It was also rumored that after all the young men in the village had been drafted, all the female virgins from thirteen to twenty-five would be drafted too. As a result, many parents hastened to get their daughters married off.

In numerous villages of Shikoku, the following note was circulated in late 1871:

Recently, the government has driven out the lord of our domain, placed evil officials, who are in favor of foreigners, in prefectural offices. They intend to sell us Japanese to foreigners so that they can extract fat from our bodies for their nourishment. . . . Unless we restore the lord to power, punish the evil officials, and drive out the foreign barbarians as soon as possible, in five years there will not be a single Japanese left in the land. We must all be prepared to drive out the evil-doers. You must collect ropes, bamboo spears, and guns to be ready to attack at any time. Anyone who refuses to join this movement will be regarded as an ally of the government, and his house will be burned down.[35]

Villagers then went on rampages, attacking the houses of officials, police stations, schools, and other public facilities. Eventually about 20,000 people were arrested and punished. Similar anticonscription riots erupted in other parts of the country and, despite vigorous efforts to instill patriotic zeal in the peasants, evasion of conscription persisted. In 1881, the minister of war bemoaned the fact that not a single person had responded to the draft in one district in Nagasaki prefecture.[36]

Resistance to the draft was not simply founded on ignorance and misconceptions as the ruling authorities charged. Most of the peasants were aware that military conscription was a form of forced labor akin to the corvée they had resented and resisted during the Tokugawa period and was, in fact, worse because it required many years' service. When questioned by the authorities, one of the leaders of the anticonscription movement said, "If we are conscripted into the military we will not be released for six to seven years and will be bound to suffer hardships."[37] The length of service was actually three years, but that was hardship enough, amounting to a serious loss of manpower for peasant families.

A booklet published in 1879 to foster "civilization" in the country featured an "ignoramus" criticizing military conscription as follows:

I am really unhappy about military conscription. As far as the *shizoku* are concerned, warfare is their way of life. They are given stipends to keep their bellies full, and they spend year after year idling their time away. So it's only natural for them to give up their lives when they are called upon to do so. But to exhort peasants and shopkeepers—who have to give up even their last grain of rice and receive nothing in return, and who can't tell left from right when it comes to public affairs—to go to war and give up their lives is asking too much of them. After all the talk about granting people their rights, freedom, and so on, to dragoon protesting recruits, the precious sons of the people, and let their corpses bleach in the fields and mountains or send them home maimed and crippled makes no sense at all.[38]

Only early in the Meiji period, before the tide of militarism swept the land, could a commonsense viewpoint like this be openly expressed.

Under the conscription system all men over the age of twenty who were physically fit were subject to the draft, but there were numerous exemptions. For example, heads of households and those in line to succeed to that position within the family—the family's sole son, and men adopted to carry on the family line—were exempt from the draft.

To prevent their younger sons from being drafted, many parents set up separate households for them or tried to have them adopted into families lacking male heirs. As an old peasant woman, recalling the early Meiji years, remarked, "In those days the practice of marrying in order to avoid the draft was common. The eldest son was exempt from the draft but the younger sons were not. So marriages were often arranged for the purpose of evading the draft. . . . [As a teenager] I was fixed up with my uncle, who was twenty-five years old."[39]

The government also allowed prospective draftees to pay their way out of the army for 270 yen, a formidable sum, which no ordinary peasant could pay. The fee was raised to 400 yen in 1879, leaving only the very rich to gain exemption by this route. The practice was terminated in 1889.

Reluctance to serve in the army began to wane with the Sino-Japanese War of 1894–1895. The patriotic fervor and militarism that were fanned by the war, and the hero's welcome accorded the victorious soldiers, aroused enthusiasm for military service even among the peasantry.[40] From this point on, the army became an important vehicle for indoctrinating young peasants in the virtues of *chūkun aikoku* ("loyalty to the emperor and love of country"). And although military service tended to broaden the perspective of the peasant draftees, taking them beyond the confines of their isolated villages, the ultimate effect on them was not a liberalizing one, for the discipline and indoctrinating techniques the army inculcated in the new draftees created chauvinists who became little more than agents of militarism in the countryside.

THE NATIONAL EDUCATION SYSTEM

In 1872, the government introduced a universal education system that in theory was compulsory, although, in the beginning, attendance was not stringently enforced. This system, too, had an increasingly profound impact on peasant life, particularly as it came to serve as a vehicle for nationalistic indoctrination.

Initially, the requirement to send their children to school presented real difficulties to the peasants. It not only meant sending children to school who could otherwise help in the house and on the farm, but it also proved a financial imposition because of the tuition charge. Depending on the locality, the tuition fees ranged from 12.5 sen to 50 sen per child per month. For peasants whose average monthly income was about 1 yen 75 sen in 1878, the burden was considerable. In some areas, the villagers became so angry that they burned down school buildings.

On the other hand, the authorities were not very exacting in collecting the fees; nor were they very strict about attendance. Only about 10 percent of all schooling costs were covered by the required tuition,[41] and peasant participation remained low despite the relatively few years of attendance—three to four years—that were supposedly compulsory. In 1872, when the new education system went into effect, only 28 percent of all school-age children enrolled. By 1878, the figure had reached 40 percent. However, attendance by girls lagged well behind that of boys. As late as 1890, boys outnumbered girls in school by better than two to one.[42] Until the end of the century, most peasant families continued to regard educating their daughters as a futile endeavor. Hence, illiteracy among rural girls of school age remained high. The vaunted success of the Japanese in virtually eradicating illiteracy by the turn of the century was a myth. Such statements as "by the early years of this century illiteracy had practically disappeared from the villages" could only be made by people who were not well acquainted with village life.[43]

PEASANT REACTION:
PAIN, BEWILDERMENT, AND ANGER

Those peasant grievances that persisted from the Tokugawa period were only aggravated by the new measures introduced in such rapid succession by the Meiji government. This led to continued peasant demonstrations and riots. In the first years of Meiji, there were 180 such disturbances. Anger over high taxes caused fifty-seven incidents; resentment of village officials and wealthy farmers touched off thirty-three disturbances; and high prices, another seventeen. In 1873, when military conscription went into effect, twelve protest demonstrations erupted. An antidraft protest in Kagawa prefecture involved about 10,000 peasants.[44] There were also complaints about the granting of equality to the *burakumin,* the introduction of Christianity, innoculation against cholera, and other new measures that aroused the peasants' fears and suspicions.[45]

Not all these incidents were minor affairs. In 1873, 300,000 people in Fukuoka prefecture rioted, incensed by the high prices they believed to be caused by wealthy merchants' hoarding of rice. They attacked the houses of wealthy farmers and merchants, public buildings, schoolhouses, telegraph offices, and other symbols of wealth and authority. In all, 4,590 buildings were destroyed or damaged by the rioters. The government called in troops against the demonstrators, and a number of rioters were killed. Those identified as leaders were executed or sent to prison, and more than 63,000 were subjected to corporal punishment.[46]

The new land tax was also among the major causes of peasant unrest. In many instances, the conversion from payment by rice to payment by currency increased the peasants' financial burden. If the price of rice fell, the peasants had to sell more rice to make enough money for the tax payments. Moreover, the government assessors and the peasants often disagreed about the value of the land, which determined the rate of taxation. The government's response to peasant protesters was to threaten them. One prefectural governor told the peasants, "Those who oppose the government's land assessment will be deemed traitors, and they and their entire families will be stripped naked and exiled to foreign lands."[47] Such threats did not, however, prevent peasant protests from erupting, and in many areas troops had to be called out to quell demonstrators.

In late 1876, peasants from four prefectures in central Japan objected to high tax assessments. The price of rice had fallen, but the government calculated the per-*koku* price of rice at higher than market value. When government officials refused to heed the peasants' plea for adjustments in the assessment, 10,000 peasants in Mie prefecture congregated in protest. They soon turned to violence, attacking and destroying public buildings. The movement spread to other communities in central Japan, but, because the protests were not coordinated and remained separate acts of violence, the authorities were able to quash them. The leaders of the Mie protestors were sentenced to life imprisonment or death. Over 50,000 people were fined or punished. Although government officials managed to subdue the agitators, they began to fear a possible alliance between discontented peasants and the disgruntled *samurai* who had lost their status during the Meiji restoration. Perhaps in response to this fear, the authorities decided to reduce the land tax from 3 percent of the land value to 2.5 percent. This led to the saying, "The bamboo spear zings and we get our 2.5 percent!"[48]

After 1877, peasant disturbances tapered off, but the economic plight of the peasants continued to worsen. The burden of the land tax and other taxes together with the declining price of what the farmers brought to market (a result of the deflationary economic policies adopted by Finance Minister Matsukata Masayoshi in the early 1880s) led to the bankruptcy of large numbers of farm households. In 1883, there were 33,845 such cases; the number rose to 108,050 in 1885. This meant that, in 1885 alone, at least 400,000 people (based on an average four-member family) were left with no means of livelihood.[49]

The rapacious behavior of the moneylenders, to whom peasant families resorted in order to pay their taxes and provide their daily necessities, only added to this crisis. One victim of a moneylender related that, when a person went to a usurer to borrow 10 yen, he was given only 8 yen, the other 2 having been deducted at the outset for interest and a processing fee. For a three-month loan, the borrower had to repay the full 10 yen, plus 66 sen in additional interest. If he failed to make the payment in three months and got a three-month extension, the repayment was raised to 12 yen 79.5 sen. When extended yet another three months, it rose to 20 yen 95.9 sen. Finally, when the borrower failed to make this payment on time and refused to apply for yet another extension at an even higher rate, the lender got the authorities to confiscate the man's property and auction it off.[50]

While this was an extreme case, most moneylenders charged usurious rates and were merciless in collecting what was due. Government officials usually sided with the moneylenders, and this often led the borrower to strike back at the moneylender with violence. But because such individual actions proved ineffective, borrowers began to organize associations under the rubrics of the Debtors' Party and the Poor People's Party in hopes of gaining a negotiating foothold. The police normally tried to disperse these groups, and, failing that, arrested and jailed the leaders.

In 1884, Sunaga Renzō, a well-to-do farmer and community leader in a village in Kanagawa prefecture, submitted a petition to the authorities, stating:

The 200,000 people of this prefecture are unable to repay their debts because of declining prices and the depressed state of the silkworm business and textile industry in general. They are plagued day and night with worries, sorrow, frustration, and hardship. People are being crushed underfoot by the usurers as if they were ants. The demonstration by the members of the Debtors' Party in this prefecture in mid-1884 proved to be fruitless; all we got was a lecture from the authorities. No leniency or generosity was forthcoming. . . . Under current conditions [the debtors] can find no way to repay their debts. I beg your excellencies to allow sentiments of morality and benevolence to come forth and, even if the letter of the law has to be distorted a little, to adopt measures that would aid the impoverished people.[51]

Otherwise, Sunaga warned, the debtors would turn to violence and attack the moneylenders' property and even the moneylenders themselves.

Neither local nor central government officials heeded the pleas of the poor, however, and peasant protests and demonstrations continued. In 1884, there were over 80 incidents in which debtor peasants and the police clashed, and, in May of that year, one such occurrence near the city of Hachiōji involved 3,000 peasants. The Kanto region, where the production of cash crops such as tea and silkworms had increased following the opening of trade with the West, became the center of the trouble, for it was the area most damaged by the government's deflationary policies.

The protest movement in the Kanto region culminated in the Chichibu Uprising of 1884. The residents of the county Chichibu in Saitama prefecture had in one year (1882–1883) suffered from a 50 percent drop in the price of raw silk, and the following year were hit by crop failures. Heavily in debt, the Chichibu peasants were subjected to particularly stringent collection tactics, the moneylenders having convinced the authorities to seize debtor property for the slightest delinquency in payment. The debtors sought to persuade county officials to effect a moratorium on repayments but failed. Their attempts to negotiate with the creditors were also futile. They thereupon organized a Poor People's Party that called for a ten-year moratorium on debts, extension of repayments over a forty-year period, reduction of local expenditures, and a rescinding of the compulsory-schooling requirement for three years.[52]

The sense of despair that permeated the Chichibu region is revealed in a poem entitled, "Making Tombstones," written by a local resident.

The wind blows,
The rain falls,
Young men die.
The groans of poverty
Flutter like flags in the wind.
When life makes no sense,
Even the old people quarrel.

The words on our tombstones,
Buried in the snowstorms of 1884,
Are not visible to the authorities.
In these times
We must cry out loudly.[53]

Among the leaders of the Chichibu Poor People's Party were radical members of the Liberal Party, a national political party committed to the cause of popular rights (though the national leadership of the party disavowed the Chichibu members, condemning them as radical extremists). Sixteen of these Chichibu Liberal Party members were convinced that the only way the poor could be helped was by overthrowing the Meiji government. To accomplish this, they believed it necessary to assassinate certain high government officials. When their plot was exposed in the fall of 1884, before they could take action, they decided to stage a "rebellion" at Mt. Kaba in Ibaraki prefecture. In their manifesto they stated,

Of primary importance in creating a nation is ensuring a fair distribution of the wealth and rights that heaven has bestowed on each individual. . . . It appears that our wise and virtuous emperor has neglected to realize that this is not the time to make heavy demands of people who are walking the road to starvation. As individuals who regard themselves as humanitarians and as patriots, we regret this pitiful situation and cannot endure it. . . . Accordingly, we will assemble an army on Mt. Kaba . . . to fight for revolution and to overthrow the despotic government.[54]

As might be expected, the "rebellion" was easily quelled. A more serious challenge was, however, facing the authorities: The Chichibu Poor People's Party was gathering an even larger force of "peasant soldiers."

Among the leaders of the would-be Chichibu rebels was Tashiro Eisuke (1834–1885), who came from a prominent Chichibu family and had become the local boss of a gang of gamblers. He too had lost his land and belongings because of the government's deflationary policy. When he was asked by the members of the Poor People's Party to help them deal with the moneylenders and government officials, he agreed to lend his support. When, after his arrest, he was questioned by the authorities about why he was chosen as the leader of the rebellion, Tashiro replied, "It is my nature to help the weak and crush the strong. When a poor or a weak person comes to me,

I take him in. For eighteen years I have served as a middleman for people in trouble. I have over 200 followers. As for the current affair, I saw the four-point program formulated by Inoue Denzō and others to help the poor, and I agreed with their position. So I was chosen as leader."[55]

Tashiro and his followers proceeded to rally the support of the Chichibu villagers and, in early November 1884, set out to confront the moneylenders and government officials. This "revolutionary army" was joined by thousands of peasants and other residents of the region, armed with rifles and swords, and marched toward Ōmiya (now Chichibu City), the county capital. En route they attacked the houses of moneylenders, vandalized public buildings, burned documents, stole weapons and money, and conscripted men for their army. By the time they reached Ōmiya, their ranks had risen to 3,000, and calls for support were sent out to outlying villages. As the number of rebels swelled to between 7,000 and 8,000, the insurgents proclaimed the establishment of a revolutionary government with Tashiro as prime minister. Up to this point the insurgents had not encountered government troops, but, when the government sent units of the Imperial Army against the rebels, the leadership panicked and their troops, except for a few contingents, dispersed. The rebellion was brought under control in about ten days. Approximately 3,000 insurgents were captured or surrendered. The authorities sentenced Tashiro and seven others to death (three in absentia), sent over thirty to prison for five to eight years each, and fined the rest. One of the leaders managed to escape and remained in hiding in the backwaters of Hokkaido for thirty-five years.[56]

Thus, the largest armed peasant uprising to confront the Meiji government ended, and the peasants learned that they could not hope to succeed in having their grievances redressed by force of rebellion. Most of the liberal leaders, champions of freedom and popular rights, condemned the uprising as the work of "hooligans, gamblers, and arsonists." A large number of these liberals had come from the *shizoku,* or wealthy farm and merchant families. They did not see themselves as committed to advancing the lot of the poor. Indeed, they saw any movement in which the poor participated as a threat to their privileged status. The newspapers associated with the Liberal Party condemned the emergence of "poor people's parties" as "a sickness that eats into the heart and guts of the nation" and "the onset of a most frightful disease."[57] Even though the liberals and other more progressive voices of the Meiji period constantly championed the "people," they usually meant only the *shizoku* and the wealthy commoners.

The suppression of the Chichibu Uprising signaled the end of any attempt on the part of the poor people's parties to rely on force to protect their interests. Although minor protest movements did occur afterward, they were readily squelched by the government. Bad weather in 1884–1885 caused crop failures, and the entire nation suffered from severe famines, but no uprisings occurred. Throughout 1885 the newspapers were full of accounts of starvation, the worst conditions prevailing in the Kanto region, where the disruptions caused by the earlier uprising aggravated the situation. Refugees from the countryside swarmed into the cities to beg and steal. Kitamura Tōkoku (1868–1894), who later gained renown as a poet, asked while observing the starving masses of the Kanto region, "While the rich and the powerful seek and acquire more wealth and power, what is to be done with the millions of destitute who have no home or food and are starving to death?" The government, whose policies had reduced countless farm families to poverty, could only respond, "They must work harder, be thrifty, and save more."[58]

For decades, impoverished peasants had no recourse but to endure their poverty and hardship in silence, permitting the government to exploit the fruits of their labor in order to pursue its policy of "building a rich and strong nation." Not until World War I and the triumph of the Bolsheviks in Russia did peasant activism directed against landlords (though not the political authorities) again come to the fore.

Thus, the condition of the peasants remained pathetic in contrast with the growing well-being of bourgeois capitalists. Farmowners continued to lose their land and the rate of tenancy steadily increased. In the years immediately following the Chichibu Uprising and the famine of 1885, the suicide rate rose precipitously, and the traditional means of "thinning out" the children by infanticide seems to have been practiced. One social observer noted that in a Kanto prefecture most peasant families had only one boy and one girl.[59] As we shall see, the only other avenue available to the desperately impoverished peasants was to send their children, especially their daughters, to work in the silk and cotton factories that were springing up, or to sell their daughters to brothels both in Japan and overseas.

FARMING

AND

FARM

LIFE

Land Use and Farm Work

Japan is an island nation of 144,000 square miles with limited arable land. Seventy-five percent of the country is hilly or mountainous with an average slope of more than fifteen degrees. Nearly 65 percent of the land with a slope of fifteen degrees or less is tilled, but even with such an intensive effort, less than 16 percent of the land mass, about 14 million acres, is cultivated today. About 30 percent of Japanese farm villages are located along foothills and 20 percent in the mountains. The other half is located in flat coastal areas.[1]

The average number of farm households in these 150,000 farming communities is small. Nonetheless, the houses are crowded into narrow, cramped areas. According to the 1960 World Agriculture Census, the average Japanese farm settlements consisted of thirty-nine farm households and twenty-eight nonfarm households. From the Meiji to the immediate postwar years, the number of farm families remained more or less constant at around 5.5 million.[2]

The plots cultivated by the Japanese farmers are neither large nor open, but consist of small strips of wet (rice) and dry fields, often terraced and climbing hillsides. Japanese farming is a labor-intensive activity—much like gardening in England or America, with practically every plant (in the case of fruits, each individual fruit) receiving close attention and care. The land tilled by the average farm family in the prewar years was miniscule by Western standards. In the early Meiji period, about 40 percent of all farm households owned 1.1 acres or less, and 70 percent cultivated less than 1.0 *chō* (2.45 acres). This included plots held in tenancy as well as those owned by the tiller. The amount of farmland sufficient to sustain a family varied from region to region. In Hokkaido, where only a single crop was harvested each year, farms of less than 5 *chō* (12.25 acres) were regarded as being especially small;[3] 73.7 percent of all Hokkaido farm families lived on such farms in the 1880s.

In the northern sections of Honshu, the main island, one crop in wet fields and two in upland fields could be harvested annually. Here, farms with less than 2 *chō* (4.9 acres) under cultivation were considered especially small. About 81.8 percent of all farm households in this region farmed such holdings. In southwestern Japan, where double-cropping was practiced in both wet and dry fields, farms of less than 1.5 *chō* fell into this category. In the 1880s, 92.6 percent of all farm households subsisted on these meager plots of land.

The size of the area tilled by the average farm family did not increase in subsequent years. The average tillage per family remained below 3.0 chō on the islands of Honshu, Shikoku, and Kyushu from the 1880s until the immediate postwar years.[4] In other words, the vast majority of the peasantry (chief among them, tenant farmers) remained in the category of "water-drinking peasants"; that is, people who had to ease their hunger pains by drinking water.

The mode of farming in the Meiji era differed very little from that of pre-Meiji years. In fact, historian Thomas Smith has pointed out that "in the course of its long history, Japanese agriculture has in some respects changed remarkably little. . . . Although a Heian [from the ninth through the twelfth centuries] peasant would no doubt be perplexed by many things about contemporary farming—above all its human relations—the main operations of planting, tilling, and harvesting he would understand."[5] One might bring the point of comparison closer by several centuries and contend that little change had taken place in Japanese farming since the Ashikaga period (from the fourteenth through the sixteenth centuries) when agricultural improvements in tools, irrigation, seeds, and fertilizers, as well as greater use of draft animals were introduced. Before World War II, much farm work was performed by combining traditional tools with human muscle power. Although draft animals were used to plow the rice fields, the tilling was done by hand and heavy objects were transported to and from the fields on people's backs and shoulders.

The Meiji leaders aspired to increase agricultural production by introducing scientific ideas and "modern" (that is, Western) methods of farming. They established experimental agricultural stations but failed to support the effort with sufficient funds because of budgetary demands from other interests, in particular industry and the military. Some officials hoped to adopt large-scale commercial farming patterned after Western farms, but Japan's topography made this impossible except on Hokkaido and in Iwate prefecture. Moreover, the production of rice, Japan's most important crop, was a labor-intensive undertaking not suited for large-scale mechanized farming.[6] As a result, traditional means of production remained basically unchanged.

During this period, however, productivity was increased somewhat by the use of more and better fertilizers, better seeds, double cropping, and some improvements in farming techniques. But production had already been maximized to such an extent by traditional intensive farming that this increase in per-acre yield was barely sufficient to keep up with population growth. From the 1870s until 1920, the annual growth rate in agriculture was only about 1.0 percent.[7]

Approximately 53 percent of all arable land was given over to the production of rice. The yield per *tan* (0.245 acre) in paddy fields varied from area to area, but the national average for 1873–1877, one economist estimates, was around 1.6 *koku*. (One *koku* equals 4.96 bushels.) This increased to about 1.9 *koku* by 1920. The production of other cereals increased more substantially, but these grains were used mainly as supplementary food and were not as crucial in the production scheme as rice was to either the peasants or to the government.[8]

Because farming alone hardly provided an adequate income, most farm families turned to other activities for additional income. Raising silkworms for the burgeoning silk industry became one of the important sources of such supplementary income. By the 1930s, 2 million, or 40 percent, of all farm households were raising silkworms.[9] In addition, peasant families used every spare minute to produce straw sandals, ropes, and mats to earn a few extra sen. Adult male villagers living near cities where industrial work was available often commuted to work in the factories, leaving the farm work to women and children. Many youngsters were sent off to the cities to work in shops, restaurants, and factories or to serve as maids in the homes of the wealthy. In times of crisis, young girls were sold to brothels.

According to a farm-household survey made in 1939, 24 percent of farm families relied less on agriculture than on other occupations for their income, while another 31 percent received some, if not their major, income from nonagricultural work. In the immediate postwar years less than half of the farm households could be categorized as full-time farm families.[10]

There was nothing idyllic, wholesome, or romantic about farm work. The peasants were engaged in a bitter struggle for survival. Long hours of painful, tortuous work reaped little in return. Typically, a young girl who came out of a rural village in Kagoshima prefecture to work in a textile plant in Osaka in 1939 commented, "Think of weeding . . . in June in the rice field with the burning sun on your back and crawling on all fours in the boiling paddy-field water. Compared to that, indoor [factory] work is easy."[11]

There was almost unanimous agreement among the old women of central Japan, who as young girls went to work in the silk filatures, that despite the strenuous working conditions in the plants, farm work in their home villages was more taxing.

If they remained at home, they would have to work longer hours, taking on more strenuous work. They would have to cut trees in the mountains and remove stones to make tillable plots for growing millet and barnyard grass. But this would not result in the production of enough food for the year. They would have to climb steep hills with firewood on their backs, burn charcoal in the snow, dig bracken roots, work all night to make bracken-root powder, and exchange it for barnyard grass. They had to continue working like this from before dawn until ten and eleven at night.[12]

Shibuya Teisuke, a young farmer in the Kanto region who became a fighter for agrarian rights in the 1920s kept a record of his feelings about his daily life. Working in the rice paddy with his ox, he noted in his diary in late May 1925: "The ox is so tired he barely moves. Red leeches cling to his and my legs. . . . My ankles are painful with holes made by the leeches, which suck my blood." On another occasion, he commented, "The weather is good so I sweat a lot. When my body touches the ears of the wheat the awns drop onto my neck. . . . My body is covered with dust and awns. . . . By the time I make two trips transporting the wheat on the oxcart, it is half past five. I then go out in the field to hoe the rice paddy. . . . When I finish hoeing 8 se (about 0.025 acre) it is dark." Again, in mid-June, he wrote, "My younger brother and I hoe the rice paddy. The rain beats on our bodies from all directions. . . . Soon we are soaking wet. Both of us began to feel stomach pains. My younger brother complains, almost in tears. I feel like crying too. Ah, such hard work! What kind of life is this? The way we work is full of contradictions. . . . At four-thirty the whistle of the silk mill blows. My brother and I leave the rice field and go [to collect the] human waste [from the mill]. . . . We transport four cartloads. By the time we return the buckets to the [railroad] station, it is eleven at night." In December, he noted an encounter with a friend who was in the army medical corps. His friend told Shibuya that "his work in the army is easier than farm work. The food is good, and second-year soldiers have considerable free time. He is more worried about the hard work that is waiting for him on the farm after he is mustered out. At first, until one gets used to the regulations in the army camp, things are tougher than on the farm, but once one gets used to things army life is a lot better than farm life."[13]

Another man who came out of the farm community and to become active in the agrarian reform movement recalled:

I used to get up early in the morning to go to the rice field and work all day, then come home and sleep. This was my daily routine. I would work day after day, and yet my condition did not improve at all. I began to think that to spend my whole life like this would be like being in prison all my life. I began to feel keenly how miserable a farmer's life is. I kept wondering if there wasn't anything I could do about my life. I was twenty-one then. In those days the schools emphasized Ninomiya Sontoku's basic principles (that is, the virtue of hard work and frugality) and the concept of enriching and strengthening the nation. In the fifty households in our village, I was the only person who had gone to school two years beyond the six years of compulsory education.[14]

Living Conditions: Rural Versus Urban Life

With the establishment of the new Meiji government, a policy of adopting Western products, ways, and institutions, insofar as they contributed to the enhancement of the nation's wealth and power, was pursued. In the urban areas, particularly in Tokyo, a mania for things Western appeared destined to overwhelm traditional attitudes and institutions. Beef-eating (a taboo among most Japanese until then), Western hairstyles, Western apparel, and even ballroom dancing were seen as signs of "civilization." Trains, gaslight, the telegraph, and newspapers were introduced quickly and hastened the pace of urban life. Western books were translated into Japanese, and books about the West were written by advocates of "civilization," by which was meant Western civilization. But these artifacts and customs were slow to reach rural communities. Thus, the introduction of Western civilization into Japanese culture only widened the gap between rural and urban Japan, in effect creating two Japans, with the latter centered on Tokyo.

This disparity was obvious even to social critics writing in the early Meiji years. Fukuzawa Yukichi wrote in a magazine in 1874:

The purpose [of the government] seems to be to use the fruits of rural labor to make flowers for Tokyo. Steel bridges glisten in the capital, and horse-drawn carriages run on the streets, but in the country the wooden bridges are so rotten that one cannot cross them. The cherry blossoms bloom in Kyōbashi [in Tokyo], but weeds grow in the country fields. Billows of smoke such as rise from city stoves do not rise from the farmer's furnace. . . . We must cease making Tokyo richer and concentrate on rural districts.[15]

A newspaper article appearing in the same period observed: "A hundred times as much gold and rice circulate in Tokyo as did in the feudal days. Consequently, the city has railways, steam engines, fine stone buildings, military ministries, gaslights, and bridges. Construction expenses for one day are astounding. Cannot something be done to cause riches to flow into the outlying provinces?"[16]

These differences continued to be remarked upon by later observers. One social historian writing around the time of the first Sino-Japanese War (1894–1895) commented that war profits benefited the urban areas while the rural communities got nothing. The rural areas remained impoverished and stayed largely untouched by Western civilization.[17] The rural-urban split had its counterpart in the growing gulf that divided the upper and lower classes. In the words of one Japanese historian: "Whatever its advantages, Western culture as imported in the Meiji period served to separate the upper classes from the lower classes in a way in which they had never before been separated. Western politics, Western economy, Western religion, Western thought, Western art, and Western social movements produced a class of politicians, capitalists, and intellectuals who had no connection with the common people."[18]

The period after World War I saw a noticeable movement toward "modernity," especially among the younger generation of the middle and upper classes in major cities like Tokyo. The 1920s was the decade of the *mo-bo* and *mo-ga* ("modern boys" and "modern girls") in the cities. Movies, phonograph records, colorful magazines, radios, neon lights, dancing, café-bars, and fancy department stores seemed to be turning these cities into gaudy replicas of Western cities. But the rural villages remained almost wholly unaffected by the changes until the end of World War II.[19]

The growing chasm between the life-styles of the "two Japans" led urban dwellers to look down on provincial "hayseeds" even more than before, while sensitive rural dwellers developed a festering antagonism toward city people. An aspiring writer had the following impression of the peasants he encountered when he went to work in a village near Sendai as a doctor's assistant (what we would now call a paramedic). Although he finally came to empathize with the impoverished peasants with whom he had daily contact, this is how he first saw them:

There is no one as miserable as a peasant, especially the impoverished peasants of northern Japan. The peasants there wear rags, eat coarse cereals, and have many children. They are as black as their dirt walls and lead grubby, joyless lives that can be compared to those of insects that crawl along the ground and stay alive by licking the dirt. They may walk upright, but most of the time their spirit crawls along the ground. When one is in a compassionate mood, one feels sorry for them. But . . . every time I come in contact with their musty, smelly, dull, miserable existence, I feel a sense of displeasure and distaste grounded on a hatred of ugly things. To tell the truth, there are among them, one feels, people who would have been better off had they not been born. In fact, in my opinion, the majority of them fall into this category.

I don't think these impressions come from my personal bias. Anyone who went into their midst and became deeply involved in their way of life would certainly feel the same way. I made the mistake of getting too close to them. If one really wishes to become their friend, one must keep a little distance from them and observe them from a detached position. I'm being honest about this. I have lived in their midst for over a year.

One can see the kind of people they are by simply looking at their faces. Just as domestic animals have an odor peculiar to them, peasants have a peculiar physiognomy. One can easily recognize a peasant. He can be identified by his ignoble face. He may try to conceal his identity by covering his sunburnt arms and legs, but that'll do him no good. . . . Peasants lack noteworthy facial expressions. They show no feelings, no energy, no strength. They all have common, vulgar faces. Many men of forty have no hair on their faces. Little wonder. They spend their days worrying about rain, wind, and insects. There is not a single day that they can claim to be free of fear from the elements. The spirit that is constantly quaking with fear makes even the fatigue that appears on their faces lifeless. These peasants do not possess the moral vigor that people who live in the mountains and by the sea possess. The latter have the willpower to battle nature and conquer it, relying solely on themselves. The life of the peasants, one might say, is the life of people who have given up hope. They resign themselves to their situation with the thought that it is the most sensible thing to do. Such is their miserable, meaningless life. The reason they have given up hope can be ascribed to the imperatives of the land. They have learned through years of experience that, regardless of how hard they struggle and kick, they will fail to free themselves from the painful fetters of the land.

They have crusty skin, which is yellowish and dry, wholly lacking in luster. This is true of the old and the young. They have big teeth and chins, and flat faces. Their eyelids are droopy and look as if a tapeworm could hide in the folds. They have ungainly, large hands and feet, but eight out of ten have no footwear. Their chests and shoulders show no muscular tension, and the skin of their lower bellies droops down gracelessly. Viewed even from the eyes of a doctor, their physique is something one can say nothing complimentary about. Many of them get sick because of their improvident way of life and lack of nutrition. It appears that even their stomachs, which are as tough as those of their cows, are incapable of coping with the practice of consuming so much food that has little nutritional value. One notices their ungainly mouths and coarse noses. In particular, I dislike the way their eyes look. They look like those of animals terrified of human beings. They constantly shift their little brown eyes in a sinister manner, with a dumb smirk on their lips.[20]

The rural dwellers' resentment of city people was expressed emphatically by Shibuya Teisuke, who felt that the big cities, particularly Tokyo, were predatory forces flourishing at the expense of the rural villages. In 1925, the proclamation of the Agriculturists' Self-Rule Society, which Shibuya helped to organize, stated:

The cities grow more luxurious day by day . . . while the villagers have to live on moldy salted fish and wear shopworn clothes. And even these are not readily available to propertyless farmers, who are covered with dirt like moles and are suffocating in poverty like homeless mice. To begin with, the cities are living off the sweat of the farmers. They pilfer and live on what the peasants have produced with their sweat and blood. While the cities and city dwellers prosper, becoming daily more used to luxury, the peasants who labor to support and keep them alive are on the verge of starvation and death.[21]

On March 1, 1926, Shibuya wrote in his diary, "Now, the tillers of the soil, tenant farmers as well as farmowners, must unite in a single body and declare war on modern industrial commercialism and urban-centered ways." On April 23 of the same year, he noted: "The prefectures in the vicinity of the metropolis called Tokyo are being sucked dry of their economic resources and human talents by the city. . . . Ah, Tokyo, you are a murderous machine that sucks out the blood of the peasants in the name of capitalistic, urban civilization." Again on October 1, 1926, he wrote:

I return home. The house is not lit and is pitch dark. My sick father is groaning. . . . The children are crying. Oh, what misery! This is the true picture of the life of the producers of food. My body is exhausted. My mother has taken off her work clothes soaked in sweat and does not move a muscle. The "people of culture" enjoy the glory of life while the producers of essential goods for human life—food, housing, and clothing—have to live like this. The skies of Tokyo light up the eastern horizon. You, together with the landlords, are leeches who bleed us.[22]

Such sentiments permeate Shibuya's diary.

Shibuya became a Marxist agrarian reformer because he was convinced that the capitalistic, urban centers were exploiting the peasants, and he remained a lifelong foe of urban encroachments into rural communities. In the 1970s, he continued his battle against the expansion of metropolitan Tokyo into the countryside and joined the fight against the construction of a huge international airport in Narita (Chiba prefecture), which, he contended, was being built for the convenience of the urban dwellers at the expense of village people.

Similar sentiments about the encroachment of urban communities into rural areas were expressed by other voices in prewar Japan. In Ishikawa Tatsuzō's story about the expropriation of village land for the construction of a reservoir for Tokyo in the mid-1930s, a village head reflects, " 'Prosperous Tokyo! Shinjuku, Kanda, Marunouchi.' As he gazed at these districts from the window of the electric train, he felt anger gush up to his dried old lips. 'So what if it is the imperial capital! What if it is the world's second largest city! How can Tokyo boast of its prosperity when it has driven its brothers in the villages into desperate straits?' This thought made him feel that the Tokyoites in the train were also coldly indifferent to the villagers' plight."[23]

By and large it was true that city dwellers, indifferent to rural communities, remained unconcerned about agrarian poverty.[24] Even more galling to sensitive rural youths was the half-concealed paternalism and snobbism of those intellectuals who were, at least theoretically, interested in helping the peasantry. Shibuya, for instance, did not completely trust the urban intellectuals who were his own associates in the agrarian reform movement. Thus, he jotted down in his diary, "The intelligentsia who live in the cities, especially thinkers and artists, tend to want to discourage young people from the rural communities from moving into Tokyo. It's as if they are telling us, 'We're enjoying our feast, but you must be content just to watch us eat.' " The urban intelligentsia are people who are cut off from the soil. They think only in abstract terms."[25]

It was true that intellectuals interested in agrarian problems often adopted a theoretical rather than practical approach to solving the peasants' problems for them.[26] At least, however, these people were making some effort to help. Most intellectuals made no effort at all to relate to the peasantry. In fact, many had originally come from the villages; and they, even more than the native urbanites, tended to set themselves apart from the "backward villages," seeking frantically to blend into the world of the "men of culture" *(bunka-jin).* [27] They left the fields to a small group of Christian, socialist, or communist reformers, and to the agrarian nationalists who propounded the principles of *nōhonshugi* ("agrarian fundamentalism").

The anti-urban sentiments that welled up in the minds of leftist farm youth like Shibuya and a right-wing *nōhonshugi* advocate were strikingly similar as the following excerpt from an article written in 1932 by Nagano Akira, an organizer of an agrarian self-help association and an advocate of *nōhonshugi,* attests:

Hitherto, Japan's economy has been centered around commerce and industry. It has placed cities at the forefront and made the farm villages secondary. All the laws have been enacted to uphold commerce and industry and to exploit the farm villages. The burden has been heavy on the farm villages and light on the cities. These are well-known facts. Representatives are elected by the votes of the peasants, but they become running dogs of the urban *zaibatsu* ("financial-industrial trusts"). The media all focus on the cities and ignore the farm villages. The villages are charged exorbitant rates of interest by the financial barons and are forced to pay commissions and fees to the merchants. The industrialists purchase raw materials cheaply from the villages and sell the finished products at high prices. The able young people of the farm villages are absorbed into the cities. Young girls are drawn into the cities. So the balance of men and women is upset in the countryside. The farm villages' right of self-rule is taken away from them by the central government, and the villages are forced to support a large number of useless bureaucrats at a rapidly increasing cost. [28]

GENERAL MATERIAL CONDITIONS

The anti-urban, anticapitalist sentiments that smoldered in the minds of young villagers like Shibuya and Nagano had been kindled mainly by the general poverty pervading agrarian communities, where the poor were reduced to the most primitive level of existence. Of course, there were many impoverished city dwellers living in terrible slums, but the cultural and technological conveniences of modern civilization had some ameliorating effect on their lives. In rural areas, these innovations of modern civilization were available to only the wealthy.

Needless to say, not all areas of rural Japan were uniformly impoverished or underdeveloped: The northeastern regions tended to have less productive farmland and a harsher climate, but the southwestern areas enjoyed more favorable conditions. Moreover, commerce and industry developed more rapidly in the cities of the southwestern prefectures, which then benefited from the advantages inherent in a money economy, among them better opportunities for cash cropping.[29] Such greater interaction between urban and rural communities also increased the opportunity for rural residents to supplement their farm income by commuting to nearby cities to work in factories. However, since economic development was uneven, there were also highly developed areas in the northeast and less developed areas in the southwest.

Tenant farmers were the most impoverished members of the farming community; in most instances, they paid high rents and tilled small plots of an acre or so. In 1899, a tenant farmer (with a family of five) tilling 1 *chō* (2.45 acres, about twice the acreage worked by most tenant farmers) had an income of 166 yen,[30] or 13.8 yen a month. Given the fact that peasants worked almost the year round—the husband, wife, and possibly one of the children full-time, and others part-time—the daily wage per person came to about 15 sen. In the same year, the average daily wage for a male weaver was 30 sen; a female weaver, 19 sen; a carpenter, 47 sen; and an urban day laborer, 33 sen.[31]

A reporter visiting the countryside in 1930 wrote, regarding the income of a tenant farmer tilling 1.0 *chō,* "If he harvests about fifty-five sacks a year, he turns over thirty-five sacks to the landlord. Of the remaining twenty sacks, he has to allot six to cover fertilizer costs. The rest . . . is what he has for living expenses. If he gets 11 yen a sack, his income will come to 150 yen. Assuming that he has only two children, the monthly income for his family of four will be 18 yen, or 60 sen a day. During the working months, he and his wife have labored at least twelve hours a day in the field."[32]

A government survey taken in 1926–1927 indicated that farm-family income was 70 percent that of the white-collar worker and 95 percent that of the urban laborer.[33] Since the average farm family was larger than the average urban family, per capita farm income was considerably lower than the income of the urban worker.[34]

A family's standard of living can be measured in part by the percentage of its income spent on food (that is, the Engel coefficient). In a government survey taken in 1926–1927, it was found that the average farmowner spent 49 percent of his income on food; the average part-owner part-tenant farmer, 52 percent; and the average tenant farmer, 57 percent.[35] In 1934–1936, the Engel coefficient for the average urban worker's household was 36.1 percent, while for the farm household it was 50.5 percent.[36] By the 1970s, it had dropped to about 30 percent for both farm and urban working-class families.[37]

FOOD

Even though a large percentage of the peasants' income was spent on food, the quality of their food was extremely poor. A survey made in a village in Gunma prefecture in 1910 showed that 65 percent of the money spent on food went for rice and other grains; only 13.5 percent was spent on vegetables, less than 2 percent on fish, 1.7 percent on eggs, and none on meat.[38] This heavy dependency on carbohydrates was typical of the peasants' diet. Although they preferred rice, most poor peasants seldom ate pure rice but mixed it instead with barley or yams, or else ate millet and barnyard grass instead. Meat was hardly ever consumed by the peasants. In fact, even in urban areas, meat was a luxury. In 1889–1893, the annual consumption of meat per capita was 0.9 pounds. This rose to 4 pounds by 1922–1926, still a miniscule 1.2 ounces per capita per week. The consumption of fish was higher: In 1900, the annual consumption per capita was 29 pounds and this rose to 82 pounds by 1924–1926, an increase from 0.5 pound to 1.6 pounds per week per capita. Sugar too was a luxury item. In 1910, 1.3 percent of the money spent on food was devoted to sugar. In 1896–1898, the annual per capita consumption was 10.4 pounds. This rose to 13 pounds by 1922–1926.[39] New fruits, such as apples and peaches, were introduced after the Meiji restoration, but they were produced primarily for urban consumers.[40]

Not only was the average peasant family's diet nutritionally lacking, it was also dull and monotonous. Peasant girls recruited for work in textile factories, or even in brothels, were often ensnared simply by the prospect of being able to eat better than they did at home. A textile worker from a village in Kyushu, who worked in Osaka in the 1930s, recalled, "What pleased me most was the fact that I could eat all I wanted. At home I used to eat a pasty mixture of yam and chestnut, and, instead of white rice, we had brown rice mixed with barley. . . . At home we got fish no more than once a year, on New Year's."[41]

Shibuya, commenting on the poor, coarse food that he had to eat, wrote in his diary, "Look at our dinner for tonight: rice mixed with wheat and chopped yam leaves. For our side dish we have the top half of *daikon* [long, white radishes] and *daikon* leaves. Wealthy villagers and city people throw these things away, or else feed them to oxen or pigs."[42]

In 1930, a newspaper reporter observed that the daily meals of a typical family of tenant farmers in western Japan consisted of rice gruel and pickles for breakfast; rice gruel, dregs of soybean cakes, and pickles for lunch; and rice mixed with barley, vegetables, and pickles for supper. The cost of the food for this family was 9 sen per person per day.[43]

The overall caloric consumption of the Japanese increased very little from the early Meiji period to the immediate prewar years. During 1878–1882, the daily per capita caloric consumption (mostly starch) is estimated to have been slightly over 2,100. By 1915–1919 it had risen to about 2,300.[44]

CLOTHING

If peasants could afford no more than a subsistence diet, they could afford to spend even less money on clothing. The villagers in Gunma prefecture, for example, spent only 2.65 yen per person on clothing in 1910. In the prewar years, the peasants wore coarse work clothes —a traditional cotton jacket, drawers, and loincloth. They usually wore homemade straw sandals, though by the 1920s and 1930s rubber-soled canvas shoes came to be worn by those who could afford them.

Peasant children of impoverished families wore ragtag, patched-up old clothes handed down from their older siblings. A writer living in a northern village in the early 1930s observed,

There was an affecting young village girl who wanted to buy a woolen jacket to wear on special occasions. Every night she wove straw ropes late into the night until her hands bled. But even though she worked late all winter long she failed to earn enough money to buy the woolen jacket. No doubt the girl was being unreasonable in trying to earn enough money to buy a woolen garment. At the current rate of earnings in the village, no matter how hard she works she could not by herself possibly make enough money to buy such a garment.

These girls slave away weaving straw ropes with their bleeding hands, not realizing that in the cities girls their age are gleefully playing cards under bright electric lights, that arty ladies are passing out leaflets for some cause or other on the streets of Ginza, or that writers like Hirabayashi Taeko [a renown writer] even exist.[45]

HOUSING

The average peasant family continued to live in a small hovel thatched with straw and miscanthus. In the Tokugawa period, the rulers had kept the peasants living in hovels by fiat, though few peasants could have afforded better in any case. From the Meiji era on, some improvement in peasant housing began to take place. For example, more families began to place *tatami* mats, instead of coarse straw mats, on the floor and to construct tile roofs instead of thatched roofs. In one prefecture, by the outbreak of World War II, 30 percent of all rural houses had tile roofs.[46]

During the Tokugawa period peasant houses did not have translucent paper on their sliding doors, so partitioned rooms remained dark. In the Meiji period, however, translucent paper as well as glass came to be used. Because the interior was now more visible some sociologists contend that the peasants kept rooms cleaner and in better order.[47]

Formerly homes had been illuminated at night by wax candles and lamps lit with vegetable and pine oil. By the end of the nineteenth century, kerosene lamps had come into use in some areas. Gaslight made its debut in large cities such as Tokyo in the 1880s, and, by the end of the nineteenth century, electricity had also been introduced. Not until the 1920s, however, did it begin to spread into the countryside, and even then one 10-watt bulb was all that could be managed.[48] Even in 1934, in the villages of Osaka prefecture where urban influence was felt rather forcefully because of the proximity of large cities, there was only an average of 1.8 electrical outlets per farmhouse, with an average wattage of 16.[49]

Electrical or gas heating did not, of course, exist. In the villages, and in the cities as well, people kept warm in the winter by sitting beside a charcoal-burning brazier. In the colder areas, a fire pit or hearth was built in or near the kitchen, and people spent much of each cold winter day huddled around it.[50]

Sanitation facilities remained primitive, and latrines, where human waste was kept in pits to be used later as fertilizer, were attached to the house, often near the kitchen. Most farm families also had a stall to house an ox (or a horse) useful as a draft animal as well as a source of manure and of supplementary income—for after it was fattened it could usually be traded in for cash and a calf.

TRANSPORTATION AND COMMUNICATION

Villages located along the arteries of the national transportation network acquired the convenience of rail or bus transportation by the turn of the century. Where this occurred, villagers' contact with towns and cities increased, and stores and other business establishments sprang up.[51] However, travel within and between villages was usually by foot. Goods were transported on one's back or in baskets, or by oxcart. Automobiles, needless to say, were nonexistent in most villages. Few villagers even saw a car pass through their community. Bicycles began to appear by the turn of the century, but they were hardly ever used by the peasants. A resident of a village in Gunma prefecture recalled, "Before the war, I doubt if there were three radios and three bicycles in all the sixty houses in the hamlet."[52] What was true in the Kanto region near metropolitan Tokyo was even more the case in villages in outlying areas. In communities where the roads were not hilly, however, bicycles came into frequent use by the 1920s and 1930s. In Suye Mura (Kumanoto prefecture), where American anthropologist John Embree did his research in 1935, there were 160 bicycles in a village of 285 households. Among other mechanical gadgets in the village there were 4 sewing machines, 5 radios, 20 phonographs, and 1 telephone, which was in the village office, or town hall.[53] At about this same period, a resident of a village in Yamagata prefecture reported that 16 of the 566 households owned a radio.[54]

The postal system, introduced in 1871, first linked Tokyo and Osaka, but soon it encompassed the entire country, offering the peasants a means of communication not hitherto available to them. The telegraph had been introduced in 1869, making swift communication possible for villagers who had children working in urban shops and factories. In addition, newspapers began to penetrate the countryside. Even though many peasants remained illiterate well into the twentieth century, modern means of communication were now at least accessible to them.

HEALTH AND SANITATION

The level of health and sanitation, and knowledge about health care remained fairly primitive among the peasantry well into the "modern" century. One of the most insalubrious practices inherited from the past was the use of human waste as fertilizer. Collecting "night soil" was one of the farmers' chief chores. European farmers also used human waste for fertilizer, but they buried it in the ground, whereas Japanese farmers put it on top of the soil. In rice paddies, the soil was prepared with the application of human and animal waste, and the field was flooded. The farmers then went into the paddies in their bare feet to plant the rice and, later, weed the fields. The water from the rice paddies ran off into ditches that in turn ran into brooks and streams where, downstream, people often washed their clothes, utensils, and vegetables. To make matters worse, the farmers often washed their night soil buckets in the same streams.[55] Little wonder that farm children were infested with roundworms, hookworms, pinworms, and tapeworms, among other parasites. A doctor trying to deal with this problem bemoaned the futility of treating the children without being able to get at the source of the contagion.[56]

Despite the present-day Japanese reputation for cleanliness, the use of human and animal waste, close living with oxen and horses, the use of common baths, and generally unsanitary conditions in the home caused a high incidence of skin diseases, trachoma, tuberculosis, and other communicable diseases. The inhabitants of the villages were more often than not tormented with fleas, bedbugs, lice, and other vermin. Blood-sucking worms and insects could even cause fatal illnesses. The presence of these insects was seen by the peasants as an inevitable part of life. Even in the postwar years, a villager visiting Tokyo was amazed to find that there were no fleas in the city.[57]

Another source of sickness was contaminated well water. Wells were often dug near the latrines and their water frequently became the source of epidemics.[58] Cholera, typhus, typhoid, diphtheria, dysentery, and smallpox plagued the nation in the nineteenth century and persisted well into the twentieth.

In 1879, an outbreak of cholera claimed more than 105,700 lives; and in 1866, 108,400 lives were lost to the same disease. In 1886, more than 20,000 people died of typhus and dysentery, 18,000 of smallpox. During that same year alone, more than 146,000 lives were lost to epidemic. In all, during the second and third decades of the Meiji restoration more than 800,000 people fell victim to these plagues.[59]

Medical treatment of epidemic victims remained appallingly primitive, even in major urban centers like Tokyo. Erwin von Baelz, a German physician teaching in Japan, wrote in his diary on March 10, 1892:

Went with my students to visit the smallpox hospital at Komagome [in Tokyo]. A scandalous state of affairs. There are 400 patients, often 50 new cases every day; 8 doctors, some of whom have had very little experience; and 20 nurses. Wooden sheds with torn-paper windows in wintertime. That's the way Tokyo treats the sick. Cholera—typhoid—smallpox! [And] not one hospital . . . where the poor wretches are as well cared for as a horse in a good stable.[60]

The victims of these epidemics were most often concentrated in crowded urban areas, but once the epidemics erupted, they spread swiftly to the rural areas. During the cholera epidemic of 1886, in Aomori prefecture, one of the remotest regions of Japan, 6,564 people were afflicted, and 3,774 died.[61]

As Baelz noted, the government did very little to cope with the outbreak of these epidemics or to help the victims. It concentrated instead on building the nation's armed forces, spending more money on a single warship than on combating disease. The central government expected local authorities to deal with the problem as best they could.[62] In the twentieth century, as preventive measures became available, the government launched innoculation and vaccination drives but still failed to contain periodic epidemics. It was not till the end of World War II, when the occupation authorities introduced massive health programs, that the incidence of epidemic and disease was sharply reduced.

Malnutrition, caused by a diet of starch and little else, kept the incidence of such diseases as tuberculosis and beriberi extremely high, while infant mortality rates remained high and life expectancy low well into the twentieth century due to lack of proper medical care and ignorance of sanitary measures. Tuberculosis was widespread in the silk filatures and other textile plants where thousands of young farm girls were sent to work. The long hours, the polluted air, poor nutrition, and crowded conditions in the dormitories only made the disease more widespread. The afflicted girls would then return to their villages and spread the disease to members of their home community. As a result, tuberculosis became a major health problem in prewar Japan. In 1889, 0.15 percent of the population died of the disease; in 1900, 0.17 percent; in 1904, 0.185 percent; and in 1935, 0.19 percent. This means that, in 1935, 132,300 people out of an overall population of 69 million, or almost 2 out of every 1,000, died of tuberculosis—and this out of the 1,300,000 people who were afflicted with the disease.[63]

If the incidence of tuberculosis is any gauge of health care in prewar Japan, one would have to conclude that, as the nation "modernized," the health of its people got worse. Again it was not until the postwar years that the disease was brought under control. In 1974, deaths resulting from tuberculosis had dropped to 104 out of every million people, or 0.01 percent.[64]

Further indication that sanitation and health in prewar Japan lagged behind its industrial growth is seen in other statistical data. For instance, the infant mortality rate (deaths of infants under 1 year of age per 1,000 live births) in 1930–1934 was 124.2, compared to 10 for 1975. Comparable figures for the United States are 60.4 in 1930–1934 and 15 in 1976. Life expectancy in Japan in 1891–1898 was 42.8 years for males and 44.3 years for females. Little change occurred in subsequent prewar years. In 1921–1925, the figures were 42.06 and 43.20 respectively, and in 1935–1936, 46.92 and 49.63. The extent of advances made in health and sanitation in the postwar years is seen in the spectacular increase in life expectancy. In 1976, the figures were 72.15 for men and 77.33 for women.[65]

The death rate for the year 1872 was 1.22 percent rising steadily to 2.09 percent in 1907. This dropped to 0.6 percent by 1976, which compares favorably with that same year's figure for the United States: 0.9 percent.[66]

Japanese villagers were slow in adopting even such a simple means of sanitation as soap. In most areas the practice persisted of cleaning washing by pounding it, and wood ash was still used more extensively than soap to clean cooking utensils. Daily bathing was deemed necessary to wash off the dust and dirt, and also to relax and recover from the day's toils; but the bath water was also a medium for the transmission of germs and diseases because the same water was used not only by the entire family but usually also by neighbors who did not have their own tubs. Even though the bathers rinsed their bodies outside the tub before stepping into it, the bath water naturally got rather murky by the time a dozen or more people had bathed in it. "The only thing that people had was a wooden tub in the yard," wrote a villager from Gunma prefecture, looking back on the prewar years. "You invited all the neighbors to share the bath. By the time the twentieth person had been in it, the bath stank. But even this was a treat."[67] This practice of sharing the bath persisted in the postwar years. In 1958, a medical doctor in the countryside tested the bath water of a farm family and found that it was "full of germs."[68]

Medical facilities and professional care were not readily available in most rural areas, particularly in villages located in out-of-the-way regions. As recently as the late 1920s, the ratio of doctors to the general populace was 1 to 1,100, or 1 doctor for every 300 households.[69] Even this figure is deceptive, since doctors tended to practice in towns and cities, not villages. In many villages even midwives were unavailable.[70] Babies were often delivered by friends and relatives, which meant serious trouble in cases of difficult deliveries. Yūki Aisoka, a writer who lived in a village in northern Japan, tells of a peasant woman's dying during childbirth because the doctor living in a neighboring community failed to respond to the call.[71]

Embree, in his study of Suye Mura, notes that in 1935 there were no doctors at all in the village. "The available doctors from the neighboring towns are expensive. Furthermore, the doctor from the next mura ["village"] is little better than a quack. None of the doctors shows any social conscience, and many a child dies in Suye for this reason."[72]

In rare instances when doctors were available, the quality of care was often inadequate. Even the peasants referred to them as quacks (yabu-isha, a doctor who practices in the bushes). Frequently they lacked adequate facilities and prescribed cure-all medicines much in the manner of medicine peddlers.

Peasants could seldom afford to send sick family members to the hospital. Not only was it too costly, but also the hospital was seen as a frightful place from which the patient often failed to return alive. Moreover, the facilities were not like those available in the West. A young boy in a remote village in northern Japan, writing about his mother's illness in the immediate postwar years (when prewar conditions still prevailed) relates:

When the doctor examined her he said that she must go to the village hospital immediately. She had a heart condition. The word "hospital" always causes difficulty in a family, for it means that someone in the family has to go to look after the patient. I have heard that, in some foreign-style hospitals, everything is done by nurses and that meals are prepared in the hospital kitchen for all the patients. This is a wonderful arrangement. I wish it were done in Japanese hospitals.

His family had no one who could be spared to go to the hospital to take care of the mother, so they had to send a nine-year-old girl with her. "We wondered how a nine-year-old girl with no experience in looking after a sick person could possibly take care of mother, prepare her own and mother's meals, and do all the other things that had to be done by an attendant."[73]

Until the end of World War II, the peasants continued to rely on peddlers who came around periodically to fill the household medicine bag with cure-all potions. In addition, moxabustion (burning of vital spots on the body with moxa weed, similar in principle to acupuncture) was used extensively to cope with minor, or even major, ailments. And as long as superstitious beliefs about the causes of sickness persisted, quacks and healers continued to ply their trade. Even in the postwar years, a medical officer in a rural community found the peasants going to healers. One such healer claimed that insects under the surface of the skin were causing a host of afflictions and insisted that he could remove the insect through the skin and effect a cure. Another healer contended that all sicknesses were caused by scum accumulating in the eye and that he could thus cure the patient by removing it.[74] Many rural dwellers continued to believe that possession by some evil or animal spirit, such as the Fox God, caused people to get sick. In the Tokugawa era, the authorities frequently executed—at times by burning them alive—people who were possessed by the Fox God and other animal spirits.[75]

This does not mean that no positive changes took place to affect the physical well-being of the peasantry from 1868 to 1941. Changes did occur. It is really a question of the degree of such changes—especially in comparison with what transpired in the urban areas—which, in fact, became increasingly noticeable, especially in the less remote areas, around the turn of the century.

One observer, who lived in a village about two and a half miles from the city of Himeji near Kobe, commented:

The industrial revolution took place at different times depending on the geographical location. In our village it appears to have swept the community like a tidal wave around the turn of the century. When I was in elementary school I used to wear hand-woven cotton apparel, but when I went to higher classes I began to wear factory-woven kimonos. Then the girls who used to spin, dye, and weave fabrics disappeared.[76]

A historian who grew up in the suburb of Nagoya recalled:

It seems that changes began to occur around the time of the first Sino-Japanese War (1894–1895). This was seen in such commonplace things as the clothing of the schoolteachers and the village officials. They began to wear Western-style apparel. This may have been the result of new developments and greater contact with the cities that came about with the war. . . . The manner of speech of our neighbors changed. I recall hearing more formal, learned words being used. . . . I think it was some years later, but when I returned to the village I noticed that the houses were beginning to look better. Sericulture was becoming more popular, and thus bigger houses were needed. But it also meant that the villagers' incomes were increasing. Houses with tile roofs, as well as two-story buildings, began to appear. The general framework of the houses as well as the interior design were improving. Most of the houses were now matted with *tatami* mats. And houses in which horses and people lived under one roof began to disappear. . . .[77]

Money came to be more widely used in the villages by the end of the nineteenth century. In 1890, 48.6 percent of farmowners' expenses entailed the use of cash; for tenant farmers, it was 21.1 percent. Nine years later, in 1899, the percentage had risen to 53.2 percent and 25.1 percent respectively.[78]

MORALS

AND

MORES

The Education and Indoctrination
of the Peasants

School attendance remained poor in the nineteenth century, especially in rural areas, and particularly among peasant girls. After the turn of the century, however, the authorities began to enforce attendance more stringently; and, in 1908, required school attendance was extended to six years. In 1911, the government claimed that enrollment for boys was 98.8 percent and 97.5 percent for girls.[1]

Despite this high enrollment record, actual attendance lagged. In the 1880s, for example, enrollment was about 50 percent, but attendance was 30 percent. In the early 1890s, when school tuition was lowered, enrollment rose, but attendance remained low. In the late 1890s, enrollment reached 72 percent, and attendance, 48 percent. In 1900, when tuition charges for elementary education were dropped completely, enrollment began to rise steadily; but in 1912, when enrollment was a near perfect 98 percent, attendance still lagged at 89 percent.[2]

Attendance by the children of poor families, both in urban and rural communities, continued to be spotty. A survey conducted by the Ministry of Education showed that, in 1905, 57.3 percent of the working population had not attended school at all. As late as the third decade of the twentieth century, a survey of textile workers (most of rural origins), in twenty-three factories showed that 17.3 percent of the 1,417 male workers and 19.5 percent of the 7,210 female workers had not attended school at all, and, of those who had, 15.5 percent of the male workers and 41.6 percent of the female workers had not completed the required years of elementary education. In Saitama prefecture, in 1925, 16 percent of the 13,500 young men of draft age had not completed their six years of compulsory education.[3]

Even in the urban areas, the literacy rate was much lower in the early years of the twentieth century than that claimed by the authorities. A survey conducted in 1912 in the poor sections of Tokyo showed that 32 percent of the people studied were illiterate. Another survey taken in 1921, again in the poorer sections of the city, revealed that 41 percent were totally illiterate and another 8 percent could read only simple phonetics. Only 5.8 percent of these people were able to read the newspaper and only 0.2 percent had gone beyond the six years of compulsory schooling.[4]

Children of poor farm families were frequently kept out of school to help on the farm and at home or to take care of their baby brothers and sisters. In many cases they went to school with their baby siblings strapped to their backs. A reporter touring the poverty-stricken mountain villages in the north in the early 1930s noted: "Many school children are dressed in dirty rags and have babies strapped to their backs during class. When one baby starts to wail, others follow suit. Then some of the children tending the babies begin to cry in frustration. So the years of compulsory education end up being merely a *pro forma* affair."[5]

In his diary, Shibuya Teisuke repeatedly comments on the fact that his brother and sister were forced to miss school to help out on the farm. "My younger brother and sister have cut school in order to help with farm work," he wrote on June 26, 1925. "Yesterday their teacher came to our home to see what was going on. He saw that my younger brother was busy weeding in the field and my younger sister was taking care of the baby and also nursing our sick father. The teacher simply said, 'You look very busy. You're working hard, aren't you?' and left." His sister had to miss school often to take care of their younger brother. "When I think about the fact that my younger sister, who likes school, cannot go to school because she has to baby-sit, I feel anger welling up from the pit of my stomach. It is too pitiful a sight to see her whimper that the baby is too heavy as she puts her two-year-old brother on her back and goes to school. Compulsory education! It certainly is a wonderful system, but I wonder if the minister of education even once thought about the fact that we can't attend school satisfactorily even for two or three years."[6]

Adults knew that the dual task of attending school and helping at home was a crushing burden for their children, even though the youngsters were taught the virtue of enduring hardships. A rural schoolteacher observed, "Children are often told, 'People who don't endure hardships when they are young will have a hard time when they grow up.' But the adults, when they were children, were not lazy loafers. And yet they are still undergoing hard times. . . . The youngsters seem to be aware of this."[7] The teacher, seeing his pupils hard at work, reflected on the dilemma facing him as a teacher and penned the following short essay.

THE LITTLE WORKERS, THE LITTLE FARMERS

Every evening when the setting sun shines upon the handle, rims, and spokes of my bicycle on my way home from a long day's work, I run into the little workers, the little farmers. This one is wearing a worn-out straw hat, and his ruddy face smiles under the wide brim. In his right hand is the kettle he had used to bring water to quench his thirst while at work, and in his left hand he grips the handle of a three-pronged hoe. He is wearing a small straw cape, and underneath he has on a striped cotton shirt patched together with rags, and a half-length jacket. Stiff, dark blue drawers cover his legs to a point just below his knees, and the bottom is tied together neatly with straw. His bulging sunburnt legs have no hair but are spotted with dirt. He is wearing his straw sandals adeptly and even walks like an adult, his legs spread out somewhat farther apart than usual. . . . This is how the worker, the little farmer, looks. Sometimes he even wears a towel to cover his cheeks. This is the picture of the little farm boy on his way home at sunset.

So he has a kettle in his right hand and his most important tool in his left hand. He bows politely to me without taking off his hat, as if he wants to say, "Please excuse me." I look at him and think in astonishment, "Ooh, it's you. You look like a splendid, full-blown farmer. I am baffled. You're Shunichi, whom I scolded for failing to recite the multiplication table even though you are in the fourth grade. Yes, you do look splendid." I think, "Didn't I scold you today again for your failure to read the lesson? You, who are doing such useful work." The little farmer smiles and laughs nervously. He laughs as if he wants to say, "Teacher, I tilled three strips of rice field today. I've got blisters on my hands." At the same time he looks as if he would like to protest, "Yeah, I do have a stupid-looking face. But when I go out in the rice paddy I do good work." And when I come across youngsters like this I always think, "While this boy was working in the rice field, what was I doing? I scribbled details in my lesson plan and filled in several useless pages in my grade book." And I asked myself, "Why can't this student understand the lessons?" So I jotted down a great big zero. In anger I wrote an X mark in red. In frustration I scribbled: 0/100. I even felt like writing "You stupid fool!" To express my bitter disappointment I drew a picture of an eye with red ink and then drew several round circles for teardrops. I felt hurt. "Why are you students so dense?" I was getting emotional.

There were days when we left the faculty meeting late in the afternoon after a debate that had little to do with the happiness and well-being of these children. While we were thus engaged, you, the little workers, the little farmers, were producing things, planting seeds. Then you went home with a smile on your face. And you bow politely to me; to me who does not deserve to be treated with such respect. You have your hands full, but you even try to take off your straw hat. You stand by the side of the road and bow down at a ninety-degree angle toward me. You try hastily to remove the towel from your face. That's all right, that's all right, little child, little farmer. Don't bother. You are on your way home from work. You've worked hard. Your father and mother must be delighted. And I scolded you as a numbskull, a ne'er-do-well in class.

A horse-drawn cart with manure buckets passes by. Sanji is steering the cart. He quickly bows his head toward me. Another cart, drawn by an ox, comes along. It appears to be transporting empty manure buckets. Tomeo is straddling the cart and beats on the buckets with his heels. The buckets go "thump, thump" like a drum. When he sees me he tries to straighten himself out on the wobbly cart and prepares to bow politely to me. He stands precariously on the cart and looks at me on the bicycle with strict attention. I have to take off my old soft hat. I take my hat off to the little workers. I must do so. "You're working hard, aren't you?" I say. His father, walking behind the cart, laughs and says, "Naw." When I visit his home the father complains, "Teacher, my son is a dumbbell." But here, by the roadside near the rice paddy, I detect a glimmer of pride in his face.

I pass by the home of a rather well-to-do farmer whose house is fenced in with black, wooden panels. I see several of mother's little helpers bending over. They have their baby brothers and sisters on their backs. Other young brothers and sisters are standing beside them. They are waiting for their parents to come home. They have been caring for their young siblings all day long. Having put in a useful day's work, they look up at the dusky sky. These, too, are little workers. Here, too, I take off my hat.

I take my hat off today but tomorrow I will get on the podium and again castigate the children saying, "Why can't you understand this?" What a dilemma! And where have the lively, energetic little workers and the little farmers disappeared? They are hunched over their desks, scrunched up into dark little figures.[8]

The difficulties faced by the children about whom this concerned teacher was writing were by no means confined to the problem of finding the time and physical energy to attend classes. Once they managed this first, often overwhelming hurdle, what sort of education did they then receive? School for these youngsters was hardly a means to enlightenment. After the initial phase of liberal education, the authorities began to use the schools as vehicles to manufacture loyal subjects who would willingly dedicate their lives to their country and to their emperor. Hence, indoctrination increasingly became the aim of education.

When the Meiji government set out to establish a system of universal education, it relied heavily on Western institutions, practices, and textbooks as models, while traditional Japanese educational ideals—heavily tilted toward morals and ethics—were almost wholly neglected. The textbooks that were used in the schools initially were either translations of Western readers, usually English or American, or books written by Japanese about the West. However, lessons about great Western leaders like Napoleon, Washington, and Peter the Great failed to arouse the enthusiasm of the schoolchildren. On the other hand, "practical learning," which was advocated by such educators as Fukuzawa Yukichi, disturbed the traditionalists, who believed that education must have a didactic purpose. "What is the point," Confucian critics of the new approach to education said, "of teaching children about peaches, chestnuts, and persimmons?"[9] Western education, they charged, was based on materialistic pragmatism. What had to be stressed, they asserted, was *shūshin,* or education in perfecting one's moral character, a stance almost completely ignored by the Education Act of 1871.[10]

The architects of the new educational system, Fukuzawa Yukichi among them, were certainly not indifferent to moral education; but they strove to introduce Western rational, utilitarian morality into the school system's teachings. Writings on moral science by such men as Francis Wayland, Robert and William Chambers, and Hubbard Winslow were what they turned to. But the ascendancy of the Western pragmatists was brief. Soon the traditionalists, those committed to Confucian moral education, began to exert greater influence on the molders of Japan's educational policies. When the Education Act of 1872 was revised in 1879 and again in 1880, *shūshin* was brought into the curriculum as a core subject.

In 1886, the government adopted a policy of textbook certification and, in 1904, it restricted the textbooks in elementary schools to those issued by the government itself. This trend toward more stringent control over the school system was both part of a growing centralization of authority by governmental leaders and a product of the growing influence of the traditionalists. Each group, believing that the exaltation of the emperor-centered, or imperial, system would further their objectives, agreed on the need to build and fortify the cult of the emperor. The principles that came to constitute the heart of the cult, the foundation upon which instruction in *shū-*

shin was to be built, were *chūkun aikoku* ("loyalty to the prince and love of nation").

The peasants, who constituted the bulk of the population, became the main target of the process of indoctrination pursued by these government leaders. Their task was made simple by the fact that the peasants were politically unsophisticated and easily indoctrinated. The long tradition of bowing to authority and looking up to important personages had conditioned them not to challenge the cult of the emperor or the process of indoctrination that was unfolding in the schools where they were required to send their children.

The process of establishing the cult of the emperor and linking it with moral education was supported by Emperor Meiji himself, who was under the strong influence of one of his tutors, Motoda Eifu, a Confucian philosopher. Motoda was convinced that the only way the influence of the Westernizers could be circumvented was to make the emperor the direct font of moral instruction.

In 1878, Emperor Meiji toured northern Japan and, upon his return to the capital, stated that the tour convinced him of the need to shore up the principle of frugality among the people and also of stressing moral education. The Confucian virtues of *jin-gi* ("benevolence and righteousness"), loyalty, and filial piety must be emphasized, he announced in an imperial injunction. The pursuit of knowledge and practical skills must be secondary. The emperor also expressed the opinion that moral concepts must be instilled in children at an early age by setting up certain loyal, righteous, and virtuous individuals as models for them to emulate. He claimed that during his tour he had observed children being instructed in lofty, grandiloquent ideas of no practical value to future peasants and merchants. Such an approach to education, he asserted, could only nurture fanciful ideas in these children, who would then cease being respectful toward their elders and superiors. Instead, they should be taught, he said, what would be appropriate to their station in society.[11] Undoubtedly, the young emperor had considerable help from Motoda in drafting his statement, but the "enlightened" emperor's ideas concerning an education appropriate to commoners were strikingly similar to those of nineteenth-century Russian tsars Nicholas I and Alexander III.

This expression of the imperial will came to constitute a sacrosanct principle of Japanese education until the end of World War II. It turned the tide against the proponents of Western liberal education and served as a prelude to the issuance of the Imperial Rescript on Education in 1890, twelve years after the emperor's original tour of northern Japan. The most immediate (1880) consequences of the emperor's earlier pronouncement, however, were the weeding out of undesirable textbooks; the publication by the Ministry of Education of a "moral" textbook for use in elementary schools; and the issuance in 1881 of instructions to elementary-school teachers, advising them that their chief task was "to foster the spirit of reverence for the emperor and love of country, purify and refine customs, enrich the people's lives, and advance the peace and well-being of the nation.[12]

Filial piety, the cornerstone of Confucian morality, was particularly emphasized by the formulators of this official morality. In fact, in his moral textbook, Motoda placed filial piety in the first chapter, ahead, even, of loyalty to the emperor. Only with the promulgation of the 1890 rescript did it become clear that loyalty to the prince was to precede filial piety.

Since schoolteachers were the key to an effective indoctrination of the schoolchildren, proper education of the teachers was recognized as being of prime importance. Teachers' colleges, or normal schools were established at key points in the country in the 1870s and, in 1881, regulations governing these schools were framed. Here, *shū-shin* was placed at the top of the curriculum, and guidelines were issued stressing the importance of its precepts.

In 1886, Minister of Education Mori Arinori, who had considerable contact with the Western world, tightened government control over the schools and stressed the importance of educating the students to serve the state, not their own interests.[13] As part of this process, he incorporated certain aspects of military training into the normal schools. Soon the same practices were introduced into the middle schools. Hence, the schools became vehicles for fostering the spirit of militarism in Japanese youth. All male students, from middle schools on up, were clothed in uniforms patterned after the army's livery. They were expected to salute upper-class students just as soldiers saluted their superiors. Should any infraction of the pseudomilitary code of conduct occur, upper-class students were to discipline lower-class students. Teachers thus indoctrinated and disciplined in the normal schools quite naturally carried into elementary-school classrooms the values and attitudes with which they had been imbued. As a result, the entire Japanese educational system was turned into a collection of ersatz military schools.

Schoolchildren—the vast majority of them, peasant children—were lined up in drill formation first thing in the morning. At the command of the principal, they bowed in the direction of the vault that housed the emperor's photograph. Then they were treated with a few words of moral edification by the principal. Next they marched into the classroom and hopped to attention at the command of the class president as the teacher entered. Still standing at attention, they recited the Imperial Rescript on Education and then took up the first subject of the day, *shūshin.*

The rescript, another brain-child of Motoda, stressed Confucian family-centered ethical principles as well as the concept of loyalty to the emperor. It begins by asserting that Japan was founded by the "imperial ancestors" and that the imperial subjects have been forever united in loyalty and filial piety. It goes on to exhort the pupils to be "respectful toward your parents, affectionate to your brothers and sisters, harmonious with husbands and wives, and true as friends; bear yourselves in modesty and moderation; extend your benevolence to all; pursue learning and cultivate the arts . . . advance public good and promote common interests. Should [an] emergency arise, offer yourselves courageously to the State; and thus guard and maintain the prosperity of Our Imperial Throne coeval with heaven and earth."[14]

The ideals embodied in the rescript were incorporated in all the "moral" textbooks either certified or issued by the government. The primary principle remained loyalty to the emperor. For example, a third-grade *shūshin* textbook published in 1892 commences with five short lessons on loyalty to the emperor. These are followed by three lessons in filial piety. The first lesson says,

Because of the profound benevolence of the emperor, we are able to live each day in peace. We must always keep in mind with deep gratitude the great debt we owe him.

Lesson two states:

We must constantly strive to work diligently at our tasks, plan for the well-being of the society, and, when an emergency arises, defend our nation, gladly sacrificing our lives. In this manner we will be able to fulfill completely our responsibility as imperial subjects.[15]

In 1904, it became mandatory for the public schools to use only textbooks issued by the Ministry of Education, and emphasis on *chū-kun aikoku* became even more pronounced. For example, a fourth-grade *shūshin* text of that day starts out with two chapters on the "great Japanese empire," followed by a lesson on *aikoku* and two on *chūkun.* Several chapters are devoted to the people's duties, and the text concludes with the chapter "Being a Good Japanese."[16] In the 1930s, a strong militaristic tone began to pervade the textbooks, with lessons exalting war heroes and Japan's great achievements in past wars.

THE MILITARY

Through most of the period that we are concerned with, then, there was a sustained and successful effort exerted to forge a nation of loyal subjects. This campaign was especially effective among peasant children, who had less exposure to diverse ideas and opinions than their urban counterparts. Moreover, the peasant ethos of obedience, submissiveness, and humility made them more than ready to be molded into loyal subjects who would unquestioningly serve emperor and country. The authorities could count on young peasant conscripts to develop into obedient and disciplined soldiers.

The armed forces also served as an instrument to "acculturate" the peasantry into the nation-state. The system of universal male conscription meant that a certain percentage of peasant youths would be drafted continuously into the army and navy, thus ensuring their exposure to an intensive form of indoctrination and discipline, one that in some ways takes place in any nation's military establishment but that seems to have been carried out in a more purposeful fashion in Japan.

The underlying philosophy that was to guide the Japanese armed forces was set forth by the founder of the modern Japanese army, Yamagata Aritomo (1838–1922) when he helped to frame the *Imperial Precepts to Soldiers and Sailors,* issued in 1882. This document states: "We rely upon you [the conscripts] as Our limbs and you look up to Us as your head. . . . The soldier and sailor should consider loyalty their essential duty . . . . With [a constant] heart, fulfill your essential duty of loyalty and bear in mind that duty is weightier than a mountain, while death is lighter than a feather." They were exhorted to live up to the ideals and principles of valor, faithfulness and righteousness, simplicity, respect for superiors and consideration for inferiors.[17]

"Consideration for inferiors," however, failed to become an integral part of the military mind. The primary emphasis was on discipline and obedience. For the lowest-ranking soldiers, this meant, in practical terms, constant abuse and beatings. Corporals and sergeants took sadistic pleasure in finding the slightest excuse to physically abuse the soldiers under them. A minute blemish on a rifle or bayonet, a button askew, shoes not polished spic and span were causes for physical beatings. One soldier related how, as raw recruits, he and his fellow soldiers were slugged and made to lick the soles of their inadequately polished shoes. Such sadistic abuses by noncommissioned officers resulted in occasional desertion and suicide. Another person recalled that, when soldiers were reprimanded for a slight infraction, they were beaten for excusing themselves if they tried to explain and beaten for being silent if they said nothing.[18]

Having been abused in this manner, the soldiers abused in turn those who came after them. In this way, sadistic mistreatment of those lower in rank was built into the system. At the same time, army leaders, who constantly called their soldiers the arms and legs of the emperor, fostered a sense that, as members of the imperial army, their men were better than civilians. As a result, the peasant boy who donned an army uniform developed a sense of superiority toward civilians and felt he could, when sent into the battlefield, commit all sorts of atrocities on the strength of his special ties with the sacrosanct emperor.

For young peasants, joining the army meant attaining an elevated status. Noted one observer in 1929, "The young men of the village consider it the greatest honor attainable, once they enter the army, to become a private superior class [a rank below that of corporal]. All the villagers share this view. As the young recruits leave the village, they all vow to come back as private superior class."[19]

Following the Sino-Japanese War of 1894–1895 and the Russo-Japanese War of 1904–1905, the number of veterans at large in the country was enormous. Army leaders decided to forge continuing links to this segment of the population in order to build a base of support at the grass-roots level, ensure their position in the power structure, and win popular support for their policies. In order to accomplish this objective the army, under the leadership of General Tanaka Giichi (1864–1929), established the Imperial Military Reserve Association in 1910. Tanaka's aim was to use "Japan's thousands of hamlets as the army's agrarian cells." By 1936, there were 14,000 branches of the association in the country, and, with its help, the army was able to make its ideals "an important layer of the rural value system."[20]

Like the armed forces, the Imperial Military Reserve Association became an instrument for reinforcing the indoctrination in *chūkun aikoku* that its members had been subjected to ever since their school-days.

Membership in the association was not restricted to ex-servicemen. Young men who had passed the army physical examination but had not been called to active duty were also eligible. In the 1920s and 1930s, 45 to 50 percent of those eligible to join did so, enrollment being close to 100 percent in the rural areas.[21]

Among the veteran association's auxiliary groups, the most important was the Seinendan (Young Men's Association). The functions of the youth groups that existed in the Tokugawa period had been taken over by the Meiji government, rendering those groups useless. However, at about the same time that he organized the military reserve association, General Tanaka decided to revive youth groups in an effort to stem the decline in "morality" among the young. He feared that growing social unrest would result in the spread of "unhealthy thought," by which he meant anarchism, socialism, and communism. His youth groups were to serve as instruments for fostering "wholesome" attitudes. Tanaka was as successful in building up the Seinendan as he was in establishing the military reserve association. By the 1930s, 2.7 million young men belonged to this nationwide network of associations. Again, enrollment in these groups was heaviest in rural areas. For example, in Kagoshima prefecture, the southernmost region of Kyushu, nearly 100 percent of those eligible were enrolled, whereas, in Tokyo, the figure was only 17.2 percent.[22]

Youth centers were established in many villages where, about once a week, members attended night classes in civic responsibility and wholesome thought and habits. At the same time, the military reserve association served as a vehicle to foster nationalistic and promilitary sentiments among the public at large. Local units sponsored lectures, movies, plays, exhibitions, and patriotic ceremonies in local communities, especially in the 1930s.[23] The proper "party line" was instilled in local unit leaders through seminars, directives, and publications issued by national headquarters.

By the end of the Meiji era, about 1912, civilian and military leaders had succeeded in their design to transform Japan's peasants into patriotic subjects. The peasants, whose perspective prior to the Meiji era had been confined largely to their own hamlets, were now conditioned to think of themselves as "Japanese," and could be aroused to defend Japan's national honor against offending foreign powers.[24]

Thus, the molders of the minds of the masses did succeed in forging a sense of direct linkage between the emperor and the people. To die on the battlefield shouting, "Long live the emperor!" was seen as the perfect fulfillment of one's life as a Japanese. It is no accident that the "three human bombs" who were glorified during the Shanghai Incident of 1932 had all been born and raised in rural communities (two peasants and one miner).[25]

For the peasant masses, the ideals of *chūkun aikoku* had a stronger emotional appeal than ideals of individual rights, freedom, and equality that the Meiji liberals sought to instill in them.[26] The altruistic idea of serving a higher entity, be it the emperor or the nation, hit them at the level of "felt truth," unlike the liberals' principles, which spoke to them in rational terms about their individual rights and interests.

Life-Style and Values

"MODERNIZATION"

Western technology slowly began to filter into the villages. Initially, certain objects astounded and frightened the populace. An item in a newspaper in 1873 reported that a young geisha fainted with fright when a customer lit a match: she thought a ghost had appeared. Another account in 1872 related that the peasants of western Japan believed the rumor that telegraph lines were infused with the blood of virgins who had been specially conscripted by the government to supply blood for the lines; to avoid a similar fate, young women shaved their eyebrows and blackened their teeth in hopes of passing for married women. It was also rumored that young girls between the ages of thirteen and twenty-five would be sent to the West to mate with Europeans and improve the Japanese racial stock.[27]

Eventually, however, even rural dwellers became accustomed to the material manifestations of Western civilization, which is not to say that efforts to transform their life-style and customs did not still encounter stubborn resistance.

The government, hoping to encourage the populace to behave in a manner that would not "shame" Japan in the eyes of Westerners, exhorted the people to refrain from relieving themselves on the roadside, bathing in public view, engaging in mixed bathing, or walking about in their loincloths. Women were told not to sit around barebreasted or feed their babies in public. In 1872, the Ministry of Justice issued ordinances regulating the social practices of the people.[28] Political and social leaders tried to discourage women from shaving their eyebrows and blackening their teeth (though many peasant women continued to blacken their teeth, in some cases well into the twentieth century). Men were told to cut their topknots and get Western-style haircuts. A popular saying asserted that "when you tap the head of a man with a crew cut, you will hear the sound of civilization and enlightenment." In some areas the authorities even felt compelled to impose fines on those who refused to change their hair-styles.[29] But many peasants continued to wear topknots until the end of the century. Men also continued to work in public in their loincloths, and urinate and spit noisily in public, even in urban areas. Generally, the peasants persisted in behaving the way they always had and up to the end of World War II many people persisted in ignoring the exhortations of the proponents of "civilized" conduct.

The peasants' reluctance to change their ways also revealed itself in their dogged adherence to the old calendar. As part of the modernizing process, in 1873 the Meiji government abandoned the lunar calendar and adopted the Gregorian calendar. This upset even the townspeople. One critic protested:

We have come along thus far with the traditional calendar, and it has caused no trouble to anyone. Why has the government suddenly decided to abolish it? The whole thing is disagreeable. The old system corresponded to the seasons, the weather, and the movement of the tides. One could plan one's work, one's clothing, and virtually everything else by it. Since the revision, the New Year and Obon [the Buddhist festival of the dead] come at crazy times. The cherry trees bloom in the sixth and seventh months, and the summer storms come in the tenth. In the fourth and fifth months, snow and frost are still on the ground. . . . Nothing is the way it should be.[30]

The Christian weekdays and the notion of Sunday as a day of rest had no meaning for the general populace. The traditional feast days and holidays remained more meaningful than the new holidays adopted by the government. Eventually city residents adjusted to the new calendar, but in rural areas people continued to live by and mark important events of the year by the lunar calendar. This practice persisted into the postwar years. Consequently, New Year's Day was observed twice in the countryside, but for the old-timers the "real" one was the day marked by the lunar calendar. A survey conducted in 1948 showed that 52 percent of the households in farm villages and

50 percent of the families in fishing villages still used the lunar calendar.[31]

Similarly the traditional way of calculating a person's age remained common practice. That is, at birth a baby was considered one year of age and on the first New Year's Day he/she became two. Birthdays meant very little to the peasants then, for the important day was New Year's. Again in the temporal realm, the peasants usually did not live by the clock. They lived and worked by the sun and the moon, and the passage of time was judged intuitively. Punctuality was not a habit essential to the villagers. If a gathering was planned for three in the afternoon, most people showed up around three-thirty or four or even later.

HŌTOKUKAI AND NŌHONSHUGI

It is much easier to change the external, physical aspects of life than the internal, moral life of a people. Not only did Japan's peasants feel the physical effects of the new age that followed the Meiji restoration much less forcefully than Japan's urban dwellers, but in the realm of values and attitudes, where change occurs more gradually, they were even less affected. To be sure, in prewar Japan traditional values persisted even in the urban areas, but in the rural communities they survived practically unscathed by the "enlightened," liberal rationalism of the modern age. Only the wealthy and prominent (the *gōnō*) were influenced to some extent by the movement to "enlighten and civilize" the people and to uphold "people's rights."[32] Freedom, equality, independence, and individual rights remained basically alien concepts to the peasantry, who remained provincial in their outlook and in their behavior. "The world of traditional values was not dead even in the early parts of this century, but was still in full sway over large parts of Tohoku [the northeast], Hokuriku [the north], Kyushu, and in some other areas."[33]

Among the values and attitudes that the Tokugawa ruling class had instilled in the peasants were frugality, diligence, obedience, self-denial, patience, humility, social harmony, knowing one's place, deference to one's betters, unquestioning submission to authority, loyalty, and a keen sense of duty. These values entailed the acceptance of the hierarchical order of things and the subordination of the individual to the group, whether it be the family, the hamlet, or the nation.[34]

The Meiji rulers differed greatly from their Tokugawa counterparts in that, rather than wishing to perpetuate the traditional order and its values, the Meiji were committed to "modernization"; their object was, however, solely to adopt the *external* aspects of Western civilization, in particular Western industry and technology (see p. oo). The new leaders were in essential agreement with the concept of combining "Eastern ethics and Western science," a slogan propounded by Sakuma Zōzan, a thinker of the late Tokugawa era. Theirs was to be a revolution from above, not a transformation of the society from below. Hence, they "spoke in terms of the traditional language of loyalty and obligation" to persuade the people to support their efforts at building a modern industrial and military power.[35] A Japanese sociologist asserts that "the Japanese government intentionally prevented farmers from becoming modern citizens in a modern society by means of particular indoctrination."[36]

Landlords also encouraged their tenants to follow the path of traditional values. Like the Tokugawa rulers, who issued injunctions to the peasants to work from dawn to dark and eat millet rather than rice, some landlords of the modern era exhorted their tenants "to work from 4 A.M. until 9 P.M., instead of 6 A.M. to 6 P.M., and . . . cut out useless breaks at midday. . . . The story is told of one Meiji landlord who insisted that his tenants get up at 3 A.M." One landlord, who in 1915 organized a welfare association—a kind of savings club—for his tenants, demanded that they take an oath to be pious, improve morals, "preserve [their] station in life, show humility and proper respect for others, be industrious and frugal," respect tradition, fulfill public duties, exercise self-denial, and engage in good works.[37] In a sense, these qualities represent what society as a whole, the peasants included, regarded as the characteristics of an ideal peasant.

Around the turn of the century, government leaders as well as "progressive" landlords encouraged the revival of Hōtokukai ("Society for the Repayment of Virtue") in order to inculcate in the peasantry the ideals propagated by the society's founder, Ninomiya Sontoku (1787–1856). Each person, Ninomiya had taught, "owes his existence and well-being to his ancestors and society and, therefore, has the obligation to adhere to the doctrine of repayment of virtue, which entails hard work, thrift, moderation, and sharing one's savings with others."[38] The absence of these qualities, he asserted, would result in the desolation of the spirit as well as the land. The principle of sharing one's savings with others was interpreted by Meiji officials to mean that everyone had the obligation to pay taxes.[39] Ninomiya's philosophy thus served the interests of both the landlords and the government. "Although the evidence is ambiguous, it seems prudent to conclude that the state, in cooperation with large landlords in some cases and small ones in others, used the Hōtokukai to foster rural stability," concludes one historian.[40] In 1924, local Hōtokukai were brought under the unifying authority of a central organization, the Dai-Nippon Hōtokukai, in order to curb what the authorities regarded as their growing moral laxity and to combat the rising tide of socialistic thought.[41]

Needless to say, the peasants required no lectures on the virtues of thrift and diligence. These qualities were essential for their survival. Peasant families have traditionally insisted on not leaving a single grain of rice in their bowls. Unnecessary consumption was looked upon as a sinful action, and daily toil was held in particularly high regard.[42]

A number of political leaders supported the advocates of *nōhonshugi* ("agrarian fundamentalism") to combat what they saw as the threat from "dangerous" ideologies, that is, socialism and communism. They also hoped to use *nōhonshugi* to prevent "unhealthy" urban influences from corrupting the rural areas. It was seen as a movement that would boost the morale of farmers who felt that their interests were being sacrificed in the name of industrialism.

One scholar defines *nōhonshugi* as "a loosely conceived farm-centered social and political ideology that emerged in response to enigmas and tensions created by Japanese modernization after 1868. Principal *nōhonshugi* beliefs included faith in an agricultural economy, affirmation of rural communalism, and a conviction that farming was indispensable to those qualities that made the nation unique."[43] One Japanese sociologist emphasized the moralistic aspects of the movement when he asserted that *nōhonshugi* "indoctrinated farmers with the idea that agriculture was the most natural and wholesome of occupations and the key industry of the nation, and that urban industrialization was an important cause of moral degradation. At the same time, such indoctrination helped to keep agriculture the servant of modern industrial development."[44]

Aside from the objectives noted above, government officials as well as nongovernment leaders favored the propagation of this philosophy for certain self-serving reasons. "Industrialists advocated [*nōhonshugi*] in order to use farm families as a source of cheap labor. Some militarists used the ideology to protect the middle-class farmers, who were supplying the nation's armed forces with strong soldiers. Landlords were not the last to advocate the ideology, as they feared a socialist-influenced farmers' movement."[45] Bureaucrats, initially seeing in the movement a possible means of relieving agrarian poverty, extolled the virtues of "frugality, duty, hard work, and the village economy as the backbone of the nation."[46] But they soon seized instead upon expansion abroad as their solution to agrarian problems, with *nōhonshugi* used as a vehicle to mobilize agrarian support for this policy. Most adherents of *nōhonshugi* were hostile to big business and aligned themselves with radical militarists and militant nationalists who were bent upon effecting a new order, the Shōwa restoration, by ridding the nation of grasping capitalistic elements.

Nōhonshugi failed, nonetheless, to become a highly centralized mass movement because the main proponents of the ideology, the masters themselves, were individualists, each of whom had his own "school" in which a small group of dedicated followers came to sit at his feet.[47] Far from galvanizing the peasantry into an army of devoted ideologues, their influence was limited to a small group of concerned activists, true believers who were, on occasion, willing to take direct action and commit acts of violence, such as the assassination of prominent business and political leaders.

One of the leading figures among the *nōhonshugi* masters was Gondō Seikyō (1868–1937), characterized by one authority as a "romantic agrarian nationalist."[48] Gondō favored local self-rule and village self-sufficiency. He opposed the establishment of a modern centralized bureaucracy (which he equated with Prussian statism), capitalist production, and urban life, which he judged to be in conflict with Japanese *kokutai* ("national polity"). His concept of self-rule had nothing, however, to do with democracy or individual rights. It was to be based on the traditional, hierarchical order of things.[49]

Gondō's anti-urban, pro-agrarian sentiments are best revealed in statements like the following:

Our villages are the foundations of the country and the source of our habits and customs. At present the farmers form half our total population; they utilize the greater portion of the land; and they produce a large proportion not only of the nation's staple foodstuffs but also of its industrial raw materials and commercial goods. . . . [At the same time,] Tokyo and the other cities have expanded out of all proportion to the villages, and are replete with great buildings that are the last word in comfort and elegance. But, with the Great Depression, villages everywhere are in financial difficulties.[50]

Nōhonshugi thinkers had mystical notions about the Japanese national polity, and expected social harmony to be attained under the spiritual guidance of the emperor. This is seen in the thoughts of another *nōhonshugi* ideologue, Katō Kanji (1884–1965), who sought to enhance the Japanese peasant's soul, which he defined as "the sincerity to find one's true life-work in the sacred occupation of agriculture . . . fusing oneself with that life force that is Great Japan, to be steadfast in devotion to the great spirit of the emperor. . . ." The purity of the Japanese peasant soul, according to Katō, had been corrupted by economists influenced by "Western individualism and materialism."[51]

Another *nōhonshugi* master, Tachibana Kōzaburō (1893–1974), associated himself with a terrorist organization headed by a radical nationalist and Buddhist priest, Inoue Nisshō (1886–1967), who organized the Ketsumeidan (Blood Pledge League) and instigated the assassination of prominent business and political leaders, including in 1932 Prime Minister Inukai. Tachibana spent eight years in prison for his involvement in Inoue's activities. He, like other *nōhonshugi* advocates, favored rebuilding Japan around agrarian communities, curbing capitalism, and enhancing Japan's national glory and interests.

The aspect of *nōhonshugi* that the peasants shared was its mystical notions regarding the emperor. In a sense this is a baffling phenomenon. Although the younger generation had been indoctrinated in the schools and elsewhere to revere and respect the emperor, the older generation, who had not attended school and had grown up when the *shōgun* and the *daimyō* were the feared and respected ruling authorities, had no reason to hold the new ruler in such awed respect and reverence. Perhaps the almost innate reverence for *kami* (gods, spirits) that prevailed among the peasants led to the worshipful reverence they accorded the emperor, for he was presented to the people as a living *kami (iki-gami)*. Be that as it may, the cult of the emperor—which was fostered by the government, the military, the schools, and local leaders—was a significant factor in shoring up the traditional virtues of obedience, submissiveness, self-denial, and humility among the peasants.

FAMILY LIFE

The other institution that remained a powerful factor in preserving traditional values and attitudes in the rural areas was the family system.

"The family's welfare continued to be of transcendant value, its authority immense. Solidarity and obedience within the family unit were taught to the young as conditions of survival, and these traditional values carried over to behavior outside the family."[52]

The family system emphasized the virtue of subordinating the individual's interests to those of the group, and of preserving an hierarchical order based on sex and age. At the top of the hierarchy was the father, who, under the civil code adopted by the Meiji government in 1898, was given full control over all family property, the right to determine the family members' place of residence, and the right to approve or disapprove marriages and divorces. Matters that affected the larger circle of relatives were decided by a council of heads of families from the extended kinship group. The same values that conditioned the thinking and behavior of family members—a sense of discipline, obedience, duty, and self-abnegation—were those that made their youths ideal servants of the emperor and the nation.

The point that should be noted in reflecting upon all this emphasis on group interests, cooperation, submissiveness, and harmony is that Japanese family members did not constitute one big happy, harmonious entity. There was a great deal of tension, frustration, bitterness, and even hatred lurking under the surface. Life was especially difficult for the young wife of the eldest son; upon joining the family, she had to live with her in-laws—including her husband's grandparents, parents, and siblings—and totally suppress her own interests, desires, and feelings, consenting to serve her husband's family as a virtual servant until her turn came to take over the role of the "mother" of the household. The difficult, almost cruel conditions that many young wives had to endure often led to suicide or a nervous breakdown. (Cf., "Bog Rhubarb Shoots" in chapter 4). The young wife was not the only member of the family who suffered under such family imperatives. Marriages were most often arranged by the parents, and daughters, in particular, were often compelled to marry against their will. At times this led to tragic consequences: The girl might commit suicide or run away rather than enter into an abhorrent marriage. A writer living in a northern village took note of the following conversation among his fellow villagers, Osen and Okane, who were gossiping by the fireplace.

"I hear Yoshie-san took rat poison and died yesterday."
"Why did she do that? She was so young!"
"She didn't want to have to marry her uncle."[53]

Even greater misery and hardship befell the young girls who, for the sake of the family, were sent off to the filatures and textile plants as virtual indentured servants or, even worse, sold to brothels at home and abroad.

It wasn't only female family members who experienced the emotional strain of the pressure within the family system to live lives of self-denial and self-sacrifice. Sons too felt confined and restricted, and this often led to bitterness and rebellion, as Shibuya Teisuke's diary reveals. On May 11, 1925, he wrote, "We're so busy that even the little time I have to myself at night is disappearing. I think about 'myself' and the 'family' (ie). The civil code, which turns the eldest son into a virtual prisoner, must be changed." On May 16: "Today, before I left the house with the ox, I had an argument with my father. It was over a trivial matter. So I felt irritated all day. The argument was entirely my fault." On May 17: "The 'family' is what keeps me from living the kind of life I would like to live. I want to be free! I want to be liberated from the 'family.'" July 5: "I may be bound too tightly to my parents and siblings. . . . I was not born into this environment of my own free will. My parents produced and raised me without my permission." And on December 3 Shibuya recorded a conversation that reflected his growing dissatisfaction:

I want to be liberated from this "family" as soon as possible and enter a life where I can freely develop my individuality as a social being.

Today I helped the roofer all day. The roofer said to me, "You were away from your home for two or three days without telling your father, so he was worried."

"No matter how much I explain my feelings to my father, he refuses to understand, so I've given up talking to him."

"Well, . . . but your father loves you. You are his son, and naturally he worries about you. . . ."

I was distressed when the roofer spoke of a father's love for his son. The relationship between my father and me is almost one of mutual hatred.[54]

Just as the family was a breeding ground for tensions, frustrations, and bitterness; so the hamlets, despite the ideals of community harmony and cooperation, were often rife with social tensions, rivalries, jealousies, and even hatred. Historically, cooperation among community members had been necessary to carry on activities of common interests, such as watering the rice paddies; maintaining roads and bridges; planting the rice; fire fighting; house building; and organizing and attending funerals, weddings, religious events, and festivals. Moreover, in the Tokugawa period the ruling authorities held the community as a whole responsible for the payment of taxes, and answerable for infractions against the laws and regulations imposed upon them. So the actions of individuals, insofar as they might affect the interests of other members of the community, became the community's business. In addition, villagers generally lived so close together that they were, to some extent, one large family. Everyone was expected to conform to the mores of the community, and in the Tokugawa period those who violated community customs or undermined its interests were ostracized.

Approval and acceptance by fellow villagers, then, were important to the members of the community. Villagers usually went along with the crowd to avoid breaking the "cake of custom." The wish not to incur the disapproval of fellow villagers made the preservation of proper appearances and reputation—or "saving face"—essential.

An agrarian village was not, then, a place where smiling, courteous peasants lived together in idyllic harmony. Because of the poverty, the social constraints, and the almost hermetic isolation of many villages, the tensions and frustrations of life in the rural areas may, in fact, have been more acute than in urban Japan. For example, anyone whose lot was bettered by some stroke of good fortune was likely to become the immediate target of other villagers' envy. In Shibuya's community, one family—a sick old man, an old woman, and a widow with a young baby—was on the verge of starvation, and Shibuya took the initiative in getting help for them. As, with outside aid, their plight improved, their fellow villagers became increasingly upset.

Recently money, rice, and bean paste have been arriving for the Wakabayashi family almost every day. Seeing this, it is said that their impoverished neighbors have begun to resent them. . . . This shows the desperate state of the poor peasants. When the Wakabayashi family was in desperate straits, the others felt that, compared to them, they were still well off. But now that the Wakabayashi family began receiving money and goods, their neighbors have become envious because they feel . . . worse off. . . .[55]

Yūki Aisoka tells a similar story about villagers in northern Japan in the 1930s. When a peasant's house was destroyed by fire, people from the neighboring villages brought food and clothing to help out, but soon the impoverished neighbors became envious and began to complain that the victim, after causing a lot of trouble to the villagers in connection with the fire, was profiting from it.[56]

Describing life in a village in western Japan in the late 1930s, Ibuse Masuji, the novelist, depicts the villagers as endlessly fighting, squabbling, and complaining about water rights, property rights, or drunkenness. Husbands and wives quarrel, and an unmarried pregnant woman commits suicide, as does a lonely old woman.[57]

In effect, then, the self-denial instilled in the peasants did not entirely supplant their desire for wealth and profit. A temporary resident of a village near Tokyo during the immediate postwar years wrote: "Even ties of kinship are extremely weak. When it comes to money matters, they become greedy as crows, and blood ties are instantly forgotten."[58] Parents tended to name their children in accordance with their aspirations for them. One observer noted that in a village of 500 households, 40 percent of the children had the word *kin* ("gold" or "money") in their names.[59]

Conservative political as well as military leaders were interested in keeping rural communities from falling prey not only to what they considered the degenerate ways of the cities but also to the "insidious" ideas represented by socialism, communism, and even Western liberalism. The military commander of the Hiroshima district reported in 1913:

Kure [the former naval base in Hiroshima Bay] has developed rapidly, and there we find factories, naval officers, and soldiers. The city looks like a new colony because factory laborers have immigrated here from almost every district of Japan, and more than a few outlaws are in evidence. The city appears to be lively, but the people are full of frivolity and fraud . . . blinded by immediate profits. This lamentable tendency cannot but have a bad influence on the neighboring villages, and in fact the good habits and simple customs of the rural communities are gradually being destroyed.[60]

The military reserve association and the young men's societies had, of course, been established to combat this tendency and make certain that wholesome, patriotic sentiments would be fostered and preserved among village youths. The advocates of *nōhonshugi,* as we noted earlier, had also set out to defend traditional virtues against the inimical influences of the urban, capitalistic world. One *nōhonshugi* advocate spoke of "the anger that seized him when he went to the country and saw a substance called 'lemonade' in the shops; restaurants where none were before; peasants who bought umbrellas and clogs, which they used to make themselves." He was indignant at "the luxurious idealism of rural education, which serves only to increase the tax burden of the peasants, give them ideas above their station, and siphon off the most talented of them to the towns."[61]

With the advent of the 1930s, and the growing tide of militarism and ultranationalism, excoriation of frivolous, decadent Western ways grew increasingly strident. Villagers, suspicious of those who returned from the cities, looked for signs that they had become part of the "modern" set. In the rural community depicted by Ibuse, a village councilman says of a young woman who had been a waitress in the city, "It is really mortifying that a frivolous 'modern girl' like that comes into the village and gets the young men all excited. Really, the permanent waves and synthetic fibers prevalent today cheapen the spirit of people much more than the painted faces of the girls." The girl's boyfriend "has his hair shiny with pomade, is wearing a necktie and a double-breasted suit. The scent of cream exudes from his clean-shaven face. The villagers call such young men 'modern boys.' . . . The city is full of young men like him. It's strange that in my eyes these young men all seem to fit in the same mold."[62]

NOMA SEIJI AND THE SHŌNEN KURABU

Despite the concerns of the authorities about the corruption of rural youths by the decadent influences of "modern" urban elements, the encroachment of "modern" ideas and values was not extensive. The educational level of the peasantry, as noted in chapter 2 remained low, and the media that brought "bourgeois" ideas into the villages were limited. Newspapers were not much read among the peasants. Although newspaper circulation reached 300,000 by the turn of the century, these papers were read mainly by the urban populace and by well-off rural residents.[63] For the poorer peasants, newspapers were a luxury they could not readily afford. In outlying villages, readership remained low even in the 1930s. For example, in a northern village of 566 households, only 158—28 percent of the households—subscribed to a newspaper.[64]

Although in the 1920s popular mass-circulation magazines began to appear in urban communities, their circulation in the villages remained limited, and even then they were read only by the better educated, wealthier rural families. These popular mass-circulation magazines took on an increasingly "modern" appearance, with colorful covers, photographs, drawings, cartoons and comics, informative articles and entertaining stories. But most of their contents, predictably, dealt with urban life. The younger generation began to read the popular children's magazines that were being published by magazine king Noma Seiji, but most peasant families were too poor to buy them.

The magazine that was directed toward the peasantry was *Ie no Hikari (Light of the Family)*, published by the farmers' cooperative, which, as might be expected, remained staid, conservative, and mundane, stressing the virtues of frugality and hard work. For example, one article asserted, "When luxury becomes widespread, debauchery overwhelms the cities and the countryside, and young men and women who, infected by Westernism, thoughtlessly pose at being atuned to the 'new' are becoming evident everywhere." The way to combat this trend and resist urban consumerism, the author argued, was to be frugal, save, and increase production.[65]

The most influential publisher of the 1920s and 1930s was Noma Seiji, whose many magazines gained a phenomenal readership. Unlike other publishers, he included the peasantry in the circle of those he wanted to reach. To achieve his aim of capturing the widest possible spectrum of readers, he pitched the contents of his magazines at the level of those who had had only the minimum six years of elementary education. He excluded "high brow" articles from his magazines and made certain that ideas not in tune with the times did not appear in his publications. The secret of his success, he once said, was his policy of publishing articles that were one step behind the times. On another occasion, he said that he planned to give his readers a mixture of 70 percent old and 30 percent new ingredients. Others said that it was 70 percent entertainment and 30 percent edification. Noma succeeded in achieving his goal of capturing a mass readership. By 1930, he was publishing nine magazines with a total monthly circulation of 7 million.[66]

Of Noma's magazines, the one that had the greatest influence on the youths of Japan, even rural youngsters, was his boys' magazine, *Shōnen Kurabu (Young Boys' Club)*. It was directed at sixth-graders but had readers both below and above this age group. His aim, he asserted, was to produce "real men," and to build the moral character of the youths of Japan. In addition to entertaining stories, he published "success stories" to encourage the young to make something of themselves, as well as tales of swashbuckling warriors in which virtue triumphed over evil. He also valued heuristic and hortatory stories based on the lives of such people as Ninomiya Sontoku (see p. 65) and exemplifying the virtues of diligence, dedication, and frugality.[67] Right and wrong were clearly defined, while the subtleties and fine nuances of real life were hardly ever addressed.

As the tide of militarism and nationalism rose, Noma trimmed his sails to fit the national trend and began to stress the virtues of *chūkun aikoku.* Stories of military heroes who accomplished great feats of derring-do came to the fore in his magazines, particularly in *Shōnen Kurabu.* He also sponsored the propagation of a comic-strip hero, a dog-soldier called Nora-Kura (Black Mutt) who was unquestionably the best-known character among the many fictional figures known to prewar Japanese children. It would not be an exaggeration to say that not a single child of school age was unfamiliar with the exploits of Nora-Kura, who started out as a bumbling underdog private but ended up becoming a vehicle to justify and glorify Japanese military actions against the Chinese (who were depicted as pigs). After the war, the creator of Nora-Kura admitted, "In retrospect it could be said that I was in the vanguard of military aggression."[68]

Perhaps it could be said that Noma, more than any other single individual, was responsible for fostering militaristic thinking among Japanese youths by oversimplifying issues and glamorizing Japanese military exploits. In this respect he was not simply adapting to the times but helping to chart a course of events. The profound influence that his magazines had on the minds of the young led some critics to contend that his magazine had a greater impact on them than did prewar school textbooks.[69] In 1935, *Shōnen Kurabu* enjoyed a monthly circulation of 500,000. That it even reached youngsters in out-of-the-way villages is revealed in the words of a man who years later recalled:

I spent my boyhood in a small mountain village in Niigata prefecture, about four kilometers inland from Kashiwazaki. It snowed a great deal there. When there was a heavy snowfall even the mail tended to get delayed in these mountain villages. But my older brother used to go downhill to pick up the *Shōnen Kurabu,* no matter how deep the snow was. He would plow through the snow where roads had disappeared. He went without fail. And I would await his return nervously, looking constantly at the clock. Those nights became the happiest moments of our lives. I still remember this vividly.[70]

The other media of modern society—such as radio and movies, which began to gain popularity in the cities in the 1920s—did not find their way into the rural areas until the postwar years. Radios were rarities in the villages, and, since the only broadcasting station in existence then was the government-operated NHK, it remained essentially a vehicle for official propaganda. By the 1930s, when the radio diffusion was becoming more widespread, government censorship had become more stringent.

Movies were, for the vast majority of the peasants, an inaccessible luxury. In the 1930s, on the rare occasions when they did reach certain villages, it was usually under the auspices of organizations like the military reserve association, and the pictures shown were those that would elicit support for the policies of the government and the military. Such films did little to "modernize" the thinking of the peasant masses.

For their entertainment most peasants relied on traditional village festivals: Bon dances, Buddhist festivals of the dead; and Shinto festivals. Older people might occasionally manage to go off to a hot-spring inn for a rest, and, in the 1930s, schoolchildren sometimes went off on an "educational tour" to historical sites. But these, too, were restricted to those who could afford to travel. Thus, even though we can say that, by the 1930s, the mental horizons of peasant youths were being expanded, opportunities that served this end were limited, and the values encountered were more often than not traditional ones reinforcing the demands of *chūkun aikoku.*

RURAL

WOMEN

Life on the Farm and
in the Village

Under the strong patriarchal system that prevailed in prewar Japan, women were generally deemed to be inferior beings, and according to law wives were treated like minors. Daughters had virtually no say about whom they were to marry and no legal claim to the family property; their interests were entirely subordinated to those of the men.

Ironically enough, in the feudal period there was greater equality between the husband and wife among the peasantry than there was within the warrior class, owing no doubt to the fact that the peasant wife worked just as hard in the field as her husband. Authority in the household was shared between the two. Symbolically, in many families the husband possessed the family seal as the emblem of his authority, while the wife possessed the rice scooper to signify her share of family authority. In this sense a dual authority prevailed. When a husband and wife took over family authority from the older generation (his parents) they took over their functions. "Just as her husband now took the seat at the hearth reserved for the master of the house, she took that [seat] reserved for the mistress."[1]

When the Meiji government was established and a new civil code was adopted, the authorities decided to extend the practice of primogeniture and single succession to the family "headship" that had formerly prevailed among the warrior class but not the peasants. A key legal adviser argued, "The customs of the farmers are not to receive general acceptance—instead we must follow the example of *samurai* and nobleman." Still, in practice, the peasant wife "played a large role in production and her position commanded respect."[2] John F. Embree, in his 1935 study of Suye Mura, notes: "In farm work man and wife are equal, so that in a farmer's household a woman has a comparatively higher status than in a shopkeeper's house. If a man did not get along with his wife on the farm, his own income and food supply would be endangered."[3]

This did not mean, however, that the farm wife had equal authority with her husband in deciding family affairs, for ordinarily the man had the decisive voice in important matters, and in matters that affected, directly or indirectly, members of the extended family circle, a council of relatives was convened. However, in dealing with daily household affairs and in coping with matters involving women and children, the

79

wife—as mistress of the family—played a central role.

Life for a farm family meant arduous work in the fields—and often little more. Farm women were hardly touched by the Westernized products that their counterparts in the cities were beginning to enjoy by the 1920s. The latter had the opportunity to shop in glittering department stores, see movies with glamorous stars, wear Western dresses, get a Western-style permanent wave, find employment as office girls in modern brick office buildings or in modern department stores. All this was as unreal for peasant women as the glamorous Hollywood life depicted in films was for urban working women.

For farm girls and women, life was dull, difficult, restrictive, and Spartan. Taught since childhood not to seek personal happiness and pleasure, they were bound by traditional, feudalistic mores and values. If they remained in the village they were expected to labor just as hard as the men. A city dweller residing temporarily in a farm village recalled that "the people who had gone to help in rice planting all complained of backaches. An old woman put some mulberry tree roots on the brazier, boiled some tea, and talked about the days when she was young. 'If you worked for a family that was bent on getting ahead economically it was very hard. We worked so hard that we weren't able to squat in the toilet because our legs were so sore.' "[4]

In villages where the men went to work in nearby factories, women and children were left behind to tend the fields on their own. In 1939, a farmer in Chiba prefecture told an inquiring visitor:

As you can see, this area is governed by the concept of respecting men and holding women in low regard. Women have to do much work. . . . If you look in the fields, you will see mostly women working. From around the late 1890s on, men from this area began to find work in factories making winnowing machines. At first the men went to work during the slack season on the farm, but as the factories got more business their sons began to join them. The women had to stay behind and work hard on the farm. . . . So a woman has to carry a load that weighs fifteen to sixteen *kan* [about twenty-five pounds] on her back. As a result her rear end protrudes and she walks bent over. When she wears a kimono she looks misshapen. Nowadays young men want as wives, good looking girls who don't work. This makes no sense. In the old days people used to hand the prospective bride a handful of beans [*mame*]. When she stuck out her hand for the beans, [the groom's family] looked to see if her hands were full of calluses [*mame*]. If so, she was seen as a hardworker who would turn out to be a good young wife. Today few girls work as hard as girls formerly did. They want to imitate the ways of the well-off city girls who dress and make up nicely. They are thoughtless and worry about keeping their hands and feet from getting coarse.[5]

An old woman in a village in the Kanto region observed in 1945:

In families that are fairly well off, the man has work outside the house and does not do much farm work. So the wife has to take charge of field work and keep everything in order. . . . She works hard at everything. The husband, imitating his mother, treats his wife heartlessly, as if she is a servant, but if we go behind the scenes it soon becomes clear that the wife has the real authority. When you have business with a family, if you give the children presents you can quickly make a deal. The farmer's wife does a full-time job in the field and somehow finds time to raise her children.[6]

Because the farm woman had her hands full, peasants usually frowned upon any woman interested in culture or "book learning." Such activities, especially for women and girls, were regarded as time wasters, that led to unrealistic aspirations and discontent. One old woman recalled that whenever her mother caught her reading she would take the book away from her saying, "It's pretentious for girls to read books."[7]

The belief that farm girls need not be educated contributed to their low rate of school attendance before the turn of the century. A few years before World War II, a man in a farm community not far from Tokyo told a visitor, "Education? Around here we don't believe it's necessary to educate girls. . . . Nowadays some families send their daughters to school to prepare them for marriage. I guess it's a form of vocationalism."[8] If a city girl married into a farm family, she was looked upon as a completely useless person because all her "education and culture" did nothing to make her a useful farm worker.

The other function of farm women, aside from working in the fields and on household chores, was to produce children. One old farm woman asserted, "Farmers must have children. Three children are not enough. There must be at least five. If a farmer has too few children, the world will close in on him. If he has too many, he will have trouble supporting them, but there must be at least five working hands in the family."[9] In fact, most farm families did not limit the number of their offspring. A villager near Tokyo observed, "The women here have lots of children. Eight or nine is not unusual. In the old days infanticide was tacitly permitted by the feudal lord, but after the Meiji restoration two or three villagers were punished for this. People were shocked and abandoned the practice."[10]

Still, in desperation, some farm women practiced infanticide. One old woman who had killed several of her infants remarked, "In order to survive I had no choice. To keep the children we already had, the others had to be sent back. Even now, rocks mark the spots where the babies were buried under the floor of the house. Every night I sleep right above where they're buried. Of course, I feel love and compassion for the babies I sent back. I know that I will go to hell when I die. I have a feeling the babies are there, too. When I die I want to go to hell so that I can protect them as best I can."[11]

Farm women, burdened with the dangerous task of giving birth to a large number of children, in most cases had little to say about whom they married. Such marriages were usually endogamous. In fact, close relatives, such as first cousins, or even uncles and nieces, were paired off. This kind of close inbreeding resulted in a high incidence of birth defects. A visitor to an island village was told, "Because marriages take place between close relatives, there are five idiots and three deaf-mutes in this village [of eighty households]."[12]

The women who had the most difficult time in farm families—in fact, in Japanese families in general—were young wives married to eldest sons, since they had to live with at least three, sometimes four, generations of the husbands' families. A young wife was treated as an outsider and as the lowliest member of the family until her mother-in-law got too old to run the household. She was referred to as the *yome* ("bride") and was expected to lead a life of total subservience. It was said in some communities that "the *yome* had to serve in that capacity for fifteen years"; that is, she was not accepted as a full-fledged family member for that length of time. According to another saying, "A *yome* does not need her mouth until she is thirty,"[13] for she was to remain silent till then.

A young wife had to be the first to rise and the last to go to bed. She might get up at three or four in the morning to cut grass for the horse or ox, work all day, and do the washing late at night after the others had gone to sleep. She had to resign herself to spending little or no time with her own children; because their care was taken over by her mother-in-law, sister-in-law, or the grandmother of the family. One old woman recalled, "Twenty-one days after the baby's birth is marked with red rice [rice cooked with red beans, eaten on felicitous occasions], the mother-in-law takes over the baby, and the wife has to go out in the fields to work. In the old days women used to go out to plant rice twelve days after giving birth to a baby."[14]

All the spare time the young wife had was to be devoted to work.

Caring for her children was viewed as an indulgence. One young girl recalled that her mother had to be deliberately cool toward her children so that they would go to her mother-in-law or sister-in-law for attention. As a result, the girl came to look upon her mother as a cold, forbidding person. One day, when she was three or four years old, she watched her mother weeping after being tormented by her in-laws. Seeing the child, her mother called her to her side, but the little girl was afraid to go to her. When her mother told her she loved her, she blurted out, "Do you mean it?" Her mother realized that she had turned her daughter into a stranger in her effort to be a good *yome.* [15]

It was an exceptional mother-in-law who did not constantly pick on her daughter-in-law. After all, when she had been a young wife, she had had to undergo harsh treatment by her in-laws, and now she expected her daughter-in-law to go through the same experience. The young wife could not get free of her mother-in-law's domination until the latter gave up her status as the mistress of the house, usually at the age of sixty to sixty-five—or twenty-odd years after the young wife had joined the family. The mother-in-law was naturally reluctant to give up her position as mistress of the house and become a dependent, relying on her daughter-in-law for pocket money. She knew she would be looked upon as an unwanted burden, tempting the new mistress of the house to get even with her for past years of torment. Soon she would long for death in order to escape the plight of being an unwanted appendage to the family. [16]

THE LOT OF THE ELDERLY

In fact, belief in the view of old people in Japan as objects of reverence and respect is a myth, at least as far as the peasantry was concerned. Respect for the wisened old man, a venerable patriarchal grandfather may have prevailed in families steeped in traditional cultural values. But, for peasants whose main concern was keeping family members fed, old people who continued to linger on in life were often regarded as burdens on the rest of the family.

There are tales that in the Tokugawa period, people in impoverished hill villages actually abandoned the old, on mountaintops or in meadows, to starve to death. In other villages the old were housed in shacks in out-of-the-way fields where they were used as "scarecrows" to chase birds and animals from the fields. [17]

Old people in peasant families in the "modern" period may not have been abandoned to starve to death, but, once they relinquished their positions as family head or mistress of the house, they lost financial control of the household. As long as they were able to go out and work in the fields, they were regarded as valuable members of the family, but as their capacity to work diminished they frequently came to be regarded as nuisances. The grandmother's chief function was to take care of the young children and perform odd jobs around the house and yard—tasks she sometimes resented. One old person remarked:

I hate being told "old folks" should stay home and watch over the house. When I'm sitting around at home I start feeling sorry for my old decrepit body. Even if I can't do much work I'd rather go out in the fields.[18]

Farm women who worked long hours in hard physical labor while consuming very little nourishment aged early. Their hands were chapped and marked by deep cracks and calluses. Their faces were wrinkled and their backs were bent over—sometimes at a ninety-degree angle—by the time they were fifty. A young girl writing about her mother noted that her "fingers are knobby at the joints and she can't straighten them out. Her rough, coarse hands do not look like a woman's. . . . When my mother first grabbed a hoe and sickle she was fifteen [fourteen by Western count]. She carried bundles of rice plants on her tiny back and slaved away covered with dirt and dust."[19]

It was said that peasant women aged ten years more quickly than urban women. Doctors treating peasants claimed that peasants aged sooner not only in outward appearance but also in terms of their inner organs.[20] One doctor asserted that he could tell whether a woman was from a village or a city simply by the way she lay on a bed. A peasant woman lay on a bed like a turtle turned upside down, because her back was so bent that her hands and feet failed to touch the bed.[21]

Of course, in the postwar period, the lot of farm women changed significantly as modern gadgets—including washing machines, refrigerators, and television sets—came into wide use. Even the plight of young wives improved as the more democratic and individualistic thinking of the cities began to affect life in farming communities. Sometimes, now, older women are dumbfounded by the changed life-style of the young. One old woman complained about the fact that the *yome* can get a permanent wave, go off to see a movie with her husband, and return in a taxi cab. "When I think of us farmers who worked day after day, from morning to night, and barely stayed alive, and then think of the young people today, I wonder if they will be able to make it as farmers."[22]

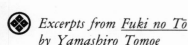

Excerpts from Fuki no Tō
by Yamashiro Tomoe

The hardships that prewar farm women, particularly young wives, had to survive are attested to by the following account of the life of an oppressed village woman. The author, Yamashiro Tomoe, came from a rural community in Hiroshima prefecture, got involved in social reform movements, married a Marxist labor organizer, and was imprisoned from 1940 to 1945 for harboring "dangerous thoughts." After the war, she played an active role in agrarian reform and antiwar movements, and began to write about people she had met in prison (as well as about the plight of rural women in general). One of the people she met in prison, a woman who was serving time for arson, is the central figure in the following story. Told like a folktale, the story depicts the hardships and abuses that the woman underwent as a young wife in a farm family. The values, attitudes, and way of life described in connection with the mother-in-law, and the husband's mistreatment of the woman, are not exaggerations or fantasies but the reality of life in many prewar Japanese families. Mitsuko, who appears in the story, is the author.[23] She was locked in the cell next to the woman prisoner whose life story was then gradually revealed to her. Filling in the gaps in that story, she wrote the following "non-fiction novelette."

BOG RHUBARB SHOOTS *Yamashiro Tomoe*

There used to be a song called "Ballad of the Bog Rhubarb Shoots." Here are the words:

The rhubarb shoots *(tō)* will be ten years old *(tō)*,
    The nursemaid is seven, she is an orphan.
The baby is a big, big boy,
    The precious, precious little heir to the family.
Lullabye baby, lullabye baby,

Go to sleep and grow up to be a big boy, go to sleep,
Your bed is being warmed by a charcoal brazier.

The rhubarb shoots on a snowy night,
   I had a dream about my wedding day.
It was spring, cheep, cheep, cheep!
   I was wearing a colorful ornamental hairpin.
Cheep, cheep, chirp, chirp.
   I shall be the first to marry,
I twirl my parasol, round and round.

This is how it was sung in some places, but the words could be changed
any way one wishes. The tune can be changed too. One could sing some parts
as if a storyteller were intoning it; other parts can be sung like a popular song
or like a school song that children sing. If we put all the parts together we
have a story. And this is the story.

A poor peasant woman and her daughter, were living in the hills on the
upper reaches of the Gō-no River. The mother worked the fields by herself.
She didn't remember when they started, but she found herself suffering
stomach pains. Her condition got steadily worse and in the spring of her
daughter's seventh year, before the camellias bloomed, she died.

One of the first things the daughter had learned was that bog rhubarb
shoots were good for stomach trouble. So from an early age she went about
hunting for rhubarb shoots. Once she nearly had a fatal accident when she
reached out for some shoots growing behind icicles formed by the waterwheel. She fell down into the gap between the waterwheel and the stone
wall. On another occasion she crawled up a cliff to pick some shoots and
tumbled down it when the snow began to slide.

The girl loved her mother, so she did not mind the cold when she went
out in the winter hunting for shoots. But, in spite of her efforts, her mother
finally died. Her relatives got together and decided to send her out to work
as a nursemaid. She was only seven then. Her family's house, yard, bamboo
grove, and rice fields passed into the hands of other people. When she left
home, the bamboo grove in the back of the house where she would no longer
be living was covered with camellia petals. Overgrown rhubarb shoots could
be spotted, and the flowers, as beautiful as ornamental hairpins, were in full
bloom.

Her aunt took her to the home of an old, prominent family, known
throughout the region, to work as a nursemaid. The spacious yard was

enclosed by a white wall. The baby she was hired to take care of was the family's precious little heir. Carrying the little baby on her back, the girl would sing the song of the rhubarb shoots. The baby seemed to like the song and his mood improved whenever she sang it.

The lady of the house provided the girl with a kimono every Obon and New Year's. By the time she finished her term of service, at the age of seventeen, she owned a formal gown and a muslin wrapper. When the term of her service was up, she was taken by her master and mistress to a far-off village in the mountains to marry into a family that lived on top of a high stone embankment.

One of her daily chores as a young wife was to fetch water from a well eighty-six feet deep. There was a clump of bog rhubarb on top of the cliff near the well. Every year when the shoots began to sprout, the young wife would think of her mother and her stomach trouble. Late in the spring, when the rhubarb shoots blossomed into flowers that reminded her of ornamental hairpins and the leaves turned into little umbrellas, she would think of the spring when she had had to leave her home and of the spring when she had come here as a young bride.

Her husband, Uichi, was six years older than she. He was a clever man, unusual for a person living in the hills. He kept saying, "I don't want to spend my whole life as a dirt farmer." Many young men from this area left the village to become policemen.

There was even a little ditty about policemen who came from this village.

Are you from Onuka again, Onuka village policeman,
　A retired policeman is a useless person,
Pension, pension, it'll choke you to death.

Uichi wanted to become a policeman too. But he did not apply for a run-of-the-mill job. He applied to go to the northernmost part of Korea as a border guard.

They had been married for three years and had one child. Now Uichi was off to Korea. The night before he left, he told his wife, almost in tears, "I'm doing this for our child. If you love our child, though it may be years before I come back, work hard just as if you were a maid serving out a term contract. Do my share of the work too. I am determined not to come back until I get my pension."

Her father-in-law was a hardworking man who went out in the fields early in the morning, before the stars disappeared, and worked until it got so dark that he couldn't see the tip of his nose. He was strong and healthy and never got sick. In the spring he couldn't wait to go out to cut brushwood, and in the fall, until he got busy with the harvest, he spent all his spare time cutting brushwood. Year after year he took care of two to three, sometimes four to five, oxen. He used brushwood and other greens to make compost, and, whenever he left the house, he transported manure to the hillside fields. He was taciturn and seldom said anything, unless it was about his work.

Once in a while he would say, "I don't care what I eat or wear. I have no desire to hold any sort of position in the village. I have no wish to see anything. I have no hobby. Making the soil produce better crops is the only pleasure I have in life."

When the young wife first came to this family, her mother-in-law told her, "There is always a chance that we will get sick. There are times when one is racked with pain or scabies. So we have to work while we're healthy. After I came to this family I worked hard and underwent a lot of hardship. This was how we managed to get the property we now have. I expect you to work hard too. I don't intend to work hard by myself and let you, the young wife, have an easy time of it. Now that you've joined our family, I want you to work hard and skimp and save with me."

When the mother-in-law stepped out of the house, she did not go beyond the village boundary, because, she said, she didn't want to waste any human manure. Whenever the young wife left the house, her mother-in-law would tell her, "If you feel like relieving yourself while you're out, be sure to run into our field." On the rare occasions when she bought fish, she would save the tails and fins and paste them on the wall as "charms." She cooked the heads, intestines, and bones until they were charred black, and mixed them with bean paste. She would say, "Now, when dirt-poor peasants like us eat fish, we have to use everything this way. Otherwise we'll be damned. So watch what I do carefully."

Every year when the time for school graduation approached, the mother-in-law would say, "I hear so-and-so's family will soon have one less mouth to feed. They're lucky!" On such occasions she and the grandmother, now over sixty, would start an argument. The old woman would repeat in a broken voice, "You keep saying you *have* to feed me. There are too many mouths to feed. Do you resent having to feed people so much? Do you want to cut down on the number of people who eat? Don't you want to feed old people? Don't you want any old people in this house?"

The mother-in-law had many bags made out of rags. She used these bags to save threads, even if they were only an inch long, bits of thread that had fallen under the hand loom, lint that had accumulated in sleeves. She saved anything that looked like a piece of thread or cotton. She would then sell them to ragpickers for 1 or 2 sen, or find some use for them. She would tell her daughters and the young wife, "For dirt-poor farmers, unless we women are frugal we won't be able to acquire any property. Unless you follow my example, you won't be able to keep your household going."

Whenever the young wife tried to wear the kimono that she had been given by her former employers, her mother-in-law would say, "It's wasteful for a wife of a family like ours to wear a kimono that's as nice as that. I hate to see you wear it." And, whenever her daughters tried to clean the house, she would say, "This isn't the temple or a doctor's house. If you have time to clean house, go out and work."

When the young wife had her baby, the mother-in-law said, "I had seven children. I didn't stay in bed for three days. No one said to me, 'You did a fine job.' Soon after childbirth I would carry a three-*to* [1 *to* equals 4.76 U.S. gallons] sack to the watermill and didn't ask anybody to help me. When I was in bed I was given just a slice of pickle. That was enough."

So she would bring only one meal to the young wife in bed. After the baby was born she would constantly repeat, "I sure hate to see a young wife wasting her time feeding the baby. She could be working the loom and making some money." No one in the house criticized her when she talked like this.

About the time that Uichi was getting ready to leave for Korea to serve as a border guard, there were twelve people in the household: old grandma, over sixty; the father and mother, about fifty; a daughter who had been married and come back, now over twenty; two marriageable daughters of nineteen and sixteen; three sons who were still in school; Uichi's baby boy; Uichi himself; and his wife.

Now, brave Uichi had gone to a far-off land, hoping to work till he got his pension. The old grandmother, still in good health, took care of the kitchen and did some spinning. People used to comment on the diligence and good sense of the father-in-law and mother-in-law. They were convinced of this themselves and worked hard as pillars of the family. The four young women—the three daughters and the young wife—worked at the loom day after day, whether it snowed or rained, in order to earn money. The boys who were still in school would take care of the baby or would wind the thread on the spindles. They just took it for granted that this was their job. Neighbors used to say, "Everybody at your place works hard, as if you're on the battlefield. You're bound to get rich."

The four young women worked the loom from early in the morning, while it was still dark, until midnight. The sound of looms filled the air of the valley. In one day they would weave three bolts of plain striped material. They would weave one bolt of patterned cloth with sixty designs or one to one and one-half bolts with forty designs. The young women earned a reputation as hardworkers, and the neighbors spoke enviously of them as the money-bags of the family.

The young wife was more skilled in weaving than the three young daughters, and she came to be recognized as the best weaver in the village. Her father-in-law and mother-in-law were pleased with her work. But because she was such an excellent weaver, they begrudged her taking any time away from the loom. They would complain, "Our young wife takes a lot of time in the toilet." Or, "She sure takes a long time feeding the baby." "She's so dumb. She's doing the washing again. It's better for the family if she let's the old woman do the washing, and does some weaving instead."

As a result, the young wife could not get away from the loom for a single minute. She didn't get a chance to vary her daily routine by doing some housework. And she had no one to talk to about how she really felt. So she began to mutter to herself. "If a young wife doesn't have any parents, she isn't appreciated for all the work she does. The more they like her work, the less time they allow her to waste. I can't even wash my underwear very often; I feel guilty if I do. It's hard to have to weave all the time."

Although she muttered to herself this way, she never uttered a single word of complaint to her in-laws. She always slaved away at the loom looking cheerful. No one told her how much money her work was bringing into the family. When she asked her mother-in-law, the older woman refused to answer. When they were asked to do weaving for other families, they would stretch the thread out and make an extra foot of fabric by not making the weave as tight as it should have been. When the young wife asked to have the extra piece to make an apron, her mother-in-law refused to answer yes or no.

Whenever the mother-in-law heard from her neighbors, "At so and so's, the wife's parents brought over a present to celebrate their daughter's pregnancy," she would say, "That must make them proud. Our wife didn't bring a single thing with her, not even a sash." When she heard stories about other young wives in the village, she would repeatedly utter mean words like, "I hear so and so's wife brought some beautiful kimonos, and dressers and bureaus with her. I hear wives are supposed to bring enough clothes with them to last a lifetime. I wonder what our wife plans to do about clothing for herself." Then she would end by saying, "I feel sorry for our grandchild. His mother doesn't have a single bureau. She can't even take her son to visit the boy's grandparents. He hasn't received a single thing—not one piece of baby clothes, or a paper carp [to celebrate Boy's Day]—from his maternal grandparents. He has nothing to show off to the neighbors. They must all be sneering at him. What a pitiful situation."

On these occasions the young wife would think, "If only somebody would say to her, 'Don't complain endlessly about the wife. When she was brought to this house as the wife, you knew that she was an orphan.'" But no one would say even that much on her behalf. There is a saying that parents bestow on their children seven blessings. She didn't want seven blessings. All she wanted was one person to whom she could divulge her feelings. Someone who would be like a parent to her. Such were the thoughts of the young, orphan wife. Then she would remember her husband Uichi's words before he left for Korea. So she continued to endure the hardships of the household, even though she was seldom permitted to hold her baby and her husband was not present—all this for the sake of her husband and her child.

With the passing years, her child grew. In other families, parents would put delicacies in their children's mouth. But here she was bound to the loom from morning to night. Now her son would quietly bring back wild, red berries that he got from his grandfather, who found them among the brush-wood, and drop them in *her* mouth. When the boy put a berry in her mouth with his cute, tiny hand, she felt a warmth in her breast that she had not known before, and her eyes filled with tears. Not until the little boy could walk around did anyone offer her a single chestnut or nutmeg that was being roasted by the fire. Now the little boy would bring tasty things for her to eat. This made her very happy.

When the snow was still deep, the little boy picked some bog rhubarb shoots from the cliff behind the well and said to her, "Mama, would you like some rhubarb shoots?" This surprised her. How did the little hands and feet manage to climb the steep cliff and reach out for the shoots? What did he see and how did he feel when he went after them? His mother mulled this question over and over while working at the loom. Ever since the boy had been a little baby she had sung the bog rhubarb song to him. He wanted it sung over and over. He never got tired of the song. She would tell him that she used to sing the song to motherless children, explaining to them, "The bog rhubarb shoots say, 'It's cold but we have to be patient for just a little while longer. Let's lift up our spirits and wait for spring. I'm an orphan left in the snow. But I don't cry. I don't cry that my feet are cold. I'm taking good care of my feet and keeping them warm. So you just wait and see. I'll be the first to make strong, beautiful flowers bloom.' " Maybe that was why the little boy went hunting for rhubarb shoots. Maybe it was because, sitting at the loom during the cold nights and early mornings, she was thinking, "It's about time for the rhubarb shoots to peek through the snow." Maybe her thoughts were transmitted to her son. Whatever the reason, he, with his tiny hands and feet, had climbed the steep cliff and picked some rhubarb shoots for her. She took them in her hands and stared at the shoots for the first time in years. She felt as if she were back in her childhood, as if the days and months of the past ten years would pour out of her throat in the form of a lullabye. While working the loom, she thought, "Maybe the spring of my life is still coming."

Then she thought, "Even if the song comes out, maybe my spring never will. Maybe the song will burst out and tell me that my spring will never come!"

Earlier, in the spring of the year when her term of service as a maid was up, and she was about to set out for a strange home to be a young wife, she had had a pleasant fantasy about her new life: It didn't matter if the new home turned out to be in the hills with only three houses. She didn't care if her husband turned out to be a charcoal burner or a woodcutter. If she could live in her own house with her husband, she would endure any hardship because life would be so joyful. She would do her best and cook and wash.

Now she had been married for ten years and for most of those years she had lived apart from her husband. She couldn't even hold her child in bed. From early in the morning till late at night, she banged away with the reed on the loom. When people asked her "Why do you work so hard?" she would reply, "My husband asked me to. And it is to build up the family property and help my husband get ahead in the world." But now she knew that if she were asked, "Will all this hard work bring happiness to you and your husband?" she would not be able to answer that it would.

Why couldn't she reply positively, she whose husband left home to earn a living? There hadn't been a single day when she didn't think about the difficult work that her husband was undertaking as a guard along the northern frontiers of Korea. When he left home he told her she had to wait until he qualified for a pension. Now, he wrote in his letter, "I can't quit simply because I can get my pension. I am determined not to return until I have become the most successful person in the whole village. I want to become a police inspector. This will take another ten years. You'll have to wait until then." When he had left for Korea she had understood why he did so. Hence, she was able to wait and work patiently; but now, when her husband notified her that it would be another ten years, she felt distressed.

When Uichi became police captain, he sent home his picture. He had a mustache, wore glasses, and had on white gloves. He looked like a different man from the person who used to farm at home. He looked like someone his wife could no longer approach. She wondered if this splendid figure would like his weaver wife, who had grown gaunt through lack of sleep. While she was working at the loom, she began to feel unsure about this.

The following lullabye tells of this wife's life and feelings. Her voice sounds like the small rivulet that runs deep in the mountains of the Chūgoku Range [in western Honshu Island]. It is sad and strained.

I wonder if spring has come nearer to me?
I didn't ask him to,

But my child has picked some rhubarb shoots
growing in the snow for me.

When Mitsuko heard this song from somewhere nearby, she began to
think of her own village, which she had not seen for a long time. Her village
too was a place where the villagers built high stone walls for their houses,
and dug deep wells. When Mitsuko was a little girl, her mother and older
sister would work at the hand loom when they were not busy on the farm.
Perhaps for this reason Mitsuko imagined hearing, together with the song,
the faint sound of the reed on the loom that used to come through the sliding
doors of her house.

Whose voice is it that's singing beside the stone wall? Is it Mii? "One, two,
three, four, five, six, seven. I'm in the first grade. Oh, I'm so happy, I'm so
happy!"

The singer's voice turned into that of a young girl's. Mitsuko could picture
the strawberry plants beginning to spread out in the spring, along the stone
wall facing south in front of the house. Mitsuko imagined herself with Mii
and his friends, standing by the stone wall. It seemed to her that her cold,
unheated cell with its temperature of fifty degrees, and the hunger pains that
came from having eaten only some barley mixed with soybeans, were beginning to ease. She felt warmer. The neighbor who was singing the song was
a prisoner too, just like her. She almost forgot that they were in solitairy,
separated by a wall, and tried to imagine the story that was being told by the
ballad.

THE HOUSE

Hardworking Uichi who used to think about his family and think about
his wife,
Must have become blinded by his uniform with gold stripes and by his
success.
He has forgotten his wife, who is getting thinner and thinner.

The wife would sing this to herself as she worked on the loom. Her in-laws
had managed to get all their children married off and had fulfilled their
responsibilities as parents. Now they were full of plans to tear down the old
house, with its straw roof, and build a new one with a tile roof. Wherever
they happened to be, in the fields or by the fireplace, the would say,

"The best thing that a human being can do is build a house."
"In this world what counts is the house. The house fixes the family's
standing in society. It fixes a person's worth."

"You can't tell when a person will get sick and have to call in a doctor. They say the doctor looks over the house carefully while he is taking your pulse. That's for sure."

"They say the priest looks over the house carefully while he is intoning his chants at a funeral. That's for sure."

"They say when the priest fixes a person's place in the nether world, he makes up his mind while he looks over the house carefully. There's no mistake about that."

"The house, the house. Everything depends on the house. When Uichi comes home we'll build a new house. We'll build a new house. We'll build a new house. We'll build everything we ever wanted. We've always been looked down on by others. They wouldn't speak to us politely. We won't forget that. Never! We'll build a new house and get even with them. We'll show them what we can do."

This is what they said day and night. Now, Uichi's wife was the only person working at the loom. When her son entered the first grade, she sang,

First grade, oh, first grade!
My son is in the first grade.
I too am in the first grade.

She looked forward everyday to her son's return from school as she worked skillfully with the reed.

When the child entered the second grade, she sang, "Second grade, oh, second grade," and passed each day joyfully as if she herself had moved up to the second grade. In this way six years passed by swiftly for her and her son. She used to sing and hum:

There's nothing as wonderful as a mother and child,
There's nothing as wonderful as a child.
My husband is starting to forget me,
But I have a son.
He is a kind boy. I wonder who he takes after?
No one has ever said the kind of nice things he says to me.
He learned to ask early in life:
"Are your feet cold? Is the fire in the brazier by your feet
    still warm?"
He would ask me these questions day and night.

But her mother-in-law never told her to go and see her son perform in a play or take part in school games. Occasionally, when she told her mother-in-law that she would like to, the woman raved that she had insulted her, and was in a bad mood all day. So Uichi's wife never managed to see her son take part in sports or school plays.

When teachers came on home visits, her mother-in-law would say, "Someone like you, who knows nothing except how to weave, would disgrace the young boy if you spoke to the teacher. You'd better stay in the back room." Everyday she would sit by the loom and imagine herself saying, "Teacher, how is my son? Will you please take good care of him." But she never did get the chance to say this to the teacher.

The first time that she got to go to the school on account of her son was at his graduation ceremony. The school yard was full of peach blossoms. The children sang:

The months and the years have come and gone, and
    now six years have passed.
We are now ready to receive our diplomas.
Nothing can match the happiness we feel!

Ever since then, whenever spring comes and the peach blossoms flower, Uichi's wife imagines she can hear this song, and tears flow.

Uichi who was far off policing the northern frontiers of Korea and working for his own advancement never mentioned his wife in his letters, but he would say he wanted his son to go to college and become a high-ranking government official. Send him to the prefectural middle school, he would write. Because of his father's wishes, Mii went to a middle school far away from home to take the entrance examination. The prefectural middle school had a reputation for being difficult to get into, but Mii passed the entrance examination on his first try. When Mii left for school, his mother went over the mountain pass and saw him off at the station. She felt the station was a sad place, and the train was a heartless vehicle. After the train left the station, she crawled through the fence, threw herself on the rail and placed her ear on it. She kept her ear there until the train disappeared around the corner of the distant hill and she could no longer hear the rumbling sound that echoed deep down inside the rail. When she finally got up, two soft rice cakes fell from the fold of her kimono and landed on the railroad bed. These had been handed to her by the mother-in-law to give to Mii to eat on the way to the station.

Her mother-in-law had been saying for some time, "I expect Mii to be by my bedside when I die. We're giving the family property to Mii. I don't begrudge Mii anything that he wants to eat. I don't feel tired when I think I'm working for Mii's benefit." She kept saying this while she was pounding the rice to make the rice cakes. She made the mugwort rice cakes before dawn. The boy's mother had intended to give them to him, but she had forgotten, she was so enraptured by what her son was saying to her on the way to the station.

The air around the rail where the two green rice cakes had fallen seemed to simmer in the heat, and the midday sun was glistening on the wheat field near the tracks. In the far distance, where the two railroad tracks merged into one, the haze made everything look blurred. While she was looking in that direction she began to feel sad again. She pressed her head on the rail once more and began to weep.

Around sunset she headed toward the mountain home where neither her son nor her husband would be home, and where there was no one she could talk with freely. Her feet and legs, used to working the loom year after year, began to feel heavy. Her legs, which for thousands of days had pumped busily, millions of times began to feel as if they were giving way. She felt as if she were walking all by herself into a dark hole on her tired legs. Her heart was heavy with apprehension and sadness.

Soon a letter arrived from her son. He wrote three times a month to his mother. Everytime she received a letter from him or wrote him, she felt a sense of well-being well up inside her.

Even after twenty years had passed, Uichi did not come home. His father and mother began to say he would probably not come back while they were alive. "We don't think he'll come back and build us a new house." So they decided to spend all their savings and rebuild the main house and roof it with tile. While the house was being rebuilt, the mother-in-law kept repeating, "When I came to this family there was nothing. Nothing at all. Soup with rye dumplings was a rarity. Fifty years have gone by since then. I turned everything that I could into money. Eggs, persimmons, everything. And I saved. We scrimped and saved. I would have used my fingernails as matches if that had been possible. This is why we can now build a new house. How could a dirt farmer build a new house without being as frugal as me?"

By the time she'd repeated this hundreds of times, the new house was finished. The mother-in-law said, "It's the fruit of our hard work. It's the product of frugality. Oh, it's bright and shiny! It's so bright and shiny, the house has a halo around it!"

When they moved in they had a house-warming party and invited the neighbors and celebrated with *sake* and fish. They cooked rice gruel and served it to everybody. It was the custom of this area to celebrate with rice gruel because rice cooked as gruel puffed up in size. It meant that the family property would increase in size with the new house. The in-laws and Uichi's married brothers and sisters greeted the guests who came to say, "Congratulations on the completion of your splendid house." Uichi's wife hitched up the sleeves of her kimono and worked by the well. She did not go out to the front rooms of the house. Earlier, when they had celebrated the completion of the house's framework, Uichi's wife had not gone out to greet the guests either. On that occasion friends and relatives came with gifts. The big gift-givers brought a big box called *hokkai* and filled it with red and white rice cakes, *sake,* and rice. The neighbors would count the gifts and say there are so many *hokkai,* so many sacks of rice, so many barrels of *sake.* Then they would compare this with what other families had received when they had celebrated the completion of their framework.

Many days before, the mother-in-law had tried to figure out what people would bring. Every time she began to count the gifts that she expected to receive, she would say, "Really, a family should not take a wife who has no parents. On occasions like this, when a house that could be built only once in a lifetime is being built, she has no relatives to bring gifts. She should be ashamed to face our neighbors. We're going to build a fine house and leave it for Mii. It hurts me to think that the wife, who has no relatives to come and offer good wishes on this auspicious occasion, will be able to take advantage of the house."

On the day when the framework was completed, the day when the *hokkai,* rice sacks and *sake* barrels began to arrive, the mother-in-law's manner of greeting the guests changed like a weather vane. Relatives who failed to bring a *hokkai* could not elicit a single word from her, even if they happened to be her own children. She refused to say a word to Uichi's wife all day. Gisuke brought the largest number of gifts. He went to talk to the old grandmother in the shack near the well and said to her in a loud voice, "Old woman, aren't you dead yet? You didn't do much in your lifetime. You couldn't even manage to own a strip of land on the hillside. Your son's wife has done a great job. She's bought rice paddies and upland fields. She's even built a house." Then he cackled. Gisuke was the younger brother of the old woman's husband. He was an old man who had left home early and had become an ox dealer. He was rich and had built his own house in town. The old woman just laughed at what Gisuke had said and nodded. Gisuke said, "Good thing she's deaf!" and left the shack.

The old woman whispered to Uichi's wife, "Did you hear what Gisuke said? It makes me feel bad."

"Grandma, don't let it bother you. No one has worked as hard as you. I was only able to keep weaving without having to get off the loom because you wound the thread on the spindles for me. The money made from weaving has surely gone into building the house. You must know that. Don't feel bad about it."

The wife took the old woman's hands and wept. The old woman said, "What you say makes me feel better." Soon after the celebration, the old woman died in her old shack. She looked like a withered tree.

On the day the family moved into the new house, Uichi's wife, working at the well, thought about the old woman who had died in the shack. The people helping with the cooking gossiped about the kind of worker the old woman had been. The front rooms of the house, where people were drinking, were filled with gaiety as the guests rejoiced at the prosperity and wealth of the family.

When Mii was drafted into the army, the in-laws hoisted banners beneath the shiny tile roof. "Our house is magnificent; so are the banners. And we have put up many banners. We're going to leave this wonderful house to Mii," they said.

Twenty-four years after he left his homeland, Uichi came home, having reached the rank of police inspector because of his superior performance and many years of diligent service. Under the new tile roof, the family celebrated Uichi's father's seventy-seventh birthday and Uichi's success in life. Relatives, prominent members of the village, and neighbors all came and drank and sang boisterously. Uichi had on his formal police uniform with its gold stripes; his eyes were framed by gold eyeglasses, and the ends of his mustache were twirled upward. He said he wanted to perform the sword dance, and he whipped the halberd around while singing the frontier guardsmen's song. They say his appearance and voice frightened the villagers.

Because she was urged to do so, Uichi's wife sang for the first time without hesitating.

The *myōga* [ginger] and *fuki* [bog rhubarb] are in our backyard,
Myōga brings good fortune, and *fuki,* prosperity.

All the guests exclaimed, "We weren't aware that the wife of this family had such a beautiful voice. It's as beautiful as a bell. Sing for us again. Let's sing and be merry."

Even before the guests left, Uichi began to say, "I'm going to build a storehouse and an annex to the house." Soon construction was started, and before two years had gone by the work was completed. The storehouse had white walls, and the living room had an alcove and open, raised corridors on all four sides. In this region, a splendid annex like this could be seen only in old established families. During the construction, Uichi never grabbed a hoe or plowed the fields with the ox. Whenever he had any free time, he went over the mountain to the town. Once he did not come home for ten days. He began to stay more in town than at home. If he stayed home for three days, he would be gone for seven days. Neighbors began to gossip that Uichi was staying with a woman in town. The woman had been sold to Korea from this area to work as a hostess. She was good-looking and clever. She spoke well and was bright, so people began to think she was too good to be merely a hostess. She was soon chosen by a prominent government official to be his mistress. It was rumored that she used to send a lot of money home to her parents, and, consequently, that her parents were quite wealthy. When her patron died, the stocks and bonds and other secret wealth that he had acquired all became his mistress's property, and she came back to her home with it all. She had so many silk kimonos, she could wear a different one every day. Her bed linens were all made of silk, and it was said that her clothing and bedding alone made her a wealthy person.

Uichi had known the woman since his days in Korea. It was rumored that he had built the annex at her suggestion. Whenever Uichi came home, he abused his wife. He even beat and kicked her. When she was being beaten, his parents made no effort to intervene. Uichi's father would say, "Unless a person has that kind of willpower, he cannot go out in the world and get ahead." His mother would agree, saying, "That's how he scared the Koreans. No wonder they were afraid of him. He really can be rough." They seemed to admire what Uichi was doing.

Because Uichi always glared at her, his wife did not have the courage to ask him, even though she wanted to, if the rumors and gossip she heard were true. Then came the day when the rumors became a reality.

On the day that the new tatami mats were laid in the annex, Uichi said sternly, "I'm going to bring my woman here from the town and let her stay in the annex." His mother told Uichi's wife, "Go and clean the annex." So she started to wipe the new tatami mats. Uichi came rushing up to her and said, "You animal! How dare you step on the tatami with your frostbitten feet!" He grabbed her and kicked her off the raised corridor. It was neither clear whether his wife was angry or was trying not to get angry, nor whether she wanted to cry but was trying not to cry. She didn't scream or cry but muttered without opening her mouth, "Mii, Mii, Mii, Mii. Where are you? Which battlefield? Mii. . . ." She kept repeating this in a senseless manner.

It seems that Uichi's father and mother had known that Uichi was planning to bring the woman home. They must have known that her belongings would be delivered that day. They were in the storehouse busily cleaning it out.

Uichi's wife wandered about near the well and the back of the storehouse, gasping faintly, "Mii, Mii. What should I do, Mii?"

Ever since the day the family had moved into the new house, the mother-in-law had said, "We built a new house but we don't have the furniture to go with it. We don't have the kimonos to match it." On the day that the chests of drawers and bureaus were delivered from town on an oxcart and transported one by one into the storehouse, Uichi's mother, who had never touched such splendid furniture, rubbed each one of them. When she saw Uichi's wife, whom she had exploited for many years, wandering around whimpering in a tiny voice, she screwed up her nose, grimaced, and said, "Go away, you crazy woman. We have no use for you."

Uichi's wife wondered if she had not lost her mind, and went near the well. There, some women from the neighborhood were saying, "He won his gold stripes by doing brutal things to the Koreans. He did shady things to get wealthy. The money he got made it possible for him to keep a mistress who herself has done shady, dishonest things. Nothing good ever comes of people who bring into their home someone who has earned the hatred of others. After all, there is a God. People who are hated will bring trouble by fire or by water. Just wait and see. Nothing good will come of this."

But when they saw Uichi's wife, they made no effort to include her in their circle and did not even speak to her.

Toward evening, the woman and her maid arrived from the town in a rickshaw. The woman stepped onto the new tatami in the annex with her pure-white silk socks and quietly closed the sliding doors. Uichi's wife could not remember anything about the house after that. The only thing she remembers is the laughter that came from the room in the annex.

She set the house on fire and grabbed the rope by the well that she had used for thirty years and slid down into the bottom, hoping to vanish from the world. She doesn't know how or by whom she was restored to this world. When she regained consciousness she was being questioned by the police.

She set the fire, but she did not see what happened. The flames shot upward through the night already darkened by the blackout to guard against air raids. The main house, the shed, the storehouse, and the annex turned into pillars of fire. They did not have time to save the town woman's chests or dressers. They all turned into ashes. When Uichi's wife, now an arsonist, was told all this, she was bewildered. Because she had set fire to the house during the blackout, she was sentenced to ten years in prison. Because of extenuating circumstances, however, the sentence was reduced to eight years, and she was sent to the Miyoshi penitentiary to serve her sentence. Here, she was dressed in red like the other prisoners.

It seems that her son worried about her in spite of what she had done. She received one letter from him from China. He wrote, "Mother, it must be cold. Stay in good health. I understand very well how you must feel." It has been a year since then, but she has not yet received a second letter. She receives no letters from anyone else either. No one comes to see her. "My son, did you die on the battlefield in far-off China? Are you alive? I wish I could find out. Even if it is by some indirect means. My son, your mother is greeting her fiftieth year on earth in this cold, snowbound penitentiary. They say there is no joy for people in the penitentiary. But even though I am past fifty, I still look forward to spring. For the first time in many years I've seen bog rhubarb shoots pushing up through the snow. I saw it in the penitentiary, on a snowy night, in my dream. I hear deep in my ears the song 'The *fuki* shoots are turning to *to.*' You remember the song.''

This then is what the arsonist says in her ballad. She is singing for no one in particular. She sings as if she were singing for her own soul. Yet she sings with passionate feeling.

Mitsuko listens intently to the faint singing that can be heard amidst the ceaseless sound of the snowy wind. The frigid wind rattles the doors and windows of the corridor, sounding like the hurried footsteps of an invisible person as it sweeps over the dirt floor.

THE

STRUGGLE

FOR

SURVIVAL

Tenant Grievances

The young farmer quoted earlier (p. 32), who bemoaned a life that required him to get up early in the morning to work long hours in the rice fields day after day without any prospect of improving his condition, was the son of a tenant farmer who rented small strips of land from two landlords. When he was twenty-one, a socialist and agrarian reformer, Ōyama Ikuo (1880-1955), came to his community in Yamagata prefecture to speak on the need for reforms. After listening to Ōyama, the youth concluded that "Japan's economic system is structured in such a way as to make the poor suffer more and more while the landlord gets richer and richer."[1] As a result, he decided to become an active fighter for agrarian reforms.

True, the tenant farmers experienced greater poverty and hardship than most other members of the rural communities. Those living in "underdeveloped" areas in particular, lived on the razor's edge, because of the constant threat of crop failure caused by bad weather. Their existence involved a continuous struggle with nature as well as a bitter struggle with the landowners to gain better terms of tenancy.

The problem of tenancy was not simply a feature of Meiji Japan, though the situation grew increasingly serious with the implementation of the new economic policies of the Meiji government. Although, in theory, land was not to be alienated in the Tokugawa period, after 1720 peasants were allowed to mortgage their land. As a result, those who lent money to impoverished peasants often ended up gaining control of it.[2] Such land tended to fall into the hands of the wealthier villagers, many of whom functioned as moneylenders and were able to reclaim wastelands over which they acquired usufruct. Villages located near towns and cities also found their land being bought up from impoverished peasants by wealthy merchants from those urban areas. The dispossessed peasants then became *de facto* tenants of these emergent landlords. By the end of the Tokugawa period, 20 to 30 percent of all arable land was held in tenancy.[3]

The process of landownership being concentrated in fewer hands actually accelerated in the early years of the Meiji era. Former feudal lords, who were granted generous pensions as compensation for relinquishing their domains, often invested their money in land. Moreover, the growing burden of taxation and the deflationary policy adopted by the government in the 1880s led to the steady impoverishment of most farmers, forcing them to give up their lands to pay their taxes and repay their debts. Their land, too, then passed into the hands of the wealthier landowners, moneylenders, and merchants.[4]

As a result, tenancy increased drastically in a short period of time. Whereas in 1872, 29 percent of the land under cultivation was under tenancy, fifteen years later the figure had risen to 40 percent. The pace then slackened, although the percentage continued to edge upward. By 1930, it was 46.7 percent.[5] A vast majority of farmers were either part-owners/part-tenants or full tenants. In 1940, 30.5 percent of all farmers were farmowners; 42.5 percent, part-owners/part-tenants; and 27.1 percent tenants.[6]

Because arable land was limited, Japanese landlords did not own immense tracts. For instance, in 1940, 94 percent of the 1,738,000 landowners in Japan possessed less than 5 *chō* (12.25 acres) of farmland.[7] If a landlord owned 30 to 50 *chō* (about 75 to 125 acres), he was a major landowner. In the prewar years there were no more than 3,000 landowners who possessed 50 *chō* or more, while 50,000 owned 10 *chō* or more, and 100,000 families held 5 *chō* or more.[8] Only a handful of families owned more than 1,000 *chō.* Most of the big landlords were located in the four northern prefectures: Niigata, Yamagata, Akita, and Miyagi.

The few biggest landholders managed their land and tenants much as feudal barons once had. One of these, Itō Bunkichi in Niigata prefecture, owned 1,345 *chō* (about 3,300 acres) in 1924. His family, which had increased their holdings of about 100 *chō* during early Meiji years to over 1,000 *chō* by the turn of the century, had merely carried to a highly lucrative extreme the practice of loaning money to impoverished peasants and eventually taking over their land when they defaulted. By the mid-twenties they had holdings in four counties encompassing over sixty villages; 900 tenant farm families worked their land and were overseen by seventy-eight stewards, many of whom had formerly been landowners themselves and were still prominent members of their communities. In fact, village standing made them particularly effective stewards. The Itō family, like many other landlords, fixed the amount of rent by evaluating the yield of each field. As did other landlords, they also graded the quality of the rice produced and insisted on accepting only high-grade rice as rent.[9]

The average rent for a tenant was a little over 50 percent of yield, but rents varied from region to region and landlord to landlord. For instance, in the early 1930s, in the Niigata-Nagano area of central Japan where the per *tan* yield of rice came to 2.8 *koku,* the rent was only 0.7 to 0.8 *koku,* or 25 to 28 percent of yield; yet, the landlords of Yamagata prefecture exacted 50 percent or more, and in extreme cases as much as 70 percent.[10]

The house rules formulated in 1892 by a major landlord in Yamagata prefecture stated that "the yield of fields classified as superior, average, and inferior should be evaluated; and, in accordance with the yield, the tenants' fee should be fixed somewhere between 45 percent and 65 percent." They held that the rate of 55 percent and above should be imposed on favorably located, productive plots, while rates below 50 percent should be imposed on less productive land located in remote places. In times of crop failure, reduction in rent was held to be unavoidable.[11]

As noted earlier, what was considered particularly small acreages varied from region to region. The tenant farmer who tilled 1.0 *chō* of farmland was fairly well off in most areas, since most tenant farmers cultivated about 0.4 to 0.5 *chō,* and some farmed as little as 1.0 *tan,* which put them below subsistence level.[12]

Despite the marginal existence that the vast majority of tenant farmers led, they tended to accept their plight fatalistically during the prewar years. Adhering to long-ingrained work ethic, they lived frugally and worked diligently. One peasant recalled, "We were taught that peasants must work from morning to night in order to stay alive. Whether bad weather caused crop failures or not, we lived believing that it was our predetermined lot to work."[13]

In general, most peasants felt that it was shameful to complain about their economic plight; poverty was regarded as an unfavorable reflection on their character, a sign of laziness or incompetence, confirmation of their failure in life. An agrarian activist trying to arouse peasants to support the tenant movement in the early 1930s complained, "They . . . try their best to pretend they are not indigent. They conceal the fact that they are in debt. If they have an income of 10 yen, they pretend it is 20 yen."[14] Conditioned not to speak up, most peasants did not ordinarily believe they had the right to question the authority of the landlords. Shibuya, lamenting the reluctance of the peasants in his village to get involved in the agrarian reform movement, records an argument he had with his father about peasant uprisings: "[My father] understood and approved of the struggle for justice against injustice, but he believed that in the end authority and power win anyway."[15]

Tenants usually behaved with deference toward the landlords, considering them to be their betters. They felt that it was their duty to pay the rent owed the landlord before they took care of their other expenses, and would default in paying off other debts in order to pay that rent.[16] One agrarian activist complained that the peasants were unaware of the fact that they were being exploited. The land belonged to the landlord and the rent he charged was rightfully his, many believed.[17] Moreover, the ethos of the society called for harmony between neighbors (and landlords with small holdings were in most instances neighbors and friends, or in some cases relatives); so the peasants—and the landlords for that matter—sought to avoid abrasive confrontations with their fellow villagers.

To complicate matters, the landlord who could afford to do so frequently sent his eldest son off to the city to get a college education. The son might then find life in the city preferable to village life and not return to the village. The land he inherited as the eldest son frequently came to be tilled by his younger brothers and sisters, who in effect became his tenants.[18]

Even when there were no familial ties to cement landlord to tenant, the personal relationships that linked them usually kept open breaches from occurring. Personal ties were, of course, stronger when the landlord lived in the village and did not have massive holdings, but even in the case of the richest landowners, efforts were made to reinforce ties with tenants by means of paternalistic personal contacts. The biggest landowners in prewar Japan, the Homma family, which in 1935 owned 1,841 chō (4,510 acres) pursued just such a paternalistic policy toward their tenants.[19] They employed a large number of stewards who were expected to serve the family with dedication. They were instructed to "be devoted to the principles of loyalty and filial piety, maintain harmony at home, work hard, and value the principle of service to the master."[20] The family's code required its members to be frugal and diligent, serve the public weal, and aid those in need of assistance. Moreover, it called for just treatment of tenants. "The prosperity of the landlord depends on his tenants. Only when all are blessed with a sufficiency can they live in peace and harmony. Reserve one quarter of your wealth for assistance to the tenants."[21] And, indeed, in times of crop failure and personal tragedy, they extended aid to their 2,500 tenants. This kind of assistance offset in part the high rent—65 percent —that they collected.[22] (In time of crop failure they lowered the rent.) The Homma family also persuaded their tenants to set aside some rice in time of plenty to use in time of famine. In return for their paternalistic approach, the tenants were expected to remain loyal to the family and shun any involvement in tenant movements or similar challenges to the family's authority. The tenants had to take what was, in effect, a pledge of allegiance. But these policies were successful. During the 1920s and 1930s, when tenant disputes were increasing, the Homma family's tenants did not challenge them at all.[23]

When tenant disputes were on the rise, some landlords took a hard line and the conflict occasionally turned violent, but in most cases the dispute was settled by compromise. Between 1920 and 1931, it has been estimated, 70 percent of all disputes were resolved through a compromise settlement in which the landlord at least partially met the tenants' demands.[24] In 1924, the government instituted a mechanism for conciliation, and local officials or the police frequently acted as mediators.

Landlords whose holdings were medium-sized and who lived in the same village as their tenants and had to associate with them as neighbors, did not relish the idea of having acrimonious disputes develop into irreparable fissures; even wealthier landowners sought to maintain amiable ties with their tenants by inviting them over for dinner on special occasions and extending help to them in times of trouble. Tenants were ordinarily grateful for any display of personal attention by their landlord, even if it took the form of the landlord's request that they help around the house and in the yard.[25] Such sentiments, founded on master-follower ties, cemented relationships between landlords and tenants. One may view this as a manifestation of a slave mentality on the part of tenants, since it worked to the advantage of the landlords, but it undeniably gave tenants a sense of security and well-being. When, as the landlords turned to other means of making money, absentee landlordism began to increase, personal ties weakened and tenancy disputes became more acrimonious.[26] Even then, however, tenants who were still linked to their landlords through personal ties normally remained loyal, siding with them against tenants who, encouraged by "radical" outsiders, challenged the landlord's authority.

Landlords, who already had an economic advantage over their tenants, were usually also members of prominent families and consequently held commanding positions in the community, both culturally and politically. During the Meiji period, landowners not only dominated village and prefectural assemblies but initially had strong representation in the national Diet. In 1890, 49 percent of the members of the House of Peers and over 50 percent in the House of

Representatives were landlords.[27] By 1920, these percentages had dropped,[28] although there was no proportional increase in the influence of tenant farmers, who still did not have the franchise. All it meant was that the industrial-commercial segments of society were gaining in wealth and power. As many rural people saw it, these groups had even less interest in improving the lot of the peasantry, and in fact where prospering at their expense.

TOIL AND TROUBLE: REFORM ATTEMPTS

For tenants to challenge the authority of landlords in society was no simple matter. Not surprisingly, then, it was not until the second decade of the twentieth century that landlord-tenant disputes began to increase in number and scale. There had been, to be sure, peasant uprisings and demonstrations in the early Meiji years, but most of these were directed against unsettling measures and taxes being introduced by the new government—although occasionally landlords had become the targets of frustrated peasants. During World War I, however, peasant disputes with landlords did begin to grow in frequency. The economic problems that arose—particularly inflation, rice shortages leading to the rice riots in 1918, and a postwar economic decline —helped create a situation in the countryside in which peasants could be induced to join together to demand better terms from their landlords, especially lower rents in years of poor harvest. For the first time, leaders from outside the villages sought to organize tenant unions with some degree of success. This initiative came from Christian reformers as well as intellectuals influenced by Marxism and stimulated by the Bolshevik revolution in Russia.

Among the early agrarian reformers were Sugiyama Motojirō, who later became a socialist member of the Diet, and Kagawa Toyohiko, a renowned Christian reformer who devoted most of his time to aiding urban slum dwellers but also involved himself in the agrarian reform movement. These two men were instrumental in organizing the first national peasants' association, the Japan Peasants' Union (Nihon Nōmin Kumiai) in 1922. Soon other socialist and communist reformers joined the fray and membership in peasant unions rose rapidly. By 1924, there were 51,806 members.[29] However, tenant-movement leaders quickly became involved in internecine doctrinal squabbles and in a fierce struggle for control of the movement, which, as a result, split into several factions whose leaders vilified each other as much as they attacked their "class enemies."

Moreover, the urban intellectuals who came into the villages to try to create and control a peasant movement had never struggled with the soil and the climate, or performed back-breaking work. They did not, in other words, speak the peasants' "language." Often, peasant activists, for whom this struggle was a matter of life and death, resented them. Nonetheless, there were a few genuine products of the soil who fell under the influence of communist ideology and sought to organize a grass-roots agrarian reform movement. Shibuya Teisuke was one of these. At the age of nineteen, while working on the farm, he wrote in his diary:

I read Lenin's *To the Village Poor* in bed [early in the morning]. 'There is no way in the world in which we can free in one fell swoop the poor people in the cities and the farm villages from their existence as workers serving the rich. The working people must not depend upon anyone but themselves. They must not count on anyone else. No one will free the workers from poverty; they must free themselves by their own efforts.' Lenin's thinking is founded on the same kind of spirit as my own ideas about the peasants and self-help. Our task is to adapt Lenin's basic principles about self-determination and self-help to the Japanese farm village and put them into practice, not as imitations of Lenin's ideas but as our own creation.[30]

Shibuya organized a peasant Self-Help Society in his community and then moved onto the national stage to work in the All Japan Peasants' Union (Zenkoku Nōmin Kumiai), the successor to the Nihon Nōmin Kumiai.[31] In 1937, he was arrested and sentenced to a five-year prison term as a "subversive" because of his Marxist notions.

Even though leaders like Shibuya may have been politically motivated, for most tenants the issues were of a purely practical nature: the need to have rents reduced or the terms of tenancy improved.

Most tenant-landlord disputes in the years 1917–1941 occurred in the more developed areas of central Japan. One authority believes this was because peasants in these areas had recourse to other sources of income in nearby towns. As a result, they felt less dependent on their landlords than tenants in less urbanized areas of Japan and were more willing to challenge them. In addition, as their economic situations improved, their expectations rose.[32]

The frequency of tenant disputes in the 1920s and 1930s is indicated in the following table:

.   .   .

TENANT DISPUTES[33]

Year	Number of Disputes	Number of Tenants Involved
1917	85	—
1918	256	—
1919	326	—
1920	408	34,605
1921	1,680	145,898
1922	1,578	125,750
1923	1,917	134,503
1924	1,532	110,920
1925	2,206	134,646
1926	2,751	151,061
1927	2,052	91,336
1928	1,866	75,136
1929	2,434	81,998
1930	2,478	58,565
1931	3,419	81,135
1932	3,414	61,499
1933	4,000	48,073
1934	5,828	121,031
1935	6,824	113,164
1936	6,804	77,187
1937	6,170	63,246
1938	4,615	52,817
1939	3,578	25,904
1940	3,165	38,614
1941	3,308	32,289

The most startling jump in tenant disputes in the post–World War I period came in 1921, when there were 1,680 incidents involving 145,898 tenant farmers. The number of incidents remained high thereafter, but the number of people involved dropped precipitously following the Great Depression. In the period 1932–1941, many disputes were caused by landlords, in particular those with smaller holdings. They sought to evict tenants from their land because the economic downturn had led to a drop in their income, making it necessary for them to farm more land themselves, seek to replace old tenants with new ones on better terms, or sell the land to buyers who wanted to farm it themselves. These disputes occurred mostly in the northeast, where economic conditions were poorest.[34] Such disputes involved few people. The famine of 1934 led, however, to a brief rise in the number of tenant-landlord disputes as well as in the number of people involved. The outbreak of war with China in 1937 engendered a demand for national unity leading to a gradual diminution, in scale and intensity, of the disputes. Membership in tenant unions, which had hit a high of 365,000 in 1927, dropped to 276,000 in 1934 and to 24,000 in 1941.[35]

In some instances, a tenant-landlord dispute could last for a number of years, creating bitter confrontations and often resulting in violence. Among the most bitter conflicts that erupted in the 1920s and 1930s was the dispute in Kisaki, a village in Niigata prefecture. It was unique in that it led to the withdrawal of the tenants' children from the public schools and the establishment of peasant schools in their place.

A tenant union had been organized in Kisaki in 1922, and the tenants asked for a 20 percent reduction in rent. All the landlords acceded to the demand except for the head of the prefectural land-lords' association, Majima Keijirō. When the tenants refused to pay the rent, Majima got a court order prohibiting the sixty-odd tenants from entering their fields. Thereupon, the head of the local union, assuming that the tenants had lost the right to work the land, committed suicide with his sword, and half of the tenants abandoned the fight and paid their rents. Majima then went to court to have those refusing to pay the rent evicted and to force payment of the rent. When the bailiffs went to enforce the court's eviction order, physical clashes occurred and twenty-nine protestors were arrested. Because Majima was the chairman of the local board of education, the union members took their children—about 600 of them—out of the public schools and established their own elementary schools.

The authorities regarded the tenants and their supporters as law-breaking troublemakers, dispersed their rallies by force, and arrested their leaders. At the same time, the national leaders of the tenant movement, who had extended their support to the Kisaki tenants, began once again to squabble among themselves over doctrinal issues and the question of leadership. This caused a fragmentation within the group in Kisaki and made enforcement of the court order evicting the tenants easier. The eight-year struggle ended in the tenants' defeat in July 1930. The peasants' elementary schools had been closed down by the prefectural authorities in 1926, but a postelementary school for peasants was allowed to remain in existence.[36]

Peasants in Japan have been characterized as docile, patient, and well disciplined. However, once their patience is strained beyond endurance and they decide to combat the social constraints that have kept them in line, they often go to an extreme of violence. An example of such behavior is seen in the tenant dispute that broke out in Okunoda, a village in Yamanashi prefecture. In this dispute the tenants demanded a rent reduction of 40 to 60 percent. The landlord, Yasusaka, procured a court order to evict the tenants, and proceeded to bring in new tenants to till the land. This led to such a ferocious attack on Yasusaka and his helpers by the dispossessed tenants that they beat him to death with their sickles and hoes.[37]

Another example of a dispute that ended in violence is the confrontation that took place in Maeda, a village in Akita prefecture. The village was dominated by the Shōji family, which owned over 1,000 acres of rice paddies tilled by seven hundred tenant families. The Shōji family controlled the village council, the police, the schools, the military reserve association, and other village institutions. The head of the Shōji family was regarded as a benevolent *tonosama* ("prince of the domain") and was held in high regard because the family had traditionally charged tenants low rents, about half the national average, in return for their efforts to help the Shōji family reclaim wasteland and woods for cultivation.[38] Then, in 1925, the tenants were unexpectedly notified that rents would be increased threefold to bring them in line with the rental charges of other landlords. The Shōji family decided on this course because their taxes had been increased and they planned to pass this increase on to their tenants.[39]

In reaction to this sudden, drastic increase, the tenants organized a union and said they would not pay the rent. Shōji then took his case to court in an attempt to evict the tenants. The case remained in litigation for several years, but eventually the court ruled in favor of the landlord. When, however, the Shōjis tried to evict the tenants from the fields and confiscate the crops, the tenants fought back with bamboo spears. This led to clashes with the police, and one of the peasants attacked the police with a sword. The ensuing melee resulted in a number of serious injuries, and in the end the tenant leaders were arrested and imprisoned. The "compromise" ultimately arrived at saw the peasants accept the rent increase. In return, the Shōjis paid for the damages resulting from the conflict and also allowed the tenants to regain use of the land.[40]

To cope with the increasing number of tenant disputes, the government passed an ordinance in 1921 drastically restricting the peasant unions' activities. For instance, the unions were banned from beating gongs, pressing their demands on the landlords by assembling a crowd of supporters, or recruiting other peasants for their movement.[41]

When disputes broke out, the local authorities and the police usually sought to act as mediators and bring about a compromise settlement. In the relatively rare cases when violence occurred, the police usually set out to quash the protesting peasants. As the leadership of the tenant movement came to be identified increasingly with socialist and communist groups, the police began to treat the leaders with particular brutality. Abuse of power by the police was particularly evident in the tenant disputes that broke out in Yamagata prefecture in 1930–1931. In the village of Odajima the police arrested 10,000 protestors. Three of those arrested were tortured to death and eighty-four leaders were sent to prison.[42]

Led by leftists, the tenant movement made little headway; the wielders of power were determined to crush socialist- and communist-inspired movements regardless of where they originated. As right-wing forces triumphed and ultranationalist, militarist, and imperialist sentiments swept the land, "subversive" and "dangerous" elements were ruthlessly subdued. The agrarian movement of the Right, *nōhonshugi,* was more in tune with the political and intellectual currents of the time. However, it became not a force for concrete agrarian reforms, but a romantic, moralistic movement that idealized the virtues of farm life.

The government did try to implement some measures to ease the crisis in the villages. These were, however, largely ineffective, since they were not designed to get at the heart of the tenancy problem by cutting into the interests of the landlords.[43]

The government did launch a rural rehabilitation program in 1932 and selected a number of villages to serve as its models, but this did little to get at the root of rural poverty. The government's main objective was simply to stabilize rural areas increasingly rocked by tenancy disputes. The program was aimed at strengthening middle-level farmers and bolstering rural communal ties by shoring up traditional communal practices as well as by introducing new institutions, such as cooperatives.[44] But funds were not sufficient to institute a meaningful rural rehabilitation program. The government budgeted 200 million yen a year for public-works projects at a time when rural indebtedness was staggeringly high. For instance, in 1931 it was 5 billion yen.[45] The debt per farm family averaged 837 yen. This far exceeded the annual income of the average farm household.[46] The Famine of 1934, of course, only increased peasant indebtedness.

Government attempts at price stabilization, reduction of debts, the fostering of cooperatives, rehabilitation through self-help, and assistance to tenants for the purchase of land were also made, but none had a significant effect on the rural socioeconomic order. In fact, "the result of all these administrative innovations was by and large to strengthen the old landlord-dominated order in the villages."[47] What affected rural life more than any of the tepid measures taken by the government was the national emergency which saw more and more young men drafted into the armed forces and taking the jobs that were opening up in the defense industry. This did not make life easier for the villagers left behind. The old, the women, and the children had to work the fields while able-bodied adult males went into the army and the defense factories. And, as the war with China led Japan into the war in the Pacific, many soldiers from the villages died in battle, leaving behind countless widows and orphans.

Agrarian Poverty

THE FAMINE OF 1934

Because the farmers in many areas, particularly the "under-developed" regions of northern Japan, were barely eking out a living under normal circumstances, when a serious crop failure occurred they were almost always faced with famine and near starvation. In fact, crop failures and famines were almost a commonplace occurrence in the northern prefectures. In the Meiji period there were twenty-four years of famine in the north, and four in the Taishō era.[48] The year after the Chichibu Uprising, peasants throughout the country experienced crop failures. People were reduced to eating the roots of plants, tree bark, and dead horses. Again the northern villages were especially hard hit. A government report stated that 70 to 80 percent of the people of Aomori prefecture were living like animals.[49]

The two most serious famines of the prewar years occurred in 1905 and 1934. The devastating famine of 1934 was preceded by several years of poor harvests, especially that of 1931, and by the adverse effects of the Great Depression.[50] Two million farm households, or 40 percent of all farmers, depended on sericulture to supplement their income.[51] When the Great Depression drastically reduced exports of raw silk—especially to the United States, the major buyer of Japanese silk—the demand for cocoons plummeted, as did their price. In 1930, the price of cocoons had dropped 80 percent below that of 1925.[52]

In 1934, when cold and wet weather ruined the crops in the north, the rice crop fell by 39 percent compared to the average yield for the previous five years, and by 47 percent compared to 1933. In some villages the yield was as low as 30 percent of normal, and in certain instances there was no yield at all.[53] In a village in Iwate prefecture where Saitō Sachiko, a teacher and poet, worked day and night teaching and scouring the countryside for food for her pupils (eventually working herself to death), the rice harvest was 12 percent of normal.[54]

Even during normal years, the diet of the poor families in the north consisted largely of millet and barnyard grass. When they did get rice to eat, they mixed it with *daikon,* including the leaves, a common practice in most farm families throughout the country.[55] In 1934, however, even millet and barnyard grass were not available in many northern villages. In Iwate prefecture about half of the 900,000 people were on the verge of starvation. Many children brought acorns and horse chestnuts to school for their lunch; others did not even have these.[56] People scoured the woods and hills in search of edible weeds. They even gathered tree bark in order to eat the inner bark, or phloem.[57] Malnutrition shortened the lives of countless people, and the infant mortality rate took a drastic leap upward in the famine-struck regions. In one village in Iwate prefecture, the infant mortality rate for 1934 rose to 50 percent. The national average was 13 percent.[58]

As a result of the famine, there was a significant increase in the number of girls sold to brothels in the cities by starving peasants who used what money they got to save other members of their families. In 1934, the number of girls sent from the six northern prefectures to work in brothels (4,521), geisha houses (2,196), restaurants where drinks and entertainment were provided, (5,952), and cafés (3,271) was enormous. In addition, 19,244 girls left these villages to work as maids and nursemaids, and 17,260 went into urban mills and factories.[59]

A newspaper reporter touring the famine-struck regions of Akita wrote:

When they have no other recourse, they sell their daughters. The parents insist that they will never let their daughters go, even if they cannot eat, but the daughters say they cannot bear to see their parents suffer and, with a greater sense of self-sacrifice than the Three Heroic Human Bombs [who purportedly went through enemy lines carrying a bomb during the Shanghai Incident of 1932], they sacrifice themselves voluntarily. . . . Just the other day six girls left the village of Takamatsu to become geishas and apprentices in a factory. Since last year, it is said, two hundred girls from the village have been sold. For November, another twenty are on the list of girls to be sold.

Even the two daughters of a former clerk in the village office have been sold into prostitution. Village officials and leaders of the Young Men's Association plead till they are hoarse to try to stop this outflow from the village, but their protestations are in vain. Some leave the village by crossing the mountain to catch the train from the neighboring village. So in many cases they have been sold out of the village before others find out about it. Even when they sell their daughters, the parents seldom get as much as 100 yen in advance.[60]

A journalist describing the situation in another village reported that "every month 50 to 60 young people disappear from the village. A survey taken last July shows that 162 girls and 54 boys have been sent out of the village to work in strange surroundings. . . ."[61]

The hardship and suffering caused by the famine led some to commit suicide. One young man who did so left a note behind saying, "Oh, what tragedy and misery crop failures cause. When I am reborn I will not come back as a farmer. I will be reborn as an important person." Another youth committed suicide with the note: "When I die you will be able to collect 1,000 yen on my insurance. Please, father and mother, lead a happy life with that money."[62]

The central and prefectural governments provided some assistance to the famine-struck region, but it was inadequate to relieve the suffering. They provided a little food and information about how to use acorns and horse chestnuts for food—which the famine-struck peasants already knew. Such "aid" was extended only to those areas where the harvest had been 50 percent below normal.[63]

Even in famine years, government leaders were usually reluctant to increase the budget to aid the agrarian sector. For instance, in late 1933 Finance Minister Takahashi Korekiyo pushed to reduce by 90 percent the agriculture and forestry department's request for additional money for fiscal year 1934.[64] In the famine year of 1934, the government and imperial court extended some financial assistance, but it was only a palliative. In fact, the bureaucrats were more interested in upholding government regulations than in helping starving peasants: When hungry villagers went scrounging in the hills for edible plants, roots, and tree bark, the government was adamant on maintaining the ban against entry into government-owned woodlands.[65]

Some landlords insisted on collecting the fixed rent due them even in years of famine. Trouble invariably resulted. One peasant recalled, "The harvest came to only 1.5 to 1.6 *koku,* but 1.2 *koku* had to be paid to the landlord as the tenant fee." This led to a tenancy dispute that ended in the tenants gaining a 40 percent reduction in rent.[66]

Numerous volunteer movements were initiated to help the famine-struck regions. Schoolchildren throughout the country were asked to donate 1 sen each, and the Salvation Army, women's organizations, and student groups set out to raise money for the famine victims, but the enormity of the disaster made the aid that was extended little more than gestures of goodwill.[67] Teachers gave a percentage of their pay to feed their schoolchildren, but in many communities the teachers' pay had already been held up because of lack of funds.[68]

Given the government's inability or unwillingness to introduce drastic measures to aid the peasantry, the rural poor could either passively accept their miserable plight, join with the Marxist and Christian urban intellectuals who were trying to get a tenant movement started, or pin their hopes on right-wing militants, including the advocates of *nōhonshugi,* who blamed the capitalistic, commercial-industrial interests for agrarian poverty.

THE RIGHT-WING RESPONSE

Perhaps it was the right-wing element that gave the privileged classes the greatest trouble; both civilian and military activists were enraged at the establishment's indifference to agrarian poverty and resorted to acts of terror in an attempt to change the order of things. Eventually this anger and frustration was directed abroad, and the solution to Japan's agrarian poverty was sought in expansion on the Asian continent.

Typically, a radical army officer, Hashimoto Kingorō (1880–1957), rationalized Japanese expansion into Manchuria in 1931–1932 by stating, "There are only three ways left to Japan to escape from the pressure of its surplus population . . . emigration, greater access to world markets, and expansion of territory. The first door, emigration, has been barred to us by the anti-Japanese immigration policies of other countries. The second door, to world markets, is being pushed shut by tariff barriers and the abrogation of commercial treaties. What should Japan do when two of the three doors have been closed against her? It is quite natural that Japan should rush upon the last remaining door."[69]

Among civilian groups the most forceful right-wing terrorists, partially motivated by the desire to protest agrarian poverty, were found among the followers of a Buddhist monk, Inoue Nisshō, the organizer of the Ketsumeidan. Inoue persuaded his followers to take a pledge in blood to assassinate the capitalists who had enriched themselves at the expense of the peasantry. They did, in fact, succeed in assassinating two key figures from the business world.[70]

Militant army officers who got involved in plots and coup attempts sought to justify their actions in terms of their desire to aid the rural poor. In 1932, Prime Minister Inukai was assassinated by a group with links to both Inoue Nisshō and *nōhonshugi* advocate Tachibana Kōzaburō. An officer on trial for taking part in the assassination stated:

The impoverishment of the farming villages is a cause of grave concern to all thoughtful people. The same is true of the fishing villages and the small merchants and industrialists. Among the troops, farmer conscripts make a good showing, and the farmers of the northeastern provinces provide the army with model soldiers. It is extremely dangerous that such soldiers should be worried about their starving families when they are at the front risking their lives. In utter disregard of poverty-stricken farmers the enormously rich *zaibatsu* pursue their private profit. Meanwhile, the young children of the impoverished farmers of the northeastern provinces attend school without having had breakfast, while their families subsist on rotten potatoes. I thought that to let a day go by without doing anything was to endanger the army for one day longer.[71]

The officers who staged the insurgency of February 26, 1936, were also partly motivated by their desire to relieve agrarian poverty. While awaiting his execution, one of the leaders, Captain Muranaka Kōji, wrote:

We did not take up the sword for the sake of increasing military expenditure, nor did we rise up to strengthen the position of the army. We did so for the sake of the peasantry, for the common people, and to save and defend the nation. . . . [We favor Kita Ikki's ten-year compulsory-education program] because it will provide lunch and school texts to the schoolchildren for a ten-year period, during which time even the children of the poorest families will be able to pursue learning. [The government's] eight-year compulsory-education plan is a direct importation of Germany's compulsory-education program. Even under the current six-year compulsory-education program local farm villages are having grave difficulty maintaining the schools. Often the teachers are not paid. Many children who cannot bring their lunch to school have had to cut school. . . . We have been asking the government to pay the full cost of compulsory education. This will aid local self-governing bodies greatly, and, if the government pays for lunch and textbooks, the children and their parents will be helped immensely.[72]

Upper-level army leaders were also concerned about agrarian poverty. In his statement to the emperor concerning the issues facing the nation in 1933, General Araki Sadao, who was seen as the leader of a militant faction of army officers, listed the agrarian problem as one of those that had most urgently to be dealt with.[73] During the famine of 1934, War Minister Hayashi Senjurō took measures to increase army procurements in the rural areas. The army pamphlet on *The Essence of National Defense (Kokubō no Hongi)* asserted that the most urgent task in the realm of the people's livelihood was the alleviation of the plight of the farm villages.[74]

The trouble with the army's position on this question was that their primary concern was national defense; military leaders' expressions of concern about agrarian poverty were founded on their desire to have the farm villages produce hardy soldiers who would be free from worries about poverty at home. Thus, when the country got involved in expansionist campaigns in China, which also tended to stimulate the rural economy, interest in agrarian poverty abated. Eventually, complaints about poverty at home came to be regarded as evidence of an absence of patriotism.

 Touring Famine-Struck Regions: A Report on the Ghastly Conditions in the Northeastern Farm Villages.[75] *by Shimomura Chiaki*

I

It is snowing again,
One foot five inches.
My fingers and toes are numb with pain,
But I must scrounge for food,
    climb the hills all alone.
I keep reminding myself: I am a man, I am a man!
    and shake off the cold,
        and desperately continue the search from hill to hill.

This poem, written by a young man who lives in a village at the foot of Mt. Hachikōda, was published in a newspaper in Aomori prefecture. I am not concerned about the quality of the poem. It is enough if this short poem makes the reader aware of the struggle for survival that the peasants plagued by this terrible famine are carrying on. Do not the pathos and wretchedness of the situation move us when the young man writes, "I keep reminding myself: I am a man, I am a man!"? All the more because his sentiments seem to be so simple and innocent.

I too was born into a poor farm village in Hitachi and have been exposed much too much to the wretched life of the peasants. And after I came to Tokyo I saw, until I could no longer bear it, the desperate, hopeless lives led by the young girls who squirmed about the dark alleys and by the many vagrants who wandered aimlessly in the streets where the unemployed loiter. I have seen on many occasions and in many places what hunger means to human beings, and what it does to them.

But the short poem cited above reveals a kind of simplicity and naïveté in the young man's struggle for survival. Especially, perhaps, because his struggle was taking place where severe crop failures and massive famine had occurred, I felt a special kind of anguish that was different from the sentiments aroused in me when I observed the women in the dark alleys and the vagrants struggling to survive. It was an anguish akin to the sad, bleak sensation one feels when one encounters an orphan crying itself to sleep.

This made me wonder: "Is this how the peasants in the famine-struck areas continue their struggle for survival through to the end? Will they continue to struggle silently without feeling any bitterness toward anyone or anything, without complaining, until all the food runs out and they finally starve to death?"

It is said that close to 450,000 peasants—30,000 plus in Iwate prefecture, 150,000 in Aomori, 15,000 in Akita, and 250,000 in Hokkaido—are beseiged in the winter ice and snow and are literally on the verge of starvation. I wanted to speak to some of these people and find answers to the questions that haunt me. Faced with the terrible crop failure and the horrendous famine, how do the peasants really feel deep in their hearts? What do they think about their way of life? How are these thoughts and sentiments manifested concretely in their lives? I wanted to find out the truth for myself. So I set out for the northeast.

I started my journey ten days ago, around one in the afternoon of December 27 of last year [1931]. I first went to an area in Iwate prefecture where the situation was said to be the worst. So I found myself in the village of Midō in Iwate. To get to the village, I took a train for about an hour from Morioka

City to a small station called Numakunai. Then I headed toward the mountain by foot for about 1 *ri* (2.44 miles). At first blue sky was visible from time to time, but soon some low gray clouds moved in from the north and snow flurries began to whip about. I pulled my coat collar around my neck and walked along the path between the rice paddies and dry fields. The road was muddy and deep enough to cover the top of my ankles. It reminded me of the muddy roads of Manchuria. My stockings were covered with mud by the time I reached the village at the foot of the mountain. Four or five children were huddled under the eaves of a house with a straw roof, and they stared at me with obvious curiosity. I asked the children how to get to the elementary school. "If I go along this road, will I get to the school?" I asked. Silence. The children looked at each other and did not reply. "Is the way to the school this way or that way?" I asked, gesturing with my hand. Then one boy raised his short hand and said, "It's that way." I took a good look at what the children were wearing. Their severely tattered kimonos were so dirty that I couldn't see the stripes. I too, with other poor farm children, had grown up wrapped in rags, but we weren't this bad off. In the winter we wore cotton shorts and drawers. But these children, standing in the snow, were shirtless and sockless. The girls had on only red drawers that reached their shins. I was reminded of the natives of Taiwan; they too wore red cloth leggings. The wild, unkempt hair and black hands and feet of these children also reminded me of Taiwan natives. Evidently they had not taken a bath for days. Their appearance was apparently not the by-product of last year's famine. This is how they lived even in normal times.

When I reached the school, the first thing I asked the principal was, "Do the peasants of this area live as primitively as the children's attire indicates?"

"That's right," the principal replied as he ran his hand over his heavy beard. "I too was appalled when I first came here. Most of the children's hands and feet are covered with dirt and mud. Not only do they not take baths, they hardly wash their hands and feet. When I criticized them for this, their reaction was, 'The new principal is an odd person. He tells us to wash our hands and feet during the day.' So I became the object of criticism instead."

"Then their level of education must be very low."

"That's right. Even when the children reach school age, unless the parents are notified by the village authorities, they make no effort to send their children to school. They may even reach the age of nine or ten unschooled. And during the busy season, many children fail to come to school because, they say, farm work is more important than schooling."

"Can you tell me anything about the village farmers' outlook and spirit?"

"They are really simple and innocent people. I think they are the most ingenuous people in all Japan. For example, recently the village young men's association sponsored a movie in order to raise money for the benefit of the soldiers in Manchuria. Each ticket cost 10 sen, and the school children were urged to buy tickets. But, because of the Depression and crop failure, the farmers could not afford a single sen. So only 6 of the almost 400 pupils could afford to buy the 10-sen ticket. Children desperately want to see movies. But they do not have the money. In this village of 600 households, they were able to raise less than 20 yen with the movie. This money was raised by squeezing the blood out of the villagers. But the entire amount was sent to the soldiers in Manchuria. The purity of their patriotism and loyalty to the emperor is unmatched. All of the farmers of this area are like the patriotic old country woman who, during the first Sino-Japanese War, sent her son off to war by exhorting him to give his life for his country."

Because of the crop failure this year, only 3 to 4 *to* (about 1.5 to 2 bushels) per *tan* (.245 acres) were harvested. Ordinarily the yield is about 2 *koku* (about 10 bushels). Twenty percent of the 200 *chō* (490 acres) tilled in this village did not produce a single grain of rice. The farmers survived by eating millet and barnyard grass. People who live farther up in the mountains ease their hunger with acorns and paste made of bracken roots. Of the 900 pupils in this area, 400 are said to do without lunch. Hearing these facts and the story about the money that was raised for the soldiers in Manchuria, I was emotionally overcome. I then asked the principal one last question.

"Then it means that the people in this area have nothing to eat and nothing to wear?"

"That's about it," the principal said with a downcast look. "Most of the children are clothed in miserable rags. Even before this they were poorly clothed, but this year's crop failure means that no one can afford to buy a single piece of clothing. When it started to snow, the children began to come to school in rubber shoes, but the soles were torn and the shoes full of mud. They have to wear the muddy shoes without socks. It's a terrible situation. If the present state of things continues, I fear that by February some people will freeze to death and some will starve to death. . . ."

After a brief silence, the principal pointed to a straw sack in the corner of the room and said, "That is the rice that was produced in the school's rice field. Ordinarily we harvest about 3 *to* (about 1.5 bushels) a year. On New Year's we use the rice to make rice cakes to celebrate. But this year we have only 1 *to* (half a bushel) of unhulled rice that is in bits and pieces. So we decided not to make rice cakes this New Year's."

In Iwate prefecture, 3 entire counties and parts of 3 more counties have been beset by famine. These areas encompass about 3,000 *chō* (7,350 acres).

Two counties, located on the mountain, face especially serious problems because they are difficult to reach from the outside. No railroads run into these counties, the roads are serpentine and bumpy, and trucks cannot travel over them. Many villages cannot even be reached by horse-drawn sleds. These counties have hardly any rice paddies, so even in normal times the people have to eat millet and barnyard grass. But this year those staples are not available. Even acorns and buckeyes are scarce. The only food they have is bracken roots, but they aren't in endless supply either. And when it snows over a foot, the people cannot dig up the roots. So there is a danger that if sufficient food is not brought into these counties from the outside . . . the people will starve to death.

On the afternoon following my visit to Midō, I went to Kozuya in the county of Futanoe. The village is located in a ravine. I spoke to an old man who makes charcoal in a small hut on the foothill. Three to four inches of snow that had fallen the previous day covered the shady areas of the hillside, and a thin layer of snow lay on the ground in the copse. The entire area was very quiet. The charcoal kiln was sheltered by the straw roof, and, from the chimney in the back, light yellow smoke poured out and disappeared after enveloping the branches of the trees in the copse. The old man, weaving straw charcoal sacks, was hunched over by the vent of the charcoal kiln to keep himself warm. After telling me stories about past years' crop failures, he said, "When we run out of food, we have to buy it. But the only way to get money to buy food in this area is to make charcoal. The wood for the charcoal must be brought from the woodlands owned by the government. But we have to pay cash for the wood. That's our first problem. Then when we manage to raise the money to buy the wood and make charcoal in our kiln, all we get is 45 sen for a 5-*kan* [about 41 pounds] sack of first-rate charcoal made of oak. It takes me five days to produce twenty sacks in this kiln. Twenty sacks in five days. They bring in 9 yen. After I pay for the wood, I have 50 to 60 sen left. That means I barely earn 10 sen a day. . . ."

I was reluctant to ask the next question, but I did anyway. "Then, are there families here that sell their daughters for a pittance?" The old man remained silent and quietly turned his head and stared at me. His face, full of reddish-black wrinkles etched by the heat of the kiln, twisted into an expression that made me wonder if he was going to laugh or cry. He then said, "I don't know if you know this or not, but when a blizzard hits the mountain not a single bird can be heard to chirp. It seems that the birds know that the hills will be racked by the storm and they fly away somewhere. The birds in this village are like that too. . . ." I couldn't question him any further.

When I went to Tsugaru Peninsula in Aomori prefecture, I heard about and saw personally the sad plight of parents who have to sell their daughters. I even had an opportunity to talk with a girl who was sold to a brothel. But I shall relate this story later. I must first describe the state of the famine-struck villages I saw when I first stepped into Aomori. The villages were Sanbongi, Shichinoe, and Uranotate—all located in Kamiji county. The coast of Sabishiro, where the plane took off to cross the Pacific Ocean, is also located in this county. I went 6 or 7 *ri* [14.6 to 17 miles] inland in the direction of Mt. Hachikōda to an inland plain. The snow that was only 3 to 4 inches deep in Iwate was 7 to 8 inches to a foot deep here. Mt. Hachikōda, which cuts across the northern sky, was wrapped completely in white.

The train goes as far as the town of Sanbongi, but from there to the town of Shichinoe and the village of Uranodate one has to take a bus. In order to look over each village carefully, I asked a young peasant to act as my guide. I decided to walk as far as possible so I wrapped leggings around my trousers. "When I get too tired to walk any farther, I shall seek lodging in some farmer's home," I told myself. So I started my hike on the morning of December 29. The young man and I talked as we walked along.

"This area is known for Nanbu horses. What's the price of horses this year?"

"It's hopeless," the young man answered as if in disgust. "A first-class two-year-old fetches about 150 yen. After the cost of feed is deducted, there is no profit left. The rest sell for about 50 yen a head. In extreme cases they go for around 30 yen. So everybody is taking a loss of about 100 yen per horse."

"How is the silkworm business?"

"The situation is hopeless in that case, too. The cocoons sell for from 1 to 1 yen 20 sen per *kan* [8.2 lbs.]. That doesn't even pay for a third of the cost of the mulberry leaves."

"Is there any other source of income?"

"There's nothing else around here. We're not in the hill country, so we can't produce charcoal, and we're too far from the sea to go fishing. Our only source of income is rice, but this year the crop is less than 30 percent of the normal yield. We have no rice to sell because we've just about eaten up all there is. There's no rice left, so every household is eating potato patties. But there's only a month's supply of potatoes left. When it runs out I don't know what we'll do. We have no money to buy rice from the outside. No matter how dumb we peasants are, we're not likely to just die quietly. At least that's how we young people feel."

"Isn't the prefectural government sending in money and rice to help out?"

"Nothing has come so far. And even if aid comes, it would barely keep us alive. It would do nothing to solve the basic problems of the farmers and ensure our security in the future. When we think about the future we feel nothing but hopeless despair."

On the way home from my journey I was told the same story by a friend who is a native of this area. It is not just the youngsters living in famine-struck Aomori who are in a state of utter despair about the peasants' livelihood. But, when I heard these sentiments expressed by a young man living in this ravished land, I felt that I had found the answer to one of the questions that I had set out to answer; that is, the nature of the feelings buried deep in the peasant's heart.

The landscape of this area had a kind of continental brightness to it. The foot-deep snow sparkled brilliantly, and the brown branches of the pine trees were intertweined to form beautiful patterns. Silver-colored Mt. Hachikōda sloped gently in the background. I suddenly found myself saying: "Isn't the scenery around here beautiful?"

The young man said, "But the fields around here produced next to nothing this year."

For the farmers, the beautiful landscape is meaningless unless it produces food in abundance. I felt that there was little more to say.

I heard what the young man was trying to express, but in a much more direct and forceful manner, in an eatery in the town of Shichinoe. It was expressed by an old man, about fifty or sixty years old. His face, coarsened by years of hardship, had hardened like the bark of a pine tree. There were two bottles of *sake* in front of him, and he seemed to be quite drunk. I thought, "Well, at least there are some people who can afford to drink *sake*," and observed the man with a feeling of relief. The man was carrying on a loud conversation with the female proprietor, gesticulating with his fist, which looked like a gnarled tree knot. He was speaking in the local dialect, and I failed to understand everything he was saying, but I got the gist of it.

"Listen, my good woman. I got only 35 yen for a horse that took me two years to raise. I turned over the horse to the buyer last July, but I still haven't been paid for it. So I set out today to get my horse back. But the man who bought the horse begged me not to take the horse away because all four members of his family would starve to death. The man runs a pack-horse business. He pulled out a 5-yen bill and begged me to take it as a down payment for this year. So I told him, 'Okay. We're all in the same boat. If we have to starve to death, let's starve together,' and left him 2 yen of the 5 he gave me and came home. Remember, last year was supposed to be a good year for the farmers, but it was just another year of crop failure. It was called bumper-crop famine. I've lived a long time but that's the first time I've heard of such a thing. I've never come across a thing like that. You know, once we have a bad year, we tend to have a series of bad years, and it gets worse each year. So a good harvest doesn't mean a damn thing. . . . And this year has been one of the worst famines. This means next year the poor farmers will dry up and starve to death; they will die in the fields. Some will end up hanging themselves. Damn it all! You know, one of my sons is in Manchuria as a soldier. I sent him a letter the other day telling him to fight bravely for our country and die on the battlefield like a man. Then, you know, we'll get some money from the government, and our family will be able to survive the winter. Families with daughters can sell them, but we have only boys. So this is the only way I can sell my son. . . ."

The man spoke as if he were spitting the words out on the dirt floor.

It is written in *All Quiet on the Western Front* that, for the soldier who is fighting on land, the earth, the ground, the soil is like his mother's bosom. Only the soil protects him. No one except the soldier who has to fight on the battlefield can really appreciate the benevolence of the earth. But a farmer would say that for him too the earth, the soil is like his mother's bosom. It is to him the be-all and end-all. No one but a farmer knows the beneficence of the soil.

But this earth, this soil, failed to produce any food at all this year. The mother's bosom turned into the bosom of a corpse. The primary reason for this was the fact that from the time the rice seedlings were planted in May until September when it was time to harvest, for well over 100 days, the temperature remained well below normal, except for a few days. Not only that, but in August and September the area was hit twice by frigid weather and snow. The rice plants and the crops on dry land barely produced shoots and hardly any grain at all. Then in October, whether people like it or not, winter comes to this region, and in November it begins to snow. The farmers feel bitter about the world because of the so-called bumper-crop famine (good yield, low price) of last year, and they have fallen into the depth of despair and depression because of this year's famine. Fatalism has overcome them. They feel sorrow at the cruelty of nature and at the same time, as victims of oppression, bitterly resent the injustice of the exploiting classes created by the existing urban-centered system, the commercial-industrial institutions.

We can look to the future with some hope and anticipation so far as the young people in the villages are concerned; they have the ability to think in these terms and possess the willpower to put their ideas into practice. But I feel nothing but sorrow when I see the simple old men and women who can no longer harbor any hope for the future.

After leaving the restaurant, I followed the young guide and walked toward Uranodate, one of the worst famine-struck villages. It was only around two in the afternoon, but it was as dark as dusk because the sky was overcast with inky clouds. The path that runs through the rice paddies had turned into a river of snow and mud because of the tracks made by the horse-drawn carts and buses. I was told that the village had no money to repair the roads, as 70 percent of the taxpayers were unable to pay their taxes. So the muddy road stays the way it is.

We were joined on this muddy path by a peasant woman who said she was returning from a shopping trip to Shichinoe. The woman had a child, about two years old, strapped on her back and was carrying a package of things she had bought. She was wearing large straw shoes; they looked like potatoes on skewers. The straws from the shoes spread out like a bird's nest. They were not shoes but were more like loose straw tied around her feet. I've seen snow shoes in Nagano and Niigata prefectures but they were more substantial. I was struck by the ineptitude, or rather the simple primitiveness, of the people of this area as revealed in such things as the way they made their straw shoes. The child on her back had a balloon tied to a small bamboo stick in his hand. This touched me and led me to speak to the mother.

"Isn't it cold!"

In fact, my shoes had got wet in the snow and my feet were so painful I felt as if they might split wide open.

"Yaa . . ." the mother answered in the local dialect, and asked me where I was headed.

"I plan to go to Uranodate," I answered.

She asked if I had relatives in the village. I said no.

"You'll have no place to stay then. Where will you stay?" she asked.

I told her, "I plan to ask some farmer to put me up." She then told me that if I didn't mind eating squash for supper and sleeping like pups huddled around the fireplace, I was welcome to stay over in her home. I was delighted. "That'll be wonderful. I certainly would like to accept your invitation."

I then decided to let the young man, who had been carrying my bag and serving as my guide, return to Sanbongi. To show my appreciation I tried to hand him two 50-sen pieces but he stubbornly refused to take both and accepted only one coin. Here too the simple honesty of the local people is evident. We stood in the muddy road arguing about the two coins for some time.

After parting with the young man, I followed the woman with the child on her back, arrived at her house around sunset, and stepped into the dirt-floor room with my muddy shoes.

Rice paddies and dry fields covered with snow spread out bleakly in the vicinity of her house. In the yard there were four or five stands on which to hang rice straws, and the house was surrounded by a straw fence designed to block the drifting snow. Along the eaves a row of icicles about a foot long were dangling in the cold. Layers of radish leaves—to be cooked with rice —and ears of corn tied up with straw cords were dangling from the eaves.

There was no electric light in the house because they had not paid their bill. The fireplace provided the only light. On one side of the fireplace was a dirt-black screen. Children's clothing and diapers were thrown over it. There was no partition other than the screen. This is where the family sat, had their meals, and slept. Facing this room, partitioned by wooden boards, was the stable. The shed was separated from the family room by only a 6-foot width of dirt floor, and was only nine feet away from where the family ate and slept. The wooden partition was so full of wide cracks that the outline of the black horse was clearly discernible. For the people of this area, the horse is a member of the family. Perhaps this is why they produce fine horses, the famous Nanbu horses. I didn't realize, however, that people and horses lived so close together.

By my pillow,
fleas and lice,
and a horse making water.

This poem is in Bashō's *The Narrow Road of Oku*. While I was sleeping by the fireside, I thought of this haiku, and could not but feel that peasant life in this region had not changed at all since Bashō's Genroku period.

Well, when I entered the house, the head of the house was sitting idly by the fireside. From behind his beard, which he had not shaved for days, I could only see his white shiny eyes. When his wife explained why she brought me home, his eyes broke into a smile and he welcomed me heartily. I took off my muddy shoes and pointed my icy feet toward the fire. Something was boiling away in the kettle hanging above the fire. When it was served at supper, I found it was bits of rice mixed with blighted squash. Normally such squash is thrown away in the rice paddy because it is mushy and has no taste or character.

The family head tried to curb his local dialect and speak standard Japanese as best he could and began to say a few words at a time. All the stories he told me were bleak, painful tales. He told me of a fellow villager who was unable to receive the letter sent to him by his soldier son serving in Manchuria because he did not have 6 sen. "Because he couldn't pay 6 sen in postage due, the letter was sent back to Manchuria. The old man spoke of it with tears in his eyes. The letter was thick and heavy, he said. It must have been full of news. The old man said he took the letter in his hands and tried to feel what his son had in mind. I don't know if it's true or not, but people say each soldier in Manchuria is allotted twenty toothbrushes and ten boxes of caramel candy. But here people can't come up with 6 sen."

I heard a similar sad tale about a family, in Watoku-mura in Naka-gun, with a son in the army. It was said that when the younger sister of the soldier died, not only did the family not have money for the funeral, they couldn't afford a stamp to put on the letter to her older brother in Manchuria to inform him of her death. Her brother in Manchuria read about this in a newspaper. His company commander saw him weeping quietly and sent 20 yen to the family in the company's name. Only then was the family able to conduct funeral services.

When it was time to eat, the head of the house said, "This rice is in bits and pieces but at least it has been hulled so it goes down easily. But, once this is gone, we have to cook unhulled rice mixed with pumpkins and potatoes. That is what we normally feed our horse, but this year we have to turn into horses." Naturally, if this kind of food is consumed for months, people succumb to malnutrition. The children are the first to get sick. I heard the following story from the chief of the agriculture bureau in the Aomori prefectural office. The prefectural medical officer touring the prefecture discovered that the health of the elementary-school children in the famine-struck areas had already seriously deteriorated. If the current situation continues into March and April, when the shortage of food reaches its nadir, the death rate caused by malnutrition among children is expected to rise drastically.

After supper, since there was no light, we had nothing to do but go to sleep. The husband, wife, and child wrapped themselves up in some old bedding that looked like a bundle of rags sewn together, and slept near the screen by the fireplace. I wrapped myself up in the bedding provided for me and lay down. I then asked them, "Do you have only one child?"

The wife replied, "No, we have another child who is seventeen this year."

I wanted to ask where the child was but felt that it was too insensitive to raise that question. So I remained silent. Then the husband said with a sigh. "Our daughter is now in Tokyo. Many girls from this village go to work in cotton mills, but we sold our daughter on a five-year contract."

What could I say? I read in the Tokyo papers that girls are sold for an advance payment of 2 to 3 yen. But that was nothing more than gossip in the newspaper. No matter how naïve the peasants are, they are not that dumb. But many girls are commonly sold to private and public houses of prostitution for anywhere from 100 to 300 yen. I came across an example of such a case in a hamlet in Kanida.

This village was located about three hours' car ride from Aomori City. One went along the mud- and snow-covered road with Mutsu Bay to the right. This area also had hardly any harvest this fall, but the farmers there are also fishermen and are managing to survive somehow by catching sardines and codfish. The fishing season lasts only through January, however; after February there will be no fishing for a while. In previous years, people from Hokkaido came to recruit fishermen from this area, but this year no one has appeared at all. So nobody knows how they will eat after February.

I rode along in the car deeply depressed. It was the afternoon of January 2. Snow began to fall steadily again, and, with the snow, the sea became invisible since a blanket of gray sealed my vision. The road ahead was visible for only 50 yards or so. The man sitting next to me said, "This could turn into a blizzard." Sure enough, 6 ri [14.6 miles] later, the snow began to swirl around like a tornado. An old man sitting behind me said, "On top of the famine, if we get a blizzard that lasts three days, all the farmers in this region will starve to death. In the famine of the Tenmei era (1782–1787), they say 30,000 people starved to death. Those who survived ate human flesh. It was said that the flesh of girls between seventeen and eighteen years of age was the best, so they waited for such girls to die and ate their flesh. If we don't watch out, we'll see the same thing happening this year. I remember well the famines of 1902 and 1913. Neither one was as bad as this year's. A famine like this shows that the end of the world is at hand."

His neighbor chimed in, "Well, if I'm going to starve to death anyway, I would like to eat my fill of white rice, just once."

"Well, if you can have one meal of rice you're lucky. They say that in the hills of Iwate prefecture they bring around a bowl of rice from house to house just so that people can have a look at it. They have to be satisfied with that. I hear that when someone gets sick they place the bowl of rice by his pillow. This is enough to cure the patient. It's like a fairy tale isn't it? That farmers who grow rice can only look worshipfully at it."

The car plowed its way through the blizzard. Everybody was silent now. Then there was a loud bang in the back. "Damn it! We finally got a blowout," said the driver, as if he had been expecting it, and stopped the car. We were still 1.5 ri [over 3.5 miles] from the inn in Kanida. There was no way we could walk there. The four of us, including myself, took refuge in a farmhouse near the road.

The inside of the house was as gloomy and wretched as the house in Uranodate. We sat by the fireside and warmed our feet. Soon the wind began to subside. The two men said that they lived only 500 or 600 yards ahead and went into the snowstorm, which was beginning to die down. That left only myself and an old woman of fifty or so. She was from Okunimura, which was about 1 *ri* (2.44 miles) farther inland from Kanida. I spent the night talking to her. She told me all sorts of tales about her life. She started out by telling me in local dialect, "To tell the truth, I am on the way home from Aomori City where I left my daughter at a brothel."

I didn't have to ask her why she had left her daughter at such a place. I felt distressed about this and remained silent. The old woman, as if she were talking to herself, began to say something like the following: "In our village we were able to harvest only 2 *to* [about 1 bushel] from 1 *tan* [0.245 acres] of rice field. So we all have to buy rice from the outside. But we need money for that. To get money we have to make charcoal. But for that we have to buy wood. Seventy percent of the wood is government owned. Even if we want to produce one sack of charcoal, we have to pay cash for the government's wood. So, the farmers in our village are at the end of their rope. . . ."

The old woman was not as ignorant as she appeared to be. She knew that 70 percent of the woodland in Aomori prefecture was government owned, and she had her own opinion about this situation. She continued, saying roughly the following: "The farmers around here can still sleep under *futon* [a comforterlike bedding] so they are lucky. If you go west from here to the villages in North Tsugaru and West Tsugaru counties, not a single *futon* can be found among the farmers. They all sleep on rice straws. They spread rice straws underneath and place a miscanthus mat on top of that. The farmers sleep on top of the mat and cover themselves with mats made of seaweed. It's warm enough but it is rough and coarse, and nothing at all like *futon.*"

A few days ago I was surprised that peasants living in the mountains of Iwate lived like primitive natives, but I was surprised again at the story of the harsh life of Aomori peasants.

The other day a peasant who also slept on a straw bed bellowed indignantly: "Of course we have to take care of the problem of famine, but we must take this opportunity to show what a primitive, miserable existence the peasants of Iwate and Aomori lead to this day, and open the eyes of the big consumers living in the cities. We must expose before the eyes of government officials the fact that in this enlightened age of Shōwa there are Japanese who even in normal times eat millet and barnyard grass and sleep on straw beds."

Listening to the old woman, I could not help but agree completely with what the man had said.

The old woman summed up her thoughts: "About what the man was saying in the car . . . it wasn't only the people of olden days who ate flesh. We too are eating the flesh of human beings. In order to make it possible for the children to survive, we have to feed them their parents' flesh. To make it possible for the parents to survive, we have to eat the children's flesh. So, right now I am trying to stay alive by eating my daughter's flesh."

I could only stare at the old woman's face. She had with her the small sum of money she got by selling her daughter, and appeared to be worried about it. She looked at me warily from time to time. This made me feel uncomfortable.

The next evening I visited the brothel in Aomori City to talk to the old woman's daughter. The snow was falling off and on. The streets were frozen thick with snow and ice, and I nearly slipped and fell several times. The house was near the sea and the cold wind blowing in from Mutsu Bay was piercing through the cold night air in the streets. Three days earlier, when I was walking through Kominato, a famine-struck village near the Asamushi hotsprings, I was afraid that I would freeze to death in the wind and the snow, but it was not as cold as this place. Perhaps I felt the cold more acutely because I was going to visit a girl in the dark streets of the city, in a den of brothels. But the den of brothels was not like a den; the houses were lined up in the dim light on both sides of the broad, barren street. Most were freestanding, two-story buildings. They looked too big for brothels run by individual entrepreneurs. This made them look all the more shoddy. Most of them had three or four girls sitting in the small room by the entrance. They would call out to the men prowling about in front of the houses. The local dialect made their words sound odd to my ears.

I was able to locate right away the house of the girl I was looking for. Four girls were standing by the entrance. I asked for the girl using her real name and went upstairs with her. The room, like all other rooms in privately run Japanese brothels, was bleak and shoddy. At first the girl was suspicious of me, but when I told her that I had met her mother she began to relax. Having been raised in a farming community, she appeared clownish and bizarre, ineptly made up with heavy rouge and powder.

"When did you come here?"

"About ten days ago."

"When did you begin working?"

"Three days ago."

After that she began to tell me things that not even her mother told me. It had to do with her father.

Her father used to commute between the village and Aomori City, carrying on a fairly extensive business. He was a wholesale dealer in dry goods. But due to poor business conditions that lasted for years, he found himself in an impossible bind. Then the famine struck, and the banks declared a moratorium on payments (now most of the banks in Aomori have declared a moratorium discontinuing all payments). So her father could not get any money and his business folded. In desperation he left for Aomori City by himself, reneging on all the obligations he had.

In Aomori he looked for work as a stevedore at the waterfront but, being a total stranger, he had no connections. So he failed to find employment. All he could do day after day was to stand near the warehouse at the waterfront and eat his lunch in the freezing wind. Finally the day came when he could not even afford to bring his lunch. One day, out of desperation, driven by hunger, he stole a stevedore's lunch and ate it. This was discovered right away and he was beaten to a pulp by the others and virtually crippled. He lay in the flophouse, all alone as if he were an abandoned waif. "Four or five days later my father died. No one knows whether he died because of the injuries or because he starved to death. . . ." Speaking in the Tsugaru dialect, the daughter ended her story.

I shall put down my pen here. I have written so much about people who are languishing on the verge of starvation, I am sure the readers cannot bear to read any more such stories.

The Aomori prefectural government is trying desperately to find the means to help the people. At the end of last year, thirty-three prefectural council members came to Tokyo desperately seeking financial assistance. I hear their plan is to save the banks in the prefecture that are on the verge of bankruptcy and make money available to the merchants and businessmen. Then they will proceed to aid the peasants in the famine-struck regions. Others say, no they are going to provide money and food for the peasants first.

It is said that the sun does not set on the night road, but the darkness of the famine-struck region is not an ordinary darkness. The prefectural authorities are well aware of this. One of the officials said: "If we allow even a single person to starve to death in Aomori prefecture, it would be a disgrace to this sacred imperial era. We are determined not to disgrace this imperial age." I would like to join the peasants in the prefecture in placing great faith and hope in his words.

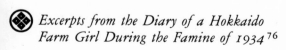

Excerpts from the Diary of a Hokkaido Farm Girl During the Famine of 1934 [76]

JULY 1:

Today some white rice is to be distributed by the village office. We in the farm villages have been eating dried potatoes and herring dregs, which are used for fertilizer, day after day, and have been on the verge of starvation. So the monthly distribution of white rice is appreciated more than anything else. Around 8 A.M. my aunt from the next village came. She says that for the past four or five days they have had nothing to eat, so she has been boiling a mixture of weeds and roots of flowering ferns. They have been eating this concoction three times a day. Maybe this is why one of her children collapsed in the hot weather. But this kind of story is not unusual in Hokkaido farm families, which are gasping under the hard times. It is really tragic, however, that we farmers who grow rice are unable to eat it.

At 10 A.M. a man from the village office brought over some rice on his bicycle. We got 3.5 *shō* [1 *shō* equals 0.476 U.S. gallons] of white rice. My father, mother, and younger sister all came out and thanked the official over and over. Their parched, wrinkled faces all smiled brightly. Now our family of six can have gruel made of white rice this noon, tonight, and then tomorrow morning and noon—four times in all. We almost cry with joy.

Lunchtime. The six members of our family, plus our aunt, had gruel made of white rice. Each one of us had one and a half bowls.

In the afternoon father went to look over the rice paddies that had just been planted with seedlings. "What do you think, Oyasu? We weren't able to use enough fertilizer again this year so we probably will not be able to harvest more than four or five sacks," my father said with a sigh as he stared out toward the rice field. They had to sell two or three of the kimonos my mother had sewn for me to put in my hope chest. But that didn't bring in enough money. I felt tears flowing down my cheeks.

On the way home from work I ran into the boss of the rice mill. He told me that Oito, the daughter of the candy store owner, was sold to a place called Terajima in Tokyo. She's the fourth person to be sold this year. From this tiny village, then, four girls have had to be sold to Tokyo to help their families survive and pay their debts. This is a terrible reality for us girls in farm villages.

At night I go with my younger sister to Mr. Tashima's to work. Our work goes toward paying off the rent we owe them from the year before last. We come home around 10:30, take a brief rest, and then start to work again, weaving straw cords. By the time we finish weaving three long cords, it is 3 A.M., and we have earned 12 sen.

JULY 2:
Today we start weeding the rice paddies. My younger sister has gone to the village head's house to work. My father and older brother have

gone to work on a project to repair the riverbank. Our mother, my older sister, and I do the field work. Our mother talks about the summer festival. My sister says with a wan smile, "But we don't have any money to buy kimonos. We might as well work to cut down our debts." She is right. We girls in the farm villages can't be bothered about festivals. All we dare think about is working hard to reduce our debts.

While we were resting after lunch, the village head came over. He said, "Heikichi's [her father's] is the only family that has not paid off the tenant rent. . . ." He is referring to the rent from the year before. My mother, kneeling, said, "Please wait until we can harvest this rice. . . ."

"Well, well. But you have such wonderful daughters. It's a shame. . . ." He's hinting that I should be sent off to Tokyo. My breast is about to burst with bitterness. But the man is the village head. My mother must have known how I felt. She turned pale and wept.

After the village head left, she said, embracing me, "We will never send you to Tokyo."

At night my younger sister and I pulled the cart to Yappari-chō, which is about 2 *ri* [2.9 miles] away, to sell the straw cords we wove. It had taken us fifteen days, working with practically no sleep, to weave the medium-sized ropes. We got 3 yen for our labor. On the way back we went to the assistant village head's home to pay him 1 yen for the straw that we had got from him. The remaining 2 yen will be turned over to the fertilizer dealer tomorrow. No matter how hard we work, our debt gets larger. My sister and I will dig up some bracken roots from the hill by the village temple, Myō'onji. This will be our substitute food tomorrow. By the time we return home with the bracken roots in our muddy hands, it will be 12:30.

JULY 3:

In order to get to work before it gets hot, we go out in the rice field around 4 A.M. At 6:30 my younger sister comes for us for breakfast, which consists of boiled fern and bracken roots. I don't feel like eating. At lunch my mother says that when the first round of weeding is done she plans to go to work on the river project. Our mother who is past fifty. . . . My older sister and I try to dissuade her.

In the evening I saw the sewing teacher. In this village of Mabu, beset with crop failures and depression, no one can afford sewing lessons.

Tonight, after our father returned from his work at the river, he told us to go sell vegetables at the Sapporo morning market beginning tomorrow morning. My younger sister and I wove straw cords until 10 P.M. and then we went to the hill by the temple for bracken roots. We ran into Ochiyo. She says she is going to Sapporo next month to work as a maid. She is pleased, she says, because she'll be able to eat white rice everyday. On the way home my younger sister kept saying that she wanted to go to work as a maid too. I can't blame her. We work all day long without any rest and still have nothing worth eating. This is our plight.

JULY 8:
We are between weeding, so my older sister, mother, and I go to the river to carry dirt in straw baskets. From 6 A.M. to 7 P.M.—for thirteen hours—we carried the heavy baskets and earned only 50 sen. But it's better than working at home.

At noon our older brother brought some millet cakes to us. This is the first time in six months we've had a taste of a millet cake. I ate it voraciously. At night I went to bed a little past 8 P.M. for the first time in a long while. Tomorrow morning I have to go to Sapporo to the market.

JULY 9:
We loaded the cart with vegetables and went to Sapporo. We sold the Chinese cabbages at 2 sen a head, 50 cucumbers for 10 sen, cherries and strawberries for 4 sen per 100 momme [1 momme equals 0.13 ounces]. It took us until 10 A.M. to sell what we had. We sold less than 1 yen's worth. At this rate we will not be able to pay for our time or fertilizer. When I think we have to do this again tomorrow I feel depressed.

—Endō Yasuko

THE

OUTCASTE

IN

JAPAN

Historical Background

Among the Japanese who did not benefit appreciably from "modernization" in the prewar years were those currently referred to as *burakumin* ("people of the hamlet"), formerly known as *eta, hinin,* and by numerous other appelations. They were in effect treated as a separate class of people somewhat similar to the outcastes in India.

At the outset of the Meiji era, when the nation's population stood at about 33 million, there were approximately 400,000 people who had some sort of "outcaste" status. The exact number of people who currently belong to the *burakumin* category is not clear, but it is estimated that in 1970 they numbered around 2 million out of an overall population of about 104 million.[1] The reason for the absence of precise figures is that, theoretically, the practice of identifying people as *eta* or *hinin* was ended when such legal distinctions were officially abandoned in 1871. In reality, such identification and discriminatory practices against them have persisted.[2]

Burakumin are today concentrated heavily in the areas centered near Kyoto and adjacent prefectures, and in the Inland Sea region, while the northeastern region has the least number of them.[3] There have been numerous theories about the origin of the outcastes. Scholars once ascribed their origin to immigrants who came to Japan from Korea sometime between the fourth and seventh centuries. These artisans, craftsmen, and workers had, it was contended, a semi-slave status; and, being non-Japanese, they were segregated and treated by the native Japanese as inferiors. Some scholars have asserted that they were descendants of Korean prisoners brought back to Japan by Japanese expeditionary forces in between the fourth and sixth centuries, while others have held that they were descendants of the Ainus. One *burakumin* recalls being insulted by his classmates, who said, "Guys like you are not Japanese! Your ancestors were brought back as prisoners when Empress Jingū [a legendary figure who was said to have led a military expedition into Korea in the third century A.D.] went to conquer the three Korean states."[4]

This tendency to ascribe the origin of people who were considered inferior to some alien race indicates the strong ethnocentrism that has persisted in Japan. It evinces a way of thinking that condemns a person to near subhuman status if he/she is not Japanese.[5] This belief that the *burakumin* are of different racial origin persisted into the postwar years. A government survey conducted in 1965 showed that 70 percent of the people polled believed that the *burakumin* were of a race and lineage different from the Japanese.[6]

This theory, however, has been rejected by most modern students of the subject; there is no evidence that the *burakumin* are racially different from the Japanese. As for the theory that the *burakumin* were accorded inferior status because of their Korean origin, the fact is that in antiquity Korean immigrants were *not* treated as lowly people. On the contrary, they achieved high social status and in many cases married into the aristocracy and noble families.[7]

However, from antiquity there has been in Japan a tradition of abhorrence of certain associations with death. It was customary to remove people near death from the house so that they would not pollute the building. Prior to the Nara period (710–784), when an emperor died the capital was moved to another location. The ceremony of cleansing people, places, and things is still an important function of Shinto priests. Those who disposed of dead people and animals were regarded as doing unclean work. The advent and diffusion of Buddhism in the early sixth century reinforced the prejudice against those who dealt with dead animals, for Buddhism condemns butchering and the consumption of animal flesh. Eventually, the circle of people who were regarded as being involved in unclean or inhuman activities enlarged. It is understandable how those who dealt with things derived from dead animals, such as tanners and leather workers, came to be regarded as *eta* ("heavily polluted") or *hinin* ("nonhuman"), but in many instances work that is not readily perceivable as "unclean" came to be reserved for them. Perhaps because bowmakers used bowstrings made of bamboo as well as leather, makers of bamboo products (*e.g.,* bamboo whisks for the tea ceremony) came to be placed in the *eta* category by mere association. Makers of military equipment who used leather in their work, cobblers, sweepers, certain entertainers, beggars, vagrants, and those afflicted with abhorrent diseases also came to be classed as *eta* or *hinin.*

Initially, such status was not hereditary and one could move out of the outcaste group by taking on "respectable" work. Certain of these occupational groups whose work was seen as essential by the ruling authorities, found themselves straddling accepted bounds of so-called respectability: The court, priests, owners of medieval estates, and feudal lords utilized their necessary services and acted as their patrons. For example, during the civil strife of the fifteenth and sixteenth centuries, makers of arms were cherished by contending warlords, who patronized and protected guilds of weapon makers. But because of ingrained beliefs about pollution, they were still segregated at the lower levels of the society.[8]

When the Tokugawa rulers established their authority over the land in the seventeenth century, they froze the social order, broadly dividing the population into four classes: *samurai,* peasants, artisans, and merchants. In reality, however, there were more than four classes. At the top of society were members of the court, aristocracy, and feudal lords, and at the very bottom there were the outcastes, people engaged in menial and "polluting" work. Segregation of and discrimination against the *eta* and *hinin* had been institutionalized by a number of feudal lords, or *daimyō,* on their own initiative before the Tokugawa rulers froze the social order, but the latter made the the *eta* and *hinin* a nationwide institution. For the first time their status was fixed.

In the early years of the Tokugawa era, a *hinin* might still be seen as a person who had fallen into his state by breaking the law or violating a serious taboo and, in theory, could eventually rise out of his situation. Ultimately, though, the *hinin,* like the *eta,* came to be consigned hereditarily to outcaste status.[9] By the Tokugawa era the *eta* were seen as people who had been, by reason of blood, relegated to their lowly status. Even though many *eta* families claimed that their ancestors had been warriors defeated in the struggle for power in the fifteenth and sixteenth centuries, who went into hiding and ended up doing menial, "unclean" work out of necessity,[10] Tokugawa scholars asserted that *eta* families were inferior aliens.[11]

Under the Tokugawa dispensation, people who committed a crime or violated the laws and customs of the land could be relegated to the status of *eta* or *hinin.* For instance, lovers who attempted double suicide but survived were consigned to the *eta* community because such acts were prohibited by the Tokugawa Bakufu.[12] But most of those who were frozen into the status of *eta* seem to have been people who happened to be engaged in occupations with a stigma attached to them at the time the Bakufu fixed the social order. Descendants of these people retained their lowly status even when they entered other, "clean" occupations. As a result, there were farmers, fishermen, weavers, dyers, and laborers who belonged to the outcaste group. In addition to the occupations already associated with the *eta,* low-level police, prison guards, and executioners of criminals were soon identified as outcastes, too.[13]

Critics of the Tokugawa rulers contend that they deliberately created a class of scapegoats for the common people to lord over and abuse, allowing a safety valve for the frustrations felt under an authoritarian, restrictive social order.[14] But the entire system of class distinctions may have emanated instead, from the Confucian world view of hierarchical order, which the Tokugawa rulers adopted when they constructed their social system. Nonetheless, just as the rulers allowed the *samurai* to abuse the commoners, they permitted the commoners to abuse the *burakumin*. All sorts of restrictive measures were imposed on the *eta-hinin*. They were restricted in where they could live, quality of housing, mobility in and out of their hamlets, clothing, hairdo, and even footwear. One *burakumin,* reflecting on the plight of his ancestors, remarked, "[They] were not treated as human beings. They were not allowed to wear any footwear but had to go about barefoot. They could use only straw ropes as belts, and only straws to tie their hair. They were forbidden to leave their hamlet from sunset to sunrise. . . . They were not allowed to associate with other people. When it was necessary to see others, for some business reason, they had to get on their hands and knees before they could speak."[15] When the *burakumin* encountered people above them in the social hierarchy, they had to get out of their way or get on their hands and knees until the others passed by. In some areas they were required to wear special identification marks, such as a yellow collar.[16] They were banned from the shrines and temples of non-*eta* communities, and intermarriage with other classes was strictly forbidden.

Magistrates did little to punish those who harmed *burakumin.* In 1859, when an *eta* youth tried to enter a Shinto shrine in Asakusa in Edo (Tokyo), he was beaten to death by the residents of that district. When the chief of the *eta* community appealed to the magistrate to punish the culprits, the magistrate is said to have responded, "The life of an *eta* is worth about one-seventh the life of a townsman. Unless seven *eta* have been killed, we cannot punish a single townsman."[17]

It could be argued that the Bakufu sought to treat the *eta* as "nonpeople." This was reflected in the policy of ignoring the very existence of *eta* communities on official maps and in calculating the distance from one point to another. Thus, in many instances the official distance given out by the Bakufu did not accord with the actual geographical distance.

As the rigid Tokugawa social order began to crumble, feudal authorities labored to shore up the disintegrating system by issuing more restrictive injunctions against the *eta* community. For example, in Tosa-han it was decreed in 1819 that peasants could not sell land to an *eta*. In the following year the *han* authorities forbade the *eta* from pawning things and from entering peasant homes, and ordered them to walk on the edge of the street. The *eta* were also prohibited from entering the city after eight at night. *Eta* women were forbidden to wear *obi* ("sashes") and were enjoined from having the windows of their houses face the street.[18]

The discriminatory treatment of the *eta* that was sanctioned by the ruling authorities implanted firmly in the minds of the populace the notion that the *eta* were lowly, despicable people who deserved to be oppressed. They were seen as dirty, vulgar, smelly, untrustworthy, dangerous, treacherous, subhuman creatures. In a typical interaction, around the turn of the century, an *eta* was taunted by his fellow students and his teacher: "Isn't it true that you *eta* have no testicles and that you are short one rib?" They then caught a hold of him and stripped his clothes off to examine him.[19]

Discrimination in the Modern Era

When the Tokugawa government fell and the new Meiji government was established, the feudal class system was abolished. In 1871, legal discrimination against the *burakumin* was ended by a government decree. When the decree emancipating the *burakumin* was proclaimed, one journalist explained it this way:

It seems that the people who are called *eta-hinin* were looked down upon because, ever since the ban on eating meat was decreed in the Middle Ages, those who slaughtered animals and ate their flesh came to be seen as odious people. It appears that this custom (of consuming meat) was introduced to Japan by Korean immigrants. Persisting in this practice, they came to be looked upon with contempt. In the modern age, European nations have concluded that meat is the best food to maintain a healthy body. This has been proven by . . . science. As a result even the most revered people, at the top of society, in Europe have started to eat meat. Since this is the case, the practice of classifying people under these categories *(eta-hinin)* should be discontinued.[20]

Needless to say, the decree of 1871 did not end discrimination or put a stop to the abuses, indignities, and cruelties that had been inflicted on the *burakumin* for centuries. Legal changes, as is so often the case, do not effect a rapid change in a people's way of thinking. In fact, the common people objected vehemently to the removal of the legal distinctions between themselves and the *burakumin*. In the three years following the decree of 1871, eleven peasant riots that included anti-*burakumin* demands erupted. Two, in particular, were large-scale uprisings.

In May 1875, 26,000 peasants in Okayama prefecture rioted, demanding that the *burakumin* be relegated to their former restrictive status. They insisted that the *burakumin* bow and scrape before them as they did in the Tokugawa era. Communities that refused to comply were attacked. Four hundred *burakumin* houses were burned or wrecked, together with other homes and public buildings. Eighteen *burakumin* were killed, eleven seriously injured.[21]

Again, in June of the same year, a massive peasant uprising involving 100,000 people broke out in Fukuoka prefecture. On this occasion, too, anti-*burakumin* demands were presented and physical attacks were perpetrated against *burakumin* communities. About 2,200 houses were burned or wrecked, mostly in *burakumin* districts.[22]

Although these attacks against the *burakumin* were sporadic, community efforts to keep the *burakumin* in "their place" persisted. In 1874, a *buraku* establishment in Nagano prefecture suffered heavy damages from a fire, and the *burakumin* had to borrow money from the main village (of which the *burakumins'* segregated hamlet was a satellite) for rehabilitation. A decade later, because they were unable to repay the debt, they were compelled to agree to the following pledge: "For many years we have worked hard to repay our debt but, being poor, we have failed to do so. Before the [Meiji] restoration, we were known as *eta* and were able to survive solely due to the kindness of the villagers. We have talked matters over and have agreed that we must revert to our former status and be guided by the village in all things and endeavor never to step out of line."[23]

The same effort to keep the *burakumin* in their place was seen half a century later in 1916, in the following declaration issued by a village in Gifu prefecture:

It is well known that the special hamlet located at the edge of this village consists of a low and vulgar race of people known as the "new commoners," formerly called *eta*. During Bakufu rule they were not allowed to own land and could only subsist as tenant farmers. When they needed firewood, they had to gather fallen branches surreptitiously in woods belonging to other people. They also survived by disposing of dead horses and oxen that were abandoned along the riverside. Hence, they were known as scavengers. Consequently, we looked down on them, and they recognized the fact that they were odious people. For example, when they came to our homes, they first removed their headgear and footwear. They then squatted on the dirt floor at the entrance and stated their business. This fact alone shows how humble they were. But after they gained the status of "new commoners," thanks to the policy of equality among the four classes brought about by the political changes that accompanied the restoration of imperial authority, their conduct has become haughtier with each passing day. One member of the special *buraku,* Maruzawa Yasokichi, has broken an ancient taboo and has purchased the plot owned by Sasaya-no-Motokihachi and is planning to build a new house there. We have repeatedly asked the *buraku* people to restrain themselves and maintain a sense of modesty. But they stubbornly refuse to comply with our wishes. If we allow them to persist in their willful ways, they will not only destroy the customs that we have inherited from antiquity, they will ultimately disrupt the social order of this village and sully our reputation and honor. This is absolutely clear to us. Spilt water cannot be recovered. So, before it is too late, we pledge to adhere to the following rules:

1. If a member of this village plans to sell to or purchase land from them [the *burakumin*], permission must first be obtained from the village. Otherwise the transaction cannot be consummated.
2. Members of this village are forbidden to eat or drink, exchange food, enter the bathhouse, or have friendly relations in any manner whatsoever with them.
3. If they set out to build houses and other buildings south of Hōjō Valley without the village's permission, the residents of the village will refuse to work for them as laborers, or assist them in any way.
4. Members of this village will not loan money to them or grant them the right to use its land.
5. The village will hire a veterinarian [so they would not have to rely on the *burakumin* for the care and disposal of their animals].
6. We will not allow them to take wood and bamboo from the village woods without our permission.
7. Those who violate this compact or act in any way to undermine and harm the order and reputation of this village will be punished in accordance with the nature of their transgression or else be removed from the rolls of the village and be ostracized.[24]

Sixty-three household heads signed the pledge, designed to repress a small group of about ten *burakumin* families.

Local communities were not the only groups that tried to suppress the rights of the *burakumin*. Higher authorities also violated their rights and interests. In 1919, for example, the government ordered an entire *burakumin* community to move from a village in Nara prefecture because their community overlooked an area in which, the authorities concluded, the tomb of the first emperor of Japan—Jimmu, a mythical figure—was located. They forced the *burakumin* to move to a narrow swampland, and this measure caused, in effect, the break-up and dispersal of the community.

In 1922, the authorities in Ōita prefecture burned down a *burakumin* hamlet, claiming that it was a nest of criminals and drifters as well as a health hazard. They provided neither relocation assistance nor any compensation to the people whose houses they had burned down. The real reason the authorities wanted the community destroyed was that it was located near the railroad, where a member of the imperial family was scheduled to pass by.[25]

Initially, then, the political authorities did very little to combat prejudice and discrimination against the *burakumin*. In fact, they perpetuated the prejudiced views that the public held. A handbook published by the Ministry of Justice in 1880 referred to the *eta* and *hinin* as "the lowliest of all people, almost like animals."[26] In 1907, Mie prefecture officials, as part of a campaign to "improve" the condition of the *burakumin*, issued this report about them:

The people of this race in this prefecture are devout believers of Buddhism, and thus they should be sincere and virtuous . . . but instead they are ruthless and cruel. Not only do they steal and kill cats and dogs, but they also steal other property. They are immoral and unruly and often defy public officials. People of this group are usually paupers. . . . This race of people stands outside society and knows nothing of morality. By and large they are lazy and addicted to gambling. Because of their perverse nature, they have a strong inclination to unite for unjust purposes. They join in groups of threes and fives, vandalize the homes of good people, and steal [anything that they can get their hands on].[27]

By the turn of the century, though, certain civic leaders had begun a movement—the Yūwakai ("Conciliation Society")—to smooth out the relationship between the *burakumin* and the general populace; and, in 1922, the leaders of the *burakumin* organized the Suiheisha ("The Levelers' Association") to combat discrimination. Their aim was to take a militant stand against those who discriminated against the *burakumin,* in hopes that this would arouse an awareness of the *burakumin*'s plight both among *burakumin* themselves and throughout the general public. The method they adopted was to confront offenders, denounce them, and force them to apologize publicly. These efforts, however, had little effect in lessening the prejudice and abuses that plagued the *burakumin* in their daily lives. For them life meant a continuous series of humiliating and degrading experiences. One old *burakumin* in Nagano prefecture recalled, "When we used to go to work for farmers, we were given tea in chipped bowls on the dirt floor by the kitchen. If we asked for a match to light our tobacco, they would throw it to us from the house. We weren't treated like human beings at all. We have lived in this community since the Edo period, but we are not allowed to bathe in the hot springs. . . . When we go and cut grass in the community woods, the villagers refuse to work by our side."[28]

"PASSING"

With the decree of 1871, one might have expected that the stigma attached to being *burakumin* would gradually disappear. However, under the system of family registration that was instituted by the Meiji government, most communities identified them in the official registrar as *shin heimin* ("new commoners"), *shin-min* ("new people"), or *moto-eta* ("former *eta*"). In most instances, then, *burakumin* could not conceal their identity and "pass" even if they wanted to, because a transcript of the family record was required to apply for jobs, to enter school, and for numerous other purposes. Moreover, outcaste villages were readily identifiable; in most cases the home address alone revealed their background.

Some *burakumin* did manage to "pass" and rise up the social ladder, but those who did so lived in mortal fear of being found out. Shimazaki Tōson (1872–1943), in his novel *Broken Commandment,* depicts the life of a schoolteacher who "passed" for a while. But his conscience plagues him and he makes a confession to his students about his *eta* background.[29] Shimazaki's inspiration for the story came from a real teacher who kept getting fired whenever his *burakumin* background was uncovered.[30]

One *burakumin* leader claims today that a number of prominent figures have succeeded in concealing their identity. "Not a few people have gotten ahead in the world by escaping from the *buraku* and blending into society at large by concealing their family origin and background. There are those, not only in the sports and entertainment fields but in political, financial, and academic circles, whose names, if known, would strain people's credulity."[31]

INTERCASTE MARRIAGES

Most resistant to change was the interdiction against intercaste marriages. For a non-*burakumin* to marry a *burakumin* meant, in effect, joining the outcaste community. Because such a social stigma adversely affected relatives as well, anyone contemplating such a marriage was vehemently discouraged by the family concerned.[32] This meant trouble for those who fell in love with a *burakumin* and vice-versa. Such an affair frequently ended in suicide.[33] If the husband or the wife had concealed the fact that he or she was a *burakumin* and the truth later came out, the marriage often ended in divorce or even suicide on the part of one of the spouses.[34] In 1927, Kitahara Taisaku, who shocked the society of his day by trying to submit a petition to the emperor in which he protested discrimination against the *burakumin* in the army (see p. 163), found that his notoriety resulted in his sister's husband finding out that she was a *burakumin*. The man abandoned his wife and four children and disappeared.[35] In one celebrated incident of the early 1930s, a district court ruled that, if a *burakumin* persuaded a woman to marry him without revealing his background to her, he was criminally liable. The trial was complicated by the fact that the girl's father charged the man with abduction. However, the man's concealment of his *burakumin* status was cited by the judge as a factor in his decision to sentence him to a year in prison. This provoked a massive protest movement by the *burakumin* community leading to the man's release, but the verdict stayed on record.[36]

Even though mixed marriages began to occur more frequently during the postwar years, opposition to such marriages continued to be strong, often causing couples to break off their relationship. For instance, when a young woman working in a small post office decided to marry a *burakumin,* the postmaster, at the request of her father, called her in and told her, "If you, an employee of this post office, were to marry someone like that, it would bring dishonor to this post office. So give up the idea."[37]

In another case, a young woman fell in love with a graduate of Kyoto University who was a *burakumin.* When she found out, she decided to marry him anyway and tried to persuade her parents to accept her decision. She insisted that her fiancé was "a splendid person who is, in fact, too good for me. I am confident that I will achieve happiness by devoting my life to him." Her parents contended, "It is not a matter of the person's moral character. [If you marry him] our ancestors and descendants will be disgraced. We will not be able to face our friends and relatives." The young woman was pregnant and was determined to go through with the marriage, but at the last minute she succumbed to the pressure from her parents. She wrote her fiancé, "I could not sleep last night for analyzing my feelings. In the end I was unable to live with the thought that I would be venturing into something impure. I concluded that, if I were to marry feeling like this, we would end up being unhappy. . . ."[38]

In 1957, the father of a young man planning to marry a *burakumin* girl committed suicide when he found that he could not persuade his son and the girl to abandon their plan.[39] Such incidents testify to the strongly embedded prejudice against the *burakumin* and the persistence of the belief that there is something inherently "unclean" about them. Thus, even in the postwar period mixed marriages have remained relatively rare. A 1967 survey showed that about 90 percent of all *burakumin* marriages were concluded with other *burakumin*.[40]

RELIGIOUS AND MILITARY INSTITUTIONS

During the Tokugawa period, both the Shinto shrines and Buddhist temples discriminated against the *burakumin*. In some places, they were neither allowed to enter the compounds of Shinto shrines nor permitted to take part in festivals that involved moving the portable altars about.[41] As noted earlier, a young man was beaten to death when he tried to enter a Shinto shrine in Asakusa in 1859.

Most *burakumin* were devout supporters of the True Pure Land Sect of Buddhism, but they were not ordinarily allowed to worship in temples attended by the general populace; they had to attend their own segregated temples. Where they were allowed to attend the "regular" temple, they were made to sit in a secluded section in the back of the hall. In bestowing posthumous Buddhist names, some temples gave the dead of the *burakumin* ignoble names like "male beast" and "female beast."[42]

Even after the emancipation decree of 1871, the two chief temples of the True Pure Land Sect did little to alleviate the woes of the *burakumin.* Critics contended that temple authorities were merely interested in gaining financial support from the *burakumin* without giving anything in return. In 1902, when a representative of one of the chief temples went on a fund-raising tour, he sought to exhort people to give generously by citing the contributions that the *burakumin* were making. "Socially they are discriminated against as people who do not belong to the realm of human beings. They are *eta,* who are just like insects. But even they give generously. [But] *you* are full-fledged human beings so [you should give even more generously]."[43]

The Suiheisha sought to persuade temple headquarters to take a more active role in improving the condition of the *burakumin.* They failed to elicit any vigorous action, however, although in the 1920s the western branch of the True Pure Land Sect issued a statement calling for equal treatment of all believers. But Suiheisha leaders believed its impact to be minimal.[44] Not until the postwar years, when occupation authorities instituted reforms and the idea of equality was given a boost, did temple headquarters begin to play a somewhat more active role in seeking to end discrimination against the *burakumin* in the temples.[45]

Another institution in which discrimination against the *burakumin* persisted was the armed forces. *Burakumin* were subject to the draft like other Japanese subjects. They were expected to shoulder their share of military duties and obligations and risk their lives in combat like everyone else. Yet only with difficulty could *burakumin* soldiers rise to the rank of superior private (the highest of the three private grades); and they could hardly ever rise to the level of a noncommissioned officer. Certainly, they could not expect to be admitted to the military academies, and they were forbidden to serve in the imperial guard division, undoubtedly because "unclean" people could not be allowed to serve in a division that guarded that purest of beings, the emperor. The navy, which was manned primarily by volunteers, did not as a rule enlist recruits from the *burakumin.*

The unit to which most *burakumin* soldiers found themselves assigned was the transportation corps. Covertly, the *burakumin* were frequently placed in all-*burakumin* squads or platoons.[46] When the army held military exercises in the field, they avoided billeting soldiers in *burakumin* homes. *Burakumin* soldiers were discriminated against even when they were killed in action in the service of their country. In the 1920s, a village in Saitama prefecture built a monument to honor those who had died in the Siberian expedition that was launched by Japan following the Bolshevik revolution. When the names were inscribed, the *burakumin* war dead were left out.[47]

The prewar Japanese army was notorious for its brutality and the way in which newly inducted men were harassed and abused by those above them in rank or length of service. The *burakumin* were usually subjected to especially severe abuse and discrimination. This led, in 1926, to a protest movement against the 24th Infantry Regiment in Fukuoka, where about 10 percent of the enlisted men were *burakumin* and where abuses had led to a number of suicides. The Suiheisha, led by Matsumoto Jiichirō, a pioneer among *burakumin* reformers, sought to get the Fukuoka army authorities to end their discriminatory practices. This confrontation ended with the arrest and imprisonment of Matsumoto and others on the trumped-up charge that they were plotting to blow up the barracks with dynamite.[48] The 24th Regiment controversy triggered Kitahara's direct petition to the emperor (see pp. 163–169).

THE ECONOMIC PLIGHT OF BURAKUMIN

The general social and economic discrimination against the *burakumin* locked them into traditional, low-paying, "unclean" jobs. This lack of opportunity to better themselves economically kept the *burakumin* the most impoverished element in modern Japan. They were forced to live in miserable shacks in the ghettoes of the cities and in segregated slums in the villages. A 1919 survey showed that there were 5,294 segregated wards or hamlets of *burakumin.* In 1935, the number had increased to 5,368.[49]

About three-quarters of the *burakumin* population was located in farm, fishing, and mountain villages; the rest in urban slums. Of the 120 *burakumin* sections in Kyoto prefecture, 36 percent were located along riverbanks, 30 percent in foothills, and 17 percent in ravines. Only 11 percent were located in flatland and only 5 percent were in the city proper. In most cities, the *burakumin* sections were located near garbage dumps, crematoriums, slaughterhouses, hospitals for communicable diseases, jails, or human-waste disposal sites.[50]

A man who, as a young boy in the 1920s, moved with his family into the *burakumin* ghetto in Kure, in Hiroshima prefecture, described the area as follows:

[It] was a ravine surrounded by hills, and through the middle ran a clear brook. Houses surrounded the brook. This was the *buraku,* and our house was located along the edge of the brook. The house, owned by the city, consisted of one four-mat room and a two-mat kitchen. It was a very small house into which our family of seven was crammed. . . . At the entrance to this section of the city there was a naval penitentiary. Across from the bridge was a place where animals were slaughtered, and nearby was a tannery. Slightly beyond that point was a large kettle where animal fat was processed. There were also mounds of oxen bones, refuse piles, a place to dispose of stray dogs, a crematorium, a graveyard, and a shop where objects were made from dog hides. Who would bother to hire people like us, living in such an odious environment? Not only did they not hire us, they treated us like subhuman creatures. They called the bridge at the entrance to our section the "Bridge of Hell." Parents told their children, "Don't go across the bridge or you'll get into terrible trouble. . . . The people who live there kill oxen and dogs and eat the meat. . . . Don't cross the bridge to the other side of the river. You can't tell what they'll do to you."[51]

In the city of Kyoto, with a traditionally large *burakumin* population, 90 percent of the *burakumin* houses in the mid-1930s were deemed unfit for habitation, and 50 percent of the households had to use community toilets. Fifty-six percent of the houses had no ventilation, 60 percent had no sunlight, and 60 percent had no sewers. Such adverse conditions led to serious health problems. The infant mortality rate was an astronomical 31 percent, 2.5 times higher than the average for the rest of the city.[52]

In the early 1930s, 50 percent of all *burakumin* were subsistence farmers, 8 percent handcraftsmen, 12 percent peddlers or small shopkeepers, 15 percent day laborers, and 13 percent were in miscellaneous jobs.[53] The urban *burakumin's* work was restricted largely to tanning, leather work, butchering, raising pigs, making and repairing footwear, rag picking, peddling, rickshaw pulling, day labor, or miscellaneous craftwork. The income derived from these activities, as one might well imagine, was meager. Only the leather workers who went into the production of Western-style shoes did relatively well, those few who got government contracts to manufacture shoes for the army developing into substantial entrepreneurs.[54] But they were the exceptions.

The family of the man from the ghetto in Kure (see above) was more typical. They eked out a living repairing footwear. They also scavenged along the riverbank picking up bits of glass and nails from the ashes that people had dumped in the river. Occasionally they managed to find some coins, but supplementing their income in this manner did not provide them with sufficient money to eat rice. "All we could afford was rice gruel, and it was mostly water with yam and only a little rice."[55] Economic necessity compelled the parents to send their eldest daughter to work in a low-class geisha house; in this case, a brothel. "My older sister has practically no education. At the age when she should have been finishing the sixth grade she was sent out as a geisha. You might say that my parents should have found a job somewhere so that they would not have had to turn their daughter into a geisha. But discrimination was a fact of life. We were insulted as cow killers, dog killers, and called four-legged animals. No one would hire us. But girls could be sent out to work as geisha to help the family. Common sense tells us that this is contrary to morality, that it is a heartless thing to do. But we had no choice if we were to eat."[56] Because this family had to call on the young geisha for money time after time, she fell deeper and deeper in debt and was finally sold abroad to Korea.

This kind of hardship was commonplace in the *burakumin* ghettoes. A survey of *burakumin* households in Kyoto in 1886 showed that, of the 1,100 households questioned, 840 survived by picking up odd jobs: 750 of these families were leading a marginal existence; 450 were selling off what few possessions they had in order to stay alive; the other 350 "have no possessions to sell. They are surviving with the help of their neighbors and the assistance of charitable people from other places. They are on the verge of starvation."[57]

The plight of the *burakumin* in Kyoto did not improve with the modernization of Japan. In fact, it may have gotten worse as population density increased; in 1937, the population density in six *burakumin* districts was six times higher than that in the rest of the city. One-fifth of the families depended on day labor and odd jobs for their living. Even with the whole family working, half of these families earned less than 40 yen a month, total, at a time when the average wage for a single laborer was 40 to 50 yen a month, and the beginning salary for schoolteachers and policemen was 35 to 40 yen a month.[58]

Rural *burakumins'* economic situation was just as harsh as urban residents'. They had to undertake equally menial jobs. A survey taken during the Great Depression showed that, of the 700 *buraku* communities checked in twenty-six prefectures, the average acreage for over 16,400 farm households was 4.4 *tan,* while the national average was 10.5 *tan.* A 1931 survey revealed that only 16 percent of *burakumin* farmers owned the farms they worked. Thirty-one percent were part-owners/part-tenants; and 53 percent, full tenants. (The national figures for non-*burakumin* were 31 percent, 42 percent, and 27 percent respectively.)[59]

The *burakumin*-owned fields were usually the most infertile plots located in the most remote areas of the village. The terms of tenancy for *burakumin* tended to be less favorable than those for non-*burakumin* peasants. For example, in a small hamlet in Nara prefecture the *burakumin* tenants paid 2 *koku* (about 10 bushels) per *tan* on plots that yielded 2.4 *koku*. This left them 0.4 *koku*, or less than 17 percent of yield, to feed their families. In many instances, they were even denied access to the village woodlands, which meant they could not supplement their income by gathering firewood.[60]

A survey of one hundred *buraku* in 1933 indicated that the *burakumin* peasants' income came to about one-quarter the national average. A 1935 survey revealed that 35 percent of the population of *buraku* communities were unemployed.[61] During the entire period of Japanese industrial expansion, job opportunities for the *burakumin* remained restricted. In the Meiji period, some *burakumin* girls and women found employment in the spinning and textile industries, but it is believed that the number was small. Often, they had to conceal their background. By the Shōwa era (beginning in 1926), an increased number of *burakumin* had gained employment in the textile industry, but they were often put in segregated dormitories.[62] Mining was another industry in which a fairly large number of *burakumin* was employed. As seen in the chapter on the mining industry, however, working conditions for all miners were harsh, but the *burakumin* were subjected to the additional humiliation of discrimination.[63]

Even in the postwar years, no significant improvement in employment opportunities for the *burakumin* materialized. A 1964 survey taken of the *burakumin* in Osaka prefecture—a highly urbanized area—showed that most were still in traditional jobs; that is, 13 percent were in the leather industry, 5 percent in rag picking, 4.3 percent in retail butchery, 2.6 percent in retail footwear, 9.4 percent in day labor or unemployed, and 30.6 percent in miscellaneous and odd jobs. In effect, about 40 percent were in a state of semi-unemployment.[64]

In a study made in Kyoto fifteen years after the end of World War II, it was found that a higher percentage of *burakumin* than non-*burakumin* school graduates were employed in small shops (29.8 percent versus 13.1 percent), and a smaller percentage in the more prestigious large-scale enterprises, where working conditions were better (1.5 percent versus 15.1 percent). *Burakumin* children were also paid less than non-*burakumin* children in these firms.[65]

The economic hardship and penury that *burakumin* experienced throughout Japan's "modern" century is reflected endlessly in the accounts of reporters and social scientists who interviewed them as well as in every memoir written by members of this group.

EDUCATION

The extreme poverty in which *burakumin* children grew up resulted not only in material deprivation but also in intense emotional stress. The continual humiliations and insults they experienced scarred many *burakumin* for life. That modernization does not necessarily create a more humane, enlightened outlook among people is indicated by the fact that even highly educated and "cultured" members of society did not overcome their prejudice against *burakumin*. For example, Yoneda Shōtarō, a *burakumin* from Nara prefecture and a U.S.-trained pioneer in sociology, was hired as a lecturer at Kyoto University. In 1920, after thirteen years of teaching, he came up for promotion to a full professorship, but a prominent colleague only agreed to his promotion on the condition that Yoneda resign the position after a year. Though Yoneda did manage to hang on to his post for five years, he was finally forced to give up his professorship and return to his former status as lecturer.[66]

However, unlike government posts or police work, which were closed to *burakumin*, teaching was an "allowed" profession. When *burakumin* were first admitted to the teaching field, their admittance was regarded as a landmark event. An early Meiji magazine reported, in 1874, on the role the governor of Nara had played in having a *burakumin* appointed to a teaching position in his prefecture. "Although he [the teacher] was a *hinin* until yesterday, today, in this age of civilization, he is able to utilize his talents and become the teacher of others. The fact that the governor used his influence and that the bureau of education agreed to employ him make this a truly commendable story."[67]

Most *burakumin* children were stunted in their desire to pursue learning early in their school life, or else their families' poverty compelled them to abandon school even before they finished the elementary grades. The *burakumin* who had the fortitude and good fortune to overcome the many obstacles in their way, finish a normal school, and gain certification to teach were exceptional people.[68] Even then, *burakumin* teachers were not ordinarily accepted in non-*buraku* schools, but were restricted to schools attended only by *burakumin* children.

Only *burakumin* children living in small pockets in the midst of non-*burakumin* school districts went to mixed schools. The rest attended schools separate from the others. The government finally moved to end this practice in 1908, but, when *burakumin* began to attend non-*buraku* schools, they were often put in segregated classes or seated in the back rows of the classroom. At the same time, many *burakumin* teachers who had been teaching in the segregated schools lost their jobs when those schools were abolished.[69]

For many *burakumin,* attending school with non-*burakumin* children was a painful and traumatic experience. This was their first encounter with naked bigotry. They became the targets of insults, taunts, and even physical attacks by their schoolmates. A study of discrimination against *burakumin* schoolchildren in two communities in Hiroshima prefecture in the second decade of this century revealed:

Children were picked on and abused in the classroom as well as on their way to and from school. *Burakumin* children reported that when they went to school they had to carry rocks with them to protect themselves. When *burakumin* and non-*burakumin* children got into fights, the teacher tended to punish the former. When assignments to clean the school were handed out, the *burakumin* children were usually the ones given the task of cleaning the latrines. The constant taunting by other children stifled their desire to go to school at all, and their schoolwork naturally suffered. Girls, plagued with a feeling of inferiority because of their wretched garments, stayed home and cared for their baby brothers and sisters.[70]

In fact, their parents, like other impoverished families, were inclined to keep the children away from school anyway, to help with the chores. As discussed earlier, the children were often sent to school with their baby siblings on their backs.

Given the adverse economic conditions and discouraging atmosphere at school, it is not surprising that the attendance record of *burakumin* children was poor. A 1937 survey conducted in Kyoto showed that among those over the age of sixteen—that is, among those who should have finished their compulsory education—35 percent had not attended elementary school at all, and 19 percent had quit school before completing the six years of compulsory education.[71]

Personal Experiences of
Burakumin Schoolchildren

A woman born in 1913 in an Osaka *buraku* recalls:

I cannot forget the discrimination I underwent in school. Often other children would tell me, "Go away, you stink"; or they would say, "That girl is from *that* village," and would not include me in whatever they were doing. They would not let me join in when they were playing jump rope. They would block my way and sneer at me. Whenever something got lost, they would pick on *buraku* children saying, "You must have taken it." Once a teacher, who had just returned from the army, told us, "It's you kids' fault," when something disappeared. It made us so mad that we spent a week looking for the real culprit.

Because I had to help with chores at home and also took care of my younger brothers and sisters, I had to cut school often. The more I missed school, the less I understood what was going on in class and got bored with my studies. So I would look out the window or do something mischievous. Then I would get scolded and be made to stand in the corridor. The pupils who were forced to stand in the corridor were mostly *buraku* children.

There were lots of *buraku* children standing around in the playground. They were supposed to have forgotten something and gone home to get what they had left at home. But, in fact, their families were too poor to bring whatever they were supposed to, such as money, and they were told by their parents to say, "I forgot."[72]

This kind of unhappy life for *buraku* children continued throughout the "modern" century, up to and through World War II. A woman born in 1934 recalled:

When I was old enough to become aware of things, I realized that I was a poor child dressed in dirty rags. My father was a day laborer without regular employment; he had no job security. We grew up in the midst of poverty. . . . My life was conditioned strongly by the fact that I was called *"buraku,"* *"eta,"* "four-legged animal." Schooling is ordinarily the most important and happiest time in a person's life. But my life was warped by elementary school. Elementary school! The mere mention of the word makes my skin crawl. I shall never forget my first day of school, for this is when I first experienced discrimination. After we heard the principal's talk in the assembly room, we started to leave, holding our classmate's hand. When I stuck out my hand to hold the hand of the girl next to me, she stubbornly refused to hold my hand.

Not knowing why, I forcefully grabbed her hand. Then she began to cry. A female teacher came by and asked her why she was crying. . . . She responded that she did not want to hold my hand. The teacher asked her why. The girl said, "Because this girl's hands are dirty." The teacher looked at my hands and said, "Her hands are clean, there's nothing on them." Then the girl said, looking straight at me, "My mother told me, 'That child is smelly so you mustn't play with her.'" At that time I did not understand why she said that. . . . I cannot forget the mother who taught her young child such things nor can I forget my confusion and bafflement as I quietly stared at the girl's face.

After that, all the children of the class said I was smelly and dirty. There were several children from my *buraku* in my class, but they too started to avoid me. The teacher too began to treat me differently than other children. With each passing day the pain inside me got worse, and I began to hate going to school. Sometimes I lied, saying I was sick, and stayed home. So I was picked on by everybody. I would cry and cower in the corner. When I went home and complained to my mother, she would not listen to me.

The first year of anger and anguish passed and I entered the second grade. Not realizing that I was to suffer even more than before, I looked forward to the second year. But I still had my old, dirty clothes, frostbitten hands and feet, and scared, skittish look and attitude. I suppose I was an eyesore for everyone.

Her second year of school was ruined from the outset: The girl who sat next to her framed her, claiming she had stolen her scissors. She was accused of being a thief and was scolded by her teacher in front of the whole class. Now, in addition to being called an *eta* who was smelly and dirty, she was called a thief by other children. Boys waylaid her on the way home from school and threw rocks at her. Harassment by her classmates and teacher continued through her third year. Then she began to lose her eyesight. The doctor told her it was caused by malnutrition, but, in fact, her eye trouble was psychosomatic. No one was aware of this, however, so she was kept at home, free from the miseries of school life. Although she gradually recovered her sight, her education was over. She was unable to read the biggest letter on the optical chart, even with glasses, until she reached the age of fifteen.[73]

Her experience was not unique. Story after story like this is related by *burakumin* who were abused, insulted, and harassed in school. During the postwar years, when a teacher was trying to arouse *burakumin* parents to fight discrimination, one mother told her to let well enough alone.

When I went to school I was forced to sit in the last row of the classroom all by myself. I went to school because my parents browbeat me into going, but on the first day, on the way home, a boy ran after me and told me, "Hey there, starting tomorrow you can't come to school. Do you understand? If you come to school, the school will get polluted." Then he threw rocks at me. This happened many times.[74]

A man who was born in 1922 and grew up in a small village in Hiroshima prefecture facing the Inland Sea recalled the time when he entered kindergarten:

In my class there were two boys and three girls from the *buraku*. During gym class boys and girls were paired off. They always paired off *buraku* boys with *buraku* girls. But in our case there was always an extra girl. We boys always had a partner but one of the girls always had to stand alone and be left out of the activities.

During the first three years of school things were pleasant because he had the same teacher who was kind and sympathetic.

In the fourth grade I got a new teacher. Then harsh discrimination began. First of all, those of us from the *buraku* were told to sit in the back row of the classroom. I was fairly tall and so I did not feel conspicuous, but others were short and yet they were made to sit in the back row. Because the teacher openly showed his bias, our classmates also began to display their bias. They constantly used a term of degradation that was used by the villagers in reference to *buraku* people. . . . I often had to take care of my older sister's child and bring the baby to school on my back. The teacher would say it was distracting and make me leave the classroom. So I had to stay outside by myself while everyone else was inside studying. I can't bear to recall my bitter feelings on those occasions.

Then one of the girls from a wealthy family lost her tennis shoes at school.

I was immediately picked as the prime suspect. Every day I was called into the faculty room and was questioned all day long about the shoes. The teachers took turns questioning me. Since I had not taken the shoes, I could not give them the answer they wanted. Frustrated, they would beat me. . . . This kind of abusive treatment lasted for ten days. On the tenth day, the principal said they might as well give up because of my refusal to tell the truth, despite the sustained questioning.

There is an epilogue to this incident. When I was forty-two, a class reunion was held. On that occasion one of my classmates, recalling the incident, mentioned the name of the real culprit. I got so mad at him that I hit him. When I was being abused for ten days for a crime that I did not commit, he did not lift a finger to help me even though he knew who had taken the shoes. I still feel that this was an outrageous case of discrimination.[75]

During the last decade of the nineteenth century and at the beginning of the twentieth, a movement was started by a group of *burakumin* leaders to enhance the status of the *burakumin*. Through "self-reform," they wanted to improve their "morals and customs." In 1903, *burakumin* leaders from six prefectures around Kyoto got together and organized the Greater Japan Fraternal Conciliation Society (Dai Nihon Dōbō Yūwakai). They called for moral discipline, improvement of customs and ways, advancement of education, improvement in sanitation, training of talented people, encouragement of savings and thrift, and fostering of economic activities.[76] Government leaders supported this movement advocating harmony and conciliation *(yūwa),* hoping it would prevent abrasive confrontations and conflicts. The movement failed, however, to gain significant support, perhaps because it placed the burden of reform on the *burakumin* themselves rather than seeking to change the outlook and attitudes of the general populace, which kept them oppressed and downtrodden. After the rice riots of 1918, in which a large number of *burakumin* were involved, government authorities and conservative social leaders supported the *yūwa* movement with greater vigor in order to offset the more militant Suiheisha movement (see p. 146), which emerged as an indirect result of the riots.[77]

The rice riots of 1918 were caused by war-time inflation. The price of 1 *koku* of rice, which was 23 yen in Osaka in January 1918, rose to 41 yen by June, or 41 sen for 1 *shō* (1.6 quarts). In Kyoto, 1 *shō* cost 52 sen. In July, the wives of fishermen in Toyama prefecture began demonstrating against the high price of rice. By August, the demonstrations had spread to wide areas of the country, and in many places turned violent as mobs attacked rice merchants and other shops, and clashed with the police. Eventually, the government was forced to call out troops. It is estimated that 700,000 people participated in the riots. The authorities were particularly harsh in their treatment of *burakumin* rioters and in some instances sought to place the entire blame on *burakumin* looters. In several prefectures, 30 to 40 percent of those arrested turned out to be *burakumin*. [78] The *burakumin* complained that the penalties imposed on them were much harsher than those imposed on non-*burakumin*. [79]

As a result of this explosion of *burakumin* anger, many of their leaders decided that "harmony" and "conciliation" would not end the abuses against them and decided to organize a more activist, militant group. Consequently, in 1922, they insisted that they be treated with as much respect and dignity as any other person. To this end, the Suiheisha leaders contended that the *burakumin* themselves must cease to cower and grovel. "The time has come when we can be proud of being *eta*. We must never again insult our ancestors and profane our humanity by slavish words and cowardly acts," the founders stated in their initial declaration. [80]

The method adopted by the Suiheisha to obtain redress—confrontation and denunciation of anyone who showed signs of harboring prejudice toward them—sometimes had the effect of confirming the general populace's prejudice that the *burakumin* were "vicious" people. It also led to frequent clashes. For instance, in 1923, in an area in Nara prefecture where discrimination was particularly severe ("They could not use public bath houses or barbershops, or rent houses in majority districts, or work at the factories."), Suiheisha members attempted to force an old man who made an insulting gesture to apologize. The result was a series of fights with members of the ultranationalist Kokusuisha (National Essence Society). [81]

A particularly vicious attack was launched upon *burakumin* in 1924 in a village in Gunma prefecture. There the Suiheisha had castigated a person for insulting a *burakumin*. In retaliation, 2,000 aroused villagers armed with bamboo spears, swords, and pistols attacked the outcaste community of some twenty houses. They burned and wrecked the houses and furniture and physically attacked the inhabitants. The *burakumin* complained that the police, though reinforced from other communities, stood by and made no attempt to stop the violence. [82]

The authorities were unsympathetic to the tactic of militant confrontation being pursued by the Suiheisha to begin with, and, when leaders of the Suiheisha sought to link their movement with the budding communist movement, they began to see the Suiheisha as a subversive organization. Those who did link up with Marxist activists were arrested, jailed, and often tortured. Among them was Kimura Keitarō, who was taken when the government made a mass arrest of "reds" on March 15, 1928 (known as the 3.15 Incident). [83] During his interrogation the police yelled at him, "We have permission to kill you if necessary. Keep that in mind." In order to make him confess that he was a communist, they beat him with a bamboo rod and an iron rod wrapped in cloth till he was black and blue. He lost his hearing when he was struck on the side of his head. After two weeks of torture, he was indicted and sent to prison for five years. Counting his two-and-a-half years of detention before sentencing, Kimura spent seven-and-a-half years in jail.[84]

An internecine struggle between Bolsheviks and anarchists in the Suiheisha movement, when added to the suppression tactics of the police and a rising tide of militarism and ultranationalism, fatally weakened the organization. By 1940, it was practically defunct.[85] The Suiheisha movement had undoubtedly raised the consciousness of *burakumin* and made them more willing to assert their rights. As far as the general public was concerned, however, its effect was mainly to increase wariness and hostility toward them. No matter what their tactics, the numerous reform movements had few means of recourse available to make life better—either materially or psychologically—for the individual *burakumin.* One old man from Nagano prefecture remarked in the postwar period:

There wasn't a single good thing about being born in the *buraku.* Nothing but bad things. We were neither allowed to worship the gods together nor allowed to join the young men's association. During Shinto festivals we were not allowed to join in the young people's activities. The situation hasn't changed much today. . . . Formally, people are aware that discrimination is bad, but I have a feeling they would like to keep discrimination alive in some form or other. I sense it. When I go to another town with a non-*buraku* person and run into someone we know, I am anxious to say hello, but the other people ignore me and say hello only to my companion. It makes you feel funny.[86]

Other old people feel that the situation has improved because of the reforms introduced by the occupation authorities. An old lady in the same prefecture commented:

Thanks to America, this has become a better society. Because America has liberated us they say Japan is now number 2 or number 3 as an economic power. It's too bad that in America there is trouble about discrimination against the blacks and that they are fighting in Vietnam. I feel that activities against discrimination in this *buraku* should be carried on quietly. But we mustn't do anything that will arouse sleeping dogs. We should not broadcast the fact that we belong to the *buraku.* We'll end up disgracing ourselves.[87]

These sentiments were expressed repeatedly by older people living in *burakumin* enclaves. They insisted, "It's better not to stir up things."[88] Although the postwar *buraku* liberation movement (the Buraku Liberation League) has become a vigorous force, the process of overcoming prejudice and improving the economic life of the *burakumin* is still moving at a snail's pace.[89]

The following are excerpts from the autobiography of Kitahara Taisaku, who won notoriety in 1927 when, as a soldier undergoing imperial review during army maneuvers, he tried to present a petition to the emperor protesting discrimination against the *burakumin* in the army.[90]

 Kitahara Taisaku

I was born on January 1, 1906, in the home of a tenant farmer in a segregated *buraku* [in Gifu prefecture]. . . . In the family register, I am recorded as the third son, but actually I am the only son of our family. My oldest brother died ten days after birth, and my second brother died only five days after birth. [Kitahara had five sisters.]

My father liked to gamble, and so our family, which was poor to begin with, suffered from poverty all the more. . . . But when I was born, he swore off gambling. . . . He, like other old people in the village, was a fatalist. They were all devout followers of the Honganji [chief temple of the True Pure Land Sect] and were influenced strongly by the Buddhist notion of karma, which held that one's destiny was determined by one's actions in a previous life. "We were born in an unlucky place. Just because we had our umbilical cord cut in this kind of *buraku,* we are looked down upon by others and suffer the hardships of poverty. There's not a single good thing about our lives. But we have to accept things as they are because it has been fixed from our previous existence. . . ." I heard these words from the old folks often. These words, I feel, eloquently describe the truth: discrimination against *burakumin* is a status distinction based on birth. Because of his place of birth, over which the individual has no choice, a *burakumin*'s position is fixed as a member of a community that is discriminated against. This status is passed on from one generation to the next. The principle of free competition that characterizes the modern age does not apply to a member of the *buraku.* Regardless of one's education, knowledge, talent, and willingness to work, a person is denied the chance to rise up the social ladder simply because he is a product of the *buraku.* As soon as the fact that he comes out of the *buraku* is uncovered, he is rejected and scorned by society even if he has managed to achieve a high position and acquire great wealth. This kind of illogical, old-fashioned social discrimination persists in Japan. I was born a *burakumin,* destined to be discriminated against.

Sixty percent of the households in our hamlet were engaged in farming. The majority of the people were impoverished peasants, farming less than a beggarly 5 *tan* (about 1.2 acres) of rice paddies and dry fields. They were unable to survive on the income derived from farming so everyone had some sort of supplementary job. In fact, there were many farm families who regarded farming as a secondary occupation. Not a single family owned all the land it farmed. Only two or three families owned as well as rented land. The rest were all tenant farmers renting their land from a landlord who lived in the next village. The farm plots, which were low-grade fields where irrigation and drainage systems were poor, were scattered about, far away from their houses. But the rents were high. . . .

The villagers called those who did not farm "craftsmen." They were people who made leather goods and footwear, day laborers who did construction work or helped farmers during busy seasons, and people who fixed *geta* ["wooden clogs"] and bought rags and junk. The lowly workers' living conditions were less secure than those of farmers who raised their own rice and vegetables. Many were having difficulty getting by. . . . The village always had a surplus of people. Even if they wanted to work they could not find it, and husky-looking men could be seen loitering in the village. . . .

In order to supplement the family income, my mother went around nearby villages peddling things. In the summer she sold the straw sandals my father made, and in the winter she peddled meat. . . . The meat she sold was dog meat. The season for dog meat ran from fall to the end of February. . . . In our village there were about twenty peddlers of dog meat. . . . I would like to comment on the Japanese prejudice about eating meat. Today no one believes such silly tales as the story that if a person eats beef a baby with horns will be born. But there are some people who, when they are confronted with beef, see the figure of a cow or bull before their eyes and find it impossible to eat the beef. So, naturally, some people feel like throwing up when they hear about eating oxtail, the organs of horses, pig's feet, and so on. For someone like me, who has consumed the innards of horses and cattle since the age of three and has no prejudice about eating meat, all this sounds comical. Among the four-legged animals I have eaten are cattle, horse, pig, deer, boar, lamb, goat, dog, cat, badger, rabbit, weasel. Aside from four-legged animals, I have tried turtle, snake, adder, frogs and so on. . . .

Deep in the souls of the Japanese lurks the Shinto concept of pollution and the Buddhist prohibition against killing. So Japanese look down on and discriminate against people who handle meat and leather . . . but they drool over *sukiyaki* and lick their chops over mixed grill. They are indeed selfish people. They let the butchers take upon their shoulders the sin of killing animals; then they wipe their mouths and pretend that they haven't done anything wrong.

My oldest sister, Fuji, had two younger sisters when she started elementary school, and so she had to take care of them. As a result, she was unable to attend the four years of elementary school with any degree of regularity. In fact, compulsory education was a heavy burden on poor families. . . . At the age of fifteen she went to work, together with several of her childhood friends, in a weaver's shop about 5 *ri* [12.2 miles] away. She was sent on a three-year contract, but during her first year as an apprentice she got paid very little. At the time the contract was concluded, my father borrowed 50 percent of her pay in advance. . . .

My third sister, Tsuya, was born in 1897, so she is seventy-five today but still in good health and sound of mind. According to her:

My parents could not afford to send me to more than two years of elementary school. When my mother went out peddling or went out to gather firewood, I had to stay home from school to help with household chores and take care of my younger brother and sisters. When I did occasionally go to school, I'd find other children sewing kimonos and undergarments, but I did not have any material and thus could not do any sewing. I felt awful about this. But on graduation day I received a certificate and rice cakes just like the other children. In those days compulsory education was four years, but I was able to attend only half of the time. When I was twelve I was sent to work as a nursemaid in another village. My employer grew rice as well as raising silkworms. Because the family was busy caring for the silkworms, I had to take care of the children till midnight and get up in the morning while it was still dark. It was a hard life and I missed my family so much I finally ran away and came home. I was then sent to work at a weaver's shop on a four-year contract. . . . We had to work all year round except for three days during the summer Obon festival and on New Year's. Even when we got sick they would not call in a doctor but told us to stay in the closet and rest. . . . [She left the weaver's shop when it went bankrupt]. After that I was sent out as a maid. . . . I had to do the cooking and washing, and father often came to get advance payments, so at the end of the year I had only 13 yen coming to me. . . . When I was a young girl there was not a single thing that I could say was fun or pleasant. . . . I experienced nothing but hardship. It's as if I were born into this world to suffer.

Sister number four, Shizu, experienced the same kind of life as my other sisters except for one atrocious experience that scarred her for life. When she was seventeen she was raped by the employer where she was working as a maid. . . . My father was furious but the incident was evidently not reported to the police. My guess is that my father agreed to an "amicable settlement" by having my sister's advance payment canceled and receiving a small amount of money in addition. . . . My sister undoubtedly was bitter toward my parents for agreeing to settle the incident in this fashion. After she returned home, she stayed for a while making sandals but soon left home again to work as a maid.

Maki, my sister right above me, died at the age of fourteen on April 13, the beginning of my third year in school. She too was working as a maid in a farm family in a neighboring village. Her employer used her not only as a nurse for his children but also as a field hand to do heavy farm work. The immediate cause of Maki's death was tetanus. She was pulling a cart on the way to a lime factory four miles away, tripped on a rock, fell, and cut herself. The cut got infected. If she had been treated by a doctor, she might have been saved. But her employer did not call in a doctor until her condition had become critical. He did not even notify my parents but left her alone. When my father went after her with a cart, Maki was already delirious. . . . On the third morning after she came home she died.

Kitahara's second sister, Kiku, also had a tragic life (see p. 00). At the age of fifteen she went to Tokyo to work in a textile factory. She fell in love with a young man who worked in the factory's office, but his parents refused to let them marry because she was a *burakumin.* Later she married a carpenter who turned out to be a wastrel and spent most of his time in the brothels.

In the fall of 1927, I [Kitahara] made my move to make a direct appeal to the emperor concerning the discrimination against the *burakumin* in the army. The papers treated this incident as sensational news, and the fact that Kiku was my sister, and hence a *burakumin,* got exposed. Her husband was shocked and castigated Kiku for having concealed her background from him all during their marriage. Within a month he left his wife and four children and vanished. Kiku was left to suffer in the pit of despair. . . .

In April of my seventh year I started elementary school. . . . It was the year [1912] when Emperor Meiji passed away and Crown Prince Yoshihito mounted the throne. The era name was changed from Meiji to Taishō. . . .

In order to build a supplementary fund at the school, every spring and fall, after the crops were harvested, each family was expected to contribute some barley and rice. . . . Each child was given a cotton sack to be filled. It took about 1 *shō* plus 2 *gō* [1 *shō* equals 1.8 litre, or .48 gallon; 1 *gō* is 0.1 of a *shō*] to fill the sack. For farm families growing barley and rice, it was not much of a burden. But most of the tenant farmers of the *buraku* were unable to produce enough rice to feed their families. For such families the children would have to beg and cry to get even 2 or 3 *gō* of grain from their angry parents. Moreover, in the *buraku* there were numerous laborers who did not even have a piece of land the size of a cat's forehead to farm. Children from these families had to bring money instead, but their parents could afford no more than 2 or 3 sen.

It is painful for me to recall those days. The farmers' children would bring bulging sacks . . . and place them on the classroom platform where the teacher was standing. . . . I used to feel ashamed and miserable. I would hide the 2 *gō* of rice that I had got from my mother in a cloth wrapper with my textbooks. But in class I had to take the rice out and give it to the teacher in front of everybody. No one said anything but I was certain that they were all sneering at me. I felt humiliated and degraded. . . . This ritual, which was repeated twice a year, was the most humiliating time of my school days.

When I was in the fifth grade, our teacher said that the class president and vice-president would be chosen by a vote of the entire class. The election resulted in my being chosen class president by a large majority. The next day the teacher told the class, "Yesterday's election was held merely to find out how the class felt. It was not held to choose the class officers." He was obviously going back on his word. I realized that he did not want to appoint me as class president. I had already been discriminated against because I was a member of the *buraku;* I knew that teacher was prejudiced against me. As I had expected, he ignored the election and appointed the son of a prominent landowner as class president, and the son of a member of the school board as vice-president. . . .

I began to be aware of discrimination against *buraku* people from about the time that I was in the third grade. Trouble often broke out among students over questions of discrimination. The teachers, showing their bias, tended to blame the *buraku* children without looking into the cause of the quarrels. Consequently, *buraku* children did not trust the teachers and even looked upon them as their oppressors. We joined hands to fight back against those who discriminated against us. This led to our being criticized and feared for ganging up on others. But those who are oppressed and abused have no other recourse but to unite to protect themselves and defend their freedom and rights. Whenever I saw my classmates and younger pupils from our *buraku* being picked on and discriminated against, I felt as if I were being abused myself and came to their defense. Sometimes the offenders would say, "Kitahara, you're different. We are not talking about you." But I would respond, "No, I'm not different. I too am a member of the *buraku*."

Kitahara's school record was excellent, but because of his family's financial situation he was unable to go to middle school. His father did manage to send him to two years of higher elementary school beyond the six years of compulsory schooling. There he had a teacher who taught the students "to think, judge, and understand" rather than rely on rote memory. He also learned from the teacher "the pleasure of writing, and was influenced by him in a spiritually important way."

After finishing two years of higher elementary school, Kitahara found employment as a mailman for 16 yen a month. But in 1922 he left his job and went to Tokyo, hoping to find employment and also attend night school. He stayed with his sister Kiku and her family. He recalls going to a movie theater and, when he saw some people viewing a newsreel of the crown prince without taking off their hats, he shouted at them to take off their hats. "At the age of seventeen I was a blind nationalist and worshipper of the emperor." With the help of his cousin Tokukichi, he applied for a schoolboy's job at the home of the then minister of education, Kamada Eikichi. Kamada's secretary told his cousin that they would have to look into Kitahara's background. This posed a dilemma for Kitahara's cousin, who had managed to become a fairly successful fabric-store owner by concealing his identity. His wife did not even know he was a *burakumin*. If Kitahara's background check revealed his *buraku* origin, the fact that his cousin Tokukichi was also a *burakumin* would become known, too. So Kitahara had to withdraw his application for a job with the Kamada household.

Beset by such difficulties, Kitahara sought solace in a philosophical-religious group led by a spiritual leader, Nishida Tenkō, who preached the doctrine of self-denial and service to others. But Kitahara left Nishida's movement after he became interested in the activities of the newly organized Suiheisha. He then returned to his village to organize a chapter of the Suiheisha, but he met with opposition from the police as well as resistance from the better-off *buraku* members who did not want to get in trouble with the authorities. Soon he came under the influence of Marxist thought, and when the Marxists split into anarchist and Bolshevik factions, Kitahara sided with the former.

In early 1927, Kitahara was drafted into the army. By this time he had long forsaken the nationalism and royalism of his youth. It was also a time when the Suiheisha was publicizing the discriminatory practices that prevailed in the army. As we saw above, in 1926 a confrontation between the Suiheisha and the 24th Regiment in Fukuoka had occurred, and a number of Suiheisha leaders were arrested. Kitahara was upset by these developments and entered the army filled with suspicion and hostility. From the outset he showed a defiant attitude toward the authorities and was soon pegged as a troublemaker. He finally went AWOL in a dispute over derogatory remarks made about *burakumin* soldiers. He was caught and put in solitary confinement for twenty days. He staged a hunger strike, giving it up, however, after seven days when his family intervened.

In November 1927, the army staged a large-scale maneuver in the Nōbi plain near Nagoya. Kitahara decided to take advantage of this occasion to petition the emperor directly in protest over discrimination against the *burakumin* in the army. He wrote the petition in brush strokes as follows:

1. The discrimination and contempt displayed toward members of the special *buraku* in the armed forces is as severe as the conditions that prevailed under feudalism. Frequently disputes are touched off by discriminatory actions. The attitude of the authorities who deal with these disputes indicates a complete absence of sincerity toward the victims of discrimination. Instead they behave repressively toward us.

2. The attitude of the authorities regarding this matter is alike in all the nation's regiments. This may be the result of confidential instructions issued by the army authorities.

3. The dispute over discrimination in the 24th Infantry Regiment has led to several victims of discrimination being cleverly framed by the police. They are about to be sent to prison.

May I petition Your Majesty to look into these situations and make your sacred wishes known.

Respectfully and Reverently,
Private Second Class
Kitahara Taisaku
68th Infantry Regiment
Company No. 5

On November 19, the day of the imperial review, Kitahara broke rank as his company was passing the emperor in review.

I ran up to a point several meters from the emperor, who was on horseback, and took a kneeling position. I then took out the petition from my pocket and raised it high in my left hand shouting, "A petition, a petition!" The emperor appeared to be baffled by this untoward occurrence and looked down at me from atop his horse with a puzzled look. The general who was on horseback behind the emperor (later I found out it was General Suzuki Sōroku, the chief of staff) was shocked and charged toward me with his saber uplifted shouting, "Arrest him, arrest him!" I was then grabbed from behind by a powerful pair of arms. When I looked around I saw Lieutenant Okuda's deathly pale face. His lips were trembling and he let out a groan and, grabbing me by my backpack, dragged me to a line to the left of the battalion. The cavalry troops under review marched in perfect formation as if nothing at all had happened. My action was a "happening" that lasted only five minutes. A military police officer and a noncommissioned officer rushed up to us and Lieutenant Okuda turned me over to them. I was put in a car and driven to the military police office in Nagoya.

For Kitahara to take the action that he did required real courage because the authorities had turned the emperor into a demigod totally secluded from the people. In the feudal period, those who made direct appeals to the *daimyō, shōgun,* or other high officials were executed. Often they were cut down on the spot. Kitahara, for all he knew, could have suffered a similar fate. In fact, he was tried by court martial and sentenced to one year in prison.

At his trial a member of the court asked him, "Did you not know that by commiting a crime of direct appeal you were getting your parents, sisters, and other people in trouble?" Kitahara replied, "The trouble that will visit my parents and sisters is a minor matter. It cannot be equated with the suffering of 3 million of my brothers and sisters. The people of the *buraku* are crying over the discrimination they are experiencing."

Kitahara succeeded in accomplishing one of his objectives; bringing the problem of discrimination against the *burakumin* to the attention of the entire nation. He did arouse the awareness and conscience of certain people, even if he did not succeed in lessening the prejudice that the masses harbored against the *burakumin.* The incident was given extensive publicity, and editorials were written condemning the evils of discrimination. But some people sought to denigrate

Kitahara's actions. For example, War Minister Ugaki Issei contended that Kitahara was merely interested in getting publicity for himself and that his supporters were using him to publicize their cause. He thought that the incident should be played down, but the army authorities did find it necessary to issue directives to division commanders instructing them to foster harmony between the *burakumin* soldiers and others. Suzuki Kisaburō, a right-wing home minister, issued directives to the prefectural governors asking them to foster harmonious relations and curb the use of discriminatory words and actions. Ultranationalist Hiranuma Kiichirō, who was active in the *yūwa* movement, also called for an end to discrimination.

After Kitahara was released from prison he joined the Suiheisha and continued to fight against discrimination.

THE

TEXTILE

FACTORY

WORKERS

When the Meiji government launched its program to "increase the wealth of the nation" *(fukoku)*, first among the industries that it sought to foster and build was the silk industry. Silk production had been an important luxury industry in Tokugawa Japan, but the market had been limited. Once, however, the country was opened to the West in the mid-nineteenth century, silk became Japan's most important export commodity. Thus, the government encouraged and supported the construction of modern silk filatures. The first such plant was established in 1870 in Gunma prefecture under the direction of a Swiss expert. In 1872, the government opened its own model plant in Tomioka in the same prefecture. The number of silk filatures increased rapidly and, before long, the region around Suwa Lake in Nagano prefecture became a flourishing center of silk production. By 1891, Nagano prefecture was producing 19 percent of the nation's raw silk, and, by 1911, 27 percent.[1]

The amount of raw silk produced in Japan jumped from 2.3 million pounds in 1868 to 10.2 million pounds in 1893. It accounted for 42 percent of Japan's exports.[2] The industry continued to grow and in the years from 1909 to 1913, annual production reached 27.9 million pounds. In 1897, 24 percent of the world's raw silk was produced in Japan, 39 percent in China, and 27 percent in Italy. By 1909, these figures had changed to 34 percent, 30.5 percent and 17.3 percent respectively.[3] The chief market for Japan's silk industry was the United States. In 1907–1908, 28.6 percent of Japan's silk exports were to the United States.[4]

The other industry that burgeoned once Japan began to industrialize was the cotton-textile industry. After a slow start because of foreign competition, the industry began to develop rapidly, and, in 1899, the production of Japanese cotton mills reached 355 million pounds of yarn. By 1913, it had risen to 672 million pounds, so that one fourth of the world's cotton-yarn exports came from Japan.[5]

Naturally, the growth of these industries entailed a rapid increase in the number of workers employed in silk and cotton plants. By 1919, it is estimated that over 300,000 workers were employed in silk filatures. If the number of people engaged in silk reeling in their homes is included, the real figure is estimated to have been well over a million.[6] A conservative estimate holds that about 800,000 workers were in the various textile industries in 1913.[7]

Escape from the Farm

The workers in the silk and cotton industries were mainly poorly paid female workers, in most cases very young girls from impoverished rural communities. When the model plants were first being built, however, at the beginning of the Meiji years, there was a degree of glamor and prestige attached to working in the modern plants. Thus, the Tomioka silk filature was staffed largely by girls of "good" families. Of the 371 girls employed there initially, 40 percent were from *shizoku* families.[8] Evidently, this situation came about because community leaders, asked by the authorities to recruit a certain number of girls for the plant, felt obligated to send their daughters and relatives to Tomioka.

At first, girls seem to have been reluctant to go to work in the new plant. A woman of *samurai* family background who was an exception wrote in her memoirs,

My father . . . was district head of Matsushiro in 1873. . . . The district heads of Shinshū [Nagano] were told by the prefectural office to supply a fixed number of girls (I believe it was sixteen) between the ages of thirteen and twenty-five from each district to work in the silk filature in Tomioka. People thought that they might be offered as human sacrifices to the gods, and no one volunteered. My father tried to encourage people in his district to send their daughters, but to no avail. They kept saying, "They're going to use the girls' blood," or "They're going to make use of their fat for oil." Some said, "The district head has a daughter of the right age, but he doesn't send her. That proves that the rumors are true." As a result, my father decided to send me to Tomioka. I had wanted to go to Tokyo to work in a muslin factory when one of my relatives went, but was not permitted to do so because I had to help at home taking care of my four younger brothers and sisters. I was feeling sorry about not being able to go to Tokyo, so I was delighted at this new opportunity and told my parents I would go even if I were the only one from our district. . . . Everything I heard about the work in Tomioka was positive. I heard I would be able to pursue learning, learn how to weave with machines, and so on. So I prepared to go to Tomioka full of joy and eagerness.[9]

The actual conditions turned out to be quite different, for the work was tedious and demanding.

As the need for workers ballooned, employers lost their concern about hiring girls from "good" families. They began to scour the countryside, at first near the factories, but eventually all over the country.

The employers favored young country girls because the work—reeling cocoon fibers or watching over weaving machines and spindles —could be performed by them, and at the same time they could be paid little and easily controlled, being normally docile and obedient. Sometimes girls as young as eight and nine were employed in these plants.

The girls' families were in most cases impoverished peasants. In 1910, 81 percent of the girl workers out of Yamanashi prefecture came from farm families that owned less than 7 *tan* of land (about 1.7 acres).[10] Noting the poverty of the families, one recruiter observed,

The farm families of Yamanashi prefecture were poorer than those of Gifu prefecture. None of the families had *tatami* mats, only straw mats, on their floors. During the Depression of the late twenties, these families incurred large debts by getting advance payments [on their daughters' contracts]. I tried not to make advance payments to extremely poor families, but often the entire family cried and begged me to do so. . . . These families subsisted mainly on *daikon* and corn. When the girls came to work in Okaya [on Lake Suwa] they could eat rice three times a day, even though it was poor-quality imported rice, so they were very pleased.[11]

For the impoverished peasants, employment for their daughters in the silk and cotton plants soon became an essential source of income. The advance payment they received to send their daughters out to work as virtual indentured servants enabled them to pay their rent and defray their daily living expenses. The terms of the contract were often stringent and exploitative, but most of the parents were illiterate and affixed their seals to the contracts without being fully aware of the terms. For example, a contract agreed to by a father of a young girl sent to work in a silk plant in Suwa in 1893 provided for the girl's employment for six months. The company paid him 1 yen in advance. The agreement prohibited the girl from seeking employment with another firm during the period of the contract. If she broke the agreement, her father was obligated to compensate the company for all expenses plus 20 yen as punitive compensation. Her salary was to be fixed by the company in accordance with the prevailing rate in the industry.[12] Another contract issued by a silk plant in Suwa gave the employer the right to dismiss the worker at his convenience, but, if the employee wished to quit, she was required not only to return the 5 yen advance payment but also to pay 50 yen in compensation and forfeit whatever pay she had coming to her.[13]

When such a long-term contract was signed, the company turned over a considerable sum of money as an advance payment to the father. For a contract extending from five to seven years, for example, the advance payment in some cases came to 200 or even 300 yen, which in the late nineteenth and early twentieth centuries amounted to a considerable sum of money.[14] "My father got an advance of 200 yen and sent me and my younger sister to work in a plant in Kawagishi," an old retired silk reeler in Nagano recalled. "He then built a house with the money." Around 1906, 100 yen could finance construction of a two-story house or two one-story houses.[15]

WAGES

In the early years of the silk industry, the girl workers often received only room and board, one or two items of clothing, and a few sen a day. The parents saw this as sufficient compensation especially since many were more interested in reducing the number of people they had to feed at home than in the welfare of those they sent away to work. However, such low wages were not only an immediate but also a long-term problem, for it took the workers years to pay off the advance payments their parents had received, particularly if the sum had been large.

A woman, born in 1873, who went to work when she was eleven, recalled, "I worked for one year and got 1 yen. In the old days we were sent out to reduce the number of people who had to be fed at home, so we didn't complain about the pay. We could eat rice, and that alone made it better than staying at home." Another woman who went to work when she was twelve, in 1884, said, "I worked one year and was given the boss's wife's old kimono. When we first started to work, we hardly got any money at all."[16]

Documents in the Okaya Municipal office show that in 1875 a superior worker was paid 9 yen 22 sen a year. By 1880, that wage had increased to 17 yen 69 sen a year. One plant in that area paid the average worker 13 sen a day; this was in 1877, but four years later, in 1881, very little had changed: It paid 20 sen to its best workers and 4.5 sen to third-rate workers. In 1883, in the government-operated Tomioka filature, the average pay was 11.4 sen.[17]

The price of rice in 1877 was 3.7 sen for 1 *shō* (0.476 gallons). The average pay for workers in the Edo period was estimated at the equivalent of 3 *shō* of rice per day. In 1876, the daily wage of a road construction worker was about 12.5 sen, so if the workers in the silk plants received 10–12 sen a day they were receiving average pay.[18] In many cases, however, the workers were not paid the stipulated wages; nor were they paid on a regular weekly or monthly basis. Instead, the company kept a record of their earnings and paid them at the end of the year, after deducting the amount that was advanced to their fathers, as well as whatever other company expenses the workers had incurred. One company's records show that, for 1891, the total earnings of the girl workers, after advance payments and other expenses had been deducted, ranged from 4 yen 30 sen to 21 yen 50 sen.[19]

Wages rose with length of service and job performance. One girl who started work at the age of 14 in 1892 received 2 yen the first year, 20 yen the next, 50 yen the third, and over 100 yen after the fifth year. A girl who started work at 13, in 1907, earned 5 yen the first year. This went up each successive year to 12, 50, 120, 125, and 135 yen.[20]

If a family managed to send several daughters to work and if they turned out to be top wage earners, they did exceedingly well financially. Five sisters who went to Suwa from the Hida region in Gifu prefecture in the 1890s brought home 600 yen at the end of one year. "Our father bought some rice paddies each year with the money we brought home," one of the sisters recalled. "In those days 1 *tan* cost 100 to 150 yen."[21] But these girls were exceptional cases. The company records of one silk plant show that, in 1909, ten of its thirty-seven workers owed the company money at the end of the year. Five of the workers earned less than 10 yen before the advance payment and other debts were deducted. One-third of the workers earned between 10 and 30 yen. Nine earned more than 50 yen, with two earning about 90 yen. But after deductions were made, the year-end take-home pay was less than 5 yen for seventeen of the workers, and ten of these wound up in debt, while another four earned less than 1 yen. Only two went home with more than 50 yen at the year's end.[22]

In the cotton industry the wages also remained low. For instance, an 1898 survey of sixty-two cotton-textile plants showed that the average monthly pay for women workers was 4.05 yen, and for men, 6.83. The average for both sexes together came to 4.67 yen. This was lower than what the textile workers in India earned in the same period. A survey of Indian workers in seven major textile firms showed that their wages ranged from equivalents of 8.07 yen to 9.18 yen a month.[23]

In 1893, a reporter who visited a plant that was regarded as a model cotton-spinning mill found that the workers, who put in twelve-hour shifts, were receiving wages as low or lower than silk-filature workers. Only 2 girls out of 1,600 workers received 22 sen a day; 200 or so earned 11 sen or more; most were paid 8 to 10 sen; some earned as little as 4 sen.[24]

The low wages of the workers were justified by one entrepreneur in terms of supply and demand:

Where do the cheap workers come from? They all come from the farming communities. . . . People from families that are working their own land, or are engaged in tenant farming but have surplus workers, come to the cities and the industrial centers to become factory workers. . . . Income from the farms provides for the family needs and subsistence of the parents and siblings. The person who takes employment in the factory is an unattached component of the family. All he or she has to do is earn enough to maintain his or her own living. This is why the workers' wages are low. This shows how important a force agriculture is for the development of our nation's commerce and industry.[25]

An ardent advocate of industrialization, Fukuzawa Yukichi, admitted in 1893 that Japanese textile workers were being paid one-tenth the wages of their British counterparts but contended that cheap labor was necessary to enable Japanese businessmen to compete effectively with the entrepreneurs of the advanced Western nations.[26]

It is true that the money the workers brought home at the end of the year was a godsend. Those who managed to bring back over 100 yen were celebrated as "hundred-yen factory women." A priest from the Hida region, where many farm girls went to work in the silk mills of Okaya, remarked,

The money that the factory girls brought back by climbing over Nomugi Pass was often more than a "water-drinking" farmer's income for the entire year. For these families, the girls were an invaluable source of income. The poor peasants of those days had to turn 60 percent of their yield over to the landlord. Thus, the peasants had only broken bits of rice mixed with weeds for food. . . . The poor peasants of this region had a saying: "Shall I hang myself or cross Nomugi Pass?" These were the only alternatives they had. Their only salvation was the girls who went to work in the factories.[27]

But the benefits these families derived were obtained from the "blood, sweat, and tears" of the girls, who had to endure hardships, abuse, and ill health to help their families.

CROSSING NOMUGI PASS

The girl workers who were recruited in the mountain villages of Hida to work in the silk mills around Lake Suwa had to make a long trek on foot over the steep pass at Nomugi. In mid-winter, they returned to celebrate New Year's in their home villages, going through deep, nearly impassable snow. In the middle of February girls from all over the Hida region gathered at the city of Takayama to head for the Suwa region. Many were only eleven or twelve years old. When they got to Nomugi Pass it would still be covered with snow and ice. One old woman recalled,

Nomugi Pass is where many factory girls fell down into the ravine. When someone slipped and fell down, we would untie our sashes, tie them together to make a rope, and lower it down to the person in the ravine. . . . I can't tell you how many girls died in that ravine. . . . We used to tie ourselves to the girls ahead of us so as not to get left behind. Each step of the way we prayed for our lives.[28]

They walked as much as 35 *ri* (about 85 miles), climbing up and down mountain passes for four to five days, before they arrived at their destination.[29] At the end of the year, when the pass was covered with several feet of snow they would retrace their steps to go home to Hida. One woman remembered the trip this way:

The wish to make my parents happy with the money I earned with my tears during the year . . . made me cross Nomugi Pass at the end of the year full of joyous expectations. I used to walk 85 miles over the pass in my straw sandals to come home. We didn't have mittens in those days, so we tucked our hands in our sleeves, linked ourselves together with cords, and crossed the pass.[30]

"Now, I have forgotten all the hardships of those days," another woman remarked. "All I remember are the pleasant things. But sometimes I dream about crossing Nomugi Pass or about being punished at Suwa, and I start crying and wake up with a start."[31]

The strenuous work, low pay, and unhealthy conditions of the factories and their dormitories no doubt seem much worse to us who view things from the vantage point of the late twentieth century than they did to the girl workers themselves. There were, however, serious abuses and sufferings that on occasion ended in suicide, so it is not just modern social critics who view the industrial plants of the postrestoration decades as being less than satisfactory. Nonetheless, former factory workers interviewed in their old age about their experiences in the mills often said, "I didn't think the work was so hard." Many said they preferred factory work to farm work in their home villages. The girls who were left behind in the villages looked with envy upon the girls who were sent off to the city factories. On occasion, Hida girls even ran away from home to seek work in the silk filatures of Okaya.[32]

Yamamoto Shigemi, who studied the lives of these girls who came out of the mountain villages of Hida, found that none of them, as old women, complained about the food or pay in the mills. Of the several hundred women he interviewed, only 3 percent complained about the long hours they had worked. Most of them said that factory work was easier than farm work.[33] Time makes bad memories fade away, so his survey may not be a true representation of how these women had felt at the time they were working in the plants. Moreover, a weeding-out process had already taken place. These people had survived the "ordeal." Many who were less hardy had fallen by the wayside, dying of tuberculosis or even committing suicide.

Nonetheless, the farm must have suffered by comparison. One old woman who regretted not having managed to go to work in Okaya described her life this way: "I stayed . . . without friends, and . . . burned the hillside to open up some farmland to grow grass and millet. . . . I used to walk 2 *ri* [about 5 miles] on a mountain road, covered with snow up to my hips, with a sack of rice and a box of flour on my back. . . . I worked beside six men and raised six children [while doing the same work as men]."[34]

The girls in the silk plants evidently dreaded more than anything else the thought of being sent back to the farm. A verse in a silk-reelers' song says:

Reel the threads, young girl, reel the threads.
If you don't reel threads, I'll make you wear straw coats [what farmers wore in the field].

Another verse read:

When I left Hida, I left in tears,
   but now I don't even long for the breeze in Hida.
When I leave Suwa, the town of hot water,
   I look back once, and go back twice.[35]

The people from Hida claimed that work in the silk filatures of Suwa was easier and paid better than work in the traditional weavers' shops in Kyoto. Work in the Suwa region paid more money than the work done by the woodcutters and stonecutters in Hida.[36]

Modern writers and scholars looking at the kind of food provided the workers in the dormitories of the silk mills find it poor and inadequate, but to the girls themselves, used to so much worse, it was more than satisfactory. (See the table in footnote 33.) One person who grew up in the hills of Hida recalled the sort of diet that the girls had experienced in their villages. "In the old days we used to put a big pot of tea on the fire, and the whole family would ladle the tea out and pour it on sorghum powder. That was our staple. Some families added bran to increase the volume. Then we had a little millet rice."[37]

By comparison, the typical factory diet, which looked so good to these farm girls, consisted of rice, bean paste soup, pickles or tofu, and occasionally bits of fish.[38] Still, peasant girls who came from other regions to work in cotton mills also found the food better than what they had had in their villages.[39] This does not mean that the life of the girls who worked in the silk and cotton mills of postrestoration Japan was easy. If we consider the fact that many of the girls who were herded into the factories were very young, some younger than ten, we cannot say that the conditions were adequate even by nineteenth-century standards. Their poor health record attests to this. Laws to protect women and children in mines and factories were being enacted in the West by the middle of the nineteenth century, and it should not have been unreasonable for the leaders of Japan who were bent upon "modernizing" the nation to emulate Western nations and introduce a modicum of worker protection. But not until 1916, when the Factory Act of 1911 actually went into effect, was a minimal degree of restraint placed on the use of child labor in the factories. Even then, many employers used underaged children illegally, concealing them when factory inspectors came around.[40]

Life in the Suwa
Silk Filatures

The work that most of the girls performed in the silk filatures involved locating the ends of the thread of several cocoons which had been steamed so that they could be unraveled, and reeling the threads onto a spinning frame. This required a delicate touch to prevent the threads from breaking into bits and pieces, and the number of threads wound together on the frame had to be just right so that the raw-silk fibers would be of uniform size. The workers also had to be careful not to let the cocoons get oversteamed; otherwise the raw silk would loose its luster and be unmarketable as high-grade silk.[41] Consequently, the work of the silk reelers was closely supervised, with the plants introducing a system of grading the employees' work that became a nightmarish experience for most workers.

Because the steam from the hot water in which the cocoons were soaking permeated the entire plant, its interior was smelly, wet, and hot. It was also noisy. Working conditions in cotton textile plants were even worse. Moisture was needed to strengthen the cotton fibers, so the interior of the factory was kept moist with sprays of mist. As a result, the workers were constantly exposed to damp air, heat, and noise. In addition, the air was filled with lint. It was estimated that in a ten-hour period a textile worker inhaled 0.12 gram of lint. These conditions accounted for the high incidence of tuberculosis in these factories.[42]

A woman who had worked in a plant in Suwa recalled:

From morning, while it was still dark, we worked in the lamplit factory till ten at night. After work, we hardly had the strength to stand on our feet. When we worked late into the night, they occasionally gave us a yam. We then had to do our washing, fix our hair, and so on. By then it would be eleven o'clock. There was no heat even in the winter, and so we had to sleep huddled together. Several of the girls ran back to Hida. I was told that girls who went to work before my time had a harder time. We were not paid the first year. In the second year I got 35 yen, and the following year, 50 yen. I felt that it was not a place for a weak-willed person like me. If we didn't do the job right we were scolded, and, if we did better than others, the others resented it. The life of a woman is really awful.[43]

A study conducted by the government in 1900 revealed that a normal work day in a plant in Okaya was thirteen to fourteen hours.

During the busy season, the workers were roused from their beds at 4:05 A.M., sent to work from 4:30 to 6, given fifteen minutes for breakfast, and sent back to work by 6:15. They were allowed fifteen minutes for lunch, between 10:30 and 10:45, and a ten-minute break from 3:30 to 3:40. Otherwise they were kept on the job till 7:30 for a total of fourteen hours and twenty minutes. When the plant was particularly busy, the workers were kept until 10 P.M.[44] Workers in the cotton-spinning plants also put in long workdays. Before the factory act went into effect in 1916, their workday averaged twelve hours, and those in cotton-textile plants worked a fourteen-hour day.[45]

The Factory Act of 1911 (see p. 181) placed a twelve-hour limit—including a one-hour rest period—per workday on women and on youngsters under the age of fifteen, and fixed the minimum employment age at twelve. For light work, however, the minimum age was fixed at ten.[46] Employers were allowed to exceed the twelve-hour limit by two hours, when necessary. The law also allowed an additional hour's extension in the busy season, which covered one hundred twenty days a year. So the workday in busy periods still remained fourteen to fifteen hours. As for the one-hour rest period that the law mandated, many employers counted the three meal periods as rest periods.[47]

While the silk-filature workers were on the job, they were under intense pressure to produce quality work at a fast pace. In order to compel the workers to produce faster and better work, the companies devised various ways to prod them. One company divided the workers into teams and made them compete for recognition as superior teams. The foreman of the winning team was given a bonus made up of money collected from a penalty imposed on teams performing poorly. This caused the foremen to apply immense pressure on the workers on their teams, in some cases abusing and beating those who did not comply with their demands.[48]

As the competition among the silk-filature companies got stiffer, the owners drove the workers ever more relentlessly. Absence from work because of sickness was looked upon as "malingering" and workers were not allowed to take time off for any other reason.

The part of their work that the workers found most onerous was quality control. At the end of each day, the performance of each worker was checked, and the silk's sheen, denier, and texture were evaluated. Workers were particularly fearful the cocoon fiber would snap into small bits, in which case they would be reprimanded severely for wastefulness. One veteran silk reeler explained the difficulty facing the workers:

The end of the cocoon fiber is visible, but inexperienced workers and those with poor eyesight had difficulty finding it. So they would use a small brush to scratch the cocoon [to find the end], which often shredded the cocoon fibers, however. If this happened, the workers were bawled out. Also we were instructed to entwine the fibers evenly, but an inexperienced worker would carelessly twine several fibers together, causing the silk thread to be uneven and have knotted spots. Also, when the cocoons were steamed too long, they lost their luster and the fibers tended to break. It really was a difficult task.[49]

A worker's pay was determined according to the rating given by the inspector. It was said, "A dagger is not needed to kill a girl worker. Just choke her to death with the texture and fineness of the fiber."[50]

The same kind of stringent quality control was enforced in the cotton-textile plants. Usually workers' performances fell into one of four categories. Those whose work was graded A received their full wages, but those with B ratings suffered a 20 percent reduction; those with C ratings a 50 percent reduction; and those at the bottom, a 100 percent reduction.[51]

The long hours and the pressure to work fast and still produce high-quality work, coupled with the absence of safety measures led to frequent accidents in the factories, particularly in the textile plants. The employers ascribed the accidents to carelessness on the part of their workers. The Factory Act of 1911 was passed under this assumption, and, consequently, no provisions were included to ensure the safety of the workers.[52]

The high accident rate is seen in the records of factory after factory. For example, in a textile plant employing 400 workers in the 1920s, 224 minor and major accidents occurred in a single year. Another plant, employing about 8,000 workers, reported 1,572 accidents in a twenty-three-month period.[53]

RESTRICTIONS, CONTROLS, AND ABUSES

In the early years of the silk and cotton industries, restrictions on the personal lives of the workers were not as stringent as they later became. But when competition for skilled workers got stiffer and strenuous conditions led some workers to run away from the plants, tight controls were imposed on the workers. Since they had come from afar, most of the girl workers were housed in company-run dormitories. The companies preferred such resident workers to commuters because they could maintain closer control over them.

Strict hours were maintained in the dormitories and the girls were not allowed to come and go as they pleased. This was done, the employers claimed, to protect the girls and also to keep them safe from exposure to diseases prevalent on the outside.[54] Like women college students of yore, those who were late returning to the dorms or broke other rules were deprived of the right to leave the dorms at all for weeks, even on special occasions, while those with good records might be allowed to step out of the dorm a number of times a month. Many did not get out of the dorms until the end of the year when they were allowed to visit their homes for New Year's. In order to keep the girls confined, factories built tall fences around the compounds—much like those of a prison camp. In fact, factory girls used to sing:

Working in a factory is like working in a prison,
The only difference is the absence of iron chains.[55]

Nor were the girls allowed to have visitors whenever they wished. Some employers even censored the letters the girls sent home, to make certain that unfavorable remarks that might adversely affect the recruitment of additional workers were not contained in them. To ensure that contaminated food did not enter the dorms, it was also a common practice to check the packages the girls received. Material from rival companies that might lure workers away was anxiously ferreted out. Books, magazines, and newspapers were also censored to make sure that subversive ideas did not filter in. This became, for the employers, a matter of urgent concern, especially after efforts to organize unions commenced in the 1920s.[56]

This kind of "benevolent" paternalism by plant owners extended into the the girls' private lives. No doubt to some extent because they felt responsible to the parents of the girls, employers were anxious to prevent the young workers from having relations with members of the opposite sex, and condemned any display of affection between young men and women as foul and obscene behavior. One unfortunate girl was punished by her employer for having fallen in love and used up her savings on her lover. This policy seems to have been motivated in part by a practical wish on the part of the companies to keep female workers from getting married and thus leaving them.[57]

Slackening the work pace or inattentiveness on the job often resulted in severe punishment by the foremen. A former textile-plant worker reported one such story of a girl who was punished for having fallen asleep on the job. As punishment, the foreman made the girl hold up bales of cotton while standing at attention. He then left for his rest period and didn't return for some time. When the foreman returned, he saw that the girl had been unable to hold up the bales properly, as he had ordered, and slapped her. The girl was staggered by this and dropped the bales on the floor, one of which hit the foreman's foot. He lost his temper and gave her a shove. The girl fell upon the teeth of the spinning wheels and was ground to death. The company reported her death as an accident caused by her carelessness.[58] It was commonplace for foremen to slap girl workers, and any foreman or supervisor who was too kind-hearted to punish the girls was seen as being unfit for his job.[59]

A 1906 government report by investigators looking into conditions in the factories includes the following dialogue between the investigators and women factory workers:

Q: Do you get scolded?
A: We are taken to a room next to the office and are reprimanded there. We are also beaten. And, until we show a change of heart, we are kept there in the dark for several days.
Q: Are you fed?
A: No.
Q: Are there other forms of punishment?
A: If anyone steals something she is stripped naked and marched around the factory with a flag attached to her shoulders. They then take her to the dining hall and report her misdeed to everybody. . . . This spring a girl in the next room took *geta* [wooden clogs], which her roommate purchased for 70 sen. She was stripped naked, had the *geta* and a red flag bearing the words *"geta* thief" strapped to her shoulders, and was then marched around the factory.
Q: Do youngsters of seven and eight work only during the day or do they work at night, too?
A: They work at night, too. Since the supervisors are strict during the day, the children clean up the plant. But at night things are less closely supervised, so they don't do much cleaning. Even in the winter we wear only one unlined kimono.
Q: Do young workers work through the night?

A: They do but sometimes they say they will not go to work unless they are given some candy. So the officials give them some. But if they ask for candy often, they are not given any. They go to work crying.

Q: Do they fall asleep in the factory?

A: If they fall asleep they are scolded and beaten.

Q: Do they get paid?

A: They are paid 8 sen. Then 7 sen is deducted for food, so they get only 1 sen.

Q: Are children charged 7 sen, too?

A: They are charged the same amount [for food as the adults].

Q: Are there many young children:

A: There are about ten workers who are seven or eight. There are many who are ten years old.[60]

The more serious abuses occurred in the small plants operated by grasping entrepreneurs who treated their employees like slaves. The 1901 government report mentioned earlier included an account of a man who operated a small textile plant in a village in a secluded area of Saitama prefecture. He employed twenty-four female workers ranging in age from fourteen to twenty-five. The workers were locked inside the plant and were forced to work until they finished producing a fixed quota, often from 5 A.M. well into the night. Those who failed to meet their quotas were deprived of their meals. One worker, who was finally blinded by the abuses inflicted on her, reported that she tried to run away twice but was caught each time and, as punishment, was stripped naked, tied up, and beaten with an iron rod. After she was released and sent back to work, she was punished over and over for failing to meet her quota. Each time she was stripped naked, tied up, and beaten. She was even stripped naked and shoved into the excrement pot. When she tried to hide from her employer, she was dragged through the snow by her hair and then made to stand in the snow for an hour. She was also burned with moksa weed, deprived of food, and her frostbitten feet were jabbed with an iron rod. In the course of these abuses her eyes got infected, but she was locked, untreated, in a small shack until she lost her eyesight completely.[61]

RUNAWAYS AND SUICIDE

There was a saying in Suwa, "There are days when the crows do not cry, but there's not a single day when female factory workers do not run away."[62] Whenever a worker ran away, the employer sent out a team of men to recapture her. The companies often used male workers to help recapture the runaway girls. In Okaya men were sent out on horseback to key passes to waylay the girls trying to return to their home villages. One male worker recalled:

Come to think of it, it was ironical, because we young boys also felt like running away, but we had to go chasing after the girl workers who were trying to run away. . . . When I caught two girls—Fumi [eighteen] and Ise [eighteen], both of whom had come from Hida near Nomugi Pass—at the Shiojiri station, they cried and begged me to let them go. I was nineteen and naïve then, so I told them I would lose face if I let them go, and asked them to please return to the plant for my sake, but they said they would not go back even if they were killed. I told them that if I let them go I'd be fired, but they wouldn't listen to me. So I told them I'd let them go but to please come back in two or three days . . . but the girls did not come back. I heard later that the company garnisheed the girls' families' entire summer cocoon harvest.[63]

Around the turn of the century a Nagano newspaper reported that three sisters—aged sixteen, nineteen, and twenty-one—had been employed in a silk filature in Okaya but because of their inexperience their performance was not satisfactory, so the foremen constantly harassed them. The youngest and most timid of the sisters was cowed by the foreman and her performance got worse, so the foreman beat her up. "As a result, the girl appeared to have become emotionally unbalanced and she cried hysterically and fell into convulsions. . . . The doctor recommended that she rest for a couple of days, but she was forced to go back to work before she had fully recovered. The foreman continued to harass her, so the sisters decided to run away. They then reported the abuses to the Kamisuwa police."[64] Such accounts appeared frequently in connection with cotton-textile workers also. At least those who tried to run away had the will to fight an oppressive system, but many others lost all hope and committed suicide.

In the silk plants in the Suwa region, despairing girls often committed suicide by jumping onto the giant waterwheels in the Tenryū River. These were used to operate the machines in the plants. One young worker, who had been beaten by the foreman for taking off from work because of illness, committed suicide in this fashion, leaving a note to her parents saying, "I am sorry that I have not yet been able to repay the debt owed the company. Please forgive me for being

a disloyal daughter, but my body is no longer of any use. Good-bye."
She was then sixteen years old and had been working in the plant for
four years. Her father had borrowed 200 yen in advance and had
hired her out on a five-year contract.[65]

The authorities were placed in an embarrassing position when, in
the fall of 1906, a member of the imperial family visited the Suwa
region. While some fishermen were demonstrating their skill with a
net, they caught the corpse of a girl who had committed suicide in
Lake Suwa. They quickly lowered the body and later hid it, but they
were reprimanded by the authorities for allowing such an inauspicious
incident to occur on that special occasion, even though the prince was
not aware of what had happened.[66] The steady increase in the number
of workers committing suicide in Lake Suwa led one early Taishō
scholar to say sarcastically that the lake was getting shallow because
the water was being drained away by the bloated bodies of the suicide
victims.

HOUSING AND HEALTH

In both the Meiji and Taishō eras, about 70 percent of the female
workers in the silk and cotton industry lived in factory-run dormitories. In 1913, a medical specialist working for the Ministry of the
Interior, Ishiwara Osamu, reported:

From what I have heard, in the West the owners try to employ people living
in the area where the factory is built. In Japan the opposite is true. The
owners show no interest in the people living in the area. They bring in
women and children from distant places and put them in dormitories. This
has a profound relationship to the prevalence of tuberculosis in the country.

Many factories—in fact, the Japanese industrial world in general—prefer
to use female workers who are housed in company dormitories. It is difficult
to ensure the regular attendance of commuting workers, and this hampers
the operation of the machines, which must function at a regular pace. Com-
mutors may decide to take time off from the plant because of work at home,
laziness, a desire to attend local festivals, or sickness. The dormitory system
is a system of detention. It restricts the free will of the workers.[67]

The female workers were lodged in spacious rooms accommodating
twenty to fifty of their number. Each worker was allotted about 1
tatami of space (about 3 feet by 6 feet). With so many people crowded
into dormitories where washing and sanitary facilities were inade-

quate, the rooms were often infested with bedbugs and lice. Disease spread very rapidly among the dorm residents. Usually two people were required to use the same bedding, and newcomers were allocated bedding that had been used by others. So the bedding itself contributed to the spread of disease,[68] the most prevalent of which was tuberculosis. Female workers in these plants were especially susceptible to tuberculosis because they were still quite young. Most were between fifteen and twenty years old, and the next highest age group was twenty to twenty-five. Thirty-eight percent of the silk-filature workers in Nagano prefecture were in the seventeen-to-twenty age group.[69]

In 1913, Ishiwara, the medical specialist from the Ministry of the Interior spoke of the high incidence of tuberculosis among the silk-filature and cotton-textile workers. He pointed out that, of the then 190,000 workers in silk filatures, 80,000 in cotton-spinning mills, and 130,000 in textile-manufacturing plants, nearly half failed to stay on their jobs for more than one year. Though they left for numerous reasons, 24 percent quit specifically because of illness, and another 5 percent due to other physical difficulties. "One out of six or seven of those who return to the villages do so in ill health. . . . This comes to about 13,000 people. Of these, one-fourth, or 3,000, have tuberculosis," reported Ishiwara.[70] He estimated that, out of 1,000 female silk- and cotton-plant workers housed in dormitories, 13 died there of sickness and another 10 after they returned home. This mortality rate of 23 out of every 1,000 is significantly higher than the ratio of 7 out of 1,000 for girls and women in the same age group (twelve to thirty-five) in the general populace.[71] Tuberculosis was responsible for the deaths of 40 percent of those who died while working at the plants, and of 70 percent of those who died after returning to their villages.[72] In one village, of the 304 girls and women who went into the silk plants, 22 died in a single five-and-half-year period. Of these, 17 died of tuberculosis.[73]

Tuberculosis almost always ended in death, and the factory owners did little to help the victims. Their solution was to send them home; that is, to abandon them, since they were no longer usable. The story of these victims was always tragic.

In the fall of 1907, several sick girls were sent back from Okaya to Hida over Nomugi Pass. One old woman recalled:

Soon after I went to work in the Yamaichi silk factory in Shinshū [Nagano prefecture], my younger sister Aki came to work there, too. I think she worked for about two years. Then she took to bed because of peritonitis. At that time there were about thirty sick people. Those who clearly had lung trouble were sent home right away. . . . Everybody feared tuberculosis and no one would come near such patients. My sister Aki was also sent home before long, and she died soon after. She was in her thirteenth year. She had come to the factory determined to become a 100 yen worker and make our mother happy. I can never forget her sad eyes as she left the factory wan and pale. . . . It would be impossible, I felt, for a person as sick as she was to travel over 30 *ri* or more and cross Nomugi Pass. But they would not let her stay in the factory. There was no money to send her to the hospital. There was nothing for her to do but go home.[74]

A man who was sent to fetch his sick younger sister gave this account:

I hurried to the factory and found my younger sister Shige was in bed and very pale. The people at the factory told me she would get well soon if she returned home and rested. But as soon as I saw Shige's face I realized that her condition was serious. She had peritonitis and her stomach was bloated; she seemed to be in agony. I believe the factory gave us a bit of money before we set out for home, but I can't remember for certain. The railroad ran part of the way, but from the end of the line we walked home slowly, taking about ten days. When we came to the mountain passes, I carried her on my back. We finally arrived in Takayama. From there I hired a rickshaw and made it home. Her condition did not improve. We caught some leeches in the rice field and placed them on her stomach to let them suck out the poison, but she didn't recover. There was no cure in those days.[75]

A former foreman remarked, "Even if female factory workers got sick, they seldom saw a doctor unless their condition was grave. Doctors' fees were comparatively high in those days, so the little money the workers had earned would have vanished in a minute. . . . The only medication the girls got was the medicine their folks had purchased from the medicine peddlers."[76]

Workers who contracted tuberculosis and returned to their villages were the carriers through which tuberculosis became the major killer in rural Japan. The villages were particularly vulnerable to its spread because it had previously been a relatively rare disease and people had not built up any resistance to it. Their poor living conditions and diet only increased their susceptibility to the disease.[77] Ishiwara reports, "In one village of fifty households, a young man who had gone to work in a spinning factory returned home with tuberculosis and died.

In five years' time, thirty people in the village had also died of tuberculosis. My friend made a study of an inland village in Miyagi prefecture. According to his study, in one short time span, thirty female factory workers returned to the village; of these, twenty-one had come back because they were sick, and fifteen or sixteen had tuberculosis."[78]

Speaking of the spread of tuberculosis from the silk and cotton mills, one man in Nagano prefecture commented: "Regardless of which hamlet one visited, one would find several people afflicted with 'lung disease,' and they were cooped up in shacks. When we were youngsters we would pass such places holding our noses. Now, I realize what pathetic victims they were."[79] A woman born in 1904 recollected:

I wanted to go to Nagano to become a silk reeler, but my father objected and I wasn't able to go. I can't forget how envious I was of my friends who returned on New Year's dressed in colorful kimonos, but many also returned as victims of tuberculosis. That was the reason my father had opposed my going to work in the silk factories. My cousin . . . came back from Okaya and died. Several of my friends died one after another with TB. . . . Tuberculosis was known as an incurable disease, and they all seemed resigned to the fact that they were going to die.[80]

People feared tuberculosis "and would not go near the sick. Every family tried to hide the fact that a family member had TB. . . . People used to worry that Hida would be destroyed by tuberculosis."[81] One recruiter went to visit a girl who had fallen victim to tuberculosis and found her "in a storeroom without windows. When I opened the door I was shocked by what I saw. Only a dim light came in from a small hole in the wall. Mizu was lying down as if she were dead. An awful odor permeated the room and a frightful atmosphere saturated the place. In those days, when a member of a family got tuberculosis no one would marry anyone else in the family. So everybody tried their best to hide the fact."[82]

Of course, the silk- and cotton-plant workers contracted other ailments as well. Beriberi was prevalent among them, a symptom of the poor nutritional balance in their diet. A general survey taken of female workers in the silk and cotton industry in 1910 revealed that 28.3 percent of the deaths in the cotton-spinning industry, 22.1 percent in the cotton-textile industry, and 11.5 percent in the silk filatures were due to beriberi.[83] No doubt because of intense work pressures and insufficient time allotted for meals, deaths resulting from gastrointestinal troubles were also prevalent (25.9 percent of the deaths among silk filature workers, and 24.6 percent among textile workers).[84] When epidemics of cholera broke out, they too spread very swiftly among the workers.

The Reform Movement

Because the vast majority of female workers in the silk and cotton industries came from impoverished peasant families located in remote villages, they were provincial in their outlook, unsophisticated, and poorly educated. In fact, in the early Meiji years most of the girls had no schooling at all. An 1898 Okaya City survey showed that, of the 1,221 silk-plant workers in that area, 840 had never attended school, 104 had one year of schooling, and only 42 had completed the four years of compulsory elementary education. Only 112 could read the simplest phonetic script. As a result, those who were literate were in great demand as letter writers for their co-workers.[85]

With the swift growth of the silk and cotton industries, however, employers began to make enticing offers to attract workers to their plants. "The recruiter promised us that once we got to the factory we would be taught how to perform the tea ceremony, flower arranging, sewing, and other arts that a girl should know, but in fact they did not teach us anything," recalled one woman.[86] Though in the twentieth century the better-established companies did provide some schooling for their workers, the focus was on practical education and the inculcation of "proper values", such as loyalty to the company.[87] Classes were usually held after work, between seven and nine at night.

Because of their poor education, as well as their tradition of bowing to authority and accepting one's place at the bottom of the social hierarchy, female factory workers were on the whole docile, submissive, and obedient. Not only did they lack the kind of aggressive individualism needed to challenge the existing order of things, they were imbued with a strong work ethic and a belief that "people are born into this world to work." They also had a strong sense of filial piety that led them, for the sake of their parents and family to enter willingly what was in effect indentured service and often to endure otherwise intolerable difficulties.[88]

Not all female workers, however, remained docile and submissive. Some did begin to believe that they had rights, and to challenge their employers. The first tenuous effort at this occurred in 1886 when more than a hundred workers in a silk filature in Yamanashi prefecture protested the plant owner's plan to extend the workday thirty minutes (to fourteen hours and thirty minutes) and at the same time reduce pay 10 sen a day. On this occasion, the workers succeeded in gaining concessions from their employer. In 1889, women workers in a cotton-spinning plant in Osaka went on strike for about a week demanding a pay raise. The company struck back, getting the police to disperse the assembly of workers and threatening to dismiss the strikers. A compromise settlement was arrived at, with the workers accepting the employer's agreement to raise wages in accordance with the performance of each worker.[89] In 1894, the workers of the same plant again went on strike demanding the dismissal of three supervisors. This strike ended in the arrest and indictment of the strike leaders.[90]

Strikes began to increase in all sectors of Japanese industry after the Sino-Japanese War of 1894–1895. In 1897, thirty-two strikes were recorded; and in 1898, forty-two strikes were staged, including a couple in the silk filatures. This increase was partly the result of greater activity by labor organizers who had returned from San Francisco where they had been exposed to U.S. labor movements.[91]

The need to enact laws to regulate the employment of women and children in the factories and mines was recognized by government officials. In the early 1880s bureaucrats in the Ministry of Agriculture and Commerce started working on draft legislation to deal with the problem. However, their efforts were blocked by business-community opposition. After the war with China, reform-minded bureaucrats began to push harder for restrictions on the use of women and children in factories and mines, and also for the establishment of a standard workday; but still they met resistance.

In 1896, the government convened a meeting between top bureaucrats concerned with economic affairs and business and financial leaders to discuss the need for such factory legislation. The government officials buttressed their arguments by pointing out that some sort of legislation was necessary to prevent socialistic movements from gaining support. The business community, led by industrial tycoon Shibuzawa Eiichi, argued that the work hours then prevalent were not beyond the ability of workers to withstand. Night work, they pointed out, was also necessary because of the economics of keeping the machines operating both day and night.[92] The first conference failed to produce a meeting of minds. A second meeting, held in 1897, also ended in a deadlock. A third conference resulted in agreement on a very innocuous draft plan that was not even submitted to the Diet.

One of the proponents of this legislation observed that he had visited textile factories where children younger than ten were tending machines they could not even leave to eat their meals. He also observed that the dormitories were unsanitary and smelled atrocious. The ill effects that these conditions were having on the health of the young workers, he remarked, made him worry that Japan's population would decline. An opponent of the same legislation argued that the use of young children in the factories fostered a spirit of enterprise in them. "In the match factories of Kobe, children five and six years old are working and earning 1 to 2 sen a day, but they say, 'Look how much we are making. Every day we go to work looking forward to receiving the money we earn.'" He went on to argue, "Needless to point out, laborers are low-class people. Japanese industry at present is like an institution set up to feed the poor. The contention that long work hours hinder education or cause people to get sick is unacceptable. If it is true that working in the factories causes many people to get sick, the law of nature will take effect and people will not go to work in the factories."[93]

Government proponents of the legislation continued their efforts to formulate proposals that would be acceptable to business leaders and bureaucratic opponents. This gave credence to the charge by labor-reform leaders and socialists that government officials were bent upon complying with the wishes of the capitalists; that there was no possibility a meaningful law would be enacted. People contended it was like making a lock by consulting thieves.

Labor disputes reached a peak in 1907: 238 strikes and disputes, compared to 38 the previous year. Because of a significant expansion of the Japanese economy, business enterpreneurs were now feeling secure enough to consider granting workers some concessions. For instance, Shibuzawa Eiichi began to say that restrictions on night work would not affect business adversely. Nonetheless, in 1910, a weak proposal the government submitted to the Diet was still opposed by the industrial community because it contained restrictions on night work. The weak factory act of 1911 was finally passed, but it applied only to factories that employed more than fifteen workers, and its provisions for protection of the young and women were minimal, offering little to improve the plight of the workers.[94]

During the years of economic boom that came with World War I, labor unrest abated, but from 1917 on, rising inflation resulted in significant increases in labor disputes.[95] General dissatisfaction with the inflationary spiral burst into massive "rice riots" in 1918, while the labor movement that had previously been inspired by Christian humanitarianism and socialism was given a strong impetus by the Bolshevik victory in Russia. Labor leaders focused their efforts primarily on heavy-industrial plants—like iron and steel factories—but some attention was also devoted to silk- and cotton-mill workers.

The first big labor dispute in the silk industry occurred in Okaya, where there were 200 plants and 40,000 workers. In March 1927, the All Japan Silk Reeling Labor Union was organized under the auspices of the Japanese Federation of Labor (Sōdōmei). In August, a chapter of the union was set up in Okaya's Yamaichi silk plant. Soon after, one of the organizers, who had worked in the firm for seventeen years, was called in by the president and told to quit the union or leave the company. Five male union leaders then submitted a demand that Yamaichi recognize the right of workers to join the union. They also demanded pay increases and better conditions in the plant and in the dormitories. When the company rejected these demands, the organizers got 1,300 women workers to support their call for a strike, closing down the Yamaichi plant for nineteen days, the longest strike in Japanese history up to that point.[96]

When the first rally was held to exhort the workers to go out on strike, a number of women workers mounted the platform. One declared, "We are not slaves! We are proud laborers who carry Japan's industries on our shoulders. We must be paid wages in accordance with our contracts. We are not pigs. We must be given food fit for human consumption. Unless our minimal demands are met, we will not retreat even if it means death." More than a thousand workers who attended the rally shouted their support for the strike and marched through the town of Okaya singing labor songs, one of which went:

Harsher than prison life is life in the dormitory. The factory is like hell. The foreman is the devil, and the spinning wheel is a wheel on fire. I wish I had wings to fly away to the other shore. I want to go home, over the mountain pass, to my sisters and parents.[97]

Almost immediately, the police moved into the factory to enforce the Peace Preservation Law, which had been enacted in 1925 to ensure that "subversive elements" would not threaten the nation's security.

The workers wrote to their parents explaining their position: "Unable to endure the harsh treatment we are subjected to in this factory, as of 10 A.M. on August 30 we have gone out on strike. Please understand and support our action, for it was brought about by the pitiful life that we lead as women factory workers." The company, however, wrote to the workers' parents stating: "The labor union has submitted to this company a seven-point demand calling for improvements in working conditions. Aside from the three items on labor unions, we have agreed to all the demands pertaining to the workers' welfare. But despite our sincere and earnest advice, the workers have chosen to follow the union's leadership and have ceased working from 10 A.M. today. The company desires that work be continued in full during the period stipulated in the workers' contracts. We hope that you, the family members, will give appropriate attention to this matter."[98]

The strike leaders urged workers in other silk mills in Suwa to support the Yamaichi strikers. "We are fed poor food and we are forced to work long hours. Our wages are so low that we can barely survive, and we are not even permitted to use as we please the pittance that we receive as pay. We have been oppressed by the capitalists. Unable to endure their tyranny and oppression any longer, we have decided to go out on strike. We ask you who are also working in silk mills not to regard our situation as a matter that does not concern you." They extended their plea, calling upon the 350,000 women textile workers throughout all of Japan to support their cause. "Workers who side with the company are monsters who are willing to let hundreds of people die. They are devils."[99]

As supporters of the strikers and backers of the company poured into Okaya, the confrontation became increasingly acrimonious. Other mill owners in the Suwa region feared that labor unrest would spread to their plants and joined in a united front against the Yamaichi workers. They agreed not to hire a single Yamaichi worker who went out on strike. To discredit the strikers, rumors were spread that men and women workers were engaging in illicit sexual relations and that the strikers were storing dynamite for future violent actions.[100]

Such rumors as well as stories of clashes between the police and strikers became a matter of grave concern to the women workers' parents, who were inclined to be upset by their daughters' radical behavior to begin with. Many parents came to Okaya to take their daughters home. Public opinion also tended to favor the company, because people were not accustomed to the idea of underlings, especially women, challenging those in positions of authority. Some townspeople handed out flyers stating: "Even a dog, if fed for three days, will not forget the debt it owes its master. Work and earn money. Griping and complaining will ruin you. It is easy to destroy, difficult to build."[101]

When Okaya schoolchildren were asked to write essays about the strike, 167 of the 600 students supported the company, while 51 favored the union; 163 were neutral and 196 expressed no opinion. The chief reason students gave for opposing the strike was that "a decline in exports will endanger the country." Those who favored the strike cited poor pay and bad food as justification.[102] These views probably reflected the opinions of the students' parents and of other adults whose views the students had heard.

The regional newspaper, *Shinano Mainichi,* was sympathetic to the strikers and editorialized, "The Okaya silk-plant operators have neglected to improve the management of their business for years and have attempted to make up for their failure by treating the workers unfairly. This primitive, barbarous mode of management has inevitably awakened the consciousness of the workers, who have long endured their miserable plight."[103]

A minority of the townspeople also supported the workers. One night a mimeographed sheet was distributed to the residents of Okaya stating:

The workers of Yamaichi are on strike. What do the people of this town demand? Times are bad. Wages continue to fall. Those on monthly salaries work for low pay, and stores are in a state of economic depression. The silkworms are unbelievably cheap. We cannot pay the electricity and water bills, but rents are sky high, and if we don't pay the rent they turn off the lights and evict us. Taxes keep going up. We can't bear it any longer. Workers, farmers, and salaried workers are all having a hard time. The only people who are raking in enormous profits are the capitalists and the landlords, choking the poor and evading tax payments. We are not surprised that the Yamaichi workers are on strike. . . . We support the Yamaichi workers. All of us townspeople must unite and ask the capitalists to engage in self-examination.[104]

The anomaly of this labor dispute was that the women workers, housed in company dormitories, had to use these as their home base; and, strangely enough, the company kept the mess halls and other facilities open for the workers while they were on strike. When the strike had continued for about twelve days, however, company officials ordered the strikers to leave the dorms because they were closing down the mess halls. This action was deemed to be inhumane and immoral. A major national newspaper, the *Asahi Shimbun,* denounced the company, accusing it of trying to starve the strikers out. Some townspeople came to the aid of the workers by bringing them food, but the ranks of the strikers dwindled gradually as worried parents arrived to take their daughters home. Those who persisted vowed to continue the strike even if they starved to death.

Then the strike leaders made a fatal miscalculation (if indeed it was an unwitting error, since it has been suggested that a few of the strike leaders may have been bought off by company officials—bribery having often been resorted to by employers to break up strikes). Saying that the workers needed their morale boosted, some leaders suggested that they all go to see a movie. When they returned they found the gates to the dormitories locked and guarded by members of the Young Men's Association and the Military Reserve Association. The workers were left to fend for themselves in the rain. Most had no choice but to return to their home villages, although a small number sought refuge in the homes of sympathetic townspeople. Due to the incredible blunder of leaving the dormitories, the struggle was now over.

From the outset there had been a lack of solidarity among the strike leaders. Bolsheviks, anarchists, syndicalists, and socialist reformers had all engaged in the sort of factional strife that was plaguing the labor movement nationally. Even before the strike was broken, certain leaders had persuaded some of the strikers to end the strike.[105]

Forty-seven of the strikers who remained to the bitter end issued a statement before they dispersed.

Our eighteen-day struggle has ended in failure, and we are now forced to accept a temporary truce. We realize more than ever that, in order to improve the miserable conditions in the factory and create a situation in which we can live like decent human beings, we have nothing to depend on but our own efforts. Were our requests so extreme as to necessitate our persecution with all the power available [to the owners]? Did the minimal requests that we, who reel silk day and night, asked for make it necessary for the capitalists and the government authorities to beat us down the way they did? Was it necessary to quash our open and just protests as if they were dealing with a political rebellion? We weep at what happened because we feel acutely the hypocrisy of our society. The Japanese spirit of chivalry, which calls for the castigation of the strong and assistance to the weak, is now dead in Okaya. But we will not give up. We will not succumb to the forces of power and money. We will continue to fight without despair and without rest until the human rights of the workers are won. We will not give up hope, because we believe that in the end we will prevail.[106]

For the Yamaichi Company the victory was short-lived. In a few years it went out of business. The company's insistence on its legalistic rights and its unwillingness to compromise had led to the sort of open confrontation the Japanese abhor. Its paternalistic position toward its employees should have required a display of "benevolence." Failing in this, the Yamaichi Company may have contributed to its eventual demise.

With the Great Depression, the export of raw silk to the United States, as well as cotton-textile goods to China and India, dropped precipitously—by 31.6 percent in 1930 and 46.6 percent in 1931. Industrialists found it necessary to curtail production and reduce their work force. The official estimate of those unemployed in 1931 was 470,000. Those who, losing their jobs in the cities, returned to their families in the villages to be "absorbed" into the family-farm work force went uncounted, so the actual number of unemployed is estimated to have actually reached about 2.5 million.[107] Given this loss of jobs and income, it is only natural that labor disputes increased, peaking in the years following 1929. Such labor trouble continued until the national emergency following the second Sino-Japanese conflict (1937) made strikes appear to be unpatriotic.

These prewar strikes and other labor union activities failed to make much progress in advancing the condition of the workers because the wielders of political power were aligned on the side of the entrepreneurs and against the workers. Union activities were hampered and strikes were often regarded as acts against the national interest. The Police Security Law of 1900 and the Peace Preservation Law of 1925 were again invoked to curb "radical" elements in the labor movement, and efforts to pass legislation protecting the rights of workers to join unions continued to be blocked in the 1920s by business interests as being contrary to the "national ethos."[108]

The authorities' practice of labeling socialists and communists as harborers of "dangerous thoughts" also discredited strike leaders and union organizers in the eyes of the public, and especially upset those workers' parents living in rural areas. The ethos of the Japanese, particularly of the peasants, favored settling disputes through mediation and conciliation, not direct confrontation. Moreover, practical considerations—the need to make certain that jobs would continue to be available to the girls and women from their communities—made parents and community leaders fear the creation of an irrevocable breach with employers, who could readily find many other eager hands to fill the jobs that might be vacated by strikers.

Because of the many restrictions placed on labor groups, and factional struggles among their leaders, the workers in most factories were poorly organized and lacked strike funds to sustain their activities. Moreover, the commitment of some strike leaders was far from unshakeable; considerable evidence exists that many leaders were bought off by the companies.[109]

Given all these factors, we cannot help but conclude that conditions must have been desperate indeed to cause women workers, nurtured in the tradition of submissiveness and obedience, to defy their employers and go out on strike. In fact, in most cases the initiative for strikes came from male workers and male union organizers. But, once women workers were drawn into the movement, a number of them became dedicated fighters for the workers' cause.

One such person was Takai Toshio, who was born into a poor charcoal maker's family in the backwoods of Gifu prefecture in 1902. She was the second of nine children and was sent out to work in a textile mill in 1914 at the age of thirteen for 13 sen a day. After changing jobs several times, she ended up in a textile mill in Nagoya. There, when she was eighteen, she had her first experience with a strike. Her initial reaction was, "What a shame. Why must they stop all the textile machines?" Then she was handed a flyer by a union leader from the Federation of Labor. She later remarked, "Isn't it amazing that a single sheet of paper can change a person's entire life. I have never forgotten the ideas contained in that flyer." The flyer included a statement by Yoshino Sakuzō (1878–1933), a professor at the University of Tokyo and a leading spokesman for liberal, democratic ideals during the Taishō era (1912–1926).

Takai recalled the message in Yoshino's statement:

Everybody is endowed with his or her individuality. But, under Japanese capitalism, individuality is not permitted to come to the surface. Occasionally there are fortunate people who can pursue learning as they wish or be trained in artistic work. But the average person, the masses, have to stick with work they dislike. Women often are forced to marry men they detest. This being the case, each person must become fully conscious of one's own individuality and must never sink into a life of self-contempt. Today in Japan there are many intelligent people who are unable to go to school and who are experiencing all sorts of hardships. To overcome this situation each person must become aware of his or her own worth, study hard, and unite with others to fight for a better society. A single person is weak, but if many people join hands even the poor can become powerful.

Takai continued, "I had not even been to elementary school and, being a girl, I was self-conscious about how homely I was. I was also shorter than most people. I always thought of myself as being inferior to others. I guess I had a warped personality. So I was unhappy about everything and did sloppy work. Being the way I was, I had few friends. To be honest, I was the type of person that people disliked. But after I read the flyer, I realized that my way of thinking had been completely wrong."[110]

She decided to change her way of life and went to Tokyo hoping to go to school there. But, lacking the means to do so, she took a job at Tōyō Muslin, a major textile plant. She worked harder than others, spent all her spare time reading, and became a "model" worker. In 1921, a strike was staged at the factory in order to gain higher wages and shorter hours. Takai was convinced that it was more important to fight for better food and better conditions in the dormitories. Not only were the dormitories unsanitary, but many workers had tuberculosis and, because they were not given medical care, they spread the disease to others. When the strike leaders at the rally failed to mention these issues, she jumped on the platform and made her maiden speech. Thus, her career as a fighter for the workers' cause was launched. She continued her work in the labor movement through years of poverty and persecution in the 1920s and 1930s, and into the postwar era. In Takai's case, as with many other labor and agrarian activists, the catalyst in the launching of her human-rights career was exposure to the ideologies of "progressive intellectuals" who did not emerge from the working class or the impoverished peasantry.[111]

While the workers' rural parents were inclined to adhere to the tradition of preserving social harmony if at all possible and were more inclined to be submissive to their "betters," the business entrepreneurs their children were up against were quick in adopting the capitalistic ways of the West and in learning to treat human labor as a "commodity." The new industrialists' approach to labor was criticized by the *Shinano Mainichi* during the Yamaichi strike. In its editorial it stated:

Humanity and human existence come first and last. This truism has been the whole story of human history. Where there is human life there is the means of production as a vehicle for human life. . . . Note carefully. The means of production does not precede human living. Living precedes the mode of production. Thus, the mode and conditions of production should be under the jurisdiction of human beings, not the other way around. . . . What were the strikers of Okaya fighting for? It is obvious that they were trying to regain their true status as human beings by ceasing to be . . . [merely] a tool of production. . . . The female workers had awakened to the fact that their existence was far more precious than the cocoons, the spindles, and the beautiful fibers that they wove with their hands.[112]

The claim of benevolent paternalism on the part of the employers was a sham, critics contended. Concerning the Kanebō strike of 1930, a critic who had been a worker in the factory wrote:

Alone among the textile manufacturers, Kanebō was seen to stand above other companies as a model firm, a company run on the principle of paternalism. I too was among those who believed in this image of Kanebō . . . until recently. But the inner workings of capitalism prevented me from remaining an obedient slave forever. The child has grown up and has begun to criticize the parents. Is Kanebō really run on the principle of paternalism? What is paternalism? Does it mean paying the workers' funeral expenses? Does it mean treating the workers to frequent movies? Does it mean providing us with cheap company housing? Does it mean imposing strenuous work on the female workers? Does it mean turning them into tubercular victims and sending them, only reluctantly, to the sanitarium? When the female workers, who have worked for many years to the point of endangering their lives, are released from their jobs they are given a pittance as severance pay, but when the president of the company retires he is given a retirement payment of 3 million yen. Ah! 3 million yen! When there is a surplus of manpower, the lower-level factory workers who have to survive from hand to mouth each day are fired, while the higher-ups who loaf around with their hands behind their backs are kept on at the plants, doing nothing. Is this what is called paternalism?[113]

The harsh conditions and exploitation that existed in Japan's factories cannot be excused with the argument that the workers would have been worse off as peasants in the villages. Paeans are sung about the great success of Japan's modernization since the Meiji restoration, but to what avail modernization if, instead of improving the lot of the vast majority of the people, it only increases the wealth and comfort of a small elite at the top?

POVERTY

AND

PROSTITUTION

Public Stigma,
Public Sanction

Among the most pitiful victims of agrarian as well as urban poverty in prewar Japan were the young farm girls who were sold to brothels. Their number increased markedly in years of crop failure and ensuing famine; but even in normal years a steady flow of young girls was being channeled into brothels at home and abroad.

The stigma attached to prostitution led the public to assume that prostitutes chose their way of life. A student of this subject notes that Meiji newspaper accounts of girls being shipped to Korea, China, and Southeast Asia refer to them as "stowaways," as if they were leaving Japan of their own accord. The fact that they had been sold into slavery or tricked into their situation through their sense of responsibility toward their poverty-stricken parents and siblings was invariably ignored.

The papers treat the prostitutes as if they were graspy vixen who bilk innocent men of their money. For example, an article about the dissection of a prostitute who died of syphilis, which afflicted her brain, states, "Whore who, when alive, sold her body, and dead still sells her body. . . ." Those who buy and sell the girls to enrich themselves are allowed to do so in the open. The girls, sold over and over to brothels in order to fatten the wallets of white-slavers, get buried under with debt, and die. But the dealers in white-slavery are not condemned; the girls are seen as having brought their misfortune upon themselves because of their vulgar greed.[1]

In the rural areas, and well into the early Shōwa period, prostitutes were considered less than human. For instance, a story was circulated in some villages that in order to be turned into a prostitute "a girl had to be put in a cage and be raped by a beast. In other words she must become a beast herself. Then she must have relations with men of all sorts. After one or two months even a backwoods girl will be endowed with the soft white skin of a prostitute. She also becomes frigid, ceasing to have any feelings about men."[2]

Even more sophisticated urban dwellers assumed prostitutes had freely chosen their profession. One female writer commented in 1916 that many girls who went overseas as prostitutes came from Amakusa and Shimabara (in Kyushu), "where, when a person returns with an enormous fortune after having sold her flesh, not just the ordinary village people but the village officials, people who are pillars of the community, treat them with respect. Consequently, when girls reach a certain age they enter this sordid profession of their own free will. It appears that, rather than eat yam and do hard physical work, they prefer this life because they can eat good food, wear soft kimonos, and make money while leading a sedate life."[3]

Although people were at least dimly aware of the fact that prostitutes were victims of poverty, they found it easier to blame the victims rather than their society.

However, these women were not simply victims of modern capitalism, as some social critics claim. When Japan opened its doors to the West in the mid-nineteenth century, officially sanctioned public brothels were already in existence, and the red-light district had long flourished under Tokugawa rule.[4] People took brothels and prostitution for granted. Even in the modern period, no government official's conscience seems to have been pricked by the sordid spectacle that the brothels presented.

Only in 1872, when the existence of prostitution resulted in an embarrassing diplomatic incident, did the government act. A Peruvian vessel, the *Maria Luz,* engaged in transporting kidnapped Chinese coolies to South America, had docked for repairs in Yokohama. Some of the coolies jumped ship and asked the Japanese authorities for help. The Japanese complied and condemned the Peruvians for running what was, in effect, a slave trade. The Peruvians countered by pointing out that slavery, in the form of girls sold to brothels, was practiced in Japan, too. This forced the Japanese government to ban the buying and selling of girls and women, but it did not prohibit "voluntary" service in the brothels.[5]

In all major cities there were sections given over to houses of prostitution, where the women were on display as if in a slave market. A Swiss official observed that the women were "publically exposed like animals on display to be freely scrutinized by all comers. After first being examined as merchandise, they are purchased and used by the first man who meets the price. The impression I got of these unfortunate creatures was one of utmost misery."[6]

In Tokyo there were six districts where brothels were licensed to operate. The most renown of these was the Yoshiwara, which had flourished since the Tokugawa era. In 1883, there were 3,156 prostitutes in about 400 houses in these six districts; in 1887, there were 4,747; and, in 1909, 6,834.[7] One mid-nineteenth–century traveler, Clement Scott, wrote:

Do they [the missionaries] not know that it is a recognized custom for parents in Japan to sell their children to a life of shame? Is it not an admitted fact that in every Yoshiwara in Japan, there are hundreds of girls who were sold originally by their parents to the keepers of these infamous places for so many hundred dollars, and [that] here they must stay until their ransom can be provided by some charitable person? . . . Girls are to them [the parents] a permanent source of income. [The girls'] savings are not put by to pay off the original deposit, but are sent home to the whining old parents who are always hat in hand, and never intend that their children shall be released at all.[8]

The root cause of this system was agrarian poverty. In the Tokugawa period, peasants had practiced infanticide when they could not afford to feed another child. A social critic writing toward the end of the Tokugawa era claimed that in the northern provinces—the area where agrarian poverty remained most extreme even in modern times —the number of children killed annually exceeded sixty or seventy thousand.[9] However, infanticide and abortion were made capital crimes in the Meiji period, while even the dissemination of information about birth control was banned. Partially as a result, the birth rate rose beyond the peasants' capacity to support new arrivals.[10] Where outright infanticide was now illegal, and birth-control information unavailable to the masses, almost as dismal a fate often awaited the children of the poor.

Child Abandonment and the Brothel Trade

One Tokugawa practice that persisted in the Meiji period was child abandonment. In the city of Tokyo alone, hundreds of babies were abandoned in public places where they were likely to be noticed and picked up. In rural areas they were commonly abandoned in front of the homes of wealthy farmers who, it was hoped, would take them in and raise them. In some areas traffickers in young children went about buying young boys in order to sell them to families in need of additional hands to work on the farms or in other occupations. For instance, in the middle Meiji period in northern Japan, an old woman known as "the hag of Mogami" bought twelve- and thirteen-year-old boys and girls for 5 to 6 yen and resold them for 7 to 8 yen or more.

Isolated fishing villages, especially on small islands, often needed additional workers, so they bought such youngsters and used them until they attained the age when they became eligible for the draft.[11]

The most common practice in the modern period, however, was the selling of daughters to brothels, a practice that continued to increase as, with the industrialization of the national economy, the cities grew in size. The defenders of the brothel system argued that in major urban centers like Tokyo, where there was a concentration of single men who had come to work in industrial and commercial institutions, such facilities were a necessity. There were, it was pointed out, 130,000 more men than women in the prefecture of Tokyo in 1891. Since Japan had a long tradition of permitting public brothels as "necessary" outlets for lustful men, the defenders of the system contended that, if public brothels were abolished, unlicensed prostitution would increase, and the wives and daughters of "refined families" would be victimized by frustrated men. They also responded to Western critics by asserting that similar practices existed among the ancient Greeks, the founders of Western culture. "There," they pointed out, "the hiring of women as sexual companions was one of the innovations of city life. Solon himself established brothels throughout Athens."[12]

As the cities grew, the number of inmates in their brothels grew, too. This was particularly noticeable after the first Sino-Japanese war, when the Japanese economy experienced rapid expansion. By 1904, there were 43,134 prostitutes in the public brothels; by 1909, 47,541; by 1912, 50,410; and by 1924, 52,325.[13]

In years of crop failure and famine the number of girls sold to brothels vaulted. For example, following the crop failures that beset the six northern prefectures in 1905, the number of girls sent into Tokyo brothels increased dramatically. Whereas 128 women from these prefectures worked in Tokyo brothels in 1902, there were 1,161 in 1907, and 1,785 in 1912. Observing this phenomenon, a British newspaper commented: "The famine that beset Hokkaido and northeastern Japan is the greatest tragedy since 1869. The peasants had no way out to cope with their families crying of hunger but to sell their daughters. The nation that officially recognizes this odious practice of publicly licensed brothels is Great Britain's ally, the land known for its *bushido,* Japan."[14]

During the famine of 1934, too, large numbers of northern girls were sent into the cities to serve as indentured workers in various entertainment facilities. By September of that year, 2,196 geishas,

4,521 servitors in brothels, and 5,952 waitresses employed to serve *sake* in Japanese-style restaurants (where they were often expected to sleep with the customers) had come into the cities from the same six prefectures. In addition, 3,271 "waitresses" to serve in bars and cafés, as well as 10,244 maids and nursemaids, were recruited from these prefectures.[15] From Yamagata prefecture alone, by November 1934, 3,298 girls had been sold into indentured service as: geishas (249), prostitutes in brothels (1,420), and *sake*-serving waitresses (1,629).[16]

Brokers who dealt in the business of buying girls for city brothels openly advertised their trade, putting up huge signs in front of their offices saying THOSE WISHING TO SELL THEIR DAUGHTERS, PLEASE CONSULT US.[17] The sum of money the parents received for a contract calling for six years' indentured service was about 600 yen. But 200 yen was deducted by the brothel keeper for the girl's kimonos, and 50 yen was retained by the middleman; so the parents received only 350 yen, or 60 yen per year. At this time, 1 *koku* of rice cost 24 yen 91 sen. On the average, the brothel keeper charged his customers 70 sen a visit. He kept 60 percent for himself and credited the remaining 40 percent, or 28 sen, to the girl. In order to repay her debt of 600 yen she would have had to accommodate 2,143 customers in those six years.[18]

The need to survive by selling their daughters to the brothels was ordinarily a tragic experience for the family members and even for those who were merely acquainted with the girls. A poet who was a teacher in a northern village wrote in her diary:

I saw with my two eyes and heard with my ears something very sad. I heard that one of my former pupils was sold to a "restaurant." The owner, it is said, asserted that "200 yen is too much; the price of everything has come down. I'll give you 150 yen." The seller complained, "That's too little." I wonder what the final price was? I hear the girl is now at the "restaurant." She was a pretty child, with a thin, sad face. I turned my face away from the person who told me the story as if it was an amusing tale, and I looked down. I have been distressed all day today. I wonder who will purge me of this gloomy mood, and when?[19]

In late 1934, a reporter from Tokyo visited a family in a village in Aomori prefecture.

As I entered the house, an old woman past seventy, the parents of the girl who was sold, and a little girl of about five were huddled around a smoky fireplace. The little girl seemed to have a cold and was wailing away. After her older sister was sold and left home, the child had turned into a crybaby, they said.

"Why did you sell your daughter," I asked.

The old woman blinked her eyes, which had been damaged by the charcoal smoke and afflicted with trachoma, and said, "Sumie has been sold and is leading a hard life. I don't care if I die. I would like to see my grandchildren have an easy life." Tears poured out of her red, festering eyes.

This family had lost their house because of debts that they had incurred, and had been living with neighbors. They then sold their fourteen-year-old daughter Sumie to a brothel in Nagoya and used the money to buy this house. They got 450 yen on a five-year contract. [After deducting commissions and expenses] they got 150 yen. Seventy yen was used to pay off the debts, 40 yen was used to build this house, and the remaining 40 yen quickly vanished.

The father did not sell his daughter willingly. But the family had no rice to eat because of the crop failure. On top of that his wife was pregnant and was afflicted with beriberi, and the moneylenders pestered him every day. . . . So he finally sold his daughter. Now all he has left is one tiny thatched hut. His daughter wrote: "My boss says that I must start taking customers after New Year's. I don't want to become a prostitute. I am so miserable!" A fourteen-year-old girl from Tsugaru is waiting for the arrival of New Year's Day with terror.[20]

Some parents may have grown callous to the imperative of selling their daughters in order to survive. One woman in her forties, who had sent her twenty-three-year-old daughter to a brothel, justified her action by explaining:

In order to pay our debts and reduce the size of our family, even by one, we sold our oldest daughter. The money we got for her was 800 yen for six years' service. Twenty percent was taken by the middleman. In addition, the cost of getting her ready [clothing] and other expenses were deducted, so we received in hand 500 yen. I don't think it's wrong to sell our own daughter, whom we raised ourselves. Other people use the money they get to go on excursions to famous sites. Some even go to hot springs to enjoy themselves. On the other hand, we sold her in order to pay our debts, so we feel we needn't be ashamed.[21]

The most atrocious aspect of the brothel experience was the fact that girls barely into puberty—some at ages twelve and thirteen—were compelled to take customers and have their bodies and spirits brutalized.[22] Many, of course, did not know what would happen to them when they went to the brothels. One woman who was sold abroad exclaimed, "If I had been given a choice between becoming a prostitute and death, I would have chosen death. I didn't know . . . what was involved when I was sold. . . ."[23]

To justify this practice, the society played up the sacrifice of the daughters as an exemplary manifestation of filial piety. The ethos of the society conditioned the girls into believing that it was their duty as daughters to become prostitutes to aid their families.[24] National political leaders did nothing to change this situation. A few advocates of Westernization, like Tsuda Mamichi (1829–1902), were early critics of publically sanctioned brothels, but they got little support from the main body of Westernizers or even from the champions of "popular rights." At the prefectural level, advocates of brothel reform did achieve some measure of success. The prefectural assembly members of Gunma prefecture initiated a reform movement in 1879 and succeeded in banning public brothels in that prefecture in 1893. Several other prefectures followed Gunma's example, but the central government failed to take any action until the end of World War II.

The Reform Movement
at Home

Among the influential exponents of brothel reform was Shimada Saburō (1852–1923), a prominent political party member and newspaper editor, but the most vocal and active opponents of public brothels were Christian reformers,[25] among them a missionary from the United States, U.G. Murphy. The most persistent and dedicated of the reformers were the members of the Salvation Army, led by Yamamuro Gunpei (1872–1940), whose efforts (however little noticed at the time) kept prewar Japan from being a land wholly without conscience or compassion about this inhumane practice. Under Yamamuro, the Salvation Army set out to abolish the institution of officially sanctioned brothels and endeavored to arouse public opinion against it by sponsoring speeches and publishing tracts. In 1911, Yamamuro explained why he took up the cause. He had been spending so much of his time helping the poor that he had had little left for his family. Then his own child, a baby, got sick and died. As he was nursing the child, the thought suddenly struck Yamamuro that "there are people in this world, just like this baby, on the edge of death, racked with pain but unable to tell people about it. So they move swiftly to their death. Since this is true, I shall devote my life to helping my fellow beings who are unable to cry out for help. Such people can be found among the prostitutes, who are imprisoned because of the vicious institution of public brothels. They are forced to lead pathetic, ignoble lives in which they are being degraded by other people."[26]

Yamamuro found out that the law gave the girls who wished to leave the brothels the right to do so. But this law was hardly known, and the brothel keepers quite naturally did their best to prevent the law from being invoked. Yamamuro and other Salvation Army members sought to spread the word among the inmates of the brothels about this legal provision and intervened on behalf of those who wished to take advantage of it.[27] The problem was that, even if the girls managed to leave the brothels, they still had to repay the debts their parents had incurred. The courts refused to allow them to leave if they were unable to repay the brothel keepers.[28] The contracts that the parents signed usually contained provisions calling for the immediate repayment of the advance payment as well as other debts incurred by the girls if they left the brothels or failed to fulfill the terms of the contract.[29]

One of the ironies of the movement to liberate the girls from the brothels was that, once driven into a profession scorned by others, they frequently found no way to rebuild their lives. Many ended up taking jobs on the fringes of the red-light district and eventually sinking back into the life from which they had escaped. A social activist who helped to liberate women in one red-light district in Tokyo during the prewar period found that, of the 400 he helped to free, only 2 managed to find employment that was not linked to the world of alcohol and sex. He was also shocked to find that many of the peasants whose daughters he had helped to return to their homes were displeased with what he had done. They said they were grateful for his good intentions, but behind his back complained that "our daughters would have been able to continue sending us money. . . . Now, we just have an extra mouth to feed when times are so hard."[30]

In a survey of a hundred prostitutes who came to the Salvation Army for help around 1910, forty-two had no schooling at all; five had one year of elementary education; nine had two years; seventeen had three years; and fourteen had four years.[31] Few could write and even fewer had access to anyone who might record their personal stories for posterity. They were, in any event, reticent to discuss their lives because of their shame that they had been reduced, in effect, to the status of outcastes. Naturally enough, then, personal accounts by victims of the brothel system are not numerous. The following are remarks by a girl whose parents sold her sister to a brothel during the Taishō era:

When my older sister fell into the pathetic world of prostitutes, I was too young to know what had happened. When I woke up one morning, my gentle sister was gone. When I asked my mother where she was, my mother told me: "Your sister has gone to a far-off place in order to save all of you. Poor thing! When you grow up you must be kind to her. You must not forget the debt you owe her." In the spring of my seventeenth year, I was invited to stay with my sister. I used to hide behind the stairway, where my sister was on display in a shameful fashion, and weep. I felt tremendous hatred toward the men who came and made lewd, insulting remarks to her. . . . I wished I could pour a pot of boiling water on these ignoble people. When my sister had to entertain a customer, I would get so angry that I had the urge to kill him. . . . My sister sacrificed her life to save our family from poverty. During the course of ten years of slavery, she surely committed many sins. If only this kind of system did not exist; if only the government would ban it, then no one could enter this way of life even if she wanted to. Since the system exists and the government permits it . . . human flesh is sold and people sink into the pit.[32]

A woman lodged in a brothel wrote in a magazine in 1921:

It is now five years since I was sold by my father and came to Kōfu City in Yamanashi prefecture. I have spent these long years behind latticed windows. . . . I must make known to the public that we are living like animals with only the veneer of human beings. In reality we are cut off from the world of humanity. We would like to ask our fellow women to think seriously about the reality of a Japan where such a system of public brothels is recognized and protected by law. My companions are writhing in the ugly sewer of life all over Japan. How do you think we feel when we, who have fallen into the pit of the society, think about our parents, brothers, sweethearts, and friends? I cannot help but curse the flaws of contemporary society. We who are weak and frail are deprived of all our rights and are forced to sell our flesh and to make indescribable sacrifices. How do you think the brothel owners treat us? They are bloodsuckers who . . . drive many of us to death. Does our society today need this kind of system, which is so clearly against the principles of morality? . . . When will the day come when people like us, who are engaged in such a shameful profession, disappear from the world? I wish to escape from this miserable, shameful abyss as soon as possible and join the community of normal human beings.[33]

A tubercular inmate of one of the brothels wrote to the Kyoto prefectural office in 1910:

Recently I went to the police to get permission to leave the brothel. For some reason the police did not allow me to leave. The reason I want to leave the brothel is my poor health. For this reason, I cannot please the customers or satisfy my master. I am thirty-three and am alone in this world. I do not have any parents or brothers. I am all alone, so my master treats me brutally. Recently one of my co-workers, Yuki, was kicked downstairs from the second floor. She died as a result of that fall. Because of this I have come to fear my master even more than before. So please, please allow me to quit the brothel. You can verify the truth about my master's cruelty by asking around.[34]

The following are excerpts from the diary of a young woman who went into a brothel in the Yoshiwara section of Tokyo in the 1920s to save her impoverished family.

What a fool I've been! I can cry and wail about what has happened to me, but there is nothing that I can do to undo what has happened. Whose fault is it that I am in this despicable state? It is the broker's fault! He took advantage of my naïveté and slyly talked me into this situation. But I am also disgusted at my own stupidity. I hate myself!

After I came to this place and, as the true state of things became clear to me, I realized that what I had feared . . . was in fact a reality. I then tried to leave, but it was no longer possible. I had already accepted a loan from them. And the money disappeared as quickly as water thrown on burning stone. So I can't leave. I can't run away. It's impossible. I'd be arrested by the police. I tried to resign myself to the situation by telling myself that this was my fate. But I couldn't resign myself to my plight. I became desperate.

I tried to kill myself. But I held back because I had to think about my feeble mother and young sister. . . .

All during this past week, I have been in a state of despair. My mind has been so full of desperate thoughts that I nearly collapsed several times. I kept telling myself, "I must kill myself, I must kill myself," and wrote endless numbers of suicide notes. But I decided against suicide for it would do me no good. All it would accomplish would be a spread in the scandal columns of the newspapers. The proprietor and the old woman boss would heap unspeakable atrocities on my corpse. The only reality would be the heartbreak of my mother and younger sister.

And I can't die without avenging myself on the broker, the proprietor, and the men who have plunged me into this dark abyss. I can't die, after having been brutalized by these people, without doing battle against them. I will not die! It may take years but I will leave this place and then I will do what has to be done. I will not cry anymore. I will not bewail my fate any longer. I must first kill my old self before I can do the work that I must do here. I am now reborn. I will [forget my past] and from now on deal with the proprietor, the old woman, and the men as the prostitute Harukoma. Years from now Harukoma will, by whatever means possible, take revenge on these people. As the first step on my road to vengeance, I shall keep this secret diary. This is my only consolation and it is also a declaration of my war of revenge against these people. Oh, diary! You are my friend, my master, my God! You shall keep my life pure and refined.[35]

Karayuki

Terrible as was the fate of the girls and women who were sold into prostitution in the brothels of Japan, they were still better off than those who were sold overseas. Those who served in Japan were at least in familiar cultural surroundings; but, sometimes cut off from their families and friends forever, the so-called *karayuki* found themselves in places where the language, culture, mores, and ambience were wholly alien.[36]

It was indeed an insensitive reporter who wrote, during the early years of this century:

[The *karayuki*] go abroad to engage in their sordid business with the same kind of attitude as a person who is out to earn some money to pay for her wedding expenses. When they earn a little money, they spend it on fancy kimonos and *obi*. They are women who are completely ignorant. The only word these pitiful women can utter is "mister" as they grab hold of some gentleman walking down the street.[37]

In fact, these women certainly were not addleheads out on a lark to earn a few quick yen. Like their counterparts in domestic brothels, they were victims of agrarian poverty and the indifference of the ruling authorities to their fate. In fact, government officials aided and abetted the perpetuation of this system: They saw value in an army of prostitutes following the vanguard of Japanese expansionists into Korea, Manchuria, China, and Southeast Asia. Although some Japanese prostitutes were sent abroad before the Russo-Japanese War of 1904–1905, their number increased dramatically after that war and peaked during the Taishō era.[38]

Most of the prostitutes sent to the Asian continent and Southeast Asia came from northern Kyushu, particularly the regions of Amakusa and Shimabara (the islands off Nagasaki and the peninsula to the east of Nagasaki). These areas, particularly the Amakusa Islands, were among the most impoverished regions of Japan. Arable land was scarce, and there were few suitable ports where the residents could engage in fishing on a scale sufficient to supplement their meager incomes. The people of Amakusa and Shimabara, many of them Christians, suffered harsh oppression and religious persecution during and following the Shimabara Rebellion of 1637–1638. Later, the Tokugawa government adopted a policy of repopulating the region, which led the population to increase three to four times over between 1691 and 1856. This increase was not accompanied by an equivalent increase in food production, and, because of centuries of Christian influence, infanticide and abortion were not widely practiced in the area.[39] However, the practice of selling children continued.

In Nagasaki, a port city where the Chinese and Dutch were allowed to come and trade, the practice of selling children abroad had existed even in the Tokugawa period and after the country was opened to the West, contact with foreigners became more extensive. One consequence was an increase in the number of children born of mixed blood. The Japanese looked down on these products of miscegenation, and the authorities treated them as aliens. They were allowed to live as Japanese until the age of ten, but after that they were required to stay in areas reserved for aliens. Since they were unwanted and had no status in the society, they were often sold overseas. In 1870, thirty-four of these children were sold to China. Publicity about this caused the government to issue a decree in 1871 prohibiting the sale of children abroad, but the practice continued surreptitiously.[40]

The selling—at first, mainly to China—of young girls from the impoverished villages of northern Kyushu was an extension of this practice. Around 1882, there were about 800 Japanese women kept in oriental "teahouses" in Shanghai.[41] The Japanese consul general in Shanghai, regarding this as a blot on Japan's national honor, apprehended and repatriated 500 of them; but this was just a temporary setback for the traffickers in this form of slavery. By 1909, there were about 3,500 Japanese prostitutes in Shanghai; and,[42] by the turn of the century, Japan had become an important supplier of prostitutes to other areas of Asia, particularly Southeast Asia with Singapore as a focal point.

As Japanese political activities intensified in Korea and Manchuria following the Russo-Japanese War, brothels also began to spring up in cities in those regions. Public brothels had not existed in Korea until the Japanese introduced them. In fact, before Japan annexed Korea in 1910, Korean authorities decapitated Korean women who consorted with Japanese men.[43] The Japanese made Dairen, on the Liaotung Peninsula, a flourishing center for public brothels. One Japanese newspaper commented, "The management of Manchuria starts with the establishment of dens of iniquity."[44] It is estimated that 30,000 prostitutes were brought into Manchuria by the Japanese.[45]

By the early twentieth century, Japanese brothels could be found in most areas of Asia including Siberia, Korea, China, Manchuria, Hong Kong, Singapore, Borneo, Cambodia, Vietnam, Thailand, Malaya, and the Philippines. Hawaii and California were also targeted by Japanese traders in prostitutes as lucrative centers for their business. In 1910, it is estimated that there were over 22,000 Japanese prostitutes abroad.[46]

A large number of the girls who were sent into brothels abroad were deceived by pimps and traders into believing that they were going to be employed as well-paid maids, waitresses, or sales clerks. A renowned prewar feminist, Yamada Waka, was victimized in this way as a young girl by a man who tricked her into believing that he would find her a respectable job in California so that she could help her impoverished family. When she arrived in California she was sent into a brothel.[47] The girls were usually slipped out of the country on board ships, as stowaways. In 1890, the Japanese consulate in Singapore reported that eight dead bodies were discovered in the hold of a Japanese freighter. A man accompanying eleven girls had hidden in the hold, but they got buried under a load of coal. The man and three of the girls survived, although they were in critical condition. The person recounting this story wrote that "their misfortune was the result of their own misdeed."[48]

An article in a Fukuoka paper in 1905 reported the uncovering of forty-eight stowaways in a Norwegian vessel that had left the port of Moji, in Kyushu, for Hong Kong. With them were eight slavers and their assistants. The vessel turned back to Moji and the slavers and the girls were turned over to the police. The girls, upon being questioned, revealed that "the abductors had told them that, once they arrived overseas, they would be able to earn fabulous sums of money. They had been transported to the Norwegian ship on coal barges and concealed in the hold. For three days, until they were discovered, they had not been fed at all. The forty-eight girls and women ranged in age from fifteen to twenty-four. All but seven were twenty years old or younger.[49] Girls who were transported to the United States were often hidden in barrels and boxes in order to get past the customs inspection. An item in a Tokyo newspaper in 1893 reported on a pimp who concealed seven girls and women in barrels but got caught in Vancouver by customs officials.[50]

The girls who were recruited for shipment overseas were usually ensnared by small-time recruiters who worked for some big boss. Women in businesses that brought them into contact with young girls looking for jobs often served as agents. For instance, in the port of Moji there was a woman known as "Old Lady Oshichi." A newspaper account states, "Oshichi saw that Osue (eighteen), who was working as a maid for a doctor, was young and attractive, so she told her, 'My daughter is working in Pusan in Korea as a maid and is making a lot of money and sends 10 yen a month home to me. Wouldn't you like to go to Pusan?' Osue took the bait, and Oshichi brought her to her home and kept her there with other girls for about a month, until she could be shipped to Korea."[51]

The life story of practically every one of the *karayuki* is an unmitigated horror story. One of these, Okimi, born in 1896, was sent to a Korean brothel at the age of fifteen. She was in a group of fourteen girls ranging in age from twelve to sixteen. Even on board the vessel, the head pimp forced them to be used by the sailors. An eleven-year-old girl was sick with tuberculosis and died on board. Her body was dumped into the sea. When Okimi went to the pimp for the name and address of the girl's parents so that she could notify them, she found out that he had legally adopted all the girls and now had parental rights over them. The girls, who had been willing to sacrifice themselves for the sake of their parents, now found that their ties to them had been severed completely.[52]

Yamasaki Tomoko, a writer who has studied the history of the *karayuki* in Southeast Asia, uncovered the story of one who was sent to Singapore around 1905 after she had been tricked by a slaver into believing he would find her a job in Osaka to help out her impoverished family. Instead she, along with three other girls, was put on board a vessel headed for Singapore. On board they were assaulted by sailors. Eventually, the other girls vanished. They had either committed suicide or been thrown overboard for resisting the sailors' demands.[53] When girls like these got to Singapore, they were usually auctioned off to the brothel keepers right on the dock.[54] Once the transaction had been concluded, the owners usually took half the money the women earned. The women then had to pay off their debts, and the interest, on those debts, as well as send some money home to their families. In reality, this meant that they had little chance of freeing themselves from the grip of the brothel keepers until they were too old to be of any further lucrative use.[55]

The greatest tragedy for many of these women was the fact they were unable to return to their families and homeland. In 1932, when a reporter came across an old *karayuki* in southern Thailand, the only thing she asked of him was to bring a strand of her gray hair back to Japan, for she had no possibility of ever returning home.[56]

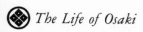 *The Life of Osaki*

In 1968, Yamasaki Tomoko spent three weeks living with an old woman in Amakusa and, by winning her friendship, got her to recount her experiences as a *karayuki* in Sandakan in Borneo.

Osaki was born into an impoverished tenant-farm family in the Amakusa Islands. Her father died when she was three. Her mother then married a man who had many children of his own, so she left her three children by her former husband behind. Osaki's older brother, only eleven, was burdened with the task of supporting his siblings. From the age of seven, Osaki worked as a baby-sitter. "I was given lunch and supper and was paid 4 yen for the year. Because I had to work, I did not set foot in school for even a single day. Neither did my older brother and older sister. Of course, it wasn't just us who did not go to school. Those days weren't like today. There were lots of children in our village who didn't attend school. It was normal not to go to school."[57]

Her older sister was persuaded by a fellow villager, whose sister ran a brothel in Rangoon, to go to work for her there. Osaki recalled:

Since the end of the war, no one goes to the South Pacific any longer, but when I was little many girls went overseas. They weren't all orphans either. From this small village about twenty girls went abroad around the time that I went. . . . I decided to go abroad when I reached my tenth birthday. We were unable to survive, with three of us children, working as tenant farmers. My older brother was now a young man, but he didn't own a single strip of land, so he was not regarded as a full-fledged member of the community. He had no chance of getting anyone to marry him. I was hoping to find a way to help him become a full-fledged man. I saw that girls from our neighborhood were going abroad after receiving a lot of money. Even though I was a mere child, I concluded that, if I went abroad to work, my older brother would be able to buy some land, build a big house, and marry a nice girl. Then he would be a real man. So I decided to go abroad.[58]

Even though she says she decided to go abroad to help her brother, it seems the real decision was made for her by her brother and a villager who had become a brothel keeper in Sandakan. Her brother was given 300 yen by the brothel keeper for permission to take her to Sandakan.

Osaki refused to go unless her best friend, Ohana, went with her. When she saw Ohana the next day, "I told her what the boss told me. 'If you go abroad, every day will be like a holiday. You can wear nice kimonos and eat as much white rice as you want. So, won't you come with me?'" Evidently the brothel keeper had persuaded Ohana's parents as well as the parents of another friend, Otsugi, to turn their daughters over to him for 300 yen each. So the three girls were sent to Borneo, arriving in Sandakan after a journey of several months.

Initially, the girls, who were barely ten at that time, were not required to serve as prostitutes but were used to do chores around the brothel. The girls who were taking customers in the brothel were, however, only thirteen or fourteen years old. According to Osaki,

The boss, Tarōzō, who was kind and gentle until we left home, turned into a ferocious demon on the ship. After we arrived in Sandakan he got even meaner. . . . He would curse us in foul language and make us work all the time. Until we were made to take customers . . . we didn't feel that being in the South Pacific was so bad. This was due in part to our ignorance about what the older girls were required to do. We were pleased that we had white rice three times a day. When we were in Amakusa we had white rice only for New Year's, Obon, and Shinto festivals. In our parentless home, we hardly ever had white rice even on these occasions. . . . And [in Sandakan] we even had fish with our rice. Amakusa is surrounded by the sea and our village is near the port of Sakitsu, but I had never eaten fish before. . . .

We were made to entertain customers two or three years after our arrival in Sandakan. I was thirteen then. I still remember the day when, after lunch, Tarōzō told us, "From tonight on, you have to entertain the customers like Ofumi." The three of us told him: "We won't entertain customers, no matter what you say." Then Tarōzō got angry like the devil and shouted, "If you're not going to entertain the customers, why did you come here?" We told him, "You brought us here as little girls without telling us what we were expected to do. You can't tell us to entertain the customers now. You lied to us."

This had no effect on the boss, who spoke to us like a cat that had cornered a mouse. "I've spent 2,000 yen on you girls. If you can pay back the 2,000 yen, you don't have to entertain the customers. So, give me back my 2,000 yen right now. If you can't, don't argue with me. Just start working with customers tonight."

How could we repay 2,000 yen when we didn't have a single sen. So we lost, and, even though we hated the idea, we had to start entertaining the customers from that night.[59]

When they asked the boss how the 300 yen advance that their families had received had turned into 2,000 yen, he told them that it included the boat fare and three years' board. They would never be able to repay the 2,000 yen: The boss kept half their earnings, and they had only the remaining half to repay the debt and pay for their kimonos, cosmetics, and other expenses.

In order to repay her debt as quickly as possible, Osaki says she took as many customers as she could. But, "No matter how much I got used to the business, once or twice a month I got so depressed at the thought of entertaining the customers that I felt like killing myself. I used to cry, wondering what sort of karma had forced me into this kind of business."

Her boss never gave the girls a day off, not even on holidays or when they were sick. A couple of years later Tarōzō died, and his sister, who took over the business, sold the girls to a brothel in Tawau, also in Borneo. Because of the stringent terms imposed on them, the three girls escaped back to Sandakan and got one of the women brothel owners, Okuni, who had a reputation for being a kind person, to intervene on their behalf. The brothel keeper from Tawau was persuaded to let two of the girls remain in Sandakan. The person to be sent back to Tawau was chosen by lot, and Ohana was forced to go back. Osaki then stayed in Sandakan and worked for Okuni's house, which, compared to other brothels, was "like being in heaven."[60]

Later, Osaki was taken out of the brothel by an Englishman who made her his mistress. A few years later she became sick, and her English master sent her back to Amakusa before the war. She was leading a solitary existence in a state of destitution when Yamasaki met her and persuaded her to tell her life story.

The Reform Movement Abroad

As with prostitution at home, Japan's leaders showed little interest in the plight of the young girls who were sent abroad as *de facto* slaves. The few people who extended a helping hand to the *karayuki* were again Christians like Yamamuro and his Salvation Army followers. In Dairen, for example, the Salvation Army established a home to help prostitutes who managed to escape the brothels.[61] In Singapore, a Japanese Christian missionary with ties to the Salvation Army, Umemuri Gōyū, did his best to undermine the brothels. Once a week, accompanied by his wife, he went into the brothel district with his tambourine and exhorted people to stay away. The brothel keepers tried to intimidate him by having him beat up by goons, but he persisted in his efforts; and, in fact, was successful in persuading some prostitutes to leave the brothels and return to Japan.[62]

A right-wing, nationalist youth who considered the brothels a national disgrace also launched a campaign against the Japanese brothels in Singapore, but his activities were quashed by the brothel keepers.[63] In 1913, the Japanese consul in Singapore convinced the authorities to expel all Japanese pimps from the city. But the expulsion order failed to rid the community of them; they simply went underground and continued to ply their trade.

The reason both the nationalist youth and the consul were so concerned about Japanese prostitutes in Singapore was that the city was seen as a crossroads between East and West, and the Japanese were especially sensitive about the West's opinion of their country. European colonial authorities had been tolerant of prostitution in their colonies, but, as public opinion grew increasingly critical of this hands-off policy, they slowly began to try to curb the brothels and the trade in prostitutes. In 1913, the governor-general of Singapore banned prostitution by white women. In 1920, the Japanese consul persuaded the British authorities to ban Japanese brothels from Singapore and Malaya.[64] In 1931, the authorities in the Dutch East Indies (Indonesia) also banned public prostitution. In response, brothel keepers simply moved their business to Japanese-controlled areas of northeastern Asia where they were allowed to carry on their trade until the end of the Pacific War. The *karayuki* who were shipped home by the Japanese authorities during this period were provided with no assistance. They were simply dropped off at the ports of arrival and forced to shift for themselves.[65]

In every area Japan conquered during World War II, prostitution was restored.[66] In fact, in 1941, the Japanese authorities actually conscripted Korean women into a corps of "entertainers" to "comfort" the Japanese troops in Manchuria. With the beginning of the Pacific War, from 50,000 to 70,000 Korean girls and women were drafted and sent to the front to "entertain" the Japanese troops.[67] It took Japan's defeat and the reforms initiated by the occupation authorities to end the practice of selling women into prostitution both at home and abroad.

THE

COAL

MINERS

Coal played a crucial role in Japan's modernization, since throughout the nineteenth century it was Japan's chief source of energy and one of the few minerals in which the country was self-sufficient. In fact, Japan was able to export a considerable amount of coal in the Meiji period. One of its largest mine complexes, the Miike coal mines in Kyushu, sent 82 percent of its yield abroad in 1883.[1]

Coal production burgeoned very swiftly because of coal's importance as an export commodity as well as the rapidly increasing domestic need for it. In the Miike mines alone, production rose from 60,000 tons in 1877 to 599,000 tons in 1893. The total national yield was 208,000 tons in 1874. By 1883, it topped the million-ton mark; by 1888, the 2-million mark, and it increased by another million tons every year or two. By 1919, it had hit 31 million tons.[2]

During the Tokugawa period, mining had been a government monopoly. The Meiji government continued this practice for a few years but soon adopted a policy of turning over the mines to favored entrepreneurs, such as Mitsui and Mitsubishi.

Early Meiji Mines

Mining had always been a hazardous occupation, and miners in many countries had been treated as virtual slaves. Roman prisoners of war and Russian political prisoners were sent into the mines, in many cases to labor away until they dropped dead. When Japan launched its program for industrialization, the Meiji leaders sent prisoners, *burakumin,* impoverished peasants,[3] and, later, colonized Koreans into the mines. By relying on prisoners to work in the mines, the government may, in effect, have established a precedent for the future abusive treatment of miners.

When the government began operating the Miike coal mines in 1873, it started out by using fifty convicts. Even though the mines were sold to the Mitsui interests in 1888, the practice of using prisoners was continued until 1933. In 1884, 53 percent of the 2,340 miners who did the actual digging in Miike were convicts. In 1896, the number had increased to 1,457 out of a total of 1,932 miners—or 75 percent. Soon afterward, the number of convicts in the mines began to decline, and in 1908 only 138 out of 2,138 miners were convicts, the drop occuring in part because more convicts began to be sent to the Hokkaido mines.[4]

The convicts used in the mines were usually those who had been sentenced to prison for ten years or more. They were bound together by heavy chains and marched into the bowels of the earth. Because lighting was poor and safety measures were worse than inadequate, accidents and deaths among the miners, particularly among the convicts, were extremely high.

The low labor cost resulting from the use of convicts gave the government-operated mines an advantage over those privately run mines that did not have ready access to convict labor. The government's position regarding the use of convict labor was stated by Kaneko Kentarō, a high official, who said in 1885,

Convicts must be used to work on these necessary [Hokkaido] construction projects. Even if they are unable to endure the hard labor, collapse, and die . . . it can be regarded as an unavoidable policy at present, when we are having difficulty defraying prison expenses. Moreover, when we compare the wages of ordinary workers and convicts in Hokkaido, the ordinary workers are paid no less than 40 sen a day while the convicts are paid only 18 sen a day. Thus, when we use convicts we can reduce the wages by more than half in these construction projects. This is like killing two birds with one stone. . . . We must drive these convicts and make them work at difficult tasks that ordinary workers are unable to undertake.[5]

In order to compete with government-operated mines using convicts, the Takashima Mining Company (which Mitsubishi had acquired from the government in 1875) was particularly ruthless in exploiting its miners who were housed in barracks as virtual prisoners and worked twelve hours a day for 30 sen. The atrocious treatment of these nonconvict miners caused them to stage several major riots against the operators between 1882 and 1888. In 1888, following one such riot, a magazine reporter was sent into the Takashima mines to look into working conditions. He found that:

The temperature got hotter the farther down in the mine I went. At the most extreme point it reached 120° to 130° F. The miners have to labor under this heat. Their bodies are constantly covered with pouring sweat. The air is stifling and it is difficult to breathe. The smell of coal makes it almost unbearable. Despite such appalling working conditions, the company rules do not allow even one second of rest. The deputy crew boss patrols the work area, and if he sees a miner slackening his pace even for an instant he beats him with his club. These deputy crew bosses are like monsters and demons. If a miner asks permission to rest because of fatigue, or if he disobeys the crew boss, he is punished as an example to others. His hands are tied behind him and he is strung up by the beam, with his feet slightly above ground. Then he is clubbed while the other miners are forced to watch the beating. If a miner, unable to bear the harsh conditions, tries to escape and is caught and brought back he is then kicked, beaten, strung up, and generally treated in a brutal and cruel fashion by the guards. No human being could behave as atrociously [as these guards]. There is no other way to identify them except to call them devils. I heard that when a cholera epidemic struck this island mine in 1844, half of the 3,000 miners, over 1,500, were struck by the epidemic and died. Whether the victims were dead or not, the day after they contracted cholera they were taken to the beach, and five to ten of them at a time were placed on an iron platform and burned.[6]

The aim of this reporter and others who revealed the atrocious conditions in the mines was to effect reforms, but the treatment of miners did not improve appreciably until the end of World War II. The mine companies denied that conditions were as bad as they were reported, and journalists friendly to the companies held that the critics' accounts were exaggerated. Among the second group of reporters was Inukai Tsuyoshi, who later became a leading parliamentary figure and eventually, in 1931, prime minister.[7]

Aside from accidents involving relatively few individuals, there were explosions, fires, cave-ins, and flooding that often caused mass deaths. Major mining accidents were almost an annual occurrence. A gas explosion in a Kyushu mine in 1914 took the lives of 669 persons, the highest toll of any disaster in Japanese mining history. As the scale of mining operations in Japan grew and the number of miners increased, the number of accidents and deaths rose also. During the Shōwa era (beginning in 1926), the number of deaths in the mines each year ranged from the 600s to a high of 1,868 in 1944. From 1935 to the end of the war, the number topped 1,000 every year but one. Even in the immediate postwar period the number of deaths remained well above 600 annually. As for injuries, about 5 percent of all miners suffered serious injuries each year.[8]

The mine companies provided only minimal compensation for the families of miners who were killed or injured on the job. In 1902, Miike paid a fixed rate of 100 yen for a death in which the miner was not at fault, and 50 yen for a death caused, in the company's opinion, by the miner's own carelessness. For major injuries, such as loss of eyesight, hearing, or limbs, the company paid 100 yen in the absence of contributory negligence; otherwise, the company paid 40 yen for damage to eyesight or hearing, and 20 yen for loss of limb.[9]

Even miners who escaped serious injury worked under extremely difficult conditions. Typically, one old woman miner recalled her days in the mines as "a living hell."[10] An account of working conditions in the early Meiji period states:

The miners work several hundred feet underground . . . with only the dim light of a hand-held lamp. . . . If by some good fortune the coal bed is thick and the passage is as much as 6 feet high, the miner can walk upright, but if the coal bed is shallow and the ceiling is less than 4 feet high, the miner has to crawl to the pit face, and dig the coal from a squatting position. In extreme cases he has to swing the pick and dig the coal lying on his back. . . . For those who transport the coal out of the mine, the situation is even more difficult. We had to grab a short wooden cane in both hands and crawl on our hands and knees to drag the coal basket out to the bin located in the main tunnel. . . . The miners were either covered with a piece of rag or were naked.[11]

The job of transporting the coal basket to the bin was usually a woman's task. In many instances, a husband and wife made up a team of digger and hod carrier.

THE CREW-BOSS SYSTEM

To keep the miners working under adverse conditions, the mine companies usually used crew or barracks bosses not only to recruit and then oversee the miners in the mines but also to act as wardens and guards in the compounds where they were housed. These crew bosses frequently came out of the underworld, many having been petty gangsters, hoodlums, or ex-convicts. The mine operators, who believed that such tough-minded thugs were needed to keep the miners (regarded as roughnecks and ne'er-do-wells) under control, endorsed the crew bosses use of regular beatings and torture to keep the miners in line and, above all, to prevent them from running away.

In return for their efforts, the crew bosses were either allowed to collect a percentage of the miners' pay or were paid company commissions based on the amount of coal their crews produced. They were also given the exclusive right to sell the miners' their daily necessities.

They were, in effect, a combination of middleman, goon, slave driver, warden, and concessionnaire.

The desperate miners often revolted against these bosses. As a result, the Takashima Mining Company abandoned the crew-boss system in 1897 and established a direct employer-employee relationship with its miners.[12] But most other companies, particularly the smaller ones, retained the crew-boss system into the twentieth century. As late as 1923, fifty of the eighty-one mines in Fukuoka prefecture still employed the crew-boss system.[13]

Run by the crew bosses, the living quarters of the miners were wretched shanties. A newspaper article from 1900 described the huts of one of the Hokkaido mines as follows:

The shacks of the miners have leaky roofs. The wooden walls are about to fall apart and the floors are rotting. Each unit is about 4 *tsubo* [about 16 square yards] and contains a kitchen, closet, [and living quarters]. It is barely large enough for the dwellers to crowd in. The entrails of fish and chickens are strewn about in the vicinity of the shacks. There is only one latrine for twenty households. When it snows, it is impossible for people to get to the latrine. The children urinate in front of their shacks. The area is afloat with excrement and urine; the filth is indescribable. Because of these conditions there is currently an outbreak of dysentery.[14]

The convicts in the Hokkaido mines were housed in what was called *tako-beya* ("octopus rooms"), which in effect were prison cells.[15] Later, the free miners too came to be housed in similar cells and were treated just like the convicts. They were denied the right to come and go as they pleased, and even their letters were censored.

Despite their strenuous and dangerous work, the miners were compensated very little. In the 1890s, in one of the major mines in northern Kyushu, the average pay was 35 sen a day, while a skilled, productive coal digger earned between 40 and 70 sen a day.[16] In a major mine in Hokkaido, a coal digger earned 95 sen for a twelve-hour day in 1903. This compared favorably with a blacksmith's earnings of 50 sen a day; but, of course, the miner was engaged in much more arduous and dangerous labor.[17] Three decades later, in 1936, the pay in the major mines in Fukuoka still came to less than 40 yen a month.

Naturally, the mine companies had difficulty recruiting workers and keeping them on the job. A woman miner, relating her life in the early decades of the twentieth century, recalled that every morning the crew boss's helper would come around the shacks with a club to get the miners out to work. If someone claimed to be ill, the enforcer would yell,

"What! You have a headache? Jackass. You had too much whiskey last night. Go to work. No?" Then he would hit the sick man.

The boss took a cut from the miners' pay. When we ran out of money the only person we could turn to was the crew boss. Then he deducted what we owed him from our earnings, and we would have to borrow again till the next payday. So we were short of money the year round. . . . Even if we got hurt they would not take care of us properly. . . . In desperation some would try to run away. Those who got away were lucky, but if you got caught that was the end. . . . The captive, with his hands tied behind his back, would be brought to the guards and crew boss, who had clubs in their hands. They then beat the victim up with all their might. When he passed out they poured water on him, revived him, and beat him again. We were all made to watch the beatings. . . . Some of the victims became crazy, some became dumb. Some were turned into cripples. But no one could do or say anything about this. The police paid no attention.[18]

One Meiji miner remembered that, in the mines of Nagasaki, he saw a man and a woman tied naked on a cross, and the other miners were required to hit them in their vital parts everytime they passed them. They were being punished for adultery.[19] Accounts of miners who were trussed up and had their feet burned with red-hot pokers,[20] and of attempted escapees who were tied and hung upside down over a fire while being clubbed[21] are not uncommon.

Despite the fact that the runaway miners knew they would be tortured in this fashion if they got caught, the number of attempted escapes remained high. A survey taken in the late 1920s by a major mining company showed that 41 percent of their 8,366 mine workers had fled or tried to flee their mines.[22]

Needless to say, not all crew bosses were sadistic monsters, and in times of need the miners could go to some of them for help. Some even cooperated with those who were planning to run away. From the crew bosses's point of view, they themselves were victims since the runaways often owed them money; and frequently the runaway miners were simply moving about to try to find mines that paid more.[23] The supervisors, foremen, and crew bosses were simply doing their dirty work for the mine operators who paid their wages and whose only goal was to increase production to fatten profits.

Having started its process of industrialization almost a century after England, Meiji Japan followed in the footsteps of the British even in the practice of using women and children in the mines. Not until 1928 did the Japanese government ban women from the mines and even then this applied only to major mining companies, not small and middle-sized ones. Moreover, the law was relaxed in 1933 to permit the use of married women in the mines, and, in 1938, the ban on women miners was revoked completely. Finally, in 1946, under the occupation authorities, a total ban on the employment of women in the mines was effected.[24]

Male miners did not regard the ban on women as a beneficial measure, for it often meant a loss of needed income. One miner went directly to the company to complain: "Why do you make my wife quit work? If you're going to fire her, fire me, too. We'll hang ourselves together at the entrance to the mine!"[25]

Children below the age of ten were also regularly brought into the mines. One woman recalled that her grandmother, who had been widowed at forty, took her children of seven, nine, eleven, and sixteen into the mines to work with her. "In those days the entire family would work as a unit to mine the coal."[26] According to another woman, as a child she couldn't wait to join her older brothers and sisters in the mines. "I wanted to be among the eleven- and twelve-year-olds. My older sister was thirteen or fourteen. She would tell me, 'I'm lonely in the mines, so why don't you come with me?' I wanted very badly to join her in the mines. The night before I was to do so, I couldn't sleep for the excitement. . . . My mother told me not to go, that it was dangerous, but I ran ahead of the others and went in."[27]

A seventy-year-old woman interviewed in the postwar years recalled that she entered the mines when she was nine, and, after working in numerous mines, finally quit at the age of sixty. "I used to think that I would go mad whenever I went down into the mines."[28] Another old woman miner related:

I was born in this mining community. The entire region along the Onga River [in Fukuoka] is mountainous, so most of the girls went into the mines to work. The mines were full of twelve- and thirteen-year-old girls. My father died in the mines when I was ten. . . . I went into the mines to work when I was thirteen. They used to say that the god of the mines was a dog. When a dog barked loud, or when it barked in the direction of the mines, it meant trouble, they would tell me. . . . But I used to hide my puppy in my lunch basket and bring him into the mines with me. . . . The mines were a danger-ous place. You were in constant danger of losing your life. A cave-in might occur at any moment. There were times when gas came out. Then a blue ball of fire would shoot through the mines. The sound was loud enough to burst your eardrums. Sometimes the beams and shafts would snap. The ground was rough, and you couldn't stand up straight and walk. The passages were narrow, too. Sometimes we had to crawl around, and water was always seeping in. The mine passages were steep . . . and it was hot.

The women's job was to transport the coal that had been mined. The coal was loaded into a 4-foot-square wooden box. The bottom of the box had metal runners. We had to pull this box with a sash over our shoulders. It was hard work. Where it was uphill, there were wooden logs to serve as rails to make it easier to pull the box. Going downhill, when the angle of the slope was over thirty degrees, we would get on our hands and knees, grab the log railings firmly, hold back the box with our heads, and slowly crawl down backward. With a lamp in our mouths and with our heads holding back the box full of coal, we would feel our way down, inch by inch, with the tip of our straw sandals. If you slipped, it wouldn't be only you who got hurt, because there were others ahead of you. Some of the women had babies on their backs while hauling coal. Since water was dripping all the time, it was slippery. [After they hauled the coal to the coal cart, they had to push a cart full of empty boxes back to where the digging was taking place.] We were really slaves. Lots of people died when the boxes fell off the cart. That was the scariest part of our work. Once a friend of mine was coming down the slope with her daughter. We were going up. All of a sudden the boxes began to tumble down and her daughter was killed. . . . That friend had been a very religious person. She said, "I was a devout believer, but my daughter died. It does no good to have faith! . . ."

It was really hard to get a loaded coal box moving. We'd push it with our heads and our rears. After struggling hard and pushing the box for hundreds of yards, we were paid 8.5 sen. . . . With both my husband and me working, we made 30 to 40 sen a day. One *shō* [.48 U.S. gallons] of rice cost 12 to 13 sen then. We used to work twelve or thirteen hours [at a time]. Sometimes they would arbitrarily deduct one box from our work. . . . But we had to accept that. If we uttered a single word of complaint we would be beaten within an inch of death. There used to be a saying that went, "Complain and you'll get a club on your back. Your towel will be dyed with blood." . . .

My first husband was killed by a runaway coal cart. . . . That was in 1923. They gave me 200 yen as compensation. That was more than what most mines paid. At another mine, five of my cousins from the same family went in the mines, and all five were killed. . . . At that time the family got 50 yen per person. Capitalists are really ruthless people. My father died [in the mines] at the time of the Russo-Japanese War. We got 5 yen then. . . .

I raised my children while working in the mines. It was really rough going into the mines then. I would get up at two in the morning and quietly prepare breakfast. . . . I would then wake my child up when it was still dark. The child would rub his eyes and complain. I would yell at him and take him to the nursery. . . . They used to take care of him for 8 sen a day. I would leave him there, wondering if I would ever see him again. . . . "Will today be the day he is going to lose his parents?" I would wonder. So I was able to see my children only at night. . . . We didn't have any *futon* for bedding. Three out of ten families had no *futon*. The shack consisted of one 4½-mat room and a 6-mat room. There were no sliding doors or screens. There was a 3-foot-wide dirt-floor opening by the entrance. A straw mat served as a curtain. It was really a pathetic place. But when my father was young, he told us, not only was there no straw mat by the entrance, the shack had no walls at all. There were only four poles holding up a grass roof. Of course, there were no mats on the floor. They burned firewood and cut a hole in the roof to let the smoke out . . . and slept on the dirt floor. . . . When we fell heavily in debt, we would sneak away at night, taking our children by their hands. . . . Even when we didn't want any more children, they kept coming. There was nothing we could do about that. Even if we spent nothing on the baby, we at least had to pay the midwife. So we fell into debt. They didn't give us any compensation worth speaking of, even if we got injured. So we would quietly get ready and sneak away.[29]

Because women miners worked as hard and produced as much as men, they had a strong sense of equal worth. According to one woman miner, "Women and men did the same kind of work. . . . It's not true that women were weaker physically. We did the same work. . . . There was a woman who used to lift up huge chunks of coal that men could not carry." Some mines paid women the same wages as men, but usually they were paid less. "My happiest time as a miner was when we went to the Nishitan mines. There, if a man was paid 1 yen, a woman was paid 1 yen, too. That's because we did the same kind of work. In fact, the women worked harder than the men." However, these mines were exceptions. "Even if women did more work than men, we were paid only 80 percent of what the men got. It really was dumb. . . . I worked very hard because I didn't want my children to have to do this kind of work, but when the war came, my youngest son had to go into the mines. I was sorry about that." When the employment of women in the mines was banned in 1928, the women who continued to go into the mines (because of the lax enforcement of the law) were paid only 50 percent of what the men got.[30]

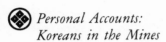

Personal Accounts:
Koreans in the Mines

In 1910, Japan annexed Korea. Soon afterward, Koreans, many of whom had had their land confiscated by the Japanese colonial authorities, began to emigrate to Japan looking for work. They usually ended up doing hard labor on road gangs or in the mines.[31] Later, the mining companies began actively to recruit Korean workers. Eventually, they were simply conscripted into the labor force by the government and forced into the mines and construction work.

The Hokkaido Mining Company got its first group of thirty-five Korean laborers in 1916. By 1928, 1,505 Koreans were employed by the company. This number declined in the early 1930s because high unemployment led the government to restrict Korean immigration to Japan. However, as Japan went onto its war footing, massive numbers of Koreans were recruited or conscripted to replace Japanese workers both in Japan and overseas in the war zones.[32] It is estimated that in 1944 there were 35,209 Korean miners in the Hokkaido mines; 74,736 in the Kyushu mines; 10,995 in the mines of Yamaguchi prefecture; and 7,250 in other mines. In all, 31.9 percent of the miners in Japan were Koreans at this time.[33]

From 1939 on, the Coal Production Board recruited Korean workers with the aid of the Korean governor-general's office. A quota was established for each county, and recruiters went into the villages to enlist Korean peasants. Because Korean farmers had suffered a serious drought and crop failure in 1939, the recruiters were initially able to meet their quotas easily.[34] But as the need for manpower grew, particularly after the outbreak of the Pacific War, the recruiters began to dragoon Koreans into the labor force. The help of government officials, Japanese police, and military gendarmes was enlisted in this effort. Often ruthless means were used to coerce the unwilling peasants into the labor force. Many were kidnapped while they were working out in the fields or asleep at home, and then taken off to Japan without even being granted the opportunity to bid their families farewell.

Between 1940 and 1945, about a million Koreans were brought to Japan to work as virtual slaves. When the war ended, there were 2,365,000 Koreans in Japan proper.[35]

Koreans dragooned into the labor force recalled with bitterness their experiences. As Choi Chun Su remembered the experience,

On October 20, 1942, I was working with some fishermen on the coast of Pusan. I was walking in front of the station with a pack on my back, when a stranger came up to me and said he wanted to talk to me and dragged me off to the inn. There were about one hundred people at the inn already. At that time I was twenty-six years old and married, with sons who were three and six, but I was not allowed to let them know where I was. I was told that I was to be taken to the Hokkaido mines. If I refused I would be sent to Taiwan [in the war zone]. I wanted to run away but I was not able to. The next day we were put on a ship and left the port of Pusan. I don't know how they found out, but before the ship left port I saw my wife and children on the dock. We were not able to exchange any words.[36]

Theoretically, these workers were on a two-year contract, but this was a meaningless formality, as their contracts were unilaterally renewed by the company officials.[37] In addition, Korean miners, who were officially paid much less than their Japanese counterparts—in many cases less than half the wage—saw all sorts of expenses deducted from their pay. This left them with very little cash, which in turn they were compelled to put in savings accounts—a means of preventing them from running away.

Korean miners were also treated with particular brutality because of racial prejudice. Their workday in the mines was supposed to be twelve hours long, but a quota was set for each day and the miners were not allowed to leave the pits until they met that quota, no matter how long it took. As one Korean miner noted, "In extreme cases we had to work from seven in the morning until three the next morning. Our meal normally consisted of bean dregs. Not even pigs would have eaten what was served us. We were so hungry that we had no strength. When we were forced to work extra hours, we were given one rice ball. . . .[38]

All the Korean miners interviewed in a postwar study complained of the poor quality and meager portions of the food they had received. One remarked, "I really had a hard time with the food. We were just given one bowl of a mixture of Chinese rice, soybeans, and broken bits of noodles. To go with it, we got some *daikon* [radishes] and bean-paste soup with *daikon* leaves. We had fish only once a month."[39]

In the mines, the Koreans were given the most difficult assignments and were constantly goaded by the club-wielding overseers. A Korean miner brought to the mines in 1942 recollected,

When I arrived at the "octopus room," the foreman told me in his dialect, "Sit down." I didn't understand what he said, so he hit me with his club. We worked in two shifts from six to six. . . . We were given an hour for lunch. . . . When we returned to our living quarters after work, the place was usually full of injured workers. They had been hurt not in the natural completion of their work but by beatings inflicted on them. The manager of the kitchen would pull out his Japanese sword and threaten us by saying, "It's nothing at all for me to cut down five or six of you peninsula men." Once a week a policeman came around and asked if we had any complaints but, since he was accompanied by the foreman, no one dared say anything. The policeman would then be treated to a feast and go home.[40]

As might be expected, the malnutrition and harsh working conditions caused the physical condition of the Korean miners to deteriorate badly. For example, there were forty-one deaths among 640 Korean miners in one Hokkaido mine in 1943. The doctor assigned to the mine was convinced that the actual figure was higher.[41]

A Korean who observed the treatment of his fellow countrymen in the mines of Fukushima prefecture recalled:

The average workday was fourteen hours. Because of the strain, even a healthy person could not sustain the pace. If a person tried to rest when he got sick, he would be charged with faking and would be brought to the office and tortured. . . . I know a worker who was thrown in jail for eight months for complaining that he did not get enough to eat. Also, for three months following our arrival at the mines, we were forced to undergo military drills after work. Those who had been on night shift would collapse with exhaustion. Those who did not march around as sharply as they were ordered to do were beaten with whips by the officials. . . . In desperation, some would try to run away. . . . Those who were recaptured were beaten half to death. Then they were turned over to the police, where they were tortured and jailed. After they were let out of jail, they were put in the company's lock-up before they were released and sent back to the mines.[42]

These stories of brutal treatment were not exaggerations. They were corroborated not only by Japanese newspaper accounts and studies made by non-Korean groups, but also by the observations of Japanese who were themselves biased against Koreans. One old Japanese woman miner held that "Koreans were a mess. . . . They didn't obey people at all. They were self-indulgent and threw things about and never cleaned up." Yet she noted: "They were beaten up all the time by the guards. They [the guards] would beat Japanese, too, but they beat up the Koreans much more severely. They were treated really brutally. [The overseers] would beat them with their rods until they bled. . . . Because they were hardly fed any food, they would stagger about. Then they would be scolded severely and be beaten up. During the war, the Koreans had practically nothing to eat . . . about two raw cucumbers. That's all. For breakfast they were given rice gruel, and so they were barely able to walk around."[43]

Choi Chun Su's story sums up much of the Korean miners' experience. Constantly abused, partly because of his inability to understand Japanese, he tried to run away. He was quickly caught and thrown in the back room of the "octopus shack." Then:

I was tied up with a rope and beaten. I fainted but was revived with a bucket of water. This happened three times. They then placed two iron rods in the stove, heated them up, and burned my back with them. When the heated rod was applied to my back the first time, I smelled my burning flesh, but after that I felt nothing because I passed out. When I regained consciousness the next morning, I asked for some water. The supervisor brought me some water and warned me, "I'll kill you if you say anything about this." For three days he watched over me and brought me my meals himself. He was afraid that the police might find out about me. Three days later he ordered me back into the mines. Yellow fluid oozed out from the blisters on my back. . . .[44]

Choi Chun Su tried again to run away. After wandering about in the snow, he was helped by some kindly peasants and managed to get on the ferry from Hokkaido to Aomori. In Aomori he was caught by the police. There he was beaten with a bamboo rod and leather strap because he refused to tell them where he had run away from. The police found out, however, and sent him back to Hokkaido. Convinced that he would be killed if he went back to the mines, he managed to escape from the train by wiggling out of the lavatory window. Again he was helped by some peasants, who got him a job with a construction crew, and again he was caught by the police.

Beaten and tortured once more, he still refused to identify his old mining company. Consequently, the police sent him to another mine where the conditions were even worse.

My head was full of lice. The burn on my back had got infected and was full of puss. If anyone spoke Korean he was not fed. . . . When we got thirsty we had to drink the polluted water found in the mines. This would be followed by diarrhea. We had to work from 6 A.M. to 11 P.M. I was paid 2 yen 15 sen but was charged 1 yen 50 sen for meals. Because our canvas shoes fell apart, we were forced to buy a new pair every day. One pair cost 3 yen 50 sen, and so our debt grew with each passing day. They knew we would try to run away if we had the money.

Many miners died. In my former mine, when the workers died, they used to call out the names of their family members just before they died. . . . In the second mine, a well-educated young man who came from a good family in Seoul tried to escape but he was recaptured and beaten brutally. He ended up going mad.[45]

Choi Chun Su was then sent to the Kuriles to work on a project to build an airfield. The end of the war saw him working in another mine as a kitchen worker.

It is interesting to note that poor peasants as well as *burakumin* were the most likely to extend a helping hand to the abused Korean workers; the wielders of power, the wealthy owners and their henchmen, were the ones who brutalized them. As another example of the weak helping the weak, there is the story of a twenty-one-year-old woman in Yamagata prefecture. When she was working in a labor-camp mess hall in 1944, the police came to her camp and instructed her to inform them if she saw any sign of runaway Korean miners. Later a young man in rags crawled out from under her house and asked for help. He explained to her:

I came to Japan to study but needed money, so in order to earn my tuition I fell for the clever tale of the recruiter and joined the miners in Hokkaido. But they paid me nothing except 2 yen for cigarette money. I had no way of saving any money for my education. Since they do not feed us Koreans adequately, my co-workers began to die, one after another, of malnutrition and hard work. Even if a person gets sick, he is forced to work or is beaten with the whip and club until he drops dead. If a person tries to resist, he is likely to be tortured to death. I have parents and brothers and sisters in my home country. I don't want to die in a foreign land.

The woman decided to help the young Korean miner and hid him for a few days. She also helped two other Koreans, who were being held by the police, to escape.[46]

It appears that, among the exploited miners themselves, the Koreans and Japanese worked together more harmoniously than one might have expected, given the atmosphere of racial mistrust on both sides. As one old woman miner said, "The biggest problem was the language barrier. But, unlike the Japanese miners, the Korean miners never made lewd remarks to the women who were assigned to them to haul out the coal. They were really principled about this. As a result, when I was a young girl, I used to like to work with Korean diggers. I could work without fear [of being molested]."[47] "The foremen made no distinction in his [harsh] treatment of Japanese and Koreans," recalled another old miner. "The miners themselves not only did not discriminate against the Koreans but we helped each other." When the war ended, a Korean miner came to say good-bye to him. " 'I'm going back to Korea, but please come and visit me there,' he said. And we departed in tears. I don't know where he got it, but he brought a sack of sugar and left it for me, saying it was a farewell gift. It was unexpected. Other young Koreans used to come and visit me often. Pak, Kim, and others. When they left, they all shed tears. They were all good young men."[48]

It is believed that Koreans and *burakumin* got along well because both were victims of prejudice. An example of cooperation between the two groups is seen in the miners' strike that took place in the Asō mines in Kyushu. Asō Mines employed about 1,000 Korean miners in conditions far worse than those of other mines. In 1932, the company found it necessary to curtail its activities and began to let Korean workers go without compensation. This led the Korean miners, with the help of union organizers, to stage a strike asking for better working conditions and higher pay. They also asked for an end to brutal treatment and for better care for the sick and injured.[49] During the course of the strike, the Suiheisha supported the Korean miners by collecting rice from *burakumin,* who themselves were in dire need because of the Depression, and donating it to the strikers.[50] While the miners got the support of other outside groups, like the right-wing socialists, in the end they failed to gain their objectives.

The *burakumin* had a reputation for being helpful to runaway miners regardless of their nationality or background. In northern Kyushu, *buraku* villages were some of the few havens for the runaways. Miners, it was said, felt as if they had reached friendly territory once they managed to hide in the outcaste community.[51]

Many *burakumin* also entered the mines, and the harsh discrimination that beset them in the society at large followed them. Until the middle of the Meiji era, some mining companies refused to employ *burakumin* at all, because, they claimed, they would pollute the mines. Those that did employ them used segregated housing, baths, and latrines.[52] Until the middle years of the Meiji era, when the *burakumin* came out of some of the northern mines, they were forced to wash off the coal dust and dirt in the same water that was used to wash the horses. In some instances, they were not even allowed to use the water until after the horses had been washed.[53]

The Reform Movement in the Mining Industry

Around the turn of the century, Christian reformers and socialists began to go among the miners to organize unions. The pioneer effort in the mining industry took place in Hokkaido in 1902 when two miners formed a self-help association designed primarily to foster a sense of self-improvement among the miners. The stated objectives of the association, known as the Rōdō Shiseikai (Association for Sincerity in Labor) included enhancement of the miners' dignity, development of a spirit of self-reliance and independence, encouragement of frugality and mutual help. But the founders also declared their aim to be the acquisition of "equal rights and freedom in our relationship with the capitalist employers."[54] A pioneer socialist and labor organizer, Katayama Sen (1859–1933), was among the supporters of the Shiseikai.[55]

In 1907, the miners of Hokkaido, led by the Shiseikai, staged a series of strikes. One of the organizers, Nagaoka Tsuruzō, wrote Katayama Sen:

I am determined to serve the interests of tens of thousands of Japanese miners by sacrificing my life and my family for the cause. I plan to turn the seven members of my family out into the snowfields of Hokkaido, sell all my household belongings and depart [to organize the Ashio copper mines in Honshu]. I feel this is the price that I must pay if I am to live up to my convictions. This is what I plan for my family members: (1) I shall put our four-year-old daughter up for adoption; (2) the eight-year-old will be the baby-sitter for the two-year-old; (3) the ten-year-old child will sell candy after school; (4) the thirteen-year-old will do the cooking and go to school; (5) the fifteen-year-old will work in a machine shop during the day and sell sweet *sake* at night; (6) my wife will work as a baggage bearer at the railroad station during the day and sell sweet *sake* at night.[56]

The Shiseikai organizers expected to negotiate with the mining company without resorting to violence. However, in early February 1907, the Ashio miners, protesting the low wages, long hours, and abuses by the foremen, took to violence, using dynamite to blow up company facilities, and indiscriminately setting fire to company buildings. The company record states that "chaos reigned in Ashio. The fire fighters failed to prevent the fire from spreading, and the police failed to protect the people. Finally the word spread that the army was coming. This gave the 30,000 residents hope. Earlier, the prefectural governor, realizing the gravity of the situation, had called on the commanding general of the First Division to send in his troops to restore order. Once the troops arrived [on February 6], our community, which had been without law and order, finally saw order restored."[57]

The next big series of violent actions by the miners broke out during the 1918 rice riots (see p. 160). The riots were triggered by the housewives of Toyama and spread rapidly to other areas and other segments of the society. The extensive involvement of the masses in these riots, the bitter feelings that were engendered by the inflation of the World War I period, and the violence led Katayama Sen to conclude that the class struggle in Japan got its true beginning during this period.[58]

Miners also joined the protest against the high price of rice and demanded higher wages. When the mining companies failed to comply with their demands, the miners in many areas also turned to violence, destroying public and company facilities, stores, and the houses of the rich. The first of these miners' riots erupted in Ube, in Yamaguchi perfecture, where the miners demanded a 30 percent increase in pay. When this was not forthcoming, the miners went on a rampage. Because the police were unable to control the rioters, the army was called in and the demonstrators were dispersed by troops, which fired into a crowd, killing thirteen persons and injuring a number of others. Hundreds of demonstrators were arrested and close to

350 of them were indicted and sentenced to prison or fined. The judge of the court of appeals commented that "the incident seems not to have any political cast, nor is there any scent of socialism. The rioters appear to have been aroused by existing conditions, and [to have] committed these crimes in a senseless manner. It may seem harsh to impose heavy sentences, but today, when the spirit of the people is turbulent, it is necessary to impose stiff sentences in order to preserve the nation's security even though we may pity those convicted."[59]

The fact that these activities lacked a "political cast" and remained merely violent outbursts of pent-up frustrations made them basically ineffective in improving the miners' conditions. On the other hand, had they possessed a "political cast," the leaders would have been charged with subversive activities and with harboring "dangerous thoughts," and would have been punished more severely—as happened to many socialist and communist labor organizers in the mass arrests of April 16, 1929. Among the victims was Yamashiro Yoshimune, the husband of the author of "The Bog Rhubarb Shoots (see p. 85)," who had led a miners' strike in 1927. After he was released from prison in 1936, he continued his "subversive" activities and persisted in harboring "dangerous thoughts," and was thus imprisoned again in 1940. He refused to renounce his Marxist views and convert to "Japanism," despite continuous pressure by the authorities. In January 1945, the authorities reported his death of "unknown causes."[60]

Following the riots of 1918, mine organizers sought to influence the miners to pursue their objectives in a more disciplined fashion. For instance, in the Miike miners' strike of 1924, the miners rigidly abstained from violence so as not to give the owners an excuse to call in police or army troops. When the owners told the strikers that their family members would be reduced to starvation if they persisted in the strike, the strikers responded, "We don't care if our family members do starve to death. We knew from the outset that we might have to accept such a development. Unless we are prepared to endure such a situation, we cannot engage the Mitsui people in a battle in which everything is at stake." The company finally succeeded in breaking the strike by bribing some of the strike leaders, but working conditions did subsequently improve in the mines.[61]

In the 1930s, as Japan went onto a semi-wartime footing, labor movements in the mines were subordinated to the imperatives of the national emergency. During the war, as noted above, miners served as virtual slave laborers.

The end of the war meant the freeing of the Korean miners. For the Japanese miners who worked for major mining companies, working conditions and pay improved as labor leaders, now free from government restrictions, were able to organize them into unions and negotiated with the mining companies on a more equitable basis. However, miners employed by small-mine operators continued to work in circumstances not much better than those that existed during the prewar years, if only because union organizers concentrated on the large mines and neglected smaller ones. Small-mine owners tried to prevent unions from penetrating their mines and fired any worker who got involved in union activities. Moreover, in the 1950s, as Japan turned to oil for its source of energy and mining became less profitable, the smaller coal mines began to shut down. The chief problem for the miners then became unemployment.[62] However, as the economy began to boom in the 1960s, former miners found employment elsewhere, and complaints of worker shortages, rather than unemployment, began to appear in the newspaper columns.

EPILOGUE:

THE

POSTWAR

YEARS

At the end of the war Japan lay in ruins. Its major cities were practically all leveled, its factories turned into rubble, its resources almost completely depleted. According to one estimate, from 1941–1945 one-fourth of Japan's national wealth was lost. Its industrial capacity at the end of the war stood at scarcely 10 percent of the normal prewar level. Industrial output during 1945–1946 was one-fourth the 1934–1936 average, and agricultural production was 50 percent of the prewar level.[1] Shortages in all the basic necessities caused serious inflation, and money rapidly lost its value. By 1948, consumer prices had risen to 200 times the prewar level.[2]

Perhaps it could be said that at this point "equality" had been achieved in Japan, for rich and poor, city and rural dwellers, all were confronted with bare cupboards. In fact, for the first time, if only briefly, the peasants were better off than bombed-out city residents, for they at least could get food from the land, while urban dwellers were given food rations of 1,050 calories per person per day which caused them to scour the countryside looking for food, bartering away whatever valuables they had. Those who failed to obtain food in these expeditions to the villages or in the black market faced starvation.[3]

This dismal state of affairs continued through the remainder of the forties. But, by 1950, the economy began to revive, and, by 1951, industrial production had climbed back to 99 percent of the 1934–1936 level. The Korean War gave the economy a shot in the arm; by 1953, industrial production had risen to 134.5 percent of the prewar level and real consumption had surpassed the prewar average.[4] After 1954, the economy began to grow by leaps and bounds, and, by 1970, Japan's gross national product had become the third largest in the world.

A Society in Flux

This rapid industrial and technological growth, together with the land reform program initiated by the occupation authorities, resulted in momentous changes in farm communities. The economic conditions and cultural life of rural Japan began steadily to approximate those of its urban population. By 1980, in most areas the differences that had sharply divided the farming and urban communities in the prewar years had become blurred.

The diffusion of television sets into the countryside has perhaps

been the single most powerful factor in changing the outlook, attitudes, and cultural life of the rural populace; but their material life too
has been technologically transformed. Washing machines, refrigerators, vacuum cleaners, propane-gas stoves, and running water have
made the lives of farm women far less difficult than they were in the
prewar years. Indicative of the radical nature of the transformation of
rural life is the widespread ownership of automobiles by farm families,
who weave their cars through narrow village roads totally unfit for
motor vehicles. By 1970, car ownership by farm families had surpassed that of nonfarm families; and, by 1975, 58 percent of all farm
families were car owners; compared to 47 percent of all nonfarm
families.[5]

Farm families' lives changed not only as a result of their relatively
sudden exposure to modern technology but also in response to the
availability of industrial and commercial jobs in the cities, which enabled farm families to supplement their income in a substantial way.
While, during the prewar and immediate postwar years, underem-
ployment and surplus labor still plagued farm communities, the economic boom of the 1960s and 1970s drew rural workers into the cities
in unprecedented numbers so that today farmers are actually faced
with a shortage of workers. Whereas, in 1950, 16 million people were
engaged in farm work (45.2 percent of the total labor force), by 1975
the figure had dropped to 6.72 million (12.6 percent of the labor
force).

The younger generation tends to be disinclined to stay on the farm.
As the flow of the young to the cities continues, the average age of
those who remain behind and undertake farm work steadily rises. In
1960, 25 percent of all farm workers were under thirty years old, and
50 percent were forty or older; by 1975, the percentage of those
under thirty had dropped to 8 percent while the percentage of those
over forty had risen to 75 percent. In contrast, in 1978, 40 percent
of all nonfarm workers were under thirty, and one-third were over
forty.

The number of farm families who rely solely on agriculture for
income has, as might be expected, also continued to decline. As early
as 1955, only 35 percent of Japan's farm families depended on agriculture alone for their livelihood. By 1978, this figure had dropped to
12 percent, with 60 percent relying on other occupations for their
chief sources of income. Because of supplementary income gained
from other sources, the per-capita household budget of small-farm
owners in 1978 was higher than that of nonfarm households.[6]

Even though, then, these improvements in the material lives of small-farm owners have clearly not been solely the consequence of the land reform program, the reforms were a contributing factor. In fact, these reforms enabled the war-ravaged rural poor to survive the economic crisis of the immediate postwar years much more comfortably than was the lot of the urban poor.

The Farm Land Reform Law, which went into effect in October 1946, banned absentee landownership and enabled tenant farmers to purchase the land that they had been farming under tenancy. A landowner living in a community where he owned land could on the average retain no more than 1 chō (2.45 acres) that he did not cultivate himself. (The actual maximum varied somewhat from area to area depending on the mean size of the farms. In Hokkaido the limit was 4 chō). He could, in addition, retain 3 cho for his own usage. Except in Hokkaido, no farmer could normally own more than 4 chō of farmland. The government purchased all surplus land held by landowners and resold it to the former tenants, who in turn were to repay the government over a thirty-year period at a low interest rate. The compensation received by the landowners turned out to be nominal, for rampant inflation caused a swift drop in the value of the yen. In some instances, the price per acre paid to the landlord was equivalent to the cost of a carton of cigarettes on the black market. The transfer of land, administered by locally elected land commissions, was completed by August 1950. About 2.8 million acres of rice paddies and 1.95 million acres of upland were transferred from 2.34 million landowners to 4.75 million tenants and farmers who possessed less than the legal maximum. This resulted in the virtual elimination of tenant farmers, who constituted 28.7 percent of all farmers in 1946, but dropped to 1.1 percent by 1957.[7]

For tenant farmers, who had struggled for years to scratch out a meager living from the soil, the notion that the landlords' possessions could be confiscated and turned over to them seemed a miracle. A novelist imagines an old tenant's musings:

In a man's lifetime, he's apt to experience incredible events. Of course, there are many things that will cause him pain and grief but there are likely to be one or two things that will make him deliriously happy. "Maybe this is just a dream," Yasuke thought, and quietly pinched himself. It hurt. It wasn't a dream after all. "The upland fields and rice paddies will all be mine! I won't have to pay any more rent. I won't have to bow and scrape to the landlord anymore." He felt as if he were dreaming. But the land reforms did not go into effect completely free of difficulties. There were some landlords who clung to the provision that allowed them to retain 1 *chō* of land and tried to hang on to all their land.[8]

Needless to say, the land reform program was a bitter pill for the landowners to swallow. A vast majority were not huge landowners, and many felt that they were being deprived of their livelihoods. A farmer in Nagano prefecture, having just returned from military service in China in 1946, found himself faced with having to give up most of his land. He took his gun and shot three members of the local land commission and set fire to six houses. An eight-year-old boy whose father died just when his family was confronted with the loss of its land recalled:

Our rice farm of 6 *chō* was reduced to 0.7 *chō,* and 0.8 *chō* of our upland was cut down to 0.3 *chō.* We were suddenly reduced to being a small-farm family. . . . But in 1946 we had to pay land taxes on our old holdings, so all the money we received as compensation for the land we lost went for the payment of taxes. . . . But it was not sufficient, so we had to sell some of our household goods. . . . Since the land reform act benefited the majority of the farmers, there was nothing we could do. But, because we had to pay heavy taxes on the land that was no longer ours, it was difficult. My father's death, the land reforms, the heavy taxes, all reduced our family to penury. We had to bid farewell to the way of life that, from the time of our ancient ancestors, saw many tenants labor for our well-being. Now we had to use our own anemic arms to work the land ourselves. . . .[9]

Some were unable to face life after they lost their possessions. In Nagano prefecture six brothers and sisters, ranging in age from nine to eighteen and who had lost their parents earlier, committed group suicide when they found that they would lose most of their family property.[10]

In many respects the plight of the former landowners in the postwar years resembled that of the *samurai* who lost their privileges at the time of the Meiji restoration and found themselves reduced to near penury. Like the former *samurai,* the landowning class accepted the new order of things without too much resistance. Only 110 "incidents" occurred over the transference of land in 1947–1948; slightly over 4,000 civil suits were filed. Considering the enormity of the undertaking, these figures do not indicate major conflicts and tensions. To be sure, village harmony and peace were disturbed to some extent as former tenants contested the claims of their former landlords who, in many cases, were their neighbors. However, the traditional practice of making concessions "to preserve the peace of the hamlet" made the drastic surgery of land reform possible without tearing apart the social fabric of the villages.[11]

Because of the enormous growth of the industrial sector, agricultural products have come to constitute less and less of the gross national income. Whereas agriculture produced 20 percent of the gross national income in 1955, it had dropped to less than 5 percent by 1978.[12] Nonetheless, even though the majority of farm families have today come to rely on earnings from nonfarm sources, increased productivity and government price supports have kept revenue from the soil at a relatively high level. Greater productivity on a given area of land was made possible by the effective use of fertilizers, insecticides, herbicides, and germicides. "Before the land reform, a rice harvest of over 3,000 kilograms per hectare [2.45 acres] was considered a bumper crop, but by 1950 that had become average. Today [1978] the average crop is 4,500 kilograms; a yield of 4,700 kilograms or more is considered a bumper crop."[13]

In the prewar years, one of the driving ambitions of the rural poor was to have a bowl of rice from time to time; so it is ironic that today there is a huge surplus of rice, a surplus brought about not only by an increase in productivity but by a change in Japanese dietary habits. Per capita consumption of rice has continued to drop drastically even in recent years. In 1960, per capita rice consumption was still 260 pounds, while, in 1978, it had declined to 178 pounds. People have turned instead to other staples, and currently Japan imports large amounts of wheat, soybeans, corn, and feed grain from the United States and other grain-producing nations. Yet the farmers keep on producing excessive amounts of rice because government price supports make it profitable for them to do so.[14]

The use of farm machines has increased substantially. In 1950, the small gasoline-engine cultivator, pushed by hand, came into use; in 1960, more than half a million were in use; in 1978, 3.3 million.[15] The use of larger cultivators has also increased, but they are counterproductive as far as energy consumption is concerned because the size of the average farm remains too small.

FARM WOMEN

Improvements in the life-style of rural residents can be seen most clearly in the changes for farm women. The life of the young farm wife during the prewar years was usually one of incessant toil and self-denial. The plight of these women, who labored for their husbands and families and then found themselves widowed by the war, was particularly bleak. One such widow, whose husband had been a charcoal maker, lamented, "No one knows our real feelings better than women like us, war widows. Now that we are getting old and seeing our children married, we long for our deceased husbands more than ever. The other day I happened to step into the neighborhood of our charcoal oven on the mountain and saw a pile of wood blackened and decaying. . . . I felt my life was like that pile of wood, decaying instead of being made into charcoal."[16]

For many young women who married into farm families after the war the situation improved considerably. Legal and political changes raised the status of women in general, and the pervasive climate of "democracy and freedom" that emerged in the postwar years as well as the improved economic state of the country also contributed to a steady enhancement of a sense of individuality in the younger generation. Naturally, many of the older generation are unsettled by the changed behavior this involves. As one old mother-in-law related:

[While I and my young daughter-in-law were working in a field] she kept stopping again and again to look up toward the sun. I asked, "Why are you looking up at the sky?"

She replied, "I'm supposed to go see a movie in town with my husband, but I forgot to bring my watch so I'm trying to make sure that I won't be late."

"If you're going to the movies can't you have an early supper and then go? There'll be plenty of time."

"Before I go to the movies, I have to go to the hairdresser in town. Then I have to stop by the public baths. So I have to go early or I'll be late for the movies."

I was really dumbfounded, but I decided that that's how young people are today, so there's nothing that can be done about it. We cut short our work and went home. I prepared an early lunch for her and sent her off.

She spent 600 yen on her hair, went to the public baths, ate supper in a restaurant with my son, and then went to the movies. After the movies they got hungry so they had some noodles and curry rice and came home by cab.

When I asked, "How can you spend that kind of money? Over 1,000 yen?" My son said, "I'm earning money as a hired worker, so it's all right."

For someone like me who had to work day after day all day long as long as there was any sunlight, and barely made a living at that, it's very troublesome. I wonder if they will make it as farmers.[17]

The postwar farm wife is better educated, more sophisticated, and more independent. The generation gap is much wider than it was in the prewar years. Mothers-in-law who led a highly constrained, self-denying lives as young wives often resent or envy the postwar generation. They complain:

When we were young, the only occasion on which we were allowed to go out was either the Girl's Festival on the third day of March or after the autumn harvest to pay a visit to our own parents.

In our day, there was not a single daughter-in-law who was allowed to read newspapers. We were too busy to do so. In contrast, nowadays there is radio to listen to anytime, and, besides, farm work is much easier than it was then.

Since the establishment of the community center, which organizes a special school for young daughters-in-law, they have come to look so superior that they are not afraid of us, the old mothers-in-law, anymore.

Everything has been changed nowadays. They tell us that, since these are the days of democracy, they are entitled to ignore old folks like us.[18]

But the tables have not been turned completely. It is not uncommon for mothers-in-law to manage to assert their authority and keep their daughters-in-law properly intimidated. One daughter-in-law of a farm family in the north complained about her mother-in-law, who watches over her son like a protective mother hen but treats her like a servant.

She makes me work nearly to death and says, because I am young and strong, it is of no matter . . . and does not give me time to rest. When I was washing my little son's hands, he said, "Look, Grandma, Mama's hands are swollen." But her attitude is that it doesn't matter, and [she] doesn't feel at all bad about the fact that my hands are bleeding because I have to work hard from dawn to dusk. She feeds her son and grandson fresh, tasty soup but tells me to finish yesterday's leftover cabbage soup because it shouldn't go to waste. Then she goes ahead and drinks the fresh tofu soup. . . . She treats me like an outsider. . . .

When her husband tries to speak on her behalf, his mother yells at him, "You've been hoodwinked by your wife! Do you intend to become a disrespectful son?" But the daughter-in-law has been influenced in more than one way by new kinds of thinking, for she berates her husband as a "jellyfish" for not standing up to his mother.[19]

The more assertive role that postwar farm wives appear to be playing is explained in part by the fact that an increasing number of them are performing full-time farm work while their husbands commute to the cities to work in shops and factories. And because a larger percentage of farm wives than of city wives is gainfully employed full-time, we can assume, paradoxically enough, that "among agrarian families there will be more . . . of the modern conjugal type of relationship and less persistence . . . of the traditional extended type of relationship" than among urban families.[20] The diffusion of the ideals of personal freedom and equality through the schools and mass media has contributed significantly toward fostering a greater sense of individuality among young farm wives.

The greater freedom of young rural women is reflected in the growing tendency for young people to choose their own mates, and also in an increasing tendency for young married couples to have their own living quarters, if not a separate house. A 1973 survey by the Ministry of Labor showed that 33 percent of marriages in rural communities were based on the young couples' choice. This is much lower than the figure for urban couples living in apartments (78 percent), but it is a radical shift from the prewar days when virtually all decisions about who would marry whom were made by parents. Even more striking is the fact that in the younger age group (twenty to twenty-four), 63 percent of rural couples exercised their own free choice in selecting a marriage partner.[21]

Another development that is easing the lives of young farm wives is the smaller size of farm families. In the prewar years, it was common for farm couples to have six, eight, ten, or even twelve children. In fact, the government encouraged such figures by honoring families of ten or more children.[22] Now, with birth-control measures readily available and abortion legalized, the number of children per couple has dropped to two or three even among farm families.[23] The weakening of the patriarchal family system and a gradual decline in the perceived need to sacrifice one's personal interests for those of the family have made it possible for the younger generation to think increasingly in terms of immediate individual well-being and happiness.

Old values, attitudes, and mores change gradually. In particular, in-grained biases and prejudices stubbornly linger on. This is seen most clearly in the bias that persists against the *burakumin* (see p. 148). While most people do not overtly reveal this prejudice for fear that they will be the object of public castigation by *burakumin* activists, prejudicial remarks are often voiced when no *burakumin* are present. The persistence of this prejudice is most strikingly reflected in the continuing resistance non-*burakumin* children encounter from their parents when they want to marry *burakumin*. Discrimination in jobs has also persisted. Even the postwar land reform program failed to benefit rural *burakumin* very much: Those who had been farming fewer than 0.3 *chō*— 90 percent of *burakumin*— were not regarded as full-fledged farmers and were not entitled to take part in the land redistribution program.[24]

In 1971, as part of the fiftieth anniversary of the founding of the Suiheisha, the Buraku Liberation League compiled a list of incidents involving discrimination or expressions of bias against *burakumin*. In Okayama prefecture alone, the League listed twenty-seven cases that called for redress.[25] In 1960, a controversy ensued when employment officers of two major firms in Kyoto indicated that their companies had a policy of not hiring *burakumin* and Koreans. In this city, with its large population of *burakumin*, a survey indicated that larger firms were less inclined to hire *burakumin* than smaller shops and plants.[26]

Spurred on by the reformist climate of the postwar years, *burakumin* leaders have stepped up their efforts to end discrimination. The movement was spearheaded by the Buraku Liberation League, which went about organizing chapters throughout the nation. In many instances, the organizers found that local *burakumin* were reluctant to join the reform movement. One mother pleaded, "Please don't disturb the sleeping children. I have had enough discrimination in my lifetime. My child has friends at school and has not experienced discrimination at all. Please don't stir things up." The organizer told her:

I understand how you feel, but though you talk about sleeping children, there is not a single child in this prefecture [Nara] who is asleep. They are all awake. The other day when a survey of high-school students was taken, 95 percent of the students indicated that they knew about the existence of the *buraku*. They know, but they don't have an accurate understanding of the situation. When the children leave for school, their parents tell them, "Don't play with those [*buraku*] children. They are dangerous and troublesome." That's what they think of the *buraku* people. . . . The only people who don't know about the *buraku* are those *buraku* children themselves whose parents conceal the truth from them, hoping to protect them from the kind of anguish and pain they themselves experienced. But you must not look upon the *burakumin* problem as somebody else's problem. You know that a girl from this community committed suicide recently. Many people have committed suicide all over the country because of discrimination over marriages. Discrimination is a reality. You cannot try to cover up its existence by silence.

The mother then admitted that her own son had been denied a job with a bank because he was a *burakumin*. [27]

The Buraku Liberation League adopted a policy of dramatizing cases of discrimination to awaken consciousness among the *burakumin* as well as in the public at large. One of the most celebrated incidents involved United States troops stationed in Japan. In 1957, a U.S. soldier shot and killed a *burakumin* woman after he encouraged her to come on base to collect empty shells. (The base had been built on land formerly owned by *burakumin* villagers.) This incident, fanned by opposition to the presence of U.S. military bases in Japan, aroused anti-American passions among the *burakumin*. [28]

The Sayama Affair, another incident that stirred up the *burakumin*'s bitterness, involved the kidnap-murder of a high-school girl in 1963. The police arrested a mentally handicapped *burakumin* youth and charged him with the crime. Critics charged that the accused was then tried and convicted on the basis of far-fetched, circumstantial evidence. The leaders of the Burakumin Liberation League saw this as a clear-cut case of bigotry in which the authorities, pressed for a speedy resolution of the case, picked on a *burakumin* youth. For almost two decades they contested the conviction and attempted, without success, to get the higher courts to overturn it. [29]

WOMEN IN THE BROTHELS

The long struggle that Yamamuro Gunpei and others carried on to end licensed prostitution did not succeed in his lifetime. But after the war, a movement was started to ban public brothels and, despite resistance by those who saw these institutions as social necessities, they were finally outlawed in 1956. Some Westerners, who romanticized the brothels and saw the women there as graceful and cultured courtesans, bemoaned the passing of these houses. Arthur Koestler is said to have observed, "[A] militant Puritan spirit . . . seems to have taken possession of a vocal minority of Japanese housewives. They demanded that the government abolish the age-old system of paid pleasure and the city of the Floating World was their target. Old guard sensualists fought in rage and bitterness to save the Yoshiwara. . . . But puritanism had come in with TV, coke, and stretch pants. The nation was dedicated to jazz, floor shows, rock and roll, Levis, and miniskirts."[30]

Those who saw these institutions as homes for exquisite courtesans who composed elegant poems to titillate their customers refused to see that these women, who had been torn away from their families and enslaved, were being degraded and humiliated. Needless to say, banning of public brothels did not eliminate prostitution, but the presence of "freelance" prostitutes is a far different matter from the legally sanctioned existence of brothels the owners of which were protected by the authorities. To be sure, postwar Japan saw prostitutes in the streets of the major cities, particularly near bases where occupation troops were stationed. The lack of food, basic necessities, and jobs had forced many young women to take to the streets. The government estimatd that, in 1947, there were 40,000 prostitutes; and, in 1952, 70,000.[31] Moreover, there were myriads of women who became "bathhouse girls, bar hostesses, nightclub and gyp-joint whores. The B-girl, the dance-hall hostess, the show girl, the chorus girl, the singer-harlot of jazz and rock and roll, all flourished in many places. . . ." In the late sixties there were 10,000 bars and cabarets in Tokyo alone.[32]

WOMEN IN THE MILLS

What about the girls and women in the Suwa silk mills? What happened in Suwa tells in part the story of the Japanese economy. The silk mills have vanished with the virtual disappearance of the silk market. What remains of the silk mills have become museums that house the machines and tools from the period when Suwa was the silk capital of Japan. Today, Suwa is flourishing as a manufacturing center of cameras, precision instruments, and electronic devices. The cotton-textile mills did not disappear immediately after the war, but they were soon replaced by plants producing synthetic fibers. In the first decade or so following the end of the war, the textile industry was relied upon to help rebuild the ruined economy. But, soon, heavy industry was revived as production of ships, machinery, automobiles, and petrochemicals began to burgeon. Cameras, precision instruments, radios, television sets, and other electronic and transistor products also came to crowd the export market. The textile industry was no longer the centerpiece of Japanese industry. By 1960, it constituted only 12.3 percent of all manufactured production, compared to 32.8 percent in the years 1934–1936, and the percentage has declined even more drastically since.[33]

In the immediate postwar years, however, the textile plants remained important sources of jobs for young women. But these workers were no longer semi-indentured employees of paternalistic companies, for the Trade Union Law of 1945 enabled unions to organize the workers without interference from employers. The workers' rights as free individuals were finally protected by law. The Labor Standard Act of 1947 stipulated, among other things, "Employers must not interfere with the freedom of the private lives of laborers who live in dormitories."[34] Some complain that employers still watch over dorm residents in a paternalistic fashion, but the latter are no longer virtual prison inmates, locked in after hours to prevent them from running away.

Of course, values and attitudes do not change overnight. One young woman wrote in the early fifties. "My Mother used to tell me: 'Do whatever your employers tell you to do. Be a good girl, and be recognized as a good girl by them.'" Then her union won a summer bonus for the workers through collective bargaining. "This was an entirely new experience for me. If we had kept quiet when the managers refused to give us the extra pay we demanded, we would have got nowhere. For the first time I realized that, if we made no demands, the company would never increase our pay of its own accord, even if the profits increased."[35] Most workers still send part of their earnings home since they consider helping out the family an important reason for their employment (some label this "family budget supplementary labor"); but, unlike their prewar counterparts, their parents do not receive payments in advance that the daughters then have to work off. With the Japanese economy booming and job opportunities in other fields increasing, farm girls are no longer so restricted in their choice of jobs. By 1959, labor shortages had become a greater concern than unemployment.[36]

It is often argued that education, though a long-term process, is the key to the elimination of prejudice. In this area significant changes have occurred. The centralized educational system of the prewar years has been replaced by a decentralized system that turns much of the responsibility for educating children over to local authorities. Ultranationalistic, militaristic textbooks have been replaced by texts that emphasize freedom, equality, democracy, and individualism. The prewar emphasis on rote memory and on acceptance of "truths" expounded by authorities from on high have been replaced by efforts to foster independent thinking and critical analysis. The prewar teacher, who usually served merely as a transmitter of "facts" and concepts promulgated from above, has in many cases been replaced by a teacher who seeks to develop analytical, critical thinking among his or her students.

One young teacher who attracted national attention in the early 1950s for his original, imaginative approach to teaching impoverished rural children in an out-of-the-way village in northern Japan was Muchaku Seikyō. His school had none of the advantages of the better-equipped urban schools. In order to get the students in his junior-high-school class to think independently and critically about their own lives, Muchaku got them to write essays about their daily experiences and thoughts. In his preface to a collection of his students' essays, published in 1951, Muchaku wrote:

The chapter on village life in Japan, in the social studies textbook, states, "Villages usually have elementary and middle schools. Children must spend nine years of compulsory education in these schools, so each village provides facilities so that the village children can receive an excellent education." But I realized that, if I taught the children the lesson as it was written, I would be teaching an untruth. In reality, our school does not have a single map, or a single apparatus to conduct scientific experiments. The roof of the school building is thatched, the classrooms are dark, and the windows are broken, letting the cold wind blow into the rooms. The teacher has only a single piece of chalk with which to conduct his classes.

But Muchaku set out to do the best he could, despite these handicaps.

I was determined to give them an authentic education. . . . I recalled that the guidelines from the Ministry of Education stated, "Children who live in the rural areas must be taught to take a fresh look at their life in the village, work toward the elimination of its defects, and create a new rural society." I thought hard about how to accomplish this and decided to use composition writing to achieve my objectives. I decided to have the students write compositions that would encourage them to probe into their way of life as they lived it, and to think and to take action [to improve their lives and their village]. As the students . . . examine their own lives, they will also be involved in studying social studies in a meaningful fashion.[37]

The contrast between prewar education and its emphasis on rote memory, and the kind of thinking that is being fostered by teachers like Muchaku is seen in the following excerpts from an essay written by one of Muchaku's pupils, then about fourteen years old. It certainly is a far cry from the platitudes about *chūkun aikoku* that formed the core of prewar education.

Newspaper articles debate whether or not the emperor is a war criminal. We discussed this question at school, too. This got me thinking about my father. . . . In 1944, when I was ten, he was drafted and went off to war. . . . The people of our village came to see him off. When the time came to say good-bye, he asked the villagers, "Please take care of my family while I am gone. . . ."

In the summer of 1945, Japan lost the war. After that, my mother and I waited day after day for our father to come home. But no word came from him. . . . Then in the fall of 1947 a lone telegram arrived with the message, "He was killed in combat." We all felt like saying "damn it," but we didn't know whom to curse. Now that we had lost the war, his death in the war made no sense at all. . . . But at that time we were too upset, in mourning over his death, to ask, "Why did Japan go to war? What was it all about?"

When we brought his ashes back home, the villagers came to greet us. They were the same people who had sent our father off four years before, telling him, "Please do your best for our country and our emperor. . . . We will take good care of your family while you are gone." But now they look upon the families of the war dead as if we are a nuisance. . . .

Later, the village officials brought us a *sake* cup and placed it on the Buddhist altar in our home, saying that it was a gift from the emperor. My younger brother said, "Why send us a *sake* cup after having killed our father?" and broke out in tears. My mother said nervously, "Now, now, you musn't talk like that," and tried to calm him down. But all of us would have preferred having our father back alive to receiving a *sake* cup. . . .

There are many, many people in Japan who are in the same position that we are in. We must work so that we ourselves will not bring misfortune upon our own families when we grow up. I believe that our father really did not want to go off to war. It is only natural for a person who cares seriously about his life and about his family not to want to go to war.[38]

Another of Muchaku's students wrote about his desire to study and about the poverty that plagued his family.

In the morning I wove straw ropes to repair the thatched roof. I worked hard to finish my chores because I wanted to do some reading. I finally used up the straws prepared for the task and thought, "Okay, now I'm finished." I grabbed my book and sat down. Then I was told, "We can use all the straw ropes you can weave." So, I couldn't read my book. . . .

[Because our family is poor], our oldest sister was persuaded by a recruiter from a spinning factory to go to work in Wakayama as soon as she finished elementary school. She decided she would be much better off working in a factory than living in poverty on the farm. My parents were not happy about letting her go so far away, but she insisted so they consented. . . . Our mother used to say, "She insisted on going off to work, but later she began to write home about how unhappy she was at the plant." Half a year later she came home because of intestinal trouble. It was the busiest time of the year then, so even though she was sick she had to help with the silkworms. Her health got worse and she was sent to a hospital. . . . In the fall she died of intestinal tuberculosis. She was nineteen then, and I was only four. I remember going with my mother to see her in the hospital, and seeing her pain-stricken face.

The young boy's desire to study was motivated in part by his wish to play an active role in determining his own destiny at the political level.

Today, compared to the days when people who are now in their thirties and forties were children, farm life has gotten a lot better. That is why I feel that I must read and study as much as I can. But, even though conditions have improved, I don't have the time to read a single book. If this keeps up, no matter how hard we try, only those who have the time to read a lot and go on to higher schools will control the government. These people will govern for the benefit of the rich . . . and people like us will have no way of improving our condition.

Even as a youngster, he was aware of the fact that urban "men of culture" ignored the interests of rural children.

Just look at the magazines, newspapers, and books written for young people! They are all written for the benefit of children with lots of free time. Nothing is written about what and how we who live in the mountain villages and have to work all year round should study and what we should be thinking about.[39]

So the clash of interests between the city and the village, the dominance of the former over the latter, and the exploitation of the latter by the former, which was noted by Fukuzawa Yukichi in the early Meiji era and which angered Shibuya Teisuke in the 1920s, has persisted in the postwar years.

THE POLLUTION PROBLEM

One of the most insidious forms of the subjugation of rural to urban interests is the continuous encroachment of industrial plants into the countryside—and the pollution that accompanies it ('though, needless to say, urban residents too are victims of the pollution of land, air, and water by industrial plants that spew out toxic fumes and liquid poison).

Industrial pollution is not, of course, a problem that has emerged only in the postwar years; it was already present in prewar Japan, but not on the scale that plagues the country today. The most controversial prewar case was the pollution of the streams and fields of the Kanto Plain area by the Ashio Copper Mining Company (founded in 1877 by an entrepreneur who had close ties to government leaders). The hazards caused by the company's toxic waste were detected as early as 1881. When the governor of Tochigi prefecture warned the people not to consume fish taken from the Watarase River, into which the company was pumping toxic waste products, he was sent off to another post.[40] As the toxic substances spread to more and more areas, not only polluting streams but damaging crops, the problem could no longer be ignored. The victims began to voice their concerns and found a champion for their cause in Tanaka Shōzō (1841–1913), a member of the national Diet. In 1891, he called on the government to take action to curb the irresponsible actions of the mining company, but the government ignored his plea. Their complaints having gone unheeded year after year, the residents of the communities affected by the pollutants staged a massive protest demonstration in the spring of 1900. The authorities responded by turning police and army troops on the protestors, arresting the leaders. Since these protest actions failed to move the government, Tanaka decided to risk his life and submit a petition directly to the emperor. When he did so in the fall of 1901, the authorities sought to dismiss his action as that of a mad man and succeeded in curbing the protest movement.[41]

Finally, the government decided to take some action, but instead of arresting the pollution at its source, officials decided to construct a dam in the upper reaches of the Watarase River, thereby checking the floods (caused by the denuding of the forests by the Ashio Mining Company) that were spreading the toxic elements. This entailed flooding one of the most fertile villages in the region—a decision that only further exacerbated the situation by forcefully evicting those villagers who resisted. Tanaka led protestors against the high-handed actions of the government but again failed to move the wielders of power.[42] Treated by the authorities as a crank and neglected by historians of the time, his life ended in seeming futility. Not until the postwar years did Tanaka's efforts come to be properly appreciated as the work of a pioneer in the fight against industrial pollution.

In recent years, industrial pollution has become such a serious problem that public opinion has forced the government to move with much greater alacrity than did prewar officials—though quite often steps to curb pollutors are only taken after irreparable damage has already been done. One of the most celebrated postwar cases involved the pollution of the waters off the coast of Kyushu, near the city of Minamata, by a nitrogen-producing plant. In this instance, residents of the area, particularly those in fishing villages, were subject to mercury poisoning and its hideous results.

Specifically, between 1953 and 1959, villagers in the coastal communities of Kagoshima and Kumamoto prefectures were puzzled by the large number of people who were beginning to suffer from paralysis of their arms and legs, loss of vision, speech defects, and other muscular disorders. A large number of babies were also being born with what appeared to be cerebral palsy. It was not till 1959 that a medical team from Kumamoto Medical School identified the cause of the afflictions. The victims were suffering from methyl mercury poisoning. In 1963, the source of the mercury was traced to the Shin Nihon Chisso Company, a nitrogen plant, which was pouring methyl mercury into Minamata Bay.[43] Strenuous public protest was launched against the company, and a decade of court action followed before the the victims and families of those who had died as a result of the poisoning were finally compensated. One person who became involved in combating this kind of industrial pollution was W. Eugene Smith, who, by means of his camera, told the story of the pathetic victims of the Minamata poisoning. In the course of his work, Smith was beaten up by company goons and suffered serious head injuries.

A writer living in the Minamata region told the following story of a young boy who fell victim to the mercury poisoning.

It was the fall of 1963. . . . I found myself in the front yard of the young boy Kyūhei's house. The boy was standing near the entrance to the house. For some time he had been concentrating earnestly on repeating a series of maneuvers. It looked as if he was engaged in baseball practice. But his actions were so serious and somber that I hesitated to call out to him. So I stood there quietly, trying to keep in tune with the actions of the young boy. His legs and hips were unstable and, regardless of whether he was standing or bending over, he appeared about to topple over. His posture was wholly inappropriate for a young person, and, if one had glanced only at the bottom half of his body, one would have thought he was an old man. . . . He was wearing a worn-out pair of *geta*. I knew that it was a physical strain for him to wear them.

He was putting pressure on his feet and, because he was straining so hard, there were signs of spasm. He then bent down and began to pound on the ground slowly with the stick he held with both hands. He then spun around as if he were drawing an arc with his body. He crawled around, tilting his crew-cut head to the side, propped himself up with one hand on the ground, and used the other hand to reach out and grope about with the stick. He seemed to be looking for something with the stick. After several tries, he hit what he was looking for, a rock, and made a cracking sound. The young boy was blind.

The boy put his stick carefully down on the ground, and held the rock in his left hand, which was resting on his knee, as if he were caressing it. His right hand was half paralyzed. Part of the rock, about the size of his fist, was protruding from his left hand. It was not a round rock but an oblong one. It seemed to fit into his left hand perfectly. It was slightly moist with the perspiration from his palm. . . . I was told later that the boy has treasured the rock ever since he found it five years ago when they were repairing the road in front of his house. He keeps the rock tucked away in a small hollow spot in the dirt floor at the entrance to the house to make sure that it doesn't roll away. . . . With his eyes half open and his face tilted skyward, he began to crawl toward the hollow spot in the floor. He put the rock away with his shaky fingers. The sight made me feel sad. I felt the weight of the rock in my heart.

The boy then lifted up his hips the way a very old person stretches his back when he gets up. With great effort, he grabbed the rock again with his left hand, and, as if he were heaving a heavy object, he threw the rock in the air. Then, displaying the swiftest motion that he had shown so far, he swung the stick around with both hands . . . but, by the time he had swung, it had already dropped to the ground, quite some distance from him. So he struck out. The boy moved silently in the direction where the rock had fallen, tilting his head to one side. He scratched the ground carefully with his bat. . . . The young boy's neck was wet with perspiration.

After waiting for what seemed like a long time, I approached the boy and called out his name. He was taken aback and dropped the stick. The rapport of silence that had been established between the hamlet and the boy was disrupted. He stood still and seemed to be trying to fix the direction of the front door of the house. Then, as if he were charging backward, he vanished behind the door.[44]

The industrial pollution of the countryside is part of an ongoing urban invasion of the rural areas. This overall urban sprawl has blighted large areas of the countryside. Factories belch noxious smoke; gaudy shopping centers are built; and highways cut through farmlands. Golf courses replacing woods and meadows have, for many rural residents, proved a symbol of the destructive "decadence" of urban status-seekers. In 1945, there were fewer than fifty golf courses, which served as playpens for court aristocrats and a small number of business tycoons; but, by the mid-1970s, there were almost 1,000 golf courses to which would-be tycoons paid inordinate membership fees in a game of one-upmanship.[45]

From time to time, inhabitants of rural areas have struck back at urban intruders who, backed by the government, have deprived them of their land in order to create some new diversion. Such was the case of the controversy over construction and opening of the huge international airport at Narita in the rural areas of Chiba prefecture. To many, the protest movement appeared to be a form of Ludditism, or politically motivated obstructionism, but the movement represented a deep-seated resentment of the way in which urban industrial-commercial interests, with government support, had from the outset of the modern age run roughshod over rural interests in the name of *fukoku kyōhei* ("enriching and strengthening the nation"). The struggle at Narita even aroused old agrarian fighters like Shibuya Teisuke to join the fray, but once again the urban forces won the battle.

The Japanese Village

In this conflict of interests between city and village, the city now appears to have subjugated the countryside almost completely. The younger generation of villagers seems eager to abandon the village and join the city folk. Rural Japan is headed for urbanism and cosmopolitanism with a vengeance. The following comment by a young farmer is the voice of a villager who knows that the battle is almost lost.

My grandfather used to say "academic learning destroys the peasants." I have now come to appreciate deeply the significance of what he was saying. Strictly speaking, of course, learning itself is not what destroys the peasants and farm communities. What is at fault are the impure values that accompany learning . . . and special privileges. The grading system that ranks one person above another is at fault.

To be successful means, evidently, the ability to earn a lot of money without doing physical work. But to earn a lot of money without laboring means living off the labor of those who do engage in physical work. Now, conventional wisdom holds that those who live off the labor of others are superior and that those who do physical work are dumb. The immediate consequence of this kind of thinking is the steady decline in the number of those who carry on farm work. A teacher at an agricultural high school lamented that children of farm families who graduate want to become authorities on agriculture rather than return to the village and work on the farm. . . . [They believe] that it is a waste of talent to permit a person in whom so much education money has been invested to become a simple farmer. People are convinced that only dumbbells work on the farm. The entire social makeup of our country encourages this kind of thought and behavior.

As a result, parents of farm children are transported with delight when their children show signs of intellectual ability, and they get puffed up with big-city dreams. Such children are needed in the village, but the parents take the initiative and eagerly send them off to the city.

Today, education is very costly. For this reason many parents take jobs outside the village or even sell their land [to pay for their children's education]. And farm children who have been provided with higher education go off, as a matter of course, to the cities. The villages that eagerly poured out money for their education receive nothing in return. It turns out to have been a fruitless investment; the cities reap the harvest. And the children from farm families who have left the village to become useful toilers for the city think of the village only as a place that supplies them with nostalgic memories. But could it be that nostalgic memory is simply a sign of vacuity? The fact that they cling to the fairy-tale image of chasing after rabbits in the hills and fishing for carp in the brooks is the consequence of their inability to become urbanites even though they live in the big city. But at the same time they are unable to preserve their identity as peasants. So, in order to assuage the loneliness that comes from the faceless existence peculiar to metropolises, they indulge in such nostalgic fantasies. It may also be the product of their need to put up a brave front toward the village and the soil. Consequently, when our friends return to the village for a visit and say, "Aah, the country-side is wonderful after all," it sounds phoney and cynical. . . .

In many instances, people who return from the city and say, "The home village is wonderful," are speaking from a sense of injured superiority. . . . A person working as a member of the mass media once said to me, "Nowadays, when I go to the villages, I don't come across the kind of simple integrity that used to be there. Villagers have become jaded with city ways; there are no longer any farmers who behave like true farmers. It makes me sad." He claims that, every time he comes to the country to gather material, he is deeply pained by the changes. Formerly the villagers would pick fresh melons, grapes, and tangerines, and urge him to have some. But now even in out-of-the-way villages people bring out instant coffee and Coca-Cola. They no longer serve him the unique country products that he longs to have. . . .

While I was listening to him speak of his love of the villages and the farmers, I was dumbfounded by the fact that he did not realize that what he was saying was a reflection of his own urban egoism; his professed goodwill toward the farmers was actually a product of his bias against them. He expects the farmers to have qualities that he himself does not possess. He wants the farmers to preserve those qualities that city people have lost or deliberately abandoned. His admiration of the peasants' simple integrity is based on his own need to feel that he would not be tricked by simple folks, that he would not be victimized by them. . . . There seems to be no connection between his admiration of the simplicity of the peasants and any personal desire of his own to possess those qualities. . . .

The ward chief of our village constantly complains, "Because parents keep saying, 'The life of a farmer is no good,' none of their children wants to carry on their work. The parents are to blame." But he himself has sent his son off to Tokyo to attend college. People who are regarded as agrarian leaders repeat until they are hoarse, "Farmers insist that their sons must marry farm girls who work hard. But they do not allow their own daughters to marry farmers. This kind of egoism is responsible for the shortage of wives for young farmers." But they themselves have either given up farming altogether and taken up another occupation, or else have at least ceased being full-time farmers. They have no intention of letting their daughters marry farmers or of allowing their sons to become farmers. When they talk about what's wrong with the villagers, they don't include themselves in that group.

It appears that there are too many people like this in our country today. Their way of thinking reflects city people's lack of identity.[46]

The desire of the young to leave the village and go to the cities where the bright lights shine seems to be a universal wish. And even those who bemoan the penetration of urban ways into the countryside are torn with ambivalence. Rural dwellers usually want the products of technology and science, for they bring material convenience and physical well-being in most instances. Industrial growth brings economic prosperity to the countryside, too, since job opportunities for rural youths become more plentiful. Of course, villagers would be best served if they could allow only what they choose to come into their community from the cities. But neither they nor the city dwellers can pick and choose what they want out of the industrial engine that is powering Japan—toward what destination, no one knows.

However, behind that industrial engine there are human beings pushing the buttons. Just as the Meiji leaders decided to move Japan toward "building a strong and rich nation," present-day business tycoons are pushing Japan toward never-ending economic expansion, which brings greater and greater wealth into their coffers. When this process—with its huge concentrations of people, pollution, and congestion—was found to be making life in the urban-industrial complex hazardous, serious consideration was given by Prime Minister Tanaka Kakuhei, in 1972, to a plan for massive dispersal of industry throughout the country; that is, he wanted to "reverse the tide of people, money, and goods" from the cities to the countryside.[47] If this plan had been adopted, the result would have been to bring the problems that plague the megalopolises to the entire nation on an unheard-of scale. Rapacious land grabbing in anticipation of this plan's adoption, plus the energy crisis, put an end to the scheme, but the spread of urban industrial blight continues apace. What is not given serious attention in this process of rampant industrial expansion, planned or unplanned, is what all this does to and means to each individual. General trends, group profiles, theoretical paradigms, and statistical data tell us nothing about what the endless pursuit of wealth and power does and means to the individual. Are his or her interests being served? We can say with near certainty that *fukoku kyōhei* was not meant to serve the interests of the masses. The peasants were seen primarily as resources to be exploited to achieve its national goals. If a modicum of benefits from the process of building a rich and powerful nation spilled over into the countryside, it was only incidental to the objectives pursued by the builders of "modern" Japan. The leaders' aim was the same as that of the Tokugawa rulers: Squeeze sesame seeds and peasants as much as you can.

Notes

MODERNIZATION AND THE PEASANTS

1. Ryusaku Tsunoda et al., *Sources of Japanese Tradition* (New York: Columbia University Press, 1958), p. 571.
2. Yanagida Kunio, *Yama no Jinsei* (Life in the Mountains) (Tokyo: Gōdo Kenyūsha, 1926), pp. 1–2; Yanagida Kunio, *Kokyō Nanajyūnen* (Seventy Years of Home Country) (Tokyo: Asahi Shimbunsha, 1974), p. 194.
3. Obata Jun, *Kinsei Shakai* (Early Modern Society) (Tokyo: Asakura Shoten, 1952), p. 292.
4. George B. Sansom, *A History of Japan,* 3 vols. (Palo Alto, Calif.: Stanford University Press, 1958), III: 186–87; Kitashima Masamoto, *Nihonshi Gaisetsu,* (Outline History of Japan), 3 vols. (Tokyo: Iwanami Shoten, 1968), II:245.
5. E. Herbert Norman, *Japan's Emergence as a Modern State* (New York: Institute of Pacific Relations, 1940), p. 23.
6. Matsunaga Goichi, ed., *Kindai Minshū no Kiroku: Nōmin* (Records of the People in the Modern Era: The Peasants) (Tokyo: Shinjinbutsu Ōraisha, 1972), Introduction, p. 13.
7. Aoki Kōji, *Hyakushō Ikki no Nenjiteki Kenkyū* (A Chronological Study of Peasant Uprisings) (Tokyo: Shinseisha, 1966), p. 13. Aoki revised his estimate upward in his later studies to 3,212. Cf. Roger W. Bowen, *Rebellion and Democracy in Meiji Japan* (Berkeley: University of California Press, 1978), pp. 72–77. A more conservative estimate lists 1,469 uprisings between 1603 and 1884. Kidota Shirō, "Ishinki no Nōmin Ikki" (Peasant Uprisings during the Meiji Restoration), in Iwanami Kōza, *Nihon Rekishi* (Japanese History), 23 vols. (Tokyo: Iwanami Shoten, 1962–1963), XIV: 183.
8. Uchida Takeshi and Miyamoto Tsuneichi, eds., *Sugae Masumi Zenshū* (Collected Works of Sugae Masumi), 12 vols. (Tokyo: Miraisha, 1971–1978), I: 274–75.
9. Furushima Toshio, *Nihon Hōken Nōgyōshi* (Japanese Feudal Agricultural History) (Tokyo: Shikai Shobō, 1931), pp. 47, 83; Matsunaga, *Kindai Minshū no Kiroku: Nōmin,* Introduction, p. 14.
10. Honjō Eijirō, *Hyakushō-Chōnin no Rekishi* (History of Peasants and Townspeople) (Tokyo: Baifūkan, 1949), p. 39.
11. Konishi Shirō, *Kaikoku to Jyōi* (Opening the Country and Expelling the Barbarians) (Tokyo: Chūō Kōronsha, 1966), pp. 82–83.
12. Sakata Yoshio, *Meiji Ishinshi* (History of the Meiji Restoration) (Tokyo: Miraisha, 1960), p. 202.
13. Arnold Toynbee, *Civilization on Trial* and *The World and the West* (New York: Meridian Books, 1958), p. 172. The opposite response is that of the Zealot who represents "an archaism evoked by foreign pressure" (p. 167).
14. *Fukuzawa Zenshū* (Collected Works of Fukuzawa), 10 vols. (Tokyo: Jiji Shimpōsha, 1925–1926), IV: 255–56.
15. Naramoto Tatsuya, ed., *Nihon no Shisōka* (The Thinkers of Japan) (Tokyo: Mainichi Shimbunsha, 1954), p. 237.
16. William Appleman Williams, *Empire as a Way of Life* (New York: Oxford University Press, 1980), pp. 152, 161.
17. William W. Lockwood, *The Economic Development of Japan* (Princeton, N.J.: Princeton University Press, 1954), pp. 141, 272.
18. Aoki, *Hyakushō Ikki no Nenjiteki Kenkyū,* p. 39.
19. The number of peasants who were brought into the initial units of the kiheitai in 1863 was insignificant. In 1864 the organization had 292 members, of which 43% were samurai, 33% were commoners (including townspeople), and 24% were of unknown social origin. Only 7% were peasants. The second kiheitai that was organized a few years later had a larger peasant representation. Of the 137 men in one unit, 78 were peasants (some townspeople and fishermen were among those counted as peasants). In another unit with

227 men, 123 were peasants. Albert M. Craig, *Chōshū in the Meiji Restoration* (Cambridge, Mass.: Harvard University Press, 1961), pp. 271–72.

20. Conrad Totman, *The Collapse of the Tokugawa Bakufu, 1862–1868* (Honolulu: University of Hawaii Press, 1980), pp. 97–98, 119, 167, 184, 187, 282.

21. Inoue Kiyoshi, *Meiji Ishin* (Meiji Restoration) (Tokyo: Chūō Kōron-sha, 1966), pp. 99–101.

22. E. Herbert Norman, *Japan's Emergence as a Modern State*, p. 79, note 80.

23. Oka Yoshitake, *Kindai Nihon no Keisei* (The Formation of Modern Japan) (Tokyo: Kōbundō, 1947), p. 301. Also Robert A. Scalapino, *Democracy and the Party Movement in Prewar Japan* (Berkeley: University of California Press, 1953), pp. 113–14.

24. Nakamura Masanori, *Nikon no Rekishi, Rōdōsha to Nōmin* (History of Japan, Laborers and Peasants) (Tokyo: Shōgakukan, 1976), pp. 75–77.

25. Tsurumi Shunsuke et al., eds., *Nihon no Hyakunen* (The Hundred Years of Japan), 10 vols. (Tokyo: Chikuma Shobō, 1961–1964), X: 277–79.

26. Yukichi Fukuzawa, *Autobiography*, trans. Eiichi Kiyooka (New York: Columbia University Press, 1966), pp. 243–44. Fukuzawa, writing about this incident years later, seems not to have seen any irony in the fact that he was ordering the peasant around and intimidating him just the way a samurai (which, in fact, is what he had been) did under the old regime.

27. *Ibid.*, p. 245.

28. Sasaki Jun'nosuke, *Yonaoshi* (Remaking the Society) (Tokyo: Iwanami Shoten, 1979), p. 185.

29. *Ibid.*, pp. 187–188.

30. *Ibid.*, pp. 189–90.

31. Shimonaka Kunihiko, ed., *Nihon Zankoku Monogatari* (Tales of Japanese Inhumanity) 5 vols. (Tokyo: Heibonsha, 1972), IV: 38–49.

32. Thomas R. Havens, *Farm and Nation in Modern Japan: Agrarian Nationalism, 1870–1940* (Princeton, N.J.: Princeton University Press, 1974), p. 36. Keizo Shibusawa, *Japanese Society in the Meiji Era*, trans. A. H. Culbertson and M. Kimura (Tokyo: Toyo Bunko, 1958), p. 410, has a table with the percentages on government revenues obtained from the land tax: 1867–75: 82%, 1875–76: 78%, 1876–77: 77%, 1877–78: 79%. Then the percentage drops because national income from other sources begins to increase, although the absolute yen income obtained from the land tax continues to edge upward.

33. Tōyama Shigeki, *Meiji Ishin* (Meiji Restoration) (Tokyo: Iwanami Shoten, 1951), p. 284.

34. Okada Akio et al., *Nihon no Rekishi* (A History of Japan), 12 vols. (Tokyo: Yomiuri Shimbunsha, 1959–1960), X: 198.

35. Shimonaka, *Nihon Zankoku Monogatari*, IV: 20.

36. Okada et al., *Nihon no Rekishi*, X: 200.

37. *Ibid.*, X: 199.

38. Yoshino Sakuzō et al., eds., *Meiji Bunka Zenshū* (A Collection on Meiji Culture), 24 vols. (Tokyo: Nihon Hyōronsha, 1927–1930), XX: 284.

39. Segawa Kiyoko, *Mura no Onna-tachi* (Women of the Village) (Tokyo: Miraisha, 1970), p. 46.

40. Tsurumi et al., *Nihon no Hyakunen*, IX: 169–173. Also Kunio Yanagida, *Japanese Manners and Customs in the Meiji Era*, trans. Charles S. Terry (Tokyo: Toyo Bunko, 1957), p. 236.

41. Kaikoku Hyakunen Bunka Jigyōkai, *Meiji Bunkashi* (A Cultural History of the Meiji Period), 14 vols. (Tokyo: Yōyōsha, 1953–1955), vol. III (Murakami Toshiaki and Sakata Yoshio, *Kyōiku Dōtoku-hen* [Education and Morals]), p. 62.

42. *Ibid.*, p. 248, has the following table on school attendance rates:

Year	Male	Female	Combined
1873	39.9%	15.1%	28.1%
1877	56.0%	22.5%	39.9%
1883	67.2%	33.6%	51.0%

1889	64.3%	30.5%	48.2%
1897	80.7%	50.9%	66.7%
1903	96.6%	89.6%	93.2%
1911	98.8%	97.5%	98.2%

43. Fukutake Tadashi, *Rural Japanese Society* (Ithaca, N.Y.: Cornell University Press, 1972), p. 209.
44. Matsunaga Goichi, ed., *Kindai Minshū no Kiroku: Nōmin*, p. 19.
45. Kidota, "Ishinki no Nōmin Ikki," pp. 187–89.
46. Inoue Kiysohi, *Meiji Ishin*, pp. 390–91
47. *Ibid.*, pp. 431–32.
48. *Ibid.*, pp. 433–35.
49. Irokawa Daikichi, *Kindai Kokka no Shuppatsu* (The Beginnings of the Modern Nation-State) (Tokyo: Chūō Kōronsha, 1966), p. 353.
50. *Ibid.*, pp. 354–55.
51. *Ibid.*, pp. 378–79.
52. *Ibid.*, pp. 361–63; Ide Magoroku, *Chichibu Konmintō Gunzō* (Group Profiles of the Chichibu Poor People's Party) (Tokyo: Shinjinbutsu Ōraisha, 1973), p. 18.
53. Bowen, *Rebellion and Democracy in Meiji Japan*, p. 259.
54. *Ibid.*, p. 251.
55. Ide Magoroku, *Chichibu Konmintō Gunzō*, p. 10.
56. Bowen, *Rebellion and Democracy in Meiji Japan*, pp. 59–62, 297; Nakazawa Ichirō, *Chichibu Konmintō ni Ikita Hitobito* (People Who Lived for the Chichibu Poor People's Party) (Tokyo: Gendaishi Shuppankai, 1977), pp. 240ff; Irokawa, *Kindai Kokka no Shuppatsu*, pp. 367–74.
57. *Ibid.*, pp. 374–76.
58. *Ibid.*, pp. 383–88.
59. *Ibid.*, pp. 320–23.

FARMING AND FARM LIFE

1. Fukutake, *Rural Japanese Society*, p. 81.
2. *Ibid.*, pp. 6, 11, 81–82.
3. The average farm family tended to be larger than the average urban family. The 1920 census revealed that the average farm household consisted of 5.44 members, while those in professional and public service occupations averaged 4.16 members. *Ibid.*, p. 35.
4. Shibusawa, *Japanese Society in the Meiji Era*, pp. 426–38. Cf. Glenn Trewartha, *Japan, A Physical & Regional Geography* (Madison: University of Wisconsin Press, 1945), pp. 196–97.
5. Thomas C. Smith, *Agrarian Origins of Modern Japan* (Stanford, Calif.: Stanford University Press, 1959), p. 1.
6. Havens, *Farm and Nation in Modern Japan*, pp. 37–38.
7. James I. Nakamura, "Growth of Japanese Agriculture, 1875–1920," in *The State and Economic Enterprise in Japan*, ed. William W. Lockwood (Princeton, N.J.: Princeton University Press, 1965), pp. 304, 316–17.
8. *Ibid.*, pp. 322–23.
9. Inomata Tsunao, "Kyūbō no Nōson," (Impoverished Farm Villiages) in *Shōwa Zenki Nōsei Keizai Meicho-shū* (Outstanding Works of Early Showa on Agrarian Economy), ed. Kondō Yasuo (Tokyo: Nōsangyoson Bunka Kyōkai, 1978), p. 301.
10. Fukutake, *Japanese Rural Society*, p. 7.
11. Shimonaka, *Nihon Zankoku Monogatari*, V: 115–16.
12. Yamamoto Shigemi, *Aa, Nomugi Tōge* (Ooh, Nomugi Pass) (Tokyo: Kadokawa Shoten, 1977), p. 328.

13. Shibuya Teisuke, *Nōmin Aishi* (The Sad History of the Peasants) (Tokyo: Keiso Shobō, 1970), pp. 45, 59, 61, 172.
14. Nakamura Masanori, *Rōdōsha to Nōmin*, pp. 330–31. Ninomiya Sontoku (1787–1856) was a Tokugawa agronomist and moralist.
15. Yanagida, *Japanese Manners and Customs in the Meiji Era*, pp. 96–97.
16. *Ibid.*, p. 97.
17. Ubukata Toshirō, *Meiji Taishō Kenbunshi* (Observations from the Meiji-Taisho Years) (Tokyo: Chūō Kōronsha, 1978), pp. 49, 54, 59.
18. Keizo Shibusawa, *Japanese Life and Culture in the Meiji Era*, trans. Charles S. Terry (Tokyo: Toyo Bunko, 1958), p. 290.
19. Yamamoto Akira, "Shakai Seikatsu no Henka to Taishū Bunka" (Transformations in Social Life and Popular Culture), in Iwanami Kōza, *Nihon Rekishi* (Japanese History), 26 vols. (Tokyo: Iwanami Shoten, 1975–1977), XIX: 328ff.
20. Mayama Seika, *Minami Koizumi-mura* (Minami Koizumi Village), in *Tsuchi to Furusato no Bungaku Zenshū* (Collection of Literature of the Soil and Home Villages), ed. Usui Yoshimi et al., 15 vols. (Tokyo: Ie-no-Hikari Kyōkai, 1976), III: 51–52.
21. Shibuya, *Nōmin Aishi*, p. 186.
22. *Ibid.*, pp. 207, 264, 440.
23. Ishikawa Tatsuzō, *Hikage no Mura* (Village in the Shadows), in *Tsuchi to Furusato*, VII: 179.
24. Yamamoto Akira, "Shakai Seikatsu no Henka," p. 331.
25. Shibuya, *Nōmin Aishi*, p. 343.
26. Matsunaga Goichi, *Kindai Minshū no Kiroku: Nōmin*, p. 27.
27. Chie Nakane, "Nihon Interii-ron" (On Japanese Intellectuals), in *Chūō Kōron* (October 1962), pp. 119ff.
28. Nakamura Masanori, *Rōdōsha to Nōmin*, pp. 333–34.
29. Fukutake, *Japanese Rural Society*, pp. 140–41.
30. Nakamura Masanori, *Rōdōsha to Nōmin*, p. 95.
31. Matsunaga Shōzō, "Shakai Mondai no Hassei" (The Origins of Social Problems), in Iwanami Kōza, *Nihon Rekishi* (1975–1977 edition), XVI: 247. In 1914 the middle-level farmer's average daily living expenses came to 16 sen per person, while for the lower-level peasant it was 8 sen. In extreme cases it fell as low as 3.5 sen. Shimonaka, *Nihon Zankoku Monogatari*, V: 285.
32. "Mura kara no Uttae" (Accusations from the Villages), in Matsunaga Goichi, *Kindai Minshū no Kiroku: Nōmin*, p. 74. Also Heibonsha editorial staff, *Dokyumento Shōwa Sesō-shi, Senzen-hen* (Documents on Showa Social Phenomena, Prewar Volume) (Tokyo: Heibonsha, 1975), pp. 92–94.
33. Fukutake Tadashi, *Japanese Society Today* (Tokyo: University of Tokyo Press, 1974), p. 51.
34. For the general population the average family size was 5 in 1930, but 38.4% of the families had 6 or more members and 15.8% had 8 or more. *Ibid.*, p. 31.
35. *Ibid.*, p. 51.
36. Fukutake, *Japanese Rural Society*, p. 206.
37. Fukutake, *Japanese Society Today*, p. 51.
38. Shibusawa, *Japanese Life and Culture in the Meiji Era*, p. 93.
39. Alan H. Gleason, "Economic Growth and Consumption in Japan," in Lockwood, *State and Economic Enterprise in Japan*, p. 401.
40. Shibusawa, *Japanese Life and Culture in the Meiji Era*, p. 74.
41. Shimonaka, *Nihon Zankoku Monogatari*, V: 115–16.
42. Shibuya, *Nōmin Aishi*, p. 150.
43. "Mura kara no Uttae," in Matsunaga Goichi, *Kindai Minshū no Kiroku: Nōmin*, p. 73.
44. James I. Nakamura, "Growth of Japanese Agriculture," pp. 297, 301. Nakamura has adjusted the official figures slightly to account for what he regards as underestimates. The figures published by the Ministry of Agriculture and Forestry indicate that in 1934–1938 caloric consumption per person per day was still 2,020; 78% consisted of starchy food. By

1969 the caloric consumption had risen to 2,447 with the percentage of starchy food down to 56.5%. The percentage of starch consumed is still high compared with Western nations. For the U.S. the percentage is 22.9 and the United Kingdom 27.3. Ichiro Yano, ed., *Nippon, A Chartered Survey of Japan, 1971* (Tokyo: Kokuseisha, 1971), pp. 76–77.

45. Yūki Aisoka, "Sonri Seikatsu-ki" (Record of Life in a Village), in *Tsuchi to Furusato*, VII: 143.

46. Yanagida, *Japanese Manners and Customs in the Meiji Era*, p. 60, and Shibusawa, *Japanese Life and Culture in the Meiji Era*, pp. 127–28.

47. Yanagida, *Japanese Manners and Customs in the Meiji Era*, pp. 60–61.

48. Shibusawa, *Japanese Life and Culture in the Meiji Era*, pp. 134–35.

49. Yamamoto Akira, "Shakai Seikatsu no Henka to Taishū-bunka," p. 330.

50. Yanagida, *Japanese Manners and Customs in the Meiji Era*, p. 51.

51. Yanagida Kunio, *Meiji Taishō-shi, Sesō-hen* (History of Meiji and Taisho, Volume on Social Phenomena) (Tokyo: Asahi Shimbunsha, 1931), p. 153.

52. Dore, *Land Reform in Japan*, p. 202.

53. John F. Embree, *Suye Mura, A Japanese Village* (Chicago: University of Chicago Press, 1939), p. 48. Shibuya records in his diary in November 1925 that he heard a radio for the first time. He longed to own one but could not afford it. Shibuya, *Nōmin Aishi*, p. 158.

54. Yūki Aisoka, *Zuihitsu* (Essay), 3 vols. (Tokyo: Chūō Shoin, 1973), I: 168.

55. Machida Toshiko, "Kankoro Meshi" (Kankoro Rice), in *Tsuchi to Furusato*, I: 373.

56. Wakatsuki Shunichi, "Inchō Nikki" (Diary of the Clinic Chief), in *Tsuchi to Furusato*, VII: 316.

57. Kida Minoru, "Kichigai Buraku Shūyū Kikō" (Notes on Touring a Crazy Hamlet), in *Tsuchi to Furusato*, I: 289. Also Shimonaka, *Nihon Zankoku Monogatari*, I: 158ff.

58. Imanishi Kinji, *Mura to Ningen* (Village and People) (Tokyo: Shin Hyōronsha, 1952), p. 135.

59. Irokawa, *Kindai Kokka no Shuppatsu*, pp. 98–102.

60. Erwin O. E. von Baelz, *Awakening Japan: The Diary of a German Doctor*, trans. Eden and Cedar Paul (New York: Viking, 1932), p. 98.

61. Tsurumi et al., *Nihon no Hyakuen*, IX: 150.

62. Irokawa, *Kindai Kokka no Shuppatsu*, p. 100.

63. Yano, ed., *Nippon, A Charted Survey of Japan, 1971*, p. 335.

64. *Ibid.*, 1976 edition, pp. 266–67.

65. *Ibid.* (1971 edition), pp. 38–41, 339. Also *Statistical Abstract of the United States* (Washington, D.C.: U.S. Department of Commerce, 1979), pp. 889–90.

66. *Ibid.* Also Shibusawa, *Japanese Society in the Meiji Era*, p. 57.

67. Dore, *Land Reform in Japan*, p. 202.

68. Wakatsuki, "Inchō Nikki," in *Tsuchi to Furusato*, VII: 318.

69. Yanagida, *Meiji-Taishō-shi: Sesō-hen*, p. 339.

70. Akita Kai-shindōsha, "Kyōsaku Chitai o Iku" (Travels in Areas Beset by Crop Failure), in *Kindai Minshū no Kiroku: Nōmin*, p. 183.

71. Yūki Aisoka, *Zoku-Sonri Seikatsu-ki* (Record of Life in a Village, A Sequel) (Tokyo: Iwanami Shoten, 1937), p. 6.

72. Embree, *Suye Mura*, p. 255.

73. Seikyo Muchaku, *Echoes from a Mountain School*, trans. G. Caulfield and M. Kimura (Tokyo: Kenkyusha, 1953), pp. 57–58.

74. Wakatsuki, "Inchō Nikki," in *Tsuchi to Furusato*, VII: 324.

75. Shimonaka, *Nihon Zankoku Monogatari*, I: 190–91.

76. Tsurumi et al., *Nihon no Hyakunen*, VIII: 231.

77. *Ibid.*, pp. 234–35.

78. *Ibid.*, p. 235.

1. Cf. note 42, Chapter I.
2. Ariizumi Sadao, "Meiji Kokka to Minshū Tōgō" (The Meiji State and the Unification of the Masses), in Iwanami Kōza, *Nihon Rekishi,* 1975–1977 edition, XVII:227.
3. Hosoi Wakizō, *Jyokō Aishi* (The Sad History of Women Factory Workers) (Tokyo: Iwanami Shoten, 1954), p. 231. Also Shibuya, *Nōmin Aishi,* p. 168; Hashimoto Tetsuya, "Toshika to Minshū Undō" (Urbanization and People's Movement), in Iwanami Kōza, *Nihon Rekishi,* 1975–1977 edition, XVII:322.
4. Shimonaka, *Nihon Zankoku Monogatari,* V:48–49.
5. Akita Kai-shinpōsha, "Kyōsaku Chitai of Iku," pp. 188–89.
6. Shibuya, *Nōmin Aishi,* pp. 69, 65.
7. Kokubun Ichitarō, "Kodomo Zuihitsu" (Children's Essays), in *Minshū no Kiroku: Nōmin,* p. 208.
8. *Ibid.,* pp. 219ff.
9. Karasawa Tomitarō, *Meiji Hyakunen no Kyōiku* (One Hundred Years of Meiji Education) (Tokyo: Nihon Keizai Shimbunsha, 1968), p. 22.
10. Murakami and Sakata, *Meiji Bunka-shi: Kyōiku Dōtoku-hen,* p. 502.
11. *Ibid.,* pp. 148, 149, 151. Also cf. George B. Sansom, *The Western World and Japan* (New York: Knopf, 1949), pp. 366ff. on "Traditionalist Reaction."
12. Murakami and Sakata, *Meiji Bunka-shi: Kyōiku Dōtoku-hen,* p. 153.
13. *Ibid.,* pp. 174–78; Ivan Parker Hall, *Mori Arinori* (Cambridge, Mass.: Harvard University Press, 1973), pp. 424ff.
14. Ryusaku Tsunoda et al., eds., *Sources of Japanese Tradition* (New York: Columbia University Press, 1958), pp. 646–47.
15. Kaigo Tokiomi, ed., *Nihon Kyōkasho Taikei* (Grand Compendium of Japanese Textbooks), 43 vols. (Tokyo: Kōdansha, 1961–1967), II:498.
16. *Ibid.,* III:26.
17. Tsunoda, *Sources of Japanese Tradition,* pp. 705–6.
18. Tsurumi et al., *Nihon no Hyakunen,* III: 79–80.
19. Yūki Aisoka, *Sonri Seikatsuki* (Record of Village Life) (Tokyo: Iwanami, 1935), p. 27.
20. Richard J. Smethurst, *A Social Basis for Prewar Japanese Militarism* (Berkeley: University of California Press, 1974), pp. xiv–xv.
21. *Ibid.,* p. 69.
22. *Ibid.,* pp. 74–76.
23. *Ibid.,* pp. 165ff.
24. A sixth-grade *shūshin* textbook issued in wartime says: "In order to establish world peace the many nations of the world must uphold moral principles and treat each other justly and fairly. A nation which does not do so and injures the honor of other nations, selfishly concerning itself only with its own interests, is an evil nation. Such a nation disrupts the peace of the world. We as imperial subjects, in order to ensure the peace of mind of the Emperor, must resolutely chastize such a nation" (Kaigo, *Nihon Kyōkasho Taikei,* III: 455).
25. They were said to have broken through enemy lines by carrying a live bomb through enemy fortifications. The authenticity of this story has been questioned in the postwar years.
26. Matsunaga, *Minshū no Kiroku: Nōmin,* p. 19.
27. Yoshino, *Meiji Bunka Zenshū,* XX: 513, 485, 500.
28. Murakami and Sakata, *Meiji Bunka-shi: Kyōiku Dōtoku-hen,* pp. 505–6. Also, Sansom, *The Western World and Japan,* p. 385. In fact many village officials felt overwhelmed by the continuous stream of directives and instructions that flowed from the government and complained of the officiousness of the bureaucrats who were determined to transform the society overnight. Cf. Yoshino, *Meiji Bunka Zenshū,* XX: 524.
29. *Ibid.,* p. 506.

30. Shibusawa, *Japanese Life and Culture in the Meiji Era,* pp. 257–58.
31. Yanagida, *Japanese Manners and Customs in the Meiji Era,* p. 259. A sociologist claims that 70% of the villages continued to live by the lunar calendar until the end of World War II. Miyamoto Jōichi, "Nōson Bunka to Toshi Bunka" (Agrarian Culture and Urban Culture in Chūō Kōron [July 1961], p. 360.
32. Some historians see the early Meiji peasant uprisings as essentially a protest movement against the path of "enlightenment and civilization" which the government leaders and the Westernizing intellectuals were following. Cf. Irokawa Daikichi, "Nihon Nasyonarizumu-ron" (On Japanese Nationalism), in Iwanami Kōza, *Nihon Rekishi,* 1975–1977 edition, XVII: 356–66.
33. Smith, *Agrarian Origins of Modern Japan,* p. 210.
34. Ronald Dore lists three salient characteristics of the prewar Japanese peasantry: "1) A submissiveness to authoritarian leadership deriving from an acceptance of hierarchical status distinctions which implied a natural right of those above to rule and a natural duty of those below to obey. 2) A willingness ot subordinate the individual to the group, to sacrifice individual interests for the good of the family, the village and the nation. 3) A tendency to interpret the 'good of the nation' largely in terms of the relative power and prestige of a Japan in aggressive competition with other powers" (Dore, *Land Reform in Japan,* p. 393).
35. Smith, *Agrarian Origins of Modern Japan,* p. 205.
36. Fukutake Tadashi, *Asian Rural Society: China, India, Japan* (Tokyo: University of Tokyo Press, 1967), p. 48.
37. Dore, *Land Reform in Japan,* p. 51.
38. Ariizumi, "Meiji Kokka to Minshū Tōgō," p. 243.
39. *Ibid.,* pp. 244–45.
40. Havens, *Farm and Nation in Modern Japan,* p. 97.
41. Murakami and Sakata, *Meiji Bunka-shi: Kyōiku Dōtōku-hen,* pp. 333–34.
42. Fukutake, *Asian Rural Society,* p. 51.
43. Havens, *Farm and Nation in Modern Japan,* p. 8.
44. Fukutake, *Asian Rural Society,* p. 53.
45. *Ibid.,* pp. 52–53.
46. Havens, *Farm and Nation in Modern Japan,* pp. 8–9.
47. Dore, *Land Reform in Japan,* p. 92.
48. Havens, *Farm and Nation in Modern Japan,* p. 164.
49. *Ibid.,* pp. 228–29.
50. Masao Maruyama, *Thought and Behaviour in Modern Japanese Politics* (London: Oxford University Press, 1963), pp. 39–40.
51. Dore, *Land Reform in Japan,* p. 102.
52. Smith, *Agrarian Origins of Modern Japan,* p. 208.
53. Yūki Aisoka, *Sonri Seikatsu-ki,* in *Tsuchi to Furusato,* VII: 145.
54. Shibuya, *Nōmin Aishi,* pp. 25, 32, 34, 76, 169.
55. *Ibid.* p. 389.
56. Yūki, *Sonri Seikatsu-ki,* in *Tsuchi to Furusato,* VII: 137, 139–40.
57. Ibuse Masuji, *Tajinko-mura* (Tajinko Village), in *Tsuchi to Furusato,* I: 169ff.
58. *Ibid.,* p. 321.
59. Yūki, *Sonri Seikatsu-ki,* in *Tsuchi to Furusato,* VII: 139.
60. Masao Maruyama, "Patterns of Individuation and the Case of Japan: A Conceptual Scheme," in Marius B. Jansen, ed., *Changing Japanese Attitudes Toward Modernization* (Princeton, N.J.: Princeton University Press, 1965), p. 508, note 12.
61. Dore, *Land Reform in Japan,* p. 61.
62. Ibuse, *Tajinko-mura,* pp. 195–96.
63. Murakami and Sakata, *Meiji Bunka-shi: Kyōiku Dōtōku-hen,* pp. 338–39.
64. Yūki, *Zuihitsu,* I: 168. The fact that newspaper consumption was largely a matter of economics is reflected in the small readership found in the urban slums. In 1915 in one

slum district of Tokyo a survey revealed that only one of 9 households read the papers. Shimonaka, *Nihon Zankoku Monogatari,* V: 49.

65. Yamamoto Akira, "Shakai Seikatsu no Henka," p. 329.
66. Okada et al., *Nihon no Rekishi,* XII: 159. Also Imai Seiichi, *Taishō Demokurashii* (Taisho Democracy) (Tokyo: Chūō Kōronsha, 1966), p. 463; Tsurumi et al., *Nihon no Hyakunen,* V: 194.
67. Katō Ken'ichi, *Shōnen Kurabu Jidai* (Years of Shonen Kurabu) (Tokyo: Kōdansha, 1968), p. 117. And Imai, *Taishō Demokurashii,* p. 463.
68. Asahi Jyaanaru staff, *Shōwashi no Shunkan* (Moments in Showa History), 2 vols. (Tokyo: Asahi Shimbunsha, 1966), I: 283.
69. Aida Yūji et al., "Nihon o Kaeta Hyakuichinin" (101 Persons Who Transformed Japan), in *Bungei Shunjū* (November 1972), p. 185.
70. Katō, *Shōnen Kurabu Jidai,* p. 128.

RURAL WOMEN

1. Yanagida, *Japanese Manners and Customs in the Meiji Era,* p. 118.
2. *Ibid.,* p. 119.
3. Embree, *Suye Mura,* p. 97.
4. Segawa, *Mura no Onna-tachi,* p. 126.
5. *Ibid.,* pp. 142–43.
6. *Ibid.,* p. 120.
7. Shibata Michiko, *Hisabetsuburaku no Denshō to Seikatsu* (Life and Tradition in the Discriminated Hamlets) (Tokyo: San'ichi Shobō, 1972), p. 152.
8. Segawa, *Mura no Onna-tachi,* p. 144.
9. *Ibid.,* p. 17.
10. *Ibid.,* p. 145.
11. Shimonaka, *Nihon Zankoku Monogatari,* I: 246.
12. Segawa, *Mura no Onna-tachi,* p. 82.
13. Shimonaka, *Nihon Zankoku Monogatari,* I: 253–54.
14. Segawa, *Mura no Onna-tachi,* pp. 122–23.
15. Wada Kinji and Takeuchi Yoshinaga, eds., "Nōson no Haha no Rekishi" (History of Farm Village Mothers), in *Tsuchi to Furusato,* VII: 328–29.
16. Shimonaka, *Nihon Zankoku Monogatari,* I: 248, 256–57.
17. *Ibid.,* pp. 230–31.
18. *Ibid.,* pp. 240–41.
19. Wada and Takeuchi, "Nōson no Haha no Rekishi," p. 330.
20. Shimonaka, *Nihon Zankoku Monogatari,* I: 257.
21. *Ibid.*
22. Segawa, *Mura no Onna-tachi,* p. 132.
23. Yamshiro Tomoe, *Fuki no Tō* (Bog Rhubarb Shoots), in *Tsuchi to Furusato,* I: 224ff, 522.

THE STRUGGLE FOR SURVIVAL

1. Nakamura Masanori, *Rōdōsha to Nōmin,* pp. 330–31.
2. Ann Waswo, *Japanese Landlords: The Decline of a Rural Elite* (Berkeley: University of California Press, 1977), p. 15.
3. Norman, *Japan's Emergence as a Modern State,* pp. 21–22; 52–53; 147–48, footnotes 24 and 25. J. W. Hall believes it was 20%; J. W. Hall and Richard K. Beardsley, *Twelve Doors to Japan* (New York: McGraw-Hill, 1965), p. 554. Waswo cites 27%; *Japanese Landlords,* p. 16.
4. *Ibid.,* p. 19.
5. Fukutake, *Japanese Rural Society,* p. 10.

6. Dore, *Land Reform in Japan,* pp. 42–43.

7. Waswo, *Japanese Landlords,* p. 8.

8. Fukutake, *Japanese Rural Society,* pp. 11–14.

9. Nakamura, *Rōdōsha to Nōmin,* pp. 60–62.

10. Inomata Tsunao, "Kyūbō no Nōson," pp. 307–9.

11. Shimonaka, *Nihon Zankoku Monogatari,* V: 269.

12. Yokoyama Gen'nosuke, *Nihon no Kasō Shakai* (The Lower Layers of Japanese Society) (Tokyo: Iwanami Shoten, 1949), p. 255.

13. Taira Shigemichi, ed., *Kindai Tōhoku Shomin no Kiroku* (Record of the Common People in the Northeast in the Modern Era), 2 vols. (Tokyo: Nihon Hōsōkyōkai, 1973), II: 189.

14. "Mura kara no Uttae," in *Kindai Minshū no Kiroku: Nōmin,* pp. 108–9.

15. Shibuya, *Nōmin Aishi,* pp. 65, 68, 264.

16. Inomata, *Kyūbō no Nōson,* pp. 412–13.

17. "Mura kara no Uttae," p. 109.

18. Miyamoto, "Nōson Bunka to Toshi Bunka," p. 358.

19. Dore, *Land Reform in Japan,* p. 44.

20. Nakamura Masanori, *Rōdōsha to Nōmin,* p. 66.

21. Dore, *Land Reform in Japan,* p. 45.

22. In the 1890s it was even higher at 75%. Waswo, *Japanese Landlords,* p. 31.

23. Nakamura Masanori, *Rōdōsha to Nōmin,* pp. 66–69.

24. Waswo, *Japanese Landlords,* pp. 108–9.

25. Nakamura Masanori, *Rōdōsha to Nōmin,* pp. 72–73.

26. Waswo, *Japanese Landlords,* pp. 103–6.

27. *Ibid.,* p. 118.

28. In 1918 the percentage of landlords in the House of Peers was 29%, and in 1920 it was 20% in the House of Representatives. *Ibid.,* p. 118.

29. Tsurumi et al., *Nihon no Hyakunen,* VI: 256.

30. Shibuya, *Nōmin Aishi,* pp. 16–17.

31. Nakamura Masanori, *Rōdōsha to Nōmin,* pp. 251–52.

32. Waswo, *Japanese Landlords,* p. 103.

33. Ashai Jyaanaru staff, *Shōwashi no Shunkan,* I: 118, 122.

34. Waswo, *Japanese Landlords,* pp. 128–30.

35. Dore, *Land Reform in Japan,* p. 72.

36. Shimonaka, *Nihon Zankoku Monogatari,* V: 289–95, and Tsurami et al., *Nihon no Hyakunen,* V: 276–80.

37. Shimonaka, *Nihon Zankoku Monogatari,* V: 298–300.

38. Asahi Jyaanaru staff, *Shōwashi no Shunkan,* I:116.

39. Taira, *Kindai Tōhoku Shomin no Kiroku,* II:175.

40. *Ibid.,* pp. 173–81, and Asahi Jyaanaru staff, *Shōwashi no Shunkan,* I: 114–21.

41. Taira, *Kindai Tōhoku Shomin no Kiroku,* II: 177–78.

42. Nakamura Masanori, *Rōdōsha to Nōmin,* pp. 327–29.

43. Cf. Dore, *Land Reform in Japan,* p. 98ff.

44. Nakamura Masanori, *Rōdōsha to Nōmin,* p. 385ff.

45. Havens, *Farm and Nation in Modern Japan,* pp. 149, 152.

46. Taira, *Kindai Tōhoku no Shomin no Kiroku,* II: 191.

47. Dore, *Land Reform in Japan,* p. 104.

48. Asahi Jyaanaru staff, *Shōwashi no Shunkan,* I:150.

49. Yanagida, *Japanese Manners and Customs in the Meiji Era,* p. 124.

50. Shimonaka, *Nihon Zankoku Monogatari,* I: 142, and Nakamura Masanori, *Rōdōsha to Nōmin,* p. 320.

51. *Ibid.*

52. Inomata, *Kyūbō no Nōson,* p. 299. If we take 1926 as index 100, we find that the price of rice dropped to 48.9 by 1931, silk to 36.7, and all farm commodities to 64.6. The cash

income of farm families dropped from 100 to 33.5 by 1931, while household expenses were 46.2. Dore, *Land Reform in Japan,* p. 88.

53. Heibonsha staff, *Dokyumento Shōwa Sesō-shi: Senzen-hen,* p. 58; and Asahi Jyaanaru staff, *Shōwashi no Shunkan,* I: 150.
54. Shimonaka, *Nihon Zankoku Monogatari,* I: 145.
55. *Ibid.,* p. 148.
56. Yūki, *Zoku-Sonri Seikatsu-ki,* pp. 7–8.
57. Tsurumi et al., *Nihon no Hyakunen,* IV: 29ff.
58. Asahi Jyaanaru staff, *Shōwashi no Shunkan,* I: 152.
59. *Ibid.,* pp. 152–53.
60. Akita Kai-shinpōsha, "Kyōsaku Chitai o Iku," in *Kindai Minshū no Kiroku: Nōmin,* p. 198.
61. *Ibid.,* p. 201.
62. Tsurumi et al., *Nihon no Hyakuen,* IV: 32–33.
63. Asahi Jyaanaru staff, *Shōwshi no Shunkan,* I: 151–53.
64. Honjō Shigeru, *Honjō Nikki* (Honjo Diary) (Tokyo: Hara Shobō, 1967), p. 168.
65. Akita Kai-shinpōsha, "Kyōsaku Chitai o Iku," p. 183.
66. Taira, *Kindai Tōhōku Shomin no Kiroku,* II: 189.
67. *Ibid.,* p. 191.
68. Shimonaka, *Nihon Zankoku Monogatari,* V: 258–59.
69. Tsunoda et al., *Sources of Japanese Tradition,* pp. 796–97.
70. Asahi Jyaanaru staff, *Shōwashi no Shunkan,* I: 143ff.
71. Maruyama, *Thought and Behavior in Modern Japanese Politics,* p. 45.
72. Kono Tsukasa, ed., *Ni-ni-roku Jiken* (2.26 Incident) (Tokyo: Kawade Shobō, 1972), p. 190.
73. Honjō, *Honjō Nikki,* p. 175.
74. Asahi Jyaanaru staff, *Shōwashi no Shunkan,* I: 157.
75. This account of agrarian poverty in northern Japan was written by Shimomura Chiaki (1893–1955) in January 1932. It is included in *Tsuchi to Furusato,* VII: 120ff. Shimomura was a novelist, essayist, and reporter who wrote about the downtrodden members of the society. His first novel dealt with the fate of the women in the brothels, and his second with urban hobos.
76. These excerpts from a diary kept by a young Hokkaido farm girl during the famine of 1934 were published in a women's magazine, *Fujin Kōron,* and were reprinted in Heibonsha staff, *Dokyumento Shōwa Sesō-shi: Senzen-hen,* pp. 71–75.

THE OUTCASTE IN JAPAN

1. Harada Tomohiko, *Hi-sabetsuburaku no Rekishi* (History of the Discriminated Hamlets) (Tokyo: Asahi Shimbunsha, 1975), p. 36.
2. The census of 1871 showed that there were 281,311 *eta,* 23,480 *hinin,* and 79,095 miscellaneous outcastes. George De Vos and Hiroshi Wagatsuma, *Japan's Invisible Race* (Berkeley: University of California Press, 1967), p. 115.

The increase in the number of *burakumin* from 400,000 to 2 million between 1871 and 1970 compared to the general population increase from 33 million to 104 million in the same period may mean that the birthrate among the *burakumin* was higher than that of the general populace. It could also mean that figures for the *burakumin* may not be completely accurate. In order to exert political pressure to gain redress, some *burakumin* leaders have exaggerated the number of *burakumin* currently present. Some have claimed that there are 3 million *burakumin,* a figure rejected by most authorities on the subject. *Ibid.,* p. 116.

A 1919 survey by the Home Ministry indicates that there were 5,294 outcaste *buraku* with 148,706 households and a population of 876,000. The national population that year was 55 million. This survey, however, did not include *burakumin* scattered in non-*burakumin* communities. Watanabe Tōru, "Buraku Kaihō Undō" (Buraku Liberation Movement), in Iwanami Kōza, *Nihon Rekishi,* 1975–1977 edition, XVIII: 185.

3. Cf. table in De Vos and Wagatsuma, *Japan's Invisible Race,* p. 116.

4. Kitahara Taisaku, *Senmin no Kōei* (A Descendant of the Pariahs) (Tokyo: Chikuma Shobō, 1974), p. 6.

5. It is believed that the kind of rigid ethnocentrism that characterizes modern Japan did not emerge as a dominant mode of thought until the Tokugawa period when the Shinto school of National Learning began to stress the sacred and unique nature of Japan and the Japanese.

6. Harada, *Hi-sabetsuburaku no Rekishi,* p. 22.

7. *Ibid.,* pp. 32–35.

8. Nagahara Keiji, "The Medieval Origins of the Eta-Hinin," *Journal of Japanese Studies,* vol. 5, no. 2 (Summer 1979), pp. 385ff.

9. "The hinin were more often associated with the transient trades such as begging, prostitution, shooting gallery keepers, peep show men, monkey masters, dog trainers, snake charmers, jugglers, acrobats and fox tamers" (De Vos and Wagatsuma, *Japan's Invisible Race,* p. 22).

10. Harada, *Hi-sabetsuburaku no Rekishi,* pp. 22–23.

11. Shibata, *Hi-sabetsuburaku no Denshō to Seikatsu,* pp. 36ff.

12. Harada, *Hi-sabetsuburaku no Rekishi,* p. 124.

13. Cf. De Vos and Wagatsuma, *Japan's Invisible Race,* p. 20, note 20.

14. Irokawa, "Nihon Nashonarizumu-ron," in Iwanami Kōza, *Nihon Rekishi,* XVII: 367.

15. Tsuchikata Tetsu, *Hi-sabetsuburaku no Tatakai* (The Struggle by the Discriminated Hamlets) (Tokyo: Shinsensha, 1973), pp. 11–12.

16. Harada, *Hi-sabetsuburaku no Rekishi,* p. 130.

17. Tsuchikata, *Hi-sabetsuburaku no Tatakai,* pp. 13–15.

18. Harada, *Hi-sabetsuburaku no Rekishi,* pp. 98, 161.

19. Shibata, *Hi-sabetsuburaku no Denshō to Seikatsu,* p. 252.

20. Yoshino, *Meiji Bunka Zenshū: Bunmei Kaika,* XX: 237.

21. De Vos and Wagatsuma, *Japan's Invisible Race,* p. 37.

22. Harada, *Hi-sabetsuburaku no Rekishi,* pp. 193–95.

23. *Ibid.,* p. 208.

24. *Ibid.,* pp. 247–48.

25. *Ibid.,* pp. 275–76.

26. Shimazaki Toson, *The Broken Commandment,* trans. Kenneth Strong (Tokyo: University of Tokyo Press, 1974), p. xiii.

27. Harada, *Hi-sabetsuburaku no Rekishi,* pp. 238–39.

28. Shibata, *Hi-sabetsuburaku no Denshō to Seikatsu,* pp. 200–201.

29. Shimazaki, *Broken Commandment,* pp. 228–29.

30. *Ibid.,* pp. xx–xxi.

31. Kitahara, *Senmin no Kōei,* p. 59.

32. The tenacity of the bias against intercaste marriages is seen in the fact that among Japanese-Americans in the United States stubborn resistance against mixed marriages with *burakumin* has persisted among non-*burakumin.* De Vos and Wagatsuma, *Japan's Invisible Race,* pp. 217–18.

33. Buraku Kaihō Dōmei Chūō Honbu staff, *Sabetsu no Naka o Ikinuite* (Carrying on through a Lifetime of Discrimination) (Tokyo: Kaihō Shuppansha, 1978), p. 64.

34. Shibata, *Hi-sabetsuburaku no Denshō to Seikatsu,* pp. 225–26.

35. Kitahara, *Senmin no Kōei,* p. 63. Also cf. De Vos and Wagatsuma, *Japan's Invisible Race,* pp. 255–56.

36. *Ibid.,* p. 57, and Harada, *Hi-sabetsuburaku no Rekishi,* pp. 319, 320.

37. Shimonaka, *Nihon Zankoku Monogatari,* V: 31.

38. *Ibid.,* p. 32.
39. De Vos and Wagatsuma, *Japan's Invisible Race,* p. 254.
40. Kitahara, *Senmin no Kōei,* p. 36.
41. Hiroshima Buraku Kaihō Kenkyūjyo, *Hiroshima-ken Hi-sabetsuburaku no Rekishi* (History of Discriminated Hamlets in Hiroshima prefecture), (Tokyo: Aki Shobō, 1975), pp. 195–97. Also Shibata, *Hi-sabetsuburaku no Denshō to Seikatsu,* p. 155.
42. *Ibid.,* pp. 86–88.
43. Harada, *Hi-sabetsuburaku no Rekishi,* p. 284.
44. *Ibid.,* pp. 284–85.
45. De Vos and Wagatsuma, *Japan's Invisible Race,* pp. 91–92.
46. Hiroshima Buraku Kaihō Kenkyūjyo, *Hiroshima-ken Hi-sabetsuburaku no Rekishi,* p. 246.
47. Kitahara, *Senmin no Kōei,* p. 100.
48. Harada, *Hi-sabetsuburaku no Rekishi,* pp. 287–88, and Tsuchikata, *Hi-sabetsuburaku no Tatakai,* p. 82.
49. Watanabe, "Buraku Kaihō Undō," p. 185.
50. *Ibid.,* pp. 225, 372–73.
51. Buraku Kaihō Dōmei Chūō Honbu, *Sabetsu no Naka o Ikinuite,* pp. 184–85.
52. Harada, *Hi-sabetsuburaku no Rekishi,* pp. 328–29.
53. *Ibid.,* p. 318.
54. *Ibid.,* pp. 205–6.
55. Buraku Kaihō Dōmei Chūō Honbu, *Sabetsu no Naka o Ikinuite,* p. 191.
56. *Ibid.,* p. 187.
57. Harada, *Hi-sabetsuburaku no Rekishi,* pp. 202–3.
58. *Ibid.,* pp. 328–29.
59. *Ibid.,* p. 314.
60. *Ibid.,* pp. 201–2.
61. *Ibid.,* p. 328.
62. Shibata, *Hi-sabetsuburaku no Denshō to Seikatsu,* p. 65.
63. Nakamura Masanori, *Rōdōsha to Nōmin,* p. 359.
64. Harada, *Hi-sabetsuburaku no Rekishi,* pp. 373–74.
65. De Vos and Wagatsuma, *Japan's Invisible Race,* p. 259.
66. Harada, *Hi-sabetsuburaku no Rekishi,* pp. 260–61.
67. Yoshino, *Meiji Bunka Zenshū: Bunmei Kaika,* XX: 517.
68. Buraku Kaihō Dōmei Chūō Honbu, *Sabetsu no Naka o Ikinuite,* p. 47.
69. Hiroshima Buraku Kaihō Kenkyūjyo, *Hiroshima-ken Hi-sabetsuburaku no Rekishi,* pp. 156–57.
70. Harada, *Hi-sabetsuburaku no Rekishi,* p. 235.
71. *Ibid.,* p. 329. Also cf. the 1903 survey in Hiroshima Buraku Kaihō Kenkyūjyo, *Hiroshima-ken Hi-sabetsuburaku no Rekishi,* pp. 158–59. The poor educational record of the *burakumin* children continued into the postwar period. IQ test scores and school grade-point averages taken in the 1950s indicated that *burakumin* pupils were still performing poorly compared to non-*burakumin* children. De Vos and Wagatsuma, *Japan's Invisible Race,* p. 261.
72. Buraku Kaihō Dōmei Chūō Honbu, *Sabetsu no Naka o Ikinuite,* p. 278.
73. *Ibid.,* pp. 238ff.
74. *Ibid.,* pp. 63–64.
75. *Ibid.,* pp. 162–66.
76. Harada, *Hi-sabetsuburaku no Rekishi,* p. 240.
77. *Ibid.,* p. 262. Also De Vos and Wagatsuma, *Japan's Invisible Race,* pp. 40–42.
78. Harada, *Hi-sabetsuburaku no Rekishi,* pp. 256–57.
79. Shimonaka, *Nihon Zankoku Monogatari,* V: 326.
80. De Vos and Wagatsuma, *Japan's Invisible Race,* pp. 44–45.
81. *Ibid.,* p. 47.
82. Harada, *Hi-sabetsuburaku no Rekishi,* pp. 277–79.

83. The government arrested 1,200 persons, held about 500 in jail, and prosecuted them. Robert A. Scalapino, *The Japanese Communist Movement, 1920–1966* (Berkeley: University of California Press, 1967), p. 34.
84. Tsuchikata, *Hi-sabetsuburaku no Tatakai*, pp. 117–22.
85. De Vos and Wagatsuma, *Japan's Invisible Race*, p. 60.
86. Shibata, *Hi-sabetsuburaku no Denshō to Seikatsu*, pp. 203–4.
87. *Ibid.*, p. 129.
88. *Ibid.*, pp. 124, 180, 264.
89. De Vos and Wagatsuma, *Japan's Invisible Race*, pp. 138–41.
90. Excerpted from Kitahara, *Senmin no Kōei*, pp. 28–32, 39–41, 43–48, 51–54, 127, 133–134, 139–40.

THE TEXTILE FACTORY WORKERS

1. Nakamura Masanori, *Rōdōsha to Nōmin*, p. 90. Other major silk-producing prefectures in 1911 were Gunma with 8% of the nation's silk production, Aichi (7.4%), Gifu (5.5%), Yamanashi (5.3%), Fukushima (4.46%), and Yamagata (3.3%). These plus Nagano prefecture produced 66.5% of the raw silk in Japan in 1911.
2. Lockwood, *Economic Development of Japan*, p. 16.
3. Ōe Shinobu, *Nihon no Sangyō Kakumei* (Japan's Industrial Revolution) (Tokyo: Iwanami Shoten, 1968), p. 283.
4. Nakamura Masanori, *Rōdōsha to Nōmin*, p. 86.
5. Lockwood, *Economic Development of Japan*, pp. 28–31.
6. Yamamoto Shigemi, *Aa Nomugi-tōge*, pp. 264–65. The number of families engaged in hand-reeling at home continued to be high. In 1894 there were estimated to be 331,257 families engaged in home silk reeling. The figure peaked in 1900 at 425,988, but was still over 400,000 in 1904. Ōe, *Nihon no Sangyō Kakumei*, p. 282.
7. Lockwood, *Economic Development of Japan*, p. 33.
8. Okada et al., *Nihon no Rekishi*, X: 211.
9. Wada Hide, *Tomioka Nikki* (Tomioka Diary) (Tokyo: Chūō Kōronsha, 1978), pp. 11–12.
10. Nakamura Masanori, *Rōdōsha to Nōmin*, p. 91.
11. *Ibid.*,
12. Yamamoto Shigemi, *Aa Nomugi-tōge*, pp. 72–73. A contract concluded with a cotton mill worker in 1923 shows that the employer reserved the right to fire the girl anytime at his convenience or if the girl made any mistake at work. The girl was not to complain and was to accept whatever action the employer took. Another contract issued by a Tokyo textile company provided for the company's right to fix the wages. The worker had to agree not to complain about the pay. Hosoi, *Jyokō Aishi*, pp. 94–95.
13. Yamamoto Shigemi, *Aa Nomugi-tōge*, p. 76.
14. The average income for a tenant farmer tilling one *chō* (2.45 acres) came to 166 yen in 1899. Nakamura Masanori, *Rōdōsha to Nōmin*, p. 95.
15. *Ibid.*, pp. 70, 77.
16. Yamamoto Shigemi, *Aa Nomugi-tōge*, pp. 40, 48–49.
17. Ōe, *Nihon no Sangyō Kakumei*, p. 175.
18. Yamamoto Shigemi, *Aa Nomugi-tōge*, pp. 180–81.
19. *Ibid.*, pp. 182–83.
20. *Ibid.*, p. 195. The base pay of the Suwa silk-plant workers did not rise much during the nineteenth century. In 1897 the lowest-paid workers received 3 sen a day and the highest-paid ones 30 sen. The average pay was 14 sen. Tsukada Masatomo, *Nagano-ken no Rekishi* (History of Nagano Prefecture) (Tokyo: Yamakawa Shuppansha, 1974), p. 248.

The following table shows the daily wages paid in other occupations between 1896 and 1903.

Year	Farm Workers (m)	Farm Workers (f)	Textile Workers (m)	Textile Workers (f)	Carpenters	Day Laborers
1896	21 sen	13 sen	19 sen	13 sen	38 sen	26 sen
1900	30	19	33	20	54	37
1903	31	19	34	19	59	40

Matsunaga Shōzo, "Shakai Mondai no Hassei," in Iwanami Kōza, *Nihon Rekishi*, XVI: 247.

21. Yamamoto Shigemi, *Aa Nomugi-tōge*, pp. 195–96.
22. *Ibid.*, p. 197.
23. Nakamura Masanori, *Rōdōsha to Nōmin*, p. 169–70.
24. Okada et al., *Nihon no Rekishi*, X: 164.
25. Nakamura Masanori, *Rōdōsha to Nōmin*, pp. 169–70.
26. *Fukuzawa Zenshū* VI: 449–50.
27. Yamamoto Shigemi, *Aa Nomugi-tōge*, pp. 330–31.
28. *Ibid.*, p. 19.
29. Nakamura Masanori, *Rōdōsha to Nōmin*, p. 80.
30. Yamamoto Shigemi, *Aa Nomugi-tōge*, p. 30.
31. *Ibid.*
32. *Ibid.*, pp. 194–95, 34–35.
33. The following table is from a survey of 580 former silk-filature workers made by Yamamoto Shigemi.

Food	poor	average	good
	0%	10%	90%
Nature of Work	hard	average	easy
	3%	75%	22%
Pay	lower than other work	average	higher
	0%	30%	70%
Inspection	harrowing	average	easy
	90%	10%	0%
Treatment When Sick	poor	average	good
	40%	50%	10%
Overall*	positive	average	negative
	90%	10%	0%

They were asked if they were glad that they had gone to work in the silk filatures.

Yamamoto Shigemi, *Aa Nomugi-tōge*, p. 328.
34. *Ibid.*, pp. 327–28.
35. *Ibid.*, pp. 329, 335.
36. *Ibid.*, pp. 331–32.
37. *Ibid.*, p. 328.
38. *Ibid.*, p. 404. In 1918 a major textile company spent about 7 to 8 sen per worker on food. This was when there was a serious inflation in rice and other food. Hosoi, *Jyokō Aishi*, pp. 174–76.
39. Shimonaka, *Nihon Zankoku Monogatari*, V: 115–16.

40. *Ibid.*, p. 89.
41. Yamamoto Shigemi, *Aa Nomugi-tōge*, p. 81.
42. Hosoi, *Jyokō Aishi*, pp. 183–87.
43. Yamamoto Shigemi, *Aa Nomugi-tōge*, pp. 176–77.
44. Nōshōmushō Shōkōkyoku, *Shokkō Jijō* (Condition of the Factory Workers) (Tokyo: Meicho Kankōkai, 1967), pp. 168–69.
45. Hosoi, *Jyokō Aishi*, pp. 106–7.
46. Lockwood, *Economic Development of Japan*, p. 557.
47. Koyama Atsuhiko, *Taishō Daizasshi* (Taishō Magazine Articles) (Tokyo: Ryūdō Shuppansha, 1978), pp. 196–97.
48. Yamamoto Shigemi, *Aa Nomugi-tōge*, pp. 82–84.
49. *Ibid.*, pp. 90–91.
50. Nakamura Masanori, *Rōdōsha to Nōmin*, p. 98.
51. Hosoi, *Jyokō Aishi*, pp. 132–33.
52. *Ibid.*, p. 302.
53. *Ibid.*, pp. 304–7.
54. *Ibid.*, p. 127.
55. Yamamoto Shigemi, *Aa Nomugi-tōge*, p. 22.
56. Hosoi, *Jyokō Aishi*, pp. 142–43, 53–54, 146–49.
57. *Ibid.*, pp. 133, 224–25.
58. *Ibid.*, pp. 131–32.
59. Yamamoto Shigemi, *Aa Nomugi-tōge*, pp. 85–86.
60. Nōshōmushō Shōkōyoku, *Shokkō Jijō*, Appendix, pp. 151–53.
61. *Ibid.*, pp. 43–50. The owner abused other workers in a similarly inhumane fashion. This led to the suicide of two girls and the indictment of the owner, who was sentenced to two years in prison and fined 30 yen. *Ibid.*, pp. 29–39. Numerous other horror stories about workers who were abused are in *Shokkō Jijō*, Appendix, pp. 1–129.
62. The cotton textile workers were also driven to running away by ruthless employers and strenuous work. In one textile firm over 50% of the workers had been brought in to take the places of workers who had run away. Ōe, *Nihon no Sangyō Kakumei*, p. 326.
63. Yamamoto Shigemi, *Aa Nomugi-tōge*, p. 98.
64. *Ibid.*, pp. 94–95.
65. *Ibid.*, pp. 82–83, 107–8.
66. *Ibid.*, pp. 134–41.
67. Shimonaka, *Nihon Zankoku Monogatari*, V: 91–92.
68. *Ibid.*, p. 97.
69. Hosoi, *Jyokō Aishi*, p. 320.
70. Nakamura Masanori, *Rōdōsha to Nōmin*, pp. 171–72.
71. Hosoi, *Jyokō Aishi*, p. 319.
72. *Ibid.*, p. 320, and Yamamoto Shigemi, *Aa Nomugi-tōge*, pp. 149–51.
73. *Ibid.*, p. 153.
74. *Ibid.*, p. 149.
75. *Ibid.*, p. 150.
76. *Ibid.*, pp. 150–51.
77. Nakamura Masanori, *Rōdōsha to Nōmin*, p. 172.
78. Shimonaka, *Nihon Zankoku Monogatari*, V: 99–100.
79. Yamamoto Shigemi, *Aa Nomugi-tōge*, p. 154.
80. *Ibid.*,
81. *Ibid.*, p. 155.
82. *Ibid.*, pp. 155–56.
83. Tsurumi et al., *Nihon no Hyakunen*, VI: 93.
84. *Ibid.*
85. Yamamoto Shigemi, *Aa Nomugi-tōge*, p. 178.

86. *Ibid.*, p. 177.

87. Hosoi, *Jyokō Aishi*, p. 233.

88. *Ibid.*, pp. 280, 284.

89. Shimonaka, *Nihon Zankoku Monogatari*, V:106–7.

90. Tsurumi et al., *Nihon no Hyakunen*, VIII: 313–14.

91. *Ibid.*, p. 316.

92. Nakamura Masanori, *Rōdōsha to Nōmin*, pp. 179–80.

93. *Ibid.*, pp. 184, 186.

94. *Ibid.*, pp. 189–91, 194. In addition to the provisions noted earlier, a 12-hour limit on night work was provided for, but this was to go into effect 15 years after the law was implemented in 1916.

95. Number of Strikes: 1914–1928

Year	Number of Strikes	Number of Workers Involved
1914	50	7,904
1915	64	7,852
1916	108	8,413
1917	398	57,309
1918	417	66,457
1919	497	63,137
1920	282	36,371
1921	246	58,225
1922	250	41,503
1923	270	36,259
1924	333	54,526
1925	293	40,742
1926	495	67,234
1927	383	46,672
1928	393	43,337

Nakamura Masanori, *Rōdōsha to Nōmin*, p. 215.

96. *Ibid.*, pp. 283–84, and Yamamoto Shigemi, *Aa Nomugi-tōge*, pp. 255ff.

97. Horie Sangorō, *Okaya Seishi Rōdōsha Sōgi no Shinsō* (The Truth about the Okaya Silk Mill Workers' Dispute) (Tokyo: Shinano Mainichi Shimbun, 1927), pp. 217–18.

98. Yamamoto Shigemi, *Aa Nomugi-tōge*, pp. 261–62.

99. *Ibid.*, pp. 262–63.

100. *ibid.*, pp. 276–77.

101. *Ibid.*, p. 285.

102. *Ibid.*, pp. 268–69.

103. *Ibid.*, p. 267.

104. *Ibid.*, pp. 275–76.

105. Nakamura Masanori, *Rōdōsha to Nōmin*, p. 293.

106. *Ibid.*, pp. 293–94.

107. Asahi Jyaanaru staff, *Shōwashi no Shunkan*, I: 78–79, and Ōkōchi Kazuo, "Rōdō," in Yanagihara Tadao, ed., *Gendai Nihon Shōshi* (A Short History of Modern Japan), 2 vols. (Tokyo: Misuzu Shobō, 1952), II: 181.

108. *Ibid.*, pp. 171–80.

109. Nakamura Masanori, *Rōdōsha to Nōmin*, pp. 241–42; Shimomura, *Zankoku Monogatari*, I: 318.

110. Nakamura Masanori, *Rōdōsha to Nōmin*, pp. 200–201.

111. *Ibid.,* pp. 209.
112. Horie, *Okaya Seishi Rōdōsha Sōgi no Shinsō,* pp. 190–93.
113. Nakamura Masanori, *Rōdōsha to Nōmin,* p. 307.

POVERTY AND PROSTITUTION

1. Morisaki Kazue, *Karayuki-san* (Miss Karayuki) (Tokyo: Asahi Shimbunsha, 1976), pp. 22–23. The Japanese public tended to treat not only the inmates of the brothels but their offspring in an inhumane fashion. The children who were born of the relationship between the prostitutes and the Westerners, who began to arrive in Japan's port cities in the mid-nineteenth century, were treated with particular cruelty. In 1873 the authorities in Yokohama buried alive at the foot of a newly built bridge four young boys who were born as a result of such relationships as human sacrifices to appease the river gods, thus reviving a practice that had been abandoned since antiquity. Shimonaka, *Nihon Zankoku Monogatari,* IV: 93.
2. *Ibid.,* I: 326–27.
3. Koyama, *Taishō Daizasshi,* pp. 202–3.
4. It is believed that officially sanctioned brothels came into existence during Toyotomi Hideyoshi's reign in the late sixteenth century. Harada, *Hi-sabetsuburaku no Rekishi,* p. 105.
5. Okada et al., *Nihon no Rekishi,* X: 193.
6. Irokawa, *Kindai Nihon no Shuppatsu,* p. 107.
7. *Ibid.,* p. 105. In 1909 there were 6,280 prostitutes in the licensed brothels of Osaka prefecture, 2,461 in Kyoto prefecture, 2,684 in Kanagawa prefecture (where Yokohama is located), 2,137 in Aichi prefecture (where Nagoya is located), 2,185 in Nagasaki prefecture, and 1,742 in Hyogo prefecture (where Kobe is (located). Yamamuro Gunpei, *Shakai Kakusei-ron* (On Cleansing the Society) (Tokyo: Chūō Kōronsha, 1977), pp. 57–60.
8. Stephen and Ethel Longstreet, *Yoshiwara, City of the Senses* (New York: David McKay Co., 1970), pp. 162–63.
9. Tsunoda et al., *Sources of Japanese Tradition,* p. 570.
10. It appears, however, that in the outlying areas of northern Japan, infanticide was still practiced around the end of the nineteenth century. Yūki, *Sonri Seiktatsu-ki,* p. 82.

When Margaret Sanger visited Japan in 1922, the Japanese authorities took strict measures to prevent her from discussing in public her ideas on birth control. Shidzue Ishimoto, *Facing Two Ways* (New York: Farrar & Rinehart, 1935), pp. 220ff.
11. Shimonaka, *Nihon Zankoku Monogatari,* I: 221–27.
12. Irokawa, *Kindai Nihon no Shuppatsu,* pp. 106–7; Yamamuro, *Shakai Kakusei-ron,* p. 143; Longstreet, *Yoshiwara,* p. 168.
13. Yamamoto Akira, "Shakai Seikatsu no Henka to Toshi Bunka," in Iwanami Kōza, *Nihon Rekishi,* XIX: 331. Also Koyama, *Taishō Daizasshi,* p. 187, and Yamamuro, *Shakai Kakusei-ron,* pp. 57–60.
14. Yamamuro, *Shakai Kakusei-ron,* pp. 66–67.
15. Asahi Jyaanaru staff, *Shōwashi no Shunkan,* I: 153.
16. Shimonaka, *Nihon Zankoku Monogatari,* V: 262. According to another source, the figures by December were 437 geishas, 2,028 prostitutes, and 1,479 *sake* waitresses. Nakamura Masanori, *Rōdōsha to Nōmin,* p. 323.
17. Tsurumi et al., *Nihon no Hyakunen,* IV: 35.
18. Shimonaka, *Nihon Zankoku Monogatari,* V: 262. Around 1910 in Yoshiwara the charge in one brothel was 35 sen. The brothel keeper kept half and credited the girl with 17 sen. Ten sen of that sum went toward the repayment of the debt. The girl had 7 sen left to pay for her necessities. Most of the 10 sen to be applied against the repayment of the debt was actually taken up by interest charges, so the tenure of service got extended year after year.

Since the brothel keeper kept the books himself, he could juggle the figures in such a way as to keep the girl under his control for as long as he wanted to. Yamamuro, *Shakai Kakusei-ron,* pp. 27–28.

19. Asahi Jyaanaru staff, *Shōwashi no Shunkan,* I: 153.
20. Nakamura Masanori, *Rōdōsha to Nōmin,* pp. 321–22.
21. Tsurumi et al., *Nihon no Hyakunen,* IV: 34.
22. In 1895, of the 5,456 prostitutes in Tokyo prefecture, 33.5% were between the ages of 16 and 19 (15 to 18 according to the Western mode of calculation), and 49.9% were between 20 and 24 (19 to 23). Matsunaga Shōzō, "Shakai Mondai no Hassei," in Iwanami Kōza, *Nihon Rekishi,* XVI: 248.
23. Morisaki, *Karayuki-san,* p. 143.
24. Yamamuro, *Shakai Kakusei-ron,* p. 94.
25. Tanaka Sumiko, ed., *Jyosei Kaihō no Shisō to Kōdō* (Thought and Behavior in the Emancipation of Women) (Tokyo: Jiji Tsūshinsha, 1975), pp. 87–94.
26. Yamamuro, *Shakai Kakusei-ron,* p. 12.
27. *Ibid.,* pp. 35ff. U.S. missionary U. G. Murphy won a victory on behalf of the inmates of the brothels when in 1899 he got the courts to uphold the women's right to leave the brothels if they so wished. Tanikawa Kenichi, ed., *Kindai Minshū no Kiroku: Shōfu* (The Record of the Masses in the Modern Era: The Prostitutes) (Tokyo: Shinjinbutsu Ōraisha, 1971), p. 525.
28. Matsumiya Kazuya, *Yamagata-ken Mogami-gun Nishi-koguni-mura* (Village of Koguni in Mogami County, Yamagata Prefecture) (Tokyo: Kakusei-kai Fujin Kyōfū-kai Haishō Renmei, 1932), p. 10.
29. Koyama Atsuhiko, *Shōwa Daizasshi,* (Collection of Showa Magazine Articles), 3 vols. (Tokyo: Ryūdō Shuppansha, 1978), II: 494.
30. *Ibid.,* pp. 499–500.
31. Yamamuro, *Shakai Kakusei-ron,* pp. 61ff., 69–70. Of these 100, only twenty-three originally came from Tokyo.
32. Koyama, *Taishō Daizasshi,* pp. 189–90.
33. *Ibid.,* p. 195.
34. Yamamuro, *Shakai Kakusei-ron,* p. 30.
35. Tanikawa, *Kindai Minshū no Kiroku: Shofū,* pp. 253–54.
36. The term *karayuki* (literally, a person going to *Kara,* that is, China or abroad) was initially employed by the people of northern Kyushu to refer to people who went overseas to work. Eventually it came to be used primarily in reference to girls who were sold abroad to work as prostitutes in the brothels of Southeast Asia. Morisaki, *Karayuki-san,* pp. 17–18.
37. Yamamuro, *Shakai Kakusei-ron,* p. 256.
38. Morisaki, *Karayuki-san,* pp. 31, 164.
39. Shimonaka, *Nihon Zankoku Monogatari,* I: 344–45; Morisaki, *Karayuki-san,* pp. 219–20.
40. *Ibid.,* pp. 86–89.
41. *Ibid.,* p. 91.
42. Shimonaka, *Nihon Zankoku Monogatari,* I: 368.
43. Morisaki, *Karayuki-san,* pp. 120–23, 127ff.
44. *Ibid.,* p. 156.
45. *Ibid.,* pp. 156–57.
46. 16,424 in China (including 8,388 in Liaotung Peninsula), 2,086 in Singapore, 980 in Batavia, 392 in Manila, 913 in Honolulu, 371 in San Francisco, and 1,087 in Vladivostok. Others were scattered from South America to India. Yamamuro, *Shakai Kakusei-ron,* pp. 252, 255.
47. Yamasaki Tomoko, "Shōfu Yamada Waka o Tazunete" (In Search of the Prostitute Yamada Waka), in *Bungei Shunjū* (April 1977), pp. 202ff.
48. Tsurumi et al., *Nihon no Hyakunen,* VIII: 109.
49. Morisaki, *Karayuki-san,* pp. 23–24.

50. *Ibid.*, pp. 101–2.
51. *Ibid.*, pp. 29–30.
52. Morisaki, *Karayuki-san*, pp. 8–16.
53. Yamasaki Tomoko, *Sandakan no Haka* (The Tombs of Sandakan) (Tokyo: Bungei Shunjū, 1977), pp. 56ff.
54. *Ibid.*, p. 49.
55. *Ibid.*, p. 50.
56. Heibonsha staff, *Dokyumento Shōwa Sesō-shi*, pp. 77ff.
57. Yamasaki, *Sandakan Hachiban Shōkan* (Brothel No. Eight in Sandakan) (Tokyo: Bungei Shunjū, 1975), p. 70.
58. *Ibid.*, pp. 74–76.
59. *Ibid.*, pp. 88–91.
60. *Ibid.*, p. 110.
61. Yamamuro, *Shakai Kakusei-ron*, p. 262. Also Morisaki, *Karayuki-san*, pp. 158ff.
62. Yamasaki, *Sandakan no Haka*, pp. 73ff.
63. *Ibid.*, p. 71
64. Morisaki, *Karayuki-san*, p. 232.
65. *Ibid.*, p. 268.
66. *Ibid.*, pp. 233, 237.
67. Chōsenjin Kyōsei Renkō Shinsō Chōsadan, *Chōsenjin Kyōsei Renkō: Kyōsei Rōdō no Kiroku* (Forced Conscription of the Koreans: A Record of Forced Labor) (Tokyo: Gendaishi Shuppankai, 1974), p. 445.

THE COAL MINERS

1. Ōe, *Nihon no Sangyō Kakumei*, p. 180. Japan's major coal mines were located in northern Kyushu and Hokkaido.
2. *Ibid.*, p. 183. Also, Nakamura Masanori, *Rōdōsha to Nōmin*, p. 109, and Trewartha, *Japan, A Physical & Regional Geography*, p. 86.
3. There was a definite link between agrarian poverty and mining, for many impoverished tenant farmers, particularly among the *burakumin*, sought to augment their income by entering the mines. Nakamura Masanori, *Rōdōsha to Nōmin*, p. 372.
4. *Ibid.*, p. 112. In 1888 in one of the major Hokkaido mines 86% of the miners were convicts. Ueno Hidenobu, *Kindai Minshū no Kiroku: Kōfu* (Record of Modern Masses, Miners) (Tokyo: Shinjinbutsu Oraisha, 1971), p. 578.
5. *Ibid.*,
6. *Ibid.*, p. 417.
7. *Ibid.*, pp. 425ff.
8. Shimonaka, *Nihon Zankoku Monogatari*, V: 236–37, 253.
9. Nakamura Masanori, *Rōdōsha to Nōmin*, pp. 112–13.
10. Morisaki Kazue, *Makkura* (Pitch Dark) (Tokyo: San'ichi Shobō, 1977), p. 228.
11. Nakamura Masanori, *Rōdōsha to Nōmin*, pp. 135–36.
12. *Ibid.*, p. 128.
13. *Ibid.*, p. 143.
14. *Ibid.*, p. 147.
15. They were called "octopus rooms" because it was said that the octopus destroyed itself by eating its own limbs. Likewise the miners who entered the mining camps were ruining their own lives. Chōsenjin Kyōsei Renkō Shinsō Chōsadan, *Chōsenjin Kyōsei Renkō*, p. 118.
16. Nakamura Masanori, *Rōdōsha to Nōmin*, p. 137. For a comparison of wages in other occupations around the turn of the century see footnote 20 in Chapter VII.
17. Nakamura Masanori, *Rōdōsha to Nōmin*, p. 146.
18. Shimonaka, *Nihon Zankoku Monogatari*, I: 312–13.

19. Ueno Hidenobu, *Chi no Soko no Warai-banashi* (Funny Tales from the Underground) (Tokyo: Iwanami Shoten, 1967), p. 68.

20. Ueno Hidenobu, *Owareyuku Kōfu-tachi* (Hunted Miners) (Tokyo: Iwanami Shoten, 1960), p. 37.

21. Ueno, *Chi no Soko no Warai-banashi*, pp. 123, 218.

22. *Ibid.*, p. 111.

23. Morisaki, *Makkura*, pp. 157–58.

24. Shimonaka, *Nihon Zankoku Monogatari*, I: 304–5.

25. Morisaki, *Makkura*, p. 217.

26. *Ibid.*, p. 34.

27. Shimonaka, *Nihon Zankoku Monogatari*, V: 203.

28. Ueno, *Chi no Soko no Warai-banashi*, pp. 85–86.

29. Shimonaka, *Nihon Zankoku Monogatari*, I: 305ff.

30. Morisaki, *Makkura*, pp. 84, 105, 51, 106, 218.

31. *Chōsenjin Kyōsei Renkō*, p. 354.

32. *Ibid.*, p. 119.

33. Nakamura Masanori, *Rōdōsha to Nōmin*, p. 417.

34. *Chōsenjin Kyōsei Renkō*, pp. 142–43.

35. Shimonaka, *Nihon Zankoku Monogatari*, V: 356.

36. *Chōsenjin Kyōsei Renkō*, pp. 148–49.

37. *Ibid.*, p. 144.

38. *Ibid.*, p. 169.

39. *Ibid.*, pp. 175–78, 191.

40. *Ibid.*, pp. 173–74.

41. *Ibid.*, pp. 183–84.

42. Shimonaka, *Nihon Zankoku Monogatari*, V: 356–57.

43. Morisaki, *Makkura*, p. 161.

44. *Chōsenjin Kyōsei Renkō* pp. 191–92.

45. *Ibid.*, pp. 194–95.

46. Shimonaka, *Nihon Zankoku Monogatari*, V: 358–60.

47. Ueno, *Kindai Minshū no Kiroku: Kōfu*, p. 24.

48. *Ibid.*, pp. 140–41.

49. *Ibid.*, pp. 336ff., 586.

50. Nakamura Masanori, *Rōdōsha to Nōmin*, p. 375.

51. Ueno, *Chi no Soko no Warai-banashi*, p. 129.

52. *Ibid.*, p. 130.

53. Nakamura Masanori, *Rōdōsha to Nōmin*, pp. 359–60.

54. *Ibid.*, pp. 150–51.

55. Katayama Sen, of peasant stock, went to the United States and worked his way through college, attending Maryville College in Tennessee, Grinnell College in Iowa, and theological school at Yale. He became a Christian, and was first drawn to socialism through his exposure to Ferdinand Lassalle's writings. He later became a staunch Marxist-Leninist, who, after he was forced to leave Japan for his attempts to organize the workers, became an active Bolshevik of world renown. Katayama Sen, *Jiden* (Autobiography) (Tokyo: Iwanami Shoten, 1954).

56. Sumiya Mikio, *Dainipponteikoku no Shiren* (The Crucible of Imperial Japan) (Tokyo: Chūō Kōronsha, 1966), p. 332.

57. *Ibid.*, p. 330.

58. Nakamura Masanori, *Rōdōsha to Nōmin*, p. 236.

59. Shimonaka, *Zankoku Monogatari*, V: 327–50.

60. Yamashiro Tomoe, "Fuki no Tō," in *Tsuchi to Furusato*, I: 250–56.

61. Nakamura Masanori, *Rōdōsha to Nōmin*, pp. 240–43.

62. Ueno, *Owareyuku Kōfutachi*, pp. 93, 145, 178–79, 183, 217.

EPILOGUE: THE POSTWAR YEARS

1. Edward F. Denison and William K. Chung, *How Japan's Economy Grew So Fast* (Washington, D.C.: Brookings Institution, 1976), pp. 10–11; Kazuo Kawakami, *Japan's American Interlude* (Chicago: University of Chicago Press, 1960), p. 135; Rōyama Masamichi, *Yomigaeru Nihon* (Reviving Japan) (Tokyo: Chūō Kōronsha, 1967), p. 106.

2. Johannes Hirschmeir and Tsunehiko Yui, *The Development of Japanese Business, 1600–1973* (Cambridge, Mass.: Harvard University Press, 1975), p. 241.

3. A judge who refused to deal in the black market because it was his duty to enforce the law against black market dealers starved to death in November 1947. He had written in his diary: "The food control law is a bad law but as long as it is the law of the land we must adhere to it stringently. No matter how much pain it causes me I shall not buy food on the black market. I have always admired Socrates, who, though he knew that the law that was used to condemn him was unjust, went willingly to his death because he believed that the law must be obeyed. Today, we who live in a land where the rule of law prevails must above all else cultivate this Socratic spirit. I am determined to fight the black market and resign myself to death by starvation." Tsurumi et al., *Nihon no Hyakunen*, II: 301–2.

4. Hirschmeir and Yui, *The Development of Japanese Business*, p. 242; William W. Lockwood, "Japan's New Capitalism," in Lockwood, *The State and Economic Enterprise in Japan*, p. 449.

5. Tadashi Fukutake, *Rural Society in Japan* (Tokyo: University of Tokyo Press, 1980), p. 19.

6. *Ibid.*, pp. 12–13, 19.

7. Kazuo Kawai, *Japan's American Interlude*, pp. 171–74; Dore, *Land Reform in Japan*, pp. 129ff.; Fukutake, *Rural Society in Japan*, p. 8.

8. Kumao Tokuhei, "Kōfū Bonchi Yori" (From Kofu Basin), in *Tsuchi to Furusato*, I: 452.

9. Tsurumi et al., *Nihon no Hyakunen*, II: 255–57.

10. *Ibid.*, pp. 248–49.

11. Dore, *Land Reform in Japan*, pp. 160–162, 170–73.

12. Fukutake, *Rural Society in Japan*, p. 11.

13. *Ibid.*, p. 9.

14. *The New York Times*, December 14, 1980, E-9.

15. Fukutake, *Rural Society in Japan*, p. 9.

16. Kazuko Tsurumi, *Social Change and the Individual* (Princeton, N.J.: Princeton University Press, 1970), p. 262.

17. Segawa, *Mura no Onna-tachi*, pp. 131–32.

18. Tsurumi, *Social Change and the Individual*, pp. 292–93.

19. Segawa, *Mura no Onna-tachi*, pp. 135–36.

20. Tsurumi, *Social Change and the Individual*, p. 301. A 1962 survey showed that 67% of the women surveyed "were the major workers on the farms. More of the part-time farmers' wives were major workers (78%) than the wives of full-time farmers (64%)." And the former had a significant voice in making decisions about managing the farm. "Of these wives engaged in farming, 11% were the major decision-makers in crop planning, while 61% at least shared such responsibilities" (*Ibid.*, p. 284).

21. Fukutake, *Rural Society in Japan*, pp. 46, 48.

22. Nozaka Akiyuki, "Shikabane-gawara Mizu-kogusa" (Water Flowers in Dead Man's Riverbed), in *Tsuchi to Furusato*, I: 508.

23. Fukutake, *Rural Society in Japan*, p. 40.

24. Harada, *Hi-sabetsuburaku no Rekishi*, p. 349.

25. *Ibid.*, pp. 360–62.

26. Tsuchikata, *Hi-sabetsuburaku no Tatakai*, pp. 192–95.

27. Buraku-kaihōdōmei Chūō-honbu, *Sabetsu no Naka o Ikinuite*, pp. 63–65.

28. De Vos and Wagatsuma, *Japan's Invisible Race*, pp. 78–80.

29. Harada, *Hi-sabetsuburaku no Rekishi*, pp. 388–92.

30. Longstreet, *Yoshiwara*, p. 219.

31. Tsurumi et al., *Nihon no Hyakunen,* II: 199. These prostitutes were known as *pan-pan* (bang-bang, a quick job).
32. Longstreet, *Yoshiwara,* pp. 217, 219, 221.
33. Tsurumi, *Social Change and the Individual,* p. 225.
34. *Ibid.,* p. 230.
35. *Ibid.,* pp. 237–38.
36. Hirschmeir and Yui, *The Development of Japanese Business,* p. 244.
37. Muchaku Seikyō, *Yamabiko Gakkō* (Echoes from a Mountain School), (Tokyo: Seidōsha, 1951) pp. 197–98. The practice of having schoolchildren write about their experiences and thoughts had, in fact, been used by some prewar teachers. It was started by some innovative teachers in 1913, but they stayed away from controversial social issues and used the compositions primarily as a means to improve the students' writing style. In the postwar period, following Muchaku's celebrated success, other teachers adopted this practice and it became an important part of the educational program. Rōyama Masamichi, *Yomigaeru Nihon,* pp. 257–59.
38. Muchaku, *Yamabiko Gakkō,* pp. 26–31.
39. *Ibid.,* pp. 119–24.
40. Arahata Kanson, "Yanaka-mura Metsubō-shi," in *Tsuchi to Furusato,* VII: 23.
41. Sumiya Mikio, *Dai-Nippon Teikoku no Shiren,* pp. 80–85.
42. Arahata, "Yanaka-mura Metsubō-shi," pp. 51, 76.
43. In 1964–1965 similar instances of mercury poisoning were reported in Niigata prefecture along the Agawa River, where an industrial plant was pumping mercury into the river, and in the early 1970s cadmium poisoning afflicted residents of Toyama prefecture, where the Mitsui Mining and Smelting Company had released toxic elements. Frank Gibney, *Japan: The Fragile Super Power* (New York: New American Library, 1980), p. 300.
44. Ishimura Michiko, *Kugai Jōdo* (The Promised Land in the Sea of Suffering), in *Tsuchi to Furusato,* I:457–58.
45. Gibney, *Japan: The Fragile Super Power,* p. 20, footnote.
46. Yamashita Sōichi, "Nihon no 'Mura' Saikō" (Further Thoughts on the Japanese Village), in *Tsuchi to Furusato,* VII:498–500.
47. Gibney, *Japan: The Fragile Super Power,* p. 298.

Index

abortions, 254
agrarian productivity, 30–31, 251
agrarian reform movements, 108–14
All-Japan Peasants' Unions, 109
All-Japan Silk Reeling Labor Union, 196
Amakusa, 208, 218, 221
arable land, 29
Araki Sadao, 119
Asahi Shimbun, 199
Ashikaga period, 30
Ashio mines, 243, 262–63
automobiles, 248

Baelz, Erwin E. O. von, 45, 274, n. 60
Bakufu. *See* Tokugawa shogunate
Bashō, 128
bathing, 46–47
beriberi, 192
birth control, 254, 286, n. 10
Bog Rhubarb Shoots, 69, 85–101, 244
Bolshevik revolution, 27, 108, 196
Broken Commandment, 147
brothel inmates, 207–25, 286, n. 16;
    age, 212–13, 220, 287, n. 22; in
    Dairen, 219; in Korea, 219; Korean
    women, 225; Okimi's story, 220–1;
    Osaki's story, 221–4; personal ac-
    counts, 215–17; postwar reforms,
    256–7; reformers, 213–14, 224–5; in
    Sandakan, 221–4; in Shanghai, 219,
    224–5; in Singapore, 219, 224–5;
    terms of service, 211–12, 214, 221,
    286, *n.* 18; trafficker in, 219–20; in
    U.S.A., 219–20
Buddhism, 140
Buraku Liberation League, 163, 255–6
burakumin, 21, 139–71, 240, 241–2,
    279, n. 2; and armed forces, 150–1;
    attacks on, 144; discrimination toward,
    146, 154, 156–60; economic condi-
    tion, 151–5; education, 155–6, 281, n.
    71; emancipation of, 143; as farmers,
    153–4; intercaste marriages, 148–9,

280, n. 32; in Kure, 151–3; in Kyoto,
    139, 151, 152, 153, 154; as miners,
    227; origin of, 139–42; "passing,"
    147–8; postwar era, 255–6; and reli-
    gion, 149–50; restrictions on, 144–5;
    in Tokugawa era, 141–3; in Tosa-han,
    142–3

calendar, 63–4, 276, n. 31
Chichibu Uprising, 24–7, 114
child abandonment, 209
child labor, 181, 186–7, 195
Choi Chun Su, 237, 239–40
Chōshū, 12
Christian reformers, 108, 117, 196, 213,
    224, 242
Christians, 218
chūkun aikoku, 20, 55, 56, 58–9, 60–1,
    62, 75, 76, 260
civil code of 1898, 69, 79
class system, 5, 14, 141–2
clothing, 41–2
coal, 227
communication, 43
communist reformers, 108, 113, 161,
    199, 244
Confucian virtues, 56
convict-miners, 227–8
cotton mill workers, 175 *passim;* chastise-
    ment of, 186–7; contracts, 282, n. 12;
    diet of, 181; health of, 190, 191–3;
    wages of, 177–8; working conditions,
    182, 184, 284, n. 62; working hours,
    183

daimyō, 5–7, 16, 68
daughters sold to brothels, 115–16,
    131–3, 134, 153
death rate, 46
Debtors' Party, 23
diet, 40–1, 181, 251, 273, n. 44
Dore, Ronald P., 276, n. 34

ABOUT THE AUTHOR

Mikiso Hane, a professor of Japanese history at Knox
College, was born in California in 1922. He went to
Japan in 1933 and grew up in a peasant village in
Hiroshima prefecture. Returning to the United States
in 1940, he was soon thereafter interned in a wartime
detention camp. He has taught at Yale and is the
author of *Japan, a Historical Survey*, among other
works.